KYŌGYŌSHINSHŌ:
ON TEACHING, PRACTICE, FAITH, AND ENLIGHTENMENT

BDK English Tripiṭaka 105-I

KYŌGYŌSHINSHŌ:
ON TEACHING, PRACTICE, FAITH,
AND ENLIGHTENMENT

by

Shinran

Translated from the Japanese
(Taishō Volume 83, Number 2646)

by

Inagaki Hisao

Numata Center
for Buddhist Translation and Research
2003

First Printing, 2003
ISBN: 1-886439-16-8
Library of Congress Catalog Card Number: 2003100179

Published by
Numata Center for Buddhist Translation and Research
2620 Warring Street
Berkeley, California 94704

Printed in thc United States of America

A Message on the Publication of the English Tripiṭaka

The Buddhist canon is said to contain eighty-four thousand different teachings. I believe that this is because the Buddha's basic approach was to prescribe a different treatment for every spiritual ailment, much as a doctor prescribes a different medicine for every medical ailment. Thus his teachings were always appropriate for the particular suffering individual and for the time at which the teaching was given, and over the ages not one of his prescriptions has failed to relieve the suffering to which it was addressed.

Ever since the Buddha's Great Demise over twenty-five hundred years ago, his message of wisdom and compassion has spread throughout the world. Yet no one has ever attempted to translate the entire Buddhist canon into English throughout the history of Japan. It is my greatest wish to see this done and to make the translations available to the many English-speaking people who have never had the opportunity to learn about the Buddha's teachings.

Of course, it would be impossible to translate all of the Buddha's eighty-four thousand teachings in a few years. I have, therefore, had one hundred thirty-nine of the scriptural texts in the prodigious Taishō edition of the Chinese Buddhist canon selected for inclusion in the First Series of this translation project.

It is in the nature of this undertaking that the results are bound to be criticized. Nonetheless, I am convinced that unless someone takes it upon himself or herself to initiate this project, it will never be done. At the same time, I hope that an improved, revised edition will appear in the future.

It is most gratifying that, thanks to the efforts of more than a hundred Buddhist scholars from the East and the West, this monumental project has finally gotten off the ground. May the rays of the Wisdom of the Compassionate One reach each and every person in the world.

NUMATA Yehan
Founder of the English

August 7, 1991

Tripiṭaka Project

v

Editorial Foreword

In January 1982, Dr. NUMATA Yehan, the founder of the Bukkyō Dendō Kyōkai (Society for the Promotion of Buddhism), decided to begin the monumental task of translating the complete Taishō edition of the Chinese Tripiṭaka (Buddhist canon) into the English language. Under his leadership, a special preparatory committee was organized in April 1982. By July of the same year, the Translation Committee of the English Tripiṭaka was officially convened.

The initial Committee consisted of the following members: (late) HANAYAMA Shōyū (Chairperson), BANDŌ Shōjun, ISHIGAMI Zennō, KAMATA Shigeo, KANAOKA Shūyū, MAYEDA Sengaku, NARA Yasuaki, SAYEKI Shinkō, (late) SHIOIRI Ryōtatsu, TAMARU Noriyoshi, (late) TAMURA Kwansei, URYŪZU Ryūshin, and YUYAMA Akira. Assistant members of the Committee were as follows: KANAZAWA Atsushi, WATANABE Shōgo, Rolf Giebel of New Zealand, and Rudy Smet of Belgium.

After holding planning meetings on a monthly basis, the Committee selected one hundred thirty-nine texts for the First Series of translations, an estimated one hundred printed volumes in all. The texts selected are not necessarily limited to those originally written in India but also include works written or composed in China and Japan. While the publication of the First Series proceeds, the texts for the Second Series will be selected from among the remaining works; this process will continue until all the texts, in Japanese as well as in Chinese, have been published.

Frankly speaking, it will take perhaps one hundred years or more to accomplish the English translation of the complete Chinese and Japanese texts, for they consist of thousands of works. Nevertheless, as Dr. NUMATA wished, it is the sincere hope of the Committee that this project will continue unto completion, even after all its present members have passed away.

It must be mentioned here that the final object of this project is not academic fulfillment but the transmission of the teaching of the

Buddha to the whole world in order to create harmony and peace among humankind. To that end, the translators have been asked to minimize the use of explanatory notes of the kind that are indispensable in academic texts, so that the attention of general readers will not be unduly distracted from the primary text. Also, a glossary of selected terms is appended to aid in understanding the text.

To my great regret, however, Dr. NUMATA passed away on May 5, 1994, at the age of ninety-seven, entrusting his son, Mr. NUMATA Toshihide, with the continuation and completion of the Translation Project. The Committee also lost its able and devoted Chairperson, Professor HANAYAMA Shōyū, on June 16, 1995, at the age of sixty-three. After these severe blows, the Committee elected me, Vice President of Musashino Women's College, to be the Chair in October 1995. The Committee has renewed its determination to carry out the noble intention of Dr. NUMATA, under the leadership of Mr. NUMATA Toshihide.

The present members of the Committee are MAYEDA Sengaku (Chairperson), BANDŌ Shōjun, ISHIGAMI Zennō, ICHISHIMA Shōshin, KANAOKA Shūyū, NARA Yasuaki, TAMARU Noriyoshi, URYŪZU Ryūshin, YUYAMA Akira, Kenneth K. Tanaka, WATANABE Shōgo, and assistant member YONEZAWA Yoshiyasu.

The Numata Center for Buddhist Translation and Research was established in November 1984, in Berkeley, California, U.S.A., to assist in the publication of the BDK English Tripiṭaka First Series. In December 1991, the Publication Committee was organized at the Numata Center, with Professor Philip Yampolsky as the Chairperson. To our sorrow, Professor Yampolsky passed away in July 1996. In February 1997, Dr. Kenneth K. Inada became Chair and served in that capacity until August 1999. The current Chair, Dr. Francis H. Cook, has been continuing the work since October 1999. All of the remaining texts will be published under the supervision of this Committee, in close cooperation with the Editorial Committee in Tokyo.

MAYEDA Sengaku
Chairperson
Editorial Committee of
the BDK English Tripiṭaka

Publisher's Foreword

The Publication Committee shares with the Editorial Committee the responsibility of realizing the vision of Dr. Yehan Numata, founder of Bukkyō Dendō Kyōkai, the Society for the Promotion of Buddhism. This vision is no less than to make the Buddha's teaching better known throughout the world, through the translation and publication in English of the entire collection of Buddhist texts compiled in the *Taishō Shinshū Daizōkyō,* published in Tokyo in the early part of the twentieth century. This huge task is expected to be carried out by several generations of translators and may take as long as a hundred years to complete. Ultimately, the entire canon will be available to anyone who can read English and who wishes to learn more about the teaching of the Buddha.

The present generation of staff members of the Publication Committee includes Marianne Dresser; Brian Nagata, president of the Numata Center for Buddhist Translation and Research, Berkeley, California; Eisho Nasu; and Reverend Kiyoshi Yamashita. The Publication Committee is headquartered at the Numata Center and, working in close cooperation with the Editorial Committee, is responsible for the usual tasks associated with preparing translations for publication.

In October 1999, I became the third chairperson of the Publication Committee, on the retirement of its very capable former chair, Dr. Kenneth K. Inada. The Committee is devoted to the advancement of the Buddha's teaching through the publication of excellent translations of the thousands of texts that make up the Buddhist canon.

Francis H. Cook
Chairperson
Publication Committee

Contents

Translator's Introduction

Kyōgyōshinshō: On Teaching, Practice, Faith, and Enlightenment is the magnum opus of Shinran Shonin, the founder of the Jōdo Shinshū school of Pure Land Buddhism, popularly known as Shin Buddhism. It is by far the most comprehensive discourse presenting the essentials of Amida's law of salvation, which is applicable to all human beings regardless of their moral qualities or spiritual capacity. As the full title indicates, this work is largely a "collection of passages"—three hundred and seventy-six quotations from sixty-two sutras, discourses, and commentaries, including non-Buddhist sources. With deep insight and meticulous care, Shinran compiled these extensive materials into an organic whole. His own notes and comments placed before or after the quotations serve as introductions to new topics and summaries of their main points. They also serve as a good guide to lead the reader from one subject to the next without confusion. In many cases, the author's comments reveal his inner thoughts formed under the influence of Amida's boundless wisdom and compassion.

By closely studying this work, one will see that Shinran successfully systematized and enhanced, to the highest point, the teaching and practice of Pure Land Buddhism which had developed in diverse forms during its transmission from India to Japan via China and Korea–mainly through the Seven Patriarchs. One will also note that Shinran had a broad perspective; his system of Shin Buddhism is not limited to general Pure Land Buddhism. He envisioned a system that would embrace all the teachings of the Buddha; indeed, he brought forth the law of salvation through "Other-Power" as the ultimate teaching of the Mahayana. Contrary to the first impression of many readers, this is not an abstract doctrinal system; those with serious

xiii

spiritual questions will find in this work appropriate answers that they may not be able to find in other religious works.

Author of the *Kyōgyōshinshō*

Shinran (1173–1262), whose parents died when he was very young, entered the priesthood at the age of nine and practiced in the Tendai school on Mount Hiei for the next two decades. At the age of twenty-nine, he left the mountain and became a disciple of Hōnen. He dedicated himself to the Nembutsu practice that Hōnen encouraged but, more importantly, he noticed that the true cause of birth in the Pure Land is the "faith of the Other-Power"—the entrusting heart endowed by Amida. He thus established a system of salvation centering on faith, which is fully explained in this text, *Kyōgyōshinshō*.

When the Nembutsu teaching was prohibited and Hōnen was banished to Shikoku in 1207, Shinran was exiled to Kokubu in northern Japan, where he married Eshin-ni. Stripped of the priesthood and given a criminal's name, he styled himself "Gutoku Shaku Shinran"—"Short-haired, ignorant person, Shinran, disciple of Śākyamuni"—with a keen awareness that he was neither a priest nor a layman. There was no longer any Buddhist precept that bound him and, consequently, no set rules of conduct prescribed for the realization of enlightenment.

Though he was pardoned four years later, Shinran stayed on in northern Japan for another three years after that and then moved to Hitachi Province, northeast of Tokyo, where he began to spread the message of Amida's salvation to the countryfolk of that region. Over the years, he perused all available Buddhist and non-Buddhist scriptures and compiled the passages from them which he found useful for his grand religious-philosophical system of salvation centering on Amida's Vow.

Shinran returned to Kyoto at the age of sixty-two or sixty-three, presumably with the intention of completing the *Kyōgyōshinshō* and writing other works for the sake of his fellow beings. He had four sons and three daughters, but in Kyoto he lived most of the time with his youngest daughter. His literary work continued up to the end of his life, at the age of ninety. Among the more than five hundred hymns in Japanese he composed, his last major collection of a hundred and fifteen hymns is believed to have been written after the age of eighty-five.

The exact year the *Kyōgyōshinshō* was complied is not known. The only date that might be considered relevant is found near the end of the last chapter, where Shinran states: "From the time of the Buddha's *parinirvāṇa* to the first year of Gennin (1224), two thousand one hundred and eighty-three years have passed." If 1224 was the year he completed this work, he was then fifty-two years old. However, studies of other sources lead to the conclusion that Shinran made the first draft of this work sometime between the ages of forty and sixty, while he was still in the Kanto area, and that after his return to Kyoto he continued revising it until the age of seventy-five to eighty.

Synopsis of the Text

Kyōgyōshinshō: On Teaching, Practice, Faith, and Enlightenment is the popular title of this text, and it precisely reflects the basic structure of the Shin Buddhist system of salvation. Chapter One, "Revealing the True Teaching," shows that the *Larger Sutra on Amitāyus* (Taishō No. 360, translated by INAGAKI Hisao with Harold Stewart, in *The Three Pure Land Sutras*, Revised Second Edition, Numata Center, 2003) is precisely the scripture that presents the true way of salvation for all beings, even the most wicked people. This sutra explains how Amida—when he was a bodhisattva called Dharmā-kara—resolved to save all beings and made Forty-eight Vows, and after completing the bodhisattva practices required for fulfilling them, attained Buddhahood. The most essential of his vows is the Eighteenth Vow, which states that anyone who entrusts oneself to Amida and calls his Name will be born in the Pure Land—the nirvana realm of the highest bliss. Shinran was firmly convinced that the primary purpose of Śākyamuni's appearance in the world was to expound the *Larger Sutra* and reveal Amida's Vow.

Chapter Two, "Revealing the True Practice," shows, in detail, how even ordinary people who lack both moral virtue and spiritual capacity can enter the Pure Land. In the prescribed method of practice in general Buddhism, one must diligently work one's way, stage by stage, toward enlightenment. In the Shin Buddhist path, all the merits and virtues accomplished by Amida are transferred to us in the form of Amida's Name. "Merit transference," therefore, is the focal point in the actualization of our salvation. By meditating on and reciting the Name, one is drawn to Amida's power and soon realizes that even the effort to recite the Name ultimately comes from Amida. In short, conventional "self-power" practice is replaced by "Other-Power" practice—the Nembutsu of the Other-Power. The second chapter thus fully explains the soteriological meaning and function of the Nembutsu and the working of the power behind it. In Shinran's view, all the teachings of the Buddha, whether of the One Vehicle or of the three vehicles, are comprised in the "One-Vehicle teaching of Amida's Vow."

Chapter Three, "Revealing the True Faith," is the pivotal part of Shinran's doctrinal system. In Buddhism generally, faith is the starting point. By establishing faith in the Buddha, Dharma, and Sangha (the Three Treasures) one can proceed along the path of salvation. In other words, correct faith precedes correct practice; blind or misguided faith will not lead us to our spiritual goal. Shinran's deep reflection on his own mind brought him face to face with the stark reality that he could not possibly have correct faith because his mind was constantly perturbed by evil passions, self-love, and attachment. Here, too, he looked for Amida's transference of true faith to him to resolve this problem. He interpreted the text of the Eighteenth Vow to mean that Amida actually transfers his sincere and true mind to practitioners. In this way, Shinran realized it is Amida's mind of wisdom and compassion that we receive as "faith." He further discovered that such faith is the *bodhi*-mind, and even Buddha-nature—the cause of enlightenment. When faith of the Other-Power is thus established, one instantly transcends samsara and attainment of birth in the Pure Land is assured.

Chapter Four, "Revealing the True Enlightenment," is divided into two parts: enlightenment as such, and the salvific activities that ensue from it. Since the Nembutsu and faith are essentially Amida's virtues and mind, they are the cause of our enlightenment. Enlightenment in the Mahayana sense is the ultimate state of spiritual perfection and is called by various names, such as nirvana, *bodhi,* Oneness, and true suchness. This is not only the final objective of all Buddhist pursuits but also the fountainhead of all altruistic activities. Those who realize enlightenment cannot enjoy only the bliss of nirvana and remain inactive. Moved by great compassion, they manifest themselves in various forms as bodhisattvas to save those who are still caught in samsara. This activity is called "the returning aspect." Since faith is the *bodhi*-mind, it naturally contains the two aspects of wisdom and compassion. When one attains wisdom, one spontaneously comes to realize compassion. Conversely, in whatever altruistic activity one may be engaged as a bodhisattva, in one's deepest mind one always dwells in the tranquil state of nirvana.

Chapter Five, "Revealing the True Buddha and Land," discloses Amida's intrinsic qualities: infinite life and light, which are identical with the fundamental virtues of nirvana and Buddha-nature. The Pure Land, as Amida's land is popularly known, describes in concrete form the ultimate nature of all that exists—it is "pure" in the sense that it is not contaminated by delusions and evil passions. Since there is no afflicting element there, those born in the Pure Land can enjoy eternal peace and bliss. Although, in essence, the Pure Land is the nirvana realm which is above the dimensions of relativity, it is also the source of all the activities of the Buddha throughout the universe, through which Amida comes in contact with us and we respond to his salvific work. In this sense, we consider the Pure Land in terms of cause and effect and accept it as the sphere of karmic perfection, which has been produced by Amida's karma-power. Hence, the Pure Land is called the Land of Recompense—rewarded for Amida's Vow and practice. This karma-power, which is known more widely as "Vow-Power," works boundlessly and endlessly to realize the Vow. It works to sustain the Pure Land on one hand, and on the other, it works to deliver living beings from samsara and bring them to the Pure Land.

Chapter Six, "Revealing the Transformed Buddhas and Lands," aims at rectifying wrong views and clarifying the right way of salvation. There are various faiths and practices within Pure Land

Buddhism propounded by Chinese and Japanese masters. Furthermore, the three Pure Land sutras present a variety of methods of salvation. Before Hōnen, all these practices, both meditative and non-meditative, had been, by and large, accepted as authentic, and so some followers practiced meditative Nembutsu, while others practiced non-meditative acts. Following Shan-tao, the Fifth Patriarch of Shin Buddhism, Hōnen declared exclusive recitation of the Nembutsu to be the "right act" or the "act of right assurance" and set aside other practices as "auxiliary acts." Shinran went a step further and distinguished all Pure Land faiths and practices into two categories: those based on one's own self-power and those based on Amida's Other-Power. He brought forth three of Amida's vows—the Eighteenth, Nineteenth, and Twentieth—as the standard for different types of practice. The Eighteenth Vow reveals the genuine Other-Power teaching as set forth in the *Larger Sutra,* and the other two vows represent the self-power teachings of the *Sutra on Contemplation of Amitāyus* and the *Smaller Sutra on Amitāyus* (Taishō Nos. 365 and 366; translated by INAGAKI Hisao with Harold Stewart, in *The Three Pure Land Sutras,* Revised Second Edition, Numata Center, 2003). Shinran, however, did not brush aside self-power teachings as totally ineffective; he considered them as "provisional" Pure Land ways leading to the Other-Power teaching. Presumably based on his own experience, Shinran envisioned the following process of conversion: from the self-power teachings of the Nineteenth and the Twentieth Vows to the Eighteenth Vow teaching.

Nineteenth Vow—*Contemplation Sutra*—meditative and non-meditative practices;

Twentieth Vow—*Smaller Sutra*—sole practice of the Nembutsu;

Eighteenth Vow—*Larger Sutra*—faith and Nembutsu of the Other-Power.

Shinran's critical eye was directed to the nature of the Pure Land. All three sutras describe the Pure Land and Amida Buddha in different and varied ways. His insightful observation revealed that "the true Buddhas and lands" should transcend numerical or spatial limitations and that the sutras' description of the Buddhas and lands in limited dimensions showed provisional manifestations of the true Buddhas and lands. It follows then that, in Shinran's view, the glorious adornments of the Pure Land as depicted in the *Amida Sutra* and the *Contemplation Sutra* are a Transformed Land; even the physical form of Amida Buddha described in the *Contemplation Sutra* in astronomical figures is, likewise, a Transformed Buddha. While maintaining this rigid distinction, Shinran had a wider and more comprehensive perspective, according to which he read all the three Pure Land sutras and other scriptures, including the Seven Patriarchs' discourses and commentaries, as presenting the "true," not "provisional," teaching—in an implicit sense. And so, the reader is led to the Other-Power teaching and made to accept even the Transformed Buddha and Land as manifesting the true ones.

The latter half of this longest chapter is dedicated to correcting the wrong views that were widespread in Shinran's time, including popular belief in spirits, astrology, and the Taoists' claim to the supremacy of Taoism over Buddhism. Shinran took great pains to demonstrate the futility of such beliefs. Astronomy had long been established in Japan under the influence of Chinese science in this area, on which basis astrological superstitions developed. In order to reject such beliefs and guide people to authentic Buddhism, Shinran relied heavily on the *Mahāvaipulyamahāsaṃnipāta-sūtra* (*Great Assembly Sutra*), which asserts that the arrangement of the constellations and stars was properly conducted through the power and influence of the Buddha. Although deeply characterized by esotericism, the *Great Assembly Sutra,* he thought, would be effective in turning people's attention away from astrological beliefs and encourage them to take refuge in the Buddha. People of his time were also considerably vulnerable to and deeply influenced by the notion of demons, devils, and other evil spirits. Shinran carefully admonished them to be on guard against such fears and superstitions by providing them with countering scriptural evidence.

Next, in refuting the Taoists' claims, Shinran quoted a series of passages from a work by a Chinese Buddhist master called Fa-lin (572–640). Although this section appears rather irrelevant, we can

understand that Shinran, in coping with the unwholesome influence
of Taoism on various phases of Japanese life, wanted to eliminate its
root cause by pointing out the fallacies of Taoist views.

To conclude the text, Shinran gratefully reflected on his deep
indebtedness to Master Hōnen and professed his wholehearted reliance
on Amida's Vow-Power.

A Note on the Translation

This English translation follows the Taishō Tripiṭaka edition. Para-
graph divisions were made as appropriate. Titles of main sections have
also been provided as a guide for the reader. The names of texts quoted
in the text have been given in English, followed by the corresponding
Sanskrit or romanized Chinese title in parentheses on first appearance. Sanskrit titles that are marked by an asterisk are provisional.

Prior to the present work, I have been involved in two translation projects of the *Kyōgyōshinshō*. I was the chief translator and edi-
tor of the *Kyō Gyō Shin Shō,* Ryukoku Translation Series V, published by Ryukoku University, Kyoto, 1966. This volume is not a
translation of the entire text of the *Kyōgyōshinshō*. Professor Kosho
Yamamoto had already published a complete translation in 1958 but
it was not considered suitable for general readers. In order to respond
to the practical need for an abridged and yet usable version of the
text, a group at the Ryukoku Translation Center decided to repro-
duce in English only Shinran's own comments and important quotations, and supply notes and explanations side by side with the original Chinese text and its romanized transcription. The desired objective
was fairly well achieved, and this version came to be used by many
interested in Shin Buddhism.

As a member of the translation committee of the Hongwanji Translation Center, I was partly responsible for translating the *Kyōgyōshinshō*
and other works of Shinran, which after nearly twenty years' joint
work resulted in the two-volume *Collected Works of Shinran* published
in 1997. The *Kyōgyōshinshō* in this volume is a translation of the
entire text and took several years to produce. The original text used
was the Japanese version published, with other Shin scriptures, in

1988 by the Hongwanji, Kyoto, and the same passage numbers in that version have been adopted in the English one. An introduction, glossary, list of passages quoted, and notes were also added to the main body of the translation—all of which no doubt renders this publication useful to specialists.

I was greatly honored by the request of the Translation Committee of the BDK English Tripiṭaka Series to produce a new translation of the *Kyōgyōshinshō* in its entirety. My long-cherished wish to make this Buddhist classic of great importance accessible to many interested people has been realized. I have carefully chosen the appropriate terminology, and have taken great pains to make the context easy to follow within the limits of translation requirements. As would naturally be expected, I have often found myself obliged to use the same terms and expressions with which I became familiar when the two previous translations were produced. In a number of cases, however, I revised the old translations and adopted different readings of the original text.

In producing this translation, I wish to acknowledge my deep indebtedness to Rev. Jokyo G. Gatenby and Rev. Nityaprabha J. Paraskevopoulos of Australia for carefully reading the draft and supplying me with valuable suggestions. I note with gratitude that their help and constant encouragement have greatly facilitated this difficult task.

As an afterthought, I would like to add that the present work is not only the result of my long association with previous translation projects but also the product of a "family enterprise." My father's fervent wish to translate the entire text of the *Kyōgyōshinshō* has now been fulfilled nearly half a century after the publication of his pioneering work in 1954. Looking ahead to the future, I am also keenly aware that more work needs to be done to make the *Kyōgyōshinshō* accessible to an even wider audience. By way of achieving this end, I have undertaken a project to post this translation in a different format on my Website, http://www.ne.jp/asahi/pureland-buddhism/amida-net.

KYŌGYŌSHINSHŌ
A COLLECTION OF PASSAGES REVEALING THE TRUE
TEACHING, PRACTICE, FAITH, AND ENLIGHTENMENT
OF THE PURE LAND WAY

by

Gutoku Shinran

Preface

When I humbly contemplate matters, I realize that the incon- 589a3
ceivable Universal Vow is the great ship that carries us across the
sea of samsara which is difficult to cross, and that the unhindered
Light is the sun of wisdom that breaks the darkness of ignorance.

When the opportunity to reveal the Pure Land Way became
ripe, Devadatta incited Ajātaśatru to commit grave offenses; and
when a person to be saved by the Pure Land practice appeared,
Śākyamuni led Vaidehī to choose her birth in the Land of Peace
and Provision. All this shows that human incarnations of sages
equally sought to deliver multitudes from suffering and that the
World Hero, out of pity, especially wished to save those who commit the five grave offenses, abusers of the [Right] Dharma, and
those without any potential for good (icchantikas).

Hence, I know clearly that the auspicious Name of the all-complete, supreme virtue is the embodiment of the perfect wisdom
that can turn evil into merit and also that joyful faith, indestructible as a diamond but difficult to accept in our hearts, is the truth
that removes our doubts and awakens us to enlightenment.

This is indeed the true teaching which is easy to practice even
for ordinary, inferior people and is the shortest way that is easy to
follow for dull and stupid people. Of all the lifetime teachings of
the Great Sage, nothing surpasses this oceanlike virtue. Those who
wish to leave this defiled world of samsara and aspire to the Pure
Land, those who are confused about religious practices and faiths,
those who are dark in mind and lacking in wisdom, and those who
are burdened with heavy evil karma and many hindrances should,
by all means, esteem the Tathāgata Śākyamuni's exhortation and
follow the supreme direct path to enlightenment; they should exclusively hold fast to this practice and only uphold faith.

How difficult it is to encounter the strong influence of the Universal Vow, even in many cycles of birth and death! How difficult

it is to attain the true pure faith, even in millions of *kalpas*! If you are fortunate enough to attain practice and faith, you should rejoice at your close relationship with Amida from the distant past. If your mind is still covered with a net of doubt, you will continue to wander about in samsara for myriads of *kalpas*.

How trustworthy are the words of truth which say that we are embraced in Amida's Light and never forsaken! How extraordinary and wonderful is the Right Dharma! Hear and reflect; be careful not to hesitate too long.

What a joy it is that I, Gutoku Shinran, disciple of Śākyamuni, have had a rare chance to meet with the Pure Land scriptures from India and the commentaries by Chinese and Japanese masters, which are difficult to encounter, and have been able to hear their teachings that we can only rarely hear!

Having respectfully accepted in faith the teaching, practice, and enlightenment of the True Pure Land Way, I deeply acknowledge the Tathāgata Amida's benevolence. Here I rejoice over what I have heard and marvel at what I have received.

Chapter I

Revealing the True Teaching

When I humbly contemplate the true essence of the Pure Land Way, I realize that [Amida's] merit transference has two aspects: one is the aspect of going forth, and the other that of returning. Concerning the aspect of going forth of merit transference, there are true teaching, practice, faith, and enlightenment.

[The *Larger Sutra* is the True Teaching]

If I am to reveal the true teaching, it is the *Larger Sutra on the Buddha of Infinite Life.* The outline of this sutra is: Amida brought forth the Vow, by which he widely opened the Dharma storehouse; out of compassion for ordinary, inferior people, he chose from among the Dharma treasures the jewel of merit and freely endows it to them. Śākyamuni appeared in the world and expounded various teachings of the Way; but he wished to save multitudes of beings by endowing them with true benefits. Therefore, to expound the Primal Vow of Amida Tathāgata is the central theme of the *Larger Sutra,* and his Name is its essence. How do we know that Śākyamuni's primary objective in appearing in this world was to expound this sutra?

It is stated in the *Larger Sutra:*

> [Ānanda said to the Buddha,] "World-honored One, today all your senses are radiant with joy, your body is serene and glorious, and your august countenance is as majestic as a clear mirror whose brightness radiates outward and inward. The magnificence of your dignified appearance is unsurpassed and beyond measure. I have never seen you look so superb and majestic as you do today. With respect, Great Sage, this

5

thought has occurred to me: 'Today, the World-honored One dwells in the rare and marvelous Dharma; today, the World Hero dwells in the Buddha's abode; today, the World Eye concentrates on the performance of the leader's duty; today, the World Valiant One dwells in the supreme *bodhi* (enlightenment); today, the One Most Honored in Heaven realizes the Tathāgata's virtue. The Buddhas of the past, present, and future contemplate each other. How can this present Buddha not contemplate the other Buddhas?' For what reason does his countenance look so majestic and brilliant?"

Then the World-honored One said to Ānanda, "Tell me, Ānanda, whether some god urged you to put this question to the Buddha or whether you asked about his glorious countenance from your own wise observation."

Ānanda replied to the Buddha, "No god came to prompt me. I asked you about this matter of my own accord."

The Buddha said, "Well said, Ānanda. I am very pleased with your question. You have shown profound wisdom and subtle insight in asking me this wise question out of compassion for sentient beings. As the Tathāgata, I regard beings of the three worlds with boundless great compassion. The reason for my appearance in the world is to expound various teachings of the Way and save multitudes of beings by endowing them with true benefits. Even in countless millions of *kalpa*s it is difficult to come upon and meet a Tathāgata. It is as difficult as seeing an *uḍumbara* flower, which blooms very rarely. Your question is of great benefit and will enlighten all heavenly and human beings. Ānanda, you should realize that the Tathāgata's perfectly enlightened wisdom is unfathomable, capable of leading innumerable beings to liberation, and that his penetrating insight cannot be obstructed."

589c

It is stated in the *Teaching Assembly of the Tathāgata of Infinite Life* (*Sukhāvatīvyūha*):

Ānanda said to the Buddha, "World-honored One, having seen the Tathāgata's countenance radiating rare, majestic glory, I have entertained this thought. No gods came to prompt me."

The Buddha said to Ānanda, "Well said, well said. Your question has pleased me. With careful observation of the Tathāgata's subtle insight, you have asked me this question. All Tathāgatas, arhats, and perfectly enlightened ones, dwelling in the great compassion, benefit multitudes of beings. To realize their wishes, this Great Being has appeared in the world like the *uḍumbara* flower which blooms very rarely. In order to help their work, you have asked me this question. Also, having pity on all sentient beings and being moved to give them spiritual benefit, you have asked me, the Tathāgata, this good question."

It is stated in the *Sutra on the Immeasurably Pure and Equal Enlightenment (Sukhāvatīvyūha-sūtra)*:

> The Buddha said to Ānanda, "We know of an *uḍumbara* tree; it bears fruit but no flowers. A Buddha appears in the world as rarely as this tree blossoms. Even if a Buddha dwells in the world, it is extremely difficult to encounter him. I have become a Buddha and here I am. Being a revered monk, wise and virtuous, you know the Buddha's intention beforehand. You never forget to stay close to me and serve me. I will answer your question. Listen well and attentively."

Master Kyeong-heung explains:[1]

> "Today, the World-honored One dwells in the rare and marvelous Dharma" describes the appearance which the Buddha manifests by his transcendent power. It is not only unusual but also unequaled.
>
> "Today, the World Hero dwells in the Buddha's abode" shows that he dwells in the *samādhi* of universal equality and subdues the king of devils, the powerful gods.

"Today, the World Eye concentrates on the performance of the leader's duty" shows that he is first and foremost in guiding sentient beings; his five eyes are called "the leader's duty."

"Today, the World Valiant One dwells in the supreme enlightenment" shows that he dwells in the four wisdoms, with which he attains the highest and peerless state.

"Today, the One Most Honored in Heaven realizes the Tathāgata's virtue" describes the Buddha as the lord of ultimate reality, for he embodies Buddha-nature which is not empty.

"Ānanda, you should realize that the Tathāgata's perfectly enlightened wisdom" describes the rare and marvelous Dharma.

"His insight cannot be obstructed" describes the supreme enlightenment.

"Nothing can hinder it" describes the Tathāgata's virtue.

The above quotations afford clear testimony of the fact that the *Larger Sutra* is the true teaching. It is indeed the correct exposition of the Dharma for which the Tathāgata appeared in the world; it is the wonderful scripture, rare and supreme; the ultimate doctrine of the One Vehicle teaching; the golden words that enable quick attainment of perfect and all-merging truth; the sincere words praised by all the Buddhas in the ten directions; the teaching of truth befitting the time and the capacities of people. Let us be clear about this.

End of Chapter I: Revealing the True Teaching

Chapter II

Revealing the True Practice

[Presentation of the Great Practice]

When I humbly contemplate the "going forth" aspect of Amida's merit transference, I realize that there are great practice and great faith. The great practice is to call the Name of the Tathāgata of Unhindered Light. This practice contains all good and roots of virtue, and is perfectly accomplished and most efficacious in bringing about liberation. It is the treasure-sea of merits of true suchness, ultimate reality. For this reason, it is called great practice. This practice comes from the vow of great compassion, the [Seventeenth] Vow, which is called the vow that the Name shall be glorified by all the Buddhas. It is also called the vow that the Name shall be praised by all the Buddhas, and the vow that the Name shall be lauded by all the Buddhas. Further, it can be called the vow accomplishing the going-forth aspect of merit transference, and also the vow of the Nembutsu chosen from among many practices.

Concerning the vow that the Name shall be praised by all the Buddhas, the *Larger Sutra* states:

> If, when I attain Buddhahood, innumerable Buddhas in the lands of the ten directions should not all praise and glorify my Name, may I not attain perfect enlightenment.

The *Larger Sutra* also states:

> When I attain Buddhahood,
> My Name shall be heard throughout the ten directions;
> Should there be any place where it is not heard,
> May I not attain perfect enlightenment....

9

I will open the Dharma storehouse for the multitudes
And endow them all with treasures of merit.
Being always among the multitudes,
I will proclaim the Dharma with the lion's roar.

Concerning the fulfillment of this vow, the [*Larger*] *Sutra* states:

All Buddha Tathāgatas, in the ten directions, as numerous as the sands of the Ganges River, together praise the inconceivable, supernal virtue of the Buddha of Infinite Life.

It also states:

The majestic virtue of the Buddha of Infinite Life is boundless. All the innumerable, countless, and inconceivable Buddha Tathāgatas in the worlds of the ten directions praise him.

It also states:

By the power of the Buddha's Original Vow,
All who hear his Name and desire birth
Will, without exception, be born in his land
And effortlessly enter the stage of non-retrogression.

It is stated in the *Teaching Assembly of the Tathāgata of Infinite Life:*

I have made great vows to the Tathāgata [Lokeśvararāja].
May he testify that they are the cause of the supreme
  enlightenment.
Should these excellent vows not be fulfilled,
May I not become a peerless Honored One possessed of the
  ten powers.

I shall endow gifts to those incapable of constant practices,
Deliver widely the poor and destitute from suffering,
And benefit the world by giving them peace and
  happiness. . . .

590b

10

Having performed the practices of the supreme and valiant
ones,
I shall become a hidden treasury for the poor and destitute;
Having also accomplished good acts, I shall be a Peerless
One.
Among the multitudes I shall preach the Dharma with a
lion's roar.

Further it is stated:

Ānanda, for this reason, Buddha Tathāgatas in the immeasurable, innumerable, inconceivable, incomparable, and limitless worlds all praise the virtue of the Buddha of Infinite Life.

It is stated in the *Sutra on the Way of Salvation of Humans
by Amida, the Perfectly Enlightened One, That Transcends All
Buddhas (Sukhāvatīvyūha-sūtra)*:[2]

The Fourth Vow: When I attain Buddhahood, my Name shall
be heard throughout the countless Buddha lands of the eight
directions, zenith, and nadir. All Buddhas shall each in their
own land explain my virtues and the excellent qualities of my
land to the multitudes of monks. All the gods, humans, and
even insects that hop, fly, crawl, or creep, having heard my
Name, will, without exception, entertain a compassionate heart.
Those who thus dance with joy in their hearts shall all be born
in my land. Having fulfilled this vow, I shall become a Buddha.
Should this vow not be fulfilled, may I not attain Buddhahood.

It is stated in the *Sutra on the Immeasurably Pure and Equal
Enlightenment,* fascicle one:

When I attain Buddhahood, my Name shall be heard throughout the innumerable Buddha lands of the eight directions,
zenith, and nadir. All Buddhas shall each praise my virtues
and the excellent qualities of my land to the multitudes of
disciples. All the gods, humans, and even insects that hop,
fly, crawl or creep, that, having heard my Name, dance with

joy in their hearts shall all be born in my land. If not, may I
not attain Buddhahood (the Seventeenth Vow).

When I attain Buddhahood, people of other Buddha lands,
who have heard my Name with evil intentions in previous
lives or aspire to be born in my land for the sake of attaining
enlightenment, may wish to be born in my land. After the
end of their lives, they shall, instead of being reborn in the
three evil realms, all be born in my land as they wish. If not,
may I not attain Buddhahood (the Nineteenth Vow).

Prince Ajātaśatru and the five hundred sons of a wealthy
man, having heard the Twenty-four Vows of the Buddha of
Infinite Purity, danced with joy in their hearts, and aspired,
"We all wish to be like the Buddha of Infinite Purity when
we attain Buddhahood."

Knowing this, the Buddha [Śākyamuni] said to the
monks, "In the future, innumerable *kalpa*s from now, Prince
Ajātaśatru and the five hundred sons of the wealthy man
shall become Buddhas like the Buddha of Infinite Purity."

The Buddha continued, "Prince Ajātaśatru and these five
hundred sons of the wealthy man have practiced the bodhisattva path for innumerable *kalpa*s, during which they each
made offerings to four hundred *koṭi*s of Buddhas. Now they
have come to make offerings to me. In a previous life, when
Buddha Kāśyapa was in the world, Prince Ajātaśatru and
the five hundred sons of the wealthy man became my disciples. Now they all have gathered and we meet here again."

When all the monks heard the Buddha's remarks, their
hearts danced with joy. . . .

Such people, having heard the Buddha's Name,
Will attain peace of heart and gain great benefit;
We ourselves will share in this virtue,
And take up the seats of blessedness in this land.

The Infinitely Enlightened One gives us the prediction of
    our enlightenment:

590c

"I made the Primal Vow in a former life,
Promising that all who hear my preaching of the Dharma
Would unfailingly come to be born in my land.

"All the vows that I made will be fulfilled;
Those who wish to come here from various lands
Will all reach my land and
Attain the stage of non-retrogression after one lifetime."

Quickly transcend this world and
Reach the Land of Peace and Bliss.
After reaching the Land of Infinite Light,
One can make offerings to innumerable Buddhas.

Those who lack merit
Are unable to hear even the name of this sutra;
Only those who have strictly observed the precepts
Can now hear the teaching of this Dharma.

Evil, arrogant, corrupt, and indolent people
Cannot readily accept this teaching.
But those who have met Buddhas in their past lives
Rejoice to hear the teaching of the World-honored One.

To obtain human life is extremely difficult;
Even if a Buddha dwells in the world, it is difficult to
    meet him;
It is hard to attain wisdom of faith;
Once you have heard the Dharma, strive to reach its heart.

If you have heard the Dharma and do not forget it
But adore and revere it with great joy,
You are my good friend. For this reason,
You should awaken aspiration for enlightenment
    (*bodhicitta*).

Even if the whole world is on fire,
Be sure to pass through it to hear the Dharma;

Then you will surely become a World-honored One
And everywhere deliver beings from birth, old age, and
  death.

It is stated in the *Sutra on the Lotus of Compassion* (*Karuṇā-pundarīka-sūtra*), fascicle two, "Chapter on Great Charity"[3] (translated by the Tripiṭaka master Dharmakṣema):

When I attain highest, perfect enlightenment (*anuttara-samyak-saṃbodhi*), all the sentient beings in immeasurable, boundless, and incalculable Buddha lands who hear my Name and wish to be born in my land by cultivating roots of good, shall, after death, be unfailingly born there. Excepted are those who commit the five grave offenses, abuse the sages, or destroy the Right Dharma.

[The Benefit of the Nembutsu]

It is thus clear that when sentient beings call the Name, all their ignorance is destroyed and all their aspirations are fulfilled. Calling the Name is the most excellent and truly wondrous right act. The right act is the Nembutsu. The Nembutsu is *Namu amida butsu*. *Namu amida butsu* is right mindfulness. This one should know.

591a

It is stated in the *Discourse on the Ten Stages* (*Daśabhūmika-vibhāṣā*):[4]

A certain [master] explains [the verse] and says, "The *pratyutpanna samādhi* and great compassion are the home of all Buddhas, because all Tathāgatas are born from them. Of the two, the *pratyutpanna samādhi* is the father, and great compassion is the mother."

He next presents a second interpretation, "The *pratyutpanna samādhi* is the father, and insight into the non-arising of all *dharmas* is the mother." The above interpretations are based on the following verse of the *Aid to Bodhi* (*Bodhi-saṃbhāra**):[5]

The *pratyutpanna samādhi* is the father;
Great compassion and insight into the non-arising [of
    all *dharmas*] are the mother;
And all Tathāgatas
Are born from these two.

"The home is free of faults" means that the home is free
of defilement. Hence, "undefiled *dharmas*" are the six perfections (*pāramitās*), the four virtues, skillful means (*upāya*),
perfection of wisdom (*prajñā-pāramitā*), goodness, wisdom,
and the *pratyutpanna samādhi*, great compassion, and various insights. These *dharmas* are free of defilement and free
of faults. For this reason, the home is said to be free of defilement. Since the bodhisattvas [of the first stage] make these
dharmas their home, they are free of faults.

"Turning from the worldly paths, they enter the superior supramundane path" means: "the worldly paths" are the
paths taken by ordinary people. "Turning from" means stopping. The paths of ordinary people do not lead ultimately to
nirvana but result in continuous coming and going in samsara. Hence, they are called "paths of ordinary people." "The
supramundane path" is the way of deliverance from the three
worlds; hence, it is called "the supramundane path." It is
described as "superior" because it is extraordinary. "Enter"
means that they unmistakably follow this path. Since they
reach the first stage with such a mind, this stage is called
"the stage of joy."

Question: Why is the first stage called "the stage of joy"?

Answer:

Just as [the *śrāvakas* of] the first fruit
Ultimately reach nirvana,
The bodhisattvas who have reached this stage
Are always full of joy in their hearts.

In them the seeds of Buddha Tathāgatas
Are able to grow naturally.
For this reason, they are called
Wise and good people.

"Just as [the *śrāvakas*] of the first fruit" means "just as
they attain the fruit of entering the stream." For them, the
gates to the three evil realms are closed forever. They discern
the principle [of the Four Noble Truths], enter it, and realize
it; dwelling in the steadfast principle of truth, they abide in
an immovable state of mind until they reach nirvana. Since
they have severed the [eighty-eight] delusions that are to be
dealt with in the path of insight, their hearts leap with great
joy. Even if they may become lax in discipline, they will not
be subject to the twenty-ninth existence in samsara.

Suppose one splits a hair into a hundred strands, and
draws water from the ocean with one of them. The few drops
of water thus drawn are compared to the amount of karmic
suffering that has already been extinguished [by the *śrāvakas*
of the first fruit]. So the remaining karmic suffering to be
dealt with is like the rest of the ocean water. Even so, their
hearts rejoice greatly.

This is also the case with bodhisattvas. When they reach
the first stage, they are called "those born into the Tathāgatas'
abode." All gods, dragons, *yakṣas*, *gandharvas*, and so on, and
also *śrāvakas* and *pratyekabuddhas*, make offerings to and
worship them. For what reason? Because this abode is free of
faults. Such bodhisattvas have turned from the worldly paths,
entered the supramundane path, joyfully revered Buddhas,
and thus attained the four virtues and the reward for the six
perfections. Since they enjoy the taste of the Dharma and keep
the seeds of Buddhahood from destruction, their hearts greatly
rejoice. The remaining karmic suffering that those bodhisattvas have yet to extinguish would appear to be only a few
drops of water. Although it takes a hundred thousand *koṭis*

591b

of *kalpa*s to attain highest, perfect enlightenment (*anuttara-samyak-sambodhi*), the remaining karmic suffering seems like a few drops of water when compared to the karmic suffering they have undergone since the beginningless past. In fact, the karmic suffering to be dealt with is like the rest of the ocean's water. For this reason, this stage is called "the stage of joy."

Question:[6] Bodhisattvas of the first stage are described as "having much joy." Since they have gained various merits, they use joy as the name for this stage. They should rejoice in the Dharma. What brings them joy?

Answer:

> To be constantly mindful of Buddhas and the supreme
>   qualities of the Buddhas
> Is the rare practice that certainly assures one's
>   enlightenment; hence, one has much joy in one's
> heart.

Such being the cause of joy, bodhisattvas of the first stage have much joy in their hearts. "To be mindful of Buddhas" means to contemplate past Buddhas, such as Dīpaṅkara; present Buddhas, such as Amida; and future Buddhas, such as Maitreya. If they constantly contemplate these Buddhas, the World-honored Ones, they feel as if these Buddhas were before their eyes. They are the most honored in the three worlds, and there is no one who excels over them. For this reason, the [bodhisattvas] have much joy.

Concerning the phrase "to be mindful of the supreme qualities of the Buddhas," I will briefly explain the forty special qualities of the Buddhas: First, they are capable of flying in the air freely as they wish; second, they are capable of transforming themselves freely and limitlessly; third, they are capable of discerning various sounds freely and without obstruction; fourth, they are capable of knowing the thoughts of all sentient beings freely by uncountable means; ...

Concerning the phrase "to be mindful of the bodhisattvas of the stage of definite assurance," such bodhisattvas have received predictions of their attainment of highest, perfect enlightenment, entered the stage of non-retrogression, and gained insight into the non-arising of all *dharmas*. An army of devils, even ten million *koṭi*s in number, could not disturb and confuse them. These bodhisattvas will attain great compassion and accomplish the Dharma of the Great Being.... This is the meaning of "being mindful of the bodhisattvas of the stage of definite assurance."

"To be mindful of the rare practice" means to contemplate the supreme, rare practice of the bodhisattvas in the stage of definite assurance. By so doing, they attain much joy in their hearts. This practice is beyond the capacities of all ordinary beings; neither *śrāvaka*s nor *pratyekabuddha*s are able to perform it. It leads to the path of nonhindrance and that of liberation of the Buddha-Dharma and awakens one to all-knowing wisdom. Again, since one contemplates all the practices to be performed in the ten stages, one attains much joy in one's heart. For this reason, if bodhisattvas can enter the first stage, they are said to be in [the stage of] joy.

Question: There are ordinary beings who have not yet awakened the aspiration for highest enlightenment (*bodhicitta*), and there are those who have awakened it but not yet reached the stage of joy. The second group of people may attain joy by contemplating the supreme qualities of the Buddhas and the rare and marvelous practices of the bodhisattvas of [the stage of] definite assurance. What difference is there between the joy of such people and that of the bodhisattvas who have reached the first stage?

Answer:

591c   Bodhisattvas who have reached the first stage have
        much joy in their hearts,

18

Thinking, "I shall definitely attain the Buddhas'
immeasurable merits."

The bodhisattvas who have reached the first stage and
are dwelling in the stage of definite assurance will attain
immeasurable merits when they contemplate Buddhas. [They
are convinced:] "I shall unfailingly attain the same merits.
Why? Because I have already reached the first stage and am
dwelling in the stage of definite assurance." Others lack this
conviction. For this reason, bodhisattvas in the first stage have
much joy in their hearts, but others have not, because even
when they contemplate the Buddhas they have no conviction
that they will certainly become Buddhas. Let us take a prince
of a wheel-turning monarch (*cakravartin*) for example; born
into the family of a wheel-turning monarch, he possesses the
physical marks of a wheel-turning monarch. When he thinks
of the virtues and noble character of past wheel-turning monarchs, he is convinced, "I have the same marks, and so I will
obtain similar wealth and noble character." And so his mind
is full of joy. Without the physical marks of a wheel-turning
monarch, he would not attain such joy. Similarly, when bodhisattvas in the stage of definite assurance contemplate Buddhas
and their great merits, dignified deportment, and noble character, they will think, "I have the same physical marks and
so I shall certainly become a Buddha." By so thinking, they
will have great joy. But other people have no such joy. With
the mind of concentration, they deeply penetrate into the
Buddha-Dharma and so their minds are unshaken.

Further, it is stated:[7]

What is "the power of faith becoming dominant"? If one
accepts without doubt what one has heard and seen, this is
called "becoming dominant" and also "excelling."

Question: Two kinds of "becoming dominant" are distinguished:

one is quantitative dominance and the other is qualitative excellence. Which applies here?

Answer: Both are implied. When bodhisattvas enter the first stage they obtain the flavor of merits, and so their power of faith increases. With the increased power of faith they contemplate the immeasurable, profound, and subtle merits of the Buddhas and accept them in faith. For this reason, their faith is both vast and superior.

"To practice great compassion deeply" means as follows: bodhisattvas' pity for sentient beings penetrates their bones; hence, "deeply." They seek the Buddha's enlightenment for the sake of all sentient beings; hence, "great." With a compassionate heart, they always seek to benefit sentient beings and bring them peace and ease. There are three kinds of compassion....

Further it is stated:[8]

There are innumerable modes of entry into the Buddha's teaching. Just as there are in the world difficult and easy paths—traveling on foot by land is full of hardship and traveling in a boat by sea is pleasant—so it is with the paths of the bodhisattvas. Some exert themselves diligently, while others quickly enter [the stage of] non-retrogression by the easy practice based on faith....

> Those who wish to enter the stage of non-retrogression
>   quickly
> Should reverently hold [the names of these Buddhas]
>   in mind and recite them.

If a bodhisattva wishes to enter the stage of non-retrogression in his present body and realize highest, perfect enlightenment, he should be mindful of those Buddhas of the ten directions. Recitation of the names is encouraged in the "Chapter on Non-retrogression" of the *Sutra on the Questions of the Youth Treasure Moon (Ratnacandra-paripṛcchā-sūtra):*...

In the land called Good in the west there dwells a
    Buddha named Infinite Light;   592a
The light of his body and his wisdom are brilliant,
    shining everywhere without limit.
Those who hear his name will enter the stage of
    non-retrogression. . . .
Innumerable *kalpa*s ago there was a Buddha named
    Oceanlike Virtue;
Under his guidance, those Buddhas of the present
    made vows, resolving:
"My life shall be limitless and my light shall shine
    with boundless intensity.
My land shall be exceedingly pure and those who hear
    my name shall definitely become Buddhas. . . . "

Question: If we hear the names of those ten Buddhas and
hold them deeply in our hearts, we shall not regress from
reaching highest, perfect enlightenment. Are there names
of other Buddhas and bodhisattvas that enable us to enter
the stage of non-retrogression?

Answer:

There are Amida and other Buddhas and various
    great bodhisattvas;
Those who recite their names and are mindful of
    them singleheartedly also enter the stage of
    non-retrogression.

You should reverently worship those Buddhas, such as
Amida, and recite their names. I will expound the Buddha of
Infinite Life. There are Buddhas such as Lokeśvararāja. These
Buddhas, World-honored Ones, dwelling in the pure realms
of the ten directions, recite Amida's Name and are mindful
of his Primal Vow, which is as follows:

If one contemplates me, recites my name, and takes refuge

in me, one will instantly enter the stage of definite assurance and subsequently attain highest, perfect enlightenment.

For this reason, you should always be mindful of him. I will now praise him in verse.

The Buddha of Infinite Light and Wisdom, whose body
is like a mountain of genuine gold,
I worship with my body, speech, and mind by joining
hands and bowing down toward him....

If one is mindful of that Buddha's infinite power and
merit,
One will instantly enter the stage of definite
assurance. So I am always mindful of Amida....

If one, aspiring to become a Buddha, contemplates
Amida in one's heart,
Amida will instantly manifest himself before this
person. So I take refuge in the Primal Vow-Power.

[By the Primal Vow-Power,] bodhisattvas of the ten
directions
Come to make offerings to him and hear the Dharma.
So I bow down to him....

If there is anyone who plants roots of good but entertains
doubts, the flower [he will be born into] will not bloom;
For those who have pure faith, the flowers [they are
born into] will bloom and they will see the Buddha.

The present Buddhas of the ten directions praise this
Buddha's merit
In various ways. So I now take refuge in him and
worship him....

Boarding the boat of the Noble Eightfold Path, he
ferries people over the sea that is difficult to cross;

He has crossed it himself and now carries others
across. So I worship the one who possesses
unrestricted power.

Even if all the Buddhas praised his merit for innumer-
able *kalpas*,   592b
They could not fully honor it. So I take refuge in the
Pure Person.

Like those Buddhas, I have praised his boundless virtue.
By this act of merit, I pray that the Buddha may
always think of me.

It is stated in the *Discourse on the Pure Land* (*Sukhāvatīvyūha-upadeśa**):

Depending on the sutras' exposition
Of the manifestation of true merit,
I compose verses of aspiration in a condensed form,
Thereby conforming to the Buddha-Dharma....

When I observe the Buddha's Primal Vow-Power,
I find that those who meet with it do not pass in vain.
They are enabled to gain quickly
The great treasure-sea of merit.

Further it is stated:

Bodhisattvas accomplish the practice for their own benefit
with the four gates in the phase of "going in." One should
realize the implication of this. Through the fifth gate of "going
out," bodhisattvas accomplish the practice of benefiting others by merit transference. One should realize the implication
of this. Thus, by performing the five mindful practices, bodhisattvas accomplish both self-benefit and benefit for others,
and so quickly attain highest, perfect enlightenment.

It is stated in the *Commentary on Vasubandhu's Discourse on
the Pure Land* (*Wang sheng lun chu*):

When I (T'an-luan) reverently read Nāgārjuna's *Discourse on the Ten Stages,* I find the following passage:

There are two paths by which bodhisattvas reach the stage of non-retrogression: 1) the path of difficult practice and 2) the path of easy practice. The path of difficult practice is a way of trying to reach the stage of non-retrogression in the period of the five defilements when no Buddha dwells in the world. It is difficult to follow this path and there are reasons for this. In order to clarify this, I shall outline several reasons as follows:

1. Non-Buddhist ways of doing what seems to be good are at variance with the bodhisattva's practice.

2. The *śrāvaka*'s pursuit of self-benefit obstructs the bodhisattva's acts of great compassion.

3. Evildoers, who have no regard for consequences, destroy the superior merit of others.

4. The results of good deeds based on deluded thinking offer a distraction from sacred practices.

5. Relying solely on our own [self-]power, we miss the support of Other-Power.

These facts are seen everywhere. The path of difficult practice is, therefore, like an overland journey painstakingly made on foot.

The path of easy practice is followed by aspiring to be born in the Pure Land through faith in Amida Buddha and quickly attaining birth in the Pure Land by his Vow-Power. In the Pure Land we are sustained by the Buddha's power and join those who are rightly established in the Mahayana path. "Rightly established" refers to the stage of non-retrogression. The path of easy practice is, therefore, like a pleasant journey on water.

The *Discourse on the Pure Land* is indeed the ultimate teaching of the Mahayana, a ship sailing before the favorable wind of non-retrogression. "Infinite Life" is another name for the Tathāgata of the Pure Land of Peace and Bliss. While he was staying in Rājagṛha and Śrāvastī, Śākyamuni expounded to the assembly the glorious virtues of the Buddha of Infinite Life. The essence of the sutras expounded at that time is the Name of Amida Buddha. Sometime later, a sage, Bodhisattva Vasubandhu, took this compassionate teaching of the Tathāgata to heart. Based upon the sutras, he composed the *Verses of Aspiration for Birth* (*Sukhāvatīvyūha-upadeśa-kārikā**) and wrote a commentary on them to explain their meaning.

Further it is stated:

Furthermore, he (Vasubandhu) has taken weighty vows. Without the support of the Tathāgata's supernatural power, how could he fulfill them? Here Vasubandhu entreats the Buddha to support him with his supernatural power, and so respectfully addresses the Buddha.   592c

"With singleness of mind" is the phrase with which Bodhisattva Vasubandhu professes his faith. It means that he is mindful of the Tathāgata of Unhindered Light, aspiring to be born in the Land of Peace and Bliss, and is continually mindful of him without the intervention of any other thought....

Concerning the line, "I take refuge in the Tathāgata of Unhindered Light Shining Throughout the Ten Directions," "take refuge in" is the gate of worship. "The Tathāgata of Unhindered Light Shining Throughout the Ten Directions" is the gate of praise. How do we know that to take refuge in the Buddha is to worship him? Bodhisattva Nāgārjuna uses phrases such as the following in his verse in praise of Amida: "I bow and worship," "I take refuge," and "I take refuge in and worship him." In the explanatory section of this *Discourse,* Vasubandhu says "performing the five mindful practices." Worship is one of the five mindful practices. Bodhisattva Vasubandhu already aspired to be born in the Pure

Land. Why then should he not worship Amida? Hence, we know that "to take refuge in him" is "to worship him." But "worshiping" can simply imply "revering"; it does not necessarily mean "taking refuge." "Taking refuge" necessarily means "worshiping." From this one can infer that "taking refuge" has a deeper meaning. On the one hand, the verses are the profession of the author's faith and so it is natural that he should say "I take refuge." On the other hand, the explanatory section gives the meaning of the verses and so here he discusses the matter generally, using the word "worship." These two expressions complement each other.

How do we know that saying "the Tathāgata of Unhindered Light Shining Throughout the Ten Directions" is the gate of praise? It is said in the explanatory section: "What is praise? I call the Name of the Tathāgata. For I wish to practice in accord with the Dharma, that is, in accord with the Tathāgata's embodiment of the light of wisdom and with the signification of his Name...."

When Bodhisattva Vasubandhu says "the Tathāgata of Unhindered Light Shining Throughout the Ten Directions," he glorifies this Tathāgata by the name that exactly describes him as the embodiment of the light of wisdom. Hence, we know that this line is the gate of praise.

"And aspire to be born in the Land of Peace and Bliss": this line is the gate of aspiration. Aspiration for birth implies Bodhisattva Vasubandhu's taking refuge in Amida....

Question: In Mahayana sutras and discourses it is repeatedly explained that sentient beings are, in the final analysis, like space, unborn. Why does Bodhisattva Vasubandhu say that he aspires to be born?

Answer: When it is explained that sentient beings are, like space, unborn, there are two possible meanings. First, sentient beings and their births and deaths conceived of as real by ordinary people are, after all, as nonexistent as the hair of

a tortoise or open space. Second, since all things are produced
by causes and conditions, they are as unproduced and as nonexistent as open space. The birth that Bodhisattva Vasubandhu
desired should be understood in the sense of "[produced by]
causes and conditions." Because birth takes place depending
on causes and conditions, it is only provisionally called "birth,"
not in the sense that there are real sentient beings and real
births and deaths as ordinary people imagine.

Question: In what sense do you speak of "birth"?

Answer: When someone among those who are thus provisionally called "human" performs the five mindful practices,
his thought in the preceding moment becomes the cause of
his thought in the following moment. The provisional "person" in this defiled land and the provisional "person" in the
Pure Land [who he is going to be] are neither exactly the
same nor definitely different. Likewise, the thought of the   593a
preceding moment and that of the following moment are neither exactly the same nor definitely different. Why is this so?
If they were the same, there would be no causality, and if
they were different, there would be no continuity. This principle is explained in detail in the discourses dealing with the
problem of "sameness" and "difference."

I (T'an-luan) have above explained the first stanza that presents the first three [of the five] mindful practices....

It is stated:[9]

> Depending on the sutras' exposition
> Of the manifestation of true merit,
> I compose verses of aspiration in a condensed form,
> Thereby conforming to the Buddha-Dharma....

What does Vasubandhu depend on, and why and how does
he depend on it? First, what does Vasubandhu depend on?
He depends on the sutras. Second, why does he depend on

them? Because the Tathāgata Amida is the manifestation of
true merit. Third, how does he depend on them? He complies
with them by performing the five mindful practices. ...

"Sutras" refers to [the Buddha's] own exposition [of the
Dharma], which is one of the twelve divisions of the Buddhist
teachings. They include the four Āgamas or the [Hinayana]
Tripiṭaka. Apart from these, Mahayana sutras are also called
"sutras." "Depending on the sutras" refers to Mahayana sutras
which are not included in the [Hinayana] Tripiṭaka. In other
words, they do not refer to such sutras as the Āgamas.

Concerning the phrase "the manifestation of true merit,"
there are two kinds of merit: 1) The merit that accrues from
the activity of a defiled mind and is not in accordance with
the Dharma-nature. Such merit arises from the various good
acts of ordinary people and heavenly beings. It also refers to
the reward of human and heavenly states of existence. Both
the cause and effect of such good acts are inverted and false;
hence they are called "false merit"; 2) The merit that is produced from the wisdom and pure karma of bodhisattvas and
which serves to glorify Buddhist action. It conforms to the
Dharma-nature and has the characteristic of purity. This
Dharma is not inverted and false; hence it is called "true
merit." Why is it not inverted? Because it conforms to the
Dharma-nature and agrees with the twofold truth. Why is it
not false? Because it takes in sentient beings and leads them
to the ultimate purity.

Concerning the lines,

I compose verses of aspiration in a condensed form,
Thereby conforming to the Buddha-Dharma,

"Holding [all]"[10] means "to hold something together and keep
it from dispersing." "[Holding] all" means "much [meaning]
condensed into a few [words]" ...

"Aspiration" means "to wish to be born in the Pure
Land. ... "

"Conforming to the Buddha-Dharma" means that [the verses of aspiration and the Buddha-Dharma] fit each other like a box and its lid. . . .

It is stated:[11]

How does one transfer [the merit of practice]? One does not forsake suffering beings but constantly resolves in one's mind to perfect the great compassion by putting merit transference above anything else.

Merit transference has two aspects: the "going" aspect and the "returning" aspect. The "going" aspect is that one turns one's merit over to all sentient beings with the aspiration that all will be born together into Amida Tathāgata's Pure Land of Peace and Bliss.

It is stated in the *Collection of Passages on the Land of Peace and Bliss (An le chi)*:

The *Sutra on the Buddha-Contemplation Samādhi (Buddha-dhyāna-samādhi-sūtra*)* says:

[Śākyamuni] urged his father, the king (Śuddhodana), to practice the Nembutsu *samādhi*. His father, the king, asked the Buddha, "Why do you not recommend to me, your disciple, the practice of meditating on the ultimate virtue of the Buddha's stage, which is identical with true suchness, ultimate reality, or the highest principle of emptiness (*śūnyatā*) ?"

The Buddha answered his father, the king, "The ultimate virtue of the Buddhas is the boundless and profoundly subtle state and is possessed of transcendent faculties and the wisdom of liberation. This is not a state fit to be practiced by ordinary people. So I urge you, the king, 593b to practice the Nembutsu *samādhi*."

His father, the king, asked the Buddha, "What are the characteristics of the merit of the Nembutsu?"

The Buddha replied to his father, the king, "Suppose there is a forest of *eraṇḍa* trees, forty *yojana*s square, and there is in it a single cow-headed sandalwood tree, whose roots and sprouts are still underground. The *eraṇḍa* forest is full of a foul smell and completely devoid of pleasant scent. If someone bites a flower or fruit of the *eraṇḍa* tree, he will become insane and die. Later, when the sandalwood spreads its roots and buds and is about to grow into a tree, it emits luxuriant fragrance and finally transforms this forest into a sweet-smelling one. Those who see this are wonderstruck."

The Buddha said to his father, the king, "A thought of the Nembutsu that all sentient beings hold in birth and death is like this. If only one concentrates one's thought on the Buddha without interruption, one will surely be born in the presence of the Buddha. Once this person attains birth in the Pure Land, he will transform all the evils into great compassion, just as the fragrant sandalwood tree transforms the *eraṇḍa* forest."

Here the *eraṇḍa* tree symbolizes the three poisons and the three hindrances within sentient beings and the innumerable grave karmic evils they commit. The sandalwood tree represents the thought of the Nembutsu in sentient beings. "Is about to grow into a tree" shows that if only sentient beings keep practicing the Nembutsu without interruption, the karmic cause of their birth in the Pure Land is accomplished.

Question: By the example of the merit of the Nembutsu of one sentient being (i.e., Śākyamuni's father, Śuddhodana) we can surmise that it applies to all sentient beings. How can the power of the merit of a single Nembutsu destroy all hindrances, just as a single fragrant tree transforms an *eraṇḍa* forest, forty *yojana*s square, into a sweet-smelling one?

Answer: I will clarify the inconceivable merit of the Nembutsu *samādhi* by quoting from various Mahayana scriptures. The *Garland Sutra (Avataṃsaka-sūtra)* says:

> If a man plucks a lute whose strings are made of the sinews of a lion, with one strike, all the strings of other lutes snap. Likewise, if a man practices the Nembutsu *samādhi* with *bodhi*-mind, all his evil passions and hindrances are destroyed. Again, if a drop of milk from a lion is placed in a vessel that contains milk from a cow, ewe, ass, and other animals, it penetrates the mixed milk unhindered, destroying it and transforming it into pure water. Likewise, if a man practices the Nembutsu *samādhi* with *bodhi*-mind, all the devils and various hindrances pass by without causing him any trouble.

The [*Garland*] *Sutra* further states:

> Just as a man who has taken a potion to make himself invisible travels from one place to another without being seen by others, if one practices the Nembutsu *samādhi* with *bodhi*-mind, one cannot be seen or detected by any evil spirit or anyone who might cause harassment, and so one can go anywhere without hindrance. It is because the Nembutsu *samādhi* is the king of all *samādhi*s.

593c

It is further stated:[12]

A Mahayana discourse[13] says:

> It is not that all the other *samādhi*s are not worthy of *samādhi*s. For a certain *samādhi* can eliminate greed but cannot eliminate anger and ignorance; another can eliminate anger but cannot eliminate greed and ignorance; still another can eliminate ignorance but cannot eliminate anger. There is a *samādhi* which can eliminate hindrances of the present but cannot eliminate those of the

31

past and future. If one constantly practices the Nembutsu *samādhi,* it eliminates all hindrances, past, present, or future.

It is also stated:[14]

The *Verses on the Larger Sutra (Tsan a mi t'o fo chieh)* says:

If one hears the virtuous Name of Amida,
Rejoices, praises, and takes refuge in it,
One will gain great benefit even with one Nembutsu;
That is, one will obtain the treasure of merit.

Even if the whole universe were filled with fire,
Pass through it straightaway to hear the Buddha's
  Name.
If one hears Amida's Name, one will enter the stage
  of non-retrogression.
For this reason, I bow and worship the Buddha
  singleheartedly.

It is further stated:[15]

The *Sutra on the Questions of Maudgalyāyana (Maudgalyā-yana-paripṛcchā*)* says:

The Buddha said to Maudgalyāyana, "In all rivers and streams there are floating grasses and trees. They are carried down [in the current] without regard to the objects that go before or follow, until they all merge in the great ocean. So it is in the world. Even though the rich and noble may freely enjoy pleasures, they cannot escape the cycle of birth, old age, sickness, and death. Through failure to accept the Buddha's teaching, those who may be born as humans in the life to come must undergo extreme hardships and tribulations and are unable to be born in the country where thousands of Buddhas appear. For this reason, I declare: It is easy to go to the land of the Buddha of Infinite Life and attain enlightenment there. But people fail to perform practices and attain birth there; instead, they follow the ninety-five wrong paths. I call such people 'those without eyes' and 'those without ears.'"

Such are the teachings of the scriptures. Why do people not abandon the path of difficult practice and follow the path of easy practice?

The Master of Kuang-ming Temple says:[16]

The *Sutra on the Perfection of Wisdom Expounded by Mañjuśrī* (*Mañjuśrī-bhāṣita-prajñāpāramitā-sūtra*) states:

I wish to explain the *samādhi* of the single practice. I encourage you to dwell alone in a quiet place, eliminate all distracted thoughts, and concentrate your mind on one Buddha. Do not contemplate his physical characteristics, but exclusively recite the Buddha's Name. Then, thinking mindfully, you will be able to see Amida and all the other Buddhas.

Question: For what reason do you directly encourage the exclusive recitation of the Name and not the practice of contemplation?

Answer: Because sentient beings have deep hindrances and their minds are coarse and rough, while the objects of contemplation are subtle; their thoughts are agitated and their minds disturbed, so that they cannot accomplish contemplation. Thereupon, the Great Sage, out of compassion for them, directly encouraged people to recite the Name only. For recitation of the Name is easy, and through the continuous practice of it one can attain birth in the Pure Land.

Question: When one exclusively recites the Name of a Buddha, why do so many Buddhas appear? Is this not a mixture of wrong and right contemplations and the mixed appearance of one and many Buddhas?

594a

33

Answer: All Buddhas have attained one and the same enlightenment, and so they are not different in form from each other. Even if you see many Buddhas by contemplating one, how could this run counter to the universal principle?

Further, it is stated in the *Contemplation Sutra:*

I urge people to practice contemplation while sitting, during worship, and during mindful recitation. In all these acts, it is best to face west. It is like a tree falling in the direction it leans. If for some reason you are not able to face west, you may simply imagine that you are facing west.

Question: All Buddhas have equally realized the three bodies, and their wisdom and compassion have been accomplished perfectly and without any distinction. Even if one may face any direction, worship one Buddha, be mindful of him, and recite his Name, one can still attain birth. Why do you solely praise the Buddha of the West (Amida) and encourage us to worship him and recite his Name?

Answer: Although the enlightenment of all Buddhas is one and the same, when discussed in terms of vows and practices, they have their own causes and conditions. Hereupon, Amida, the World-honored One, originally made deep and weighty vows, through which he embraces beings in the ten directions with his Light and Name. As he establishes faith in us, our birth is easily attained by the Buddha's Vow-Power while we recite the Nembutsu throughout our lives, or even ten times, or only once. That is why Śākyamuni and other Buddhas especially encourage us to turn our thoughts to the west. We should, however, understand that this does not mean that elimination of our hindrances and evil karma is not achieved through recitation of the names of other Buddhas. Those who continuously recite the Name, as explained above, until the end of their lives, will all be born in the Pure Land, ten out of ten and a hundred out of a hundred. Why? Because such people are free of obstructions from outside and dwell in the state of right mindfulness, and so they are in accord with the Buddha's Primal Vow, in harmony with the teaching, and in agreement with the Buddha's words.

Further, Shan-tao says:[17]

Since this Buddha watches over only the Nembutsu followers, embraces them, and does not forsake them, he is called "Amida."

He also says:[18]

The ocean of Amida's Vow that arose from wisdom
Is deep, vast, and unfathomable.
Those who hear the Name and aspire for birth
All, without exception, reach his land.

Even though the great thousand worlds were filled with fire,
Pass through them straightaway to hear the Buddha's
    Name.
Those who have heard the Name, rejoice, and praise
    its virtue
Will all be born in that land.

After ten thousand years the Three Treasures will perish,
But this *Larger Sutra* will remain for a hundred years more.
People during that time who hear and recite the Name
    even once
Will all attain birth there.

He also says:[19]

I am in reality an ordinary unenlightened being subject to birth and death, burdened with deep and heavy evil karma and hindrances, and transmigrating in the six realms. The suffering I have received is indescribable. Now I have encountered a good teacher and heard from him about the Name that has been brought forth by Amida's Primal Vow. I will aspire for birth by reciting the Name singleheartedly. May the Buddha, out of compassion, not abandoning the original Universal Vow, embrace me as his disciple.

He also says:[20]

Question: What merit and benefit do we acquire in the present life by calling the Name of Amida Buddha and worshiping and contemplating him?

Answer: One utterance of the Name of Amida Buddha can remove the heavy evil karma that will cause one to transmigrate in samsara for eighty *koṭi*s of *kalpa*s. Worshiping and focusing our thoughts upon Amida—along with other acts—have the same effect. The *Sutra on the Ten Ways of Attaining Birth (Shih wang sheng ching)* states:

594b
> If there are sentient beings who focus their thoughts upon Amida Buddha and aspire for birth in his land, the Buddha immediately sends twenty-five bodhisattvas to protect them, keeping evil spirits and evil gods away from them at all times and in all places, day and night, whether they are walking, standing, sitting, or lying down.

It is further stated in the *Contemplation Sutra:*

> If practitioners call the Name of Amida Buddha and worship and focus their thoughts upon him, aspiring to be born in his land, the Buddha immediately sends innumerable Transformed Buddhas and transformed bodies of Avalokiteśvara Bodhisattva and Mahāsthāmaprāpta Bodhisattva to the practitioners to protect them. Together with the twenty-five bodhisattvas mentioned before, these transformed bodies surround them a hundredfold and a thousandfold and stay with them at all times and in all places, day and night, whether they are walking, standing, sitting, or lying down.

Since there are such excellent benefits, you should accept this in faith. May all practitioners receive Amida's sincere heart and seek to attain birth in the Pure Land. It is further stated in the *Larger Sutra:*

> If, when I become a Buddha, all sentient beings in the ten directions who call my Name even ten times fail to be born in my land, may I not attain perfect enlightenment.

This Buddha, having attained Buddhahood, now dwells in the Pure Land. You should know that his weighty vows are not in vain. Sentient beings who call his Name will unfailingly attain birth. It is further stated in the *Amida Sutra:*

> If sentient beings hear of Amida Buddha, they should hold fast to his Name, calling it with a concentrated and undistracted mind for one day, two days, up to seven days. When their lives are about to end, Amida Buddha will appear before them with a host of sages. When they die, their minds will not fall into confusion and so they will be born in his land.
>
> Buddha Śākyamuni said to Śāriputra, "Since I perceive these benefits, I declare: Those sentient beings who hear this teaching should awaken aspiration and desire to be born in that land."

The sutra next states:

> The Buddhas of the eastern direction, as numerous as the sands of the Ganges River, as well as those as numerous as the sands of the Ganges River in each of other directions—south, west, north, nadir, and zenith—each in their own lands, extending their tongues and covering with them the universe of a thousand million worlds, pronounce these words of truth: "You, sentient beings, should accept this sutra that is protected by all Buddhas." Why is this sutra called "protected [by all Buddhas]"? If there are sentient beings who call the Name of Amida Buddha for seven days, or one day, even once, or even down to ten times, or think of him once, they can

unfailingly attain birth. Because [all Buddhas] testify to this, this is called "the sutra that is protected [by all Buddhas]."

The sutra next states:

Those who call the Buddha's Name and attain birth are constantly protected by Buddhas of the six directions, numerous as the sands of the Ganges River. Hence, this is called "the sutra which is protected [by all Buddhas]."

Since we have this supreme [Universal] Vow, we should trust it. Why do all the Buddhas' children not make a firm resolution and strive to go to the Pure Land? (The second fascicle of the *Collection of Liturgical Passages from Various Scriptures* [*Chi chu ching li tsan i*] by Chih-sheng consists of *Hymns of Birth in the Pure Land* [*Wang sheng li tsan chieh*] by Master Shan-tao. This passage comes from that.)

It is also stated:[21]

594c
The Universal Vow is presented in the *Larger Sutra*. All good and evil ordinary beings will not attain birth without having recourse to the karmic power of Amida Buddha's great vow as the supreme working.

[The Meaning of *Namu Amida Butsu*]

It is also stated:[22]

"*Namu*" means "to take refuge"; it also has the significance of "making aspiration and transferring [merits]." "*Amida butsu*" is the practice. For this reason, one can definitely attain birth.

It is stated:[23]

Concerning "the supreme working to embrace beings," one of the Forty-eight Vows in the *Larger Sutra* says, "If, when I become a Buddha, the sentient beings of the ten directions who, aspiring to be born in my land, call my Name even ten times, fail to be born there through my Vow-Power, may I not attain perfect enlightenment." This means that the practitioners who aspire for birth are embraced by the Vow-Power—when their lives are about to end—and are enabled to attain birth. Hence, this is called "the supreme working to embrace beings."

It is also stated:[24]

[The Buddhas] wish all good and evil ordinary people to convert their minds, perform Pure Land practices, and thereby attain birth. This is "the supreme working of all Buddhas testifying to our attainment of birth."

It is also stated:[25]

There are different Dharma gates numbering eighty-four
thousand.
The sharp sword for cutting asunder our ignorance, its
effects,
And the karmic cause of suffering in samsara, is Amida's
Name.
With a single utterance of the Name, all our evils are
removed.

Our numerous karmic evils of the past and self-power
calculations are destroyed;
Even without being taught, we are led into the gate of true
suchness.

For attaining freedom from many *kalpas*' suffering in this
Sahā world
We are especially indebted to the benevolence of
Śākyamuni, the true teacher;
Using various skillful means based on careful consideration,
He selected the teaching gate of Amida's Universal Vow
and led us into it.

We see from the above that the word *"namu"* means "to take refuge" (*kimyō*). *"Ki"* means "to come to"; it also means "to rely joyfully" (*kietsu*) and "to trust" (*kisai*). *"Myō"* means "act," "summoning," "causing," "teaching," "expounding," "exhorting with sincerity," "providing the compassionate means," and "calling." *"Kimyō,"* therefore, is the command of the Primal Vow, summoning us to trust it.

"Making aspiration and transferring [merit]" (*hotsugan ekō*) refers to the mind of the Tathāgata who already made the Vow resolving to endow the practice to sentient beings.

"The practice" (*sokuze gokyō*) is the working of the selected Primal Vow.

"One can definitely attain birth" (*hittoku ōjō*) shows that one attains the stage of non-retrogression. Concerning this, the [*Larger*] *Sutra* states, "immediately attains [birth]" (*sokutoku*) and [Nāgārjuna's] commentary says, "definitely assured" (*hitsujō*). *"Soku"* ("immediately") reveals the very instant in which the true cause of our birth in the Recompensed Land is settled through hearing and understanding the Vow-Power. *"Hitsu"* ("certainly") describes the state in which the adamantine mind has been established.

It is stated in the *Shorter Pure Land Liturgy of the Nembutsu Chant in Five Stages* (*Ching-t'u wu hui nien fo lüeh-fa shih i tsan*):

> The Tathāgata Śākyamuni provided the teaching in two ways, in full and in summary, according to the capacities of people. By so doing, he intended to lead all to ultimate reality in the end. To those who seek to realize true nonorigination, who else can give the appropriate teaching? Indeed, the Nembutsu *samādhi* is truly the supreme and most wonderful Dharma gate. With the Name realized by the Forty-eight Vows of Amida, the Dharma King, the Buddha, saves sentient beings, exercising the Vow-Power....
>
> The Tathāgata, while always dwelling in the oceanlike *samādhi,* raised his hand with webbed fingers and said to his father the king: "O king, you should now sit cross-legged and

595a

exclusively practice the Nembutsu. How can you seek non-thought by annihilating thought? How can you seek non-origination by annihilating origination? How can you seek the Dharma body (*dharmakāya*) by negating forms? How can you seek liberation by not relying on words?"...

How wonderful it is that the true Dharma of ultimate reality is Oneness and yet it transforms beings and benefits people! Since each Buddha's great vows differ from others', Śākyamuni manifested his accommodated body in the world of defilement and Amida appeared in the Pure Land. Although their lands are different—one is defiled and the other is pure—the benefit they give to beings is the same. It is indeed the teaching gate of the Pure Land alone that is easy to practice and easy to realize. The Western Land is exquisite, and that land is incomparable. It is adorned with lotuses of a hundred kinds of jewels, which open in nine different ways to take aspirants of different grades into them. This is due to the Buddha's Name....

It is stated in the hymns by Fa-chao, disciple of Śākyamuni, based on the *Sutra in Praise of the Pure Land (Sukhāvatīvyūha)*:

The sacred Name of the Tathāgata Amida is clearly
    manifest beyond measure;
It prevails everywhere in the worlds of the ten directions.
Simply by calling the Name, all can attain birth.
Avalokiteśvara and Mahāsthāmaprāpta come in person to
    welcome them.

Amida's Primal Vow is particularly superb;
With compassionate skillful means he leads ordinary
    beings to the Pure Land.
Thus all sentient beings attain liberation;
Those who recite the Name are immediately rid of karmic
    evil.

When ordinary beings reach the Western Land,

Their karmic evils, countless as particles, from long past
*kalpa*s will perish.
Endowed with the six supernatural powers, they attain
unrestricted freedom in action;
Forever freed of old age and sickness, they are liberated
from impermanence.

It is stated in the hymns by Fa-chao based on the *Sutra on the
Life of the Buddha (Buddha-carita)*:

What is called the Right Dharma?
The teaching that accords with truth is the true teaching.
Now right and wrong teachings should be distinguished;
Carefully examine each teaching and do not leave any in
obscurity.
The Right Dharma surpasses the worldly teachings.

Observance of the precepts and sitting meditation are
called the Right Dharma;
Attainment of Buddhahood through the Nembutsu is the
true teaching.
Those who do not accept the Buddha's words are non-
Buddhists;
The view that rejects the law of cause and effect is a
nihilistic view.
The Right Dharma surpasses the worldly teachings.

How can meditation and observance of the precepts be the
Right Dharma?
The Nembutsu *samādhi* is the true teaching.
To see one's true nature and realize one's mind is to
become a Buddha.
Why is this not in accord with truth?

It is stated in the hymns based on the *Amida Sutra:*

In the Western Land one advances in the Way more
quickly than in this Sahā world,

Because that land is free of the five desires and
    adversaries.
To become a Buddha, one does not require good acts;
One just sits on a lotus seat and concentrates on Amida.

Practice in this world of the five defilements is liable to
    regression;
Nothing is more advantageous than going to the Western
    Land through the Nembutsu.
Having reached [that land], one effortlessly realizes perfect
    enlightenment;
Then one returns to the world of suffering and becomes a
    bridge for others to cross to liberation.   595b

Among the myriad practices, the Nembutsu is the most
    essential;
No other teaching surpasses the Pure Land gate in
    bringing about liberation quickly.
Not only is this the exposition from the golden mouth of
    the Buddha, our Master,
But all Buddhas of the ten directions transmit this
    message and testify to its truth.

When one recites the Name of the Buddha in this world,
A lotus grows in the Western Land.
If one continues to recite it all one's life,
The flower comes here to welcome this person.

It is stated in the hymns by Master Tz'u-min based on the
Pratyutpanna Samādhi Sutra:

Those who have assembled today in the hall,
You have transmigrated everywhere in samsara for
    countless *kalpa*s, as numerous as the sands of the
    Ganges River.
As I reflect, this human existence is difficult to obtain;
It is like the blooming of an *uḍumbara* flower.

43

Through a rare chance, we have come to hear the Pure
    Land teaching;
We have encountered the opening of the Dharma gate of
    the Nembutsu.
Indeed, we have encountered the call of Amida's Universal
    Vow;
We have seen the assembly converting their minds into
    faith.

Today we have joined in praising Amida in accord with
    the sutras;
We have pledged with each other to meet on the higher
    lotus seats.
We have met in the hall free of devils' hindrances;
We have met again here without being hampered by illness.

We have accomplished the meritorious act for seven days;
The Forty-eight Vows will unfailingly take us to the
        Pure Land.
I urge all the fellow practitioners of this hall:
Strive diligently to convert your minds and go to the
        Pure Land.

Let me ask you, "Where is your home?"
It is the seven-jeweled lotus seat in the pond of the Land of
    Utmost Bliss.
Amida Buddha, in his causal stage, made the Universal Vow:
Whoever hears my Name and concentrates on me, I will
    welcome to my land.

No discrimination is made between the poor and destitute
    and the rich and noble,
Or between the inferior and the highly gifted,
Or between those who have heard much and those who
    observe the precepts,
Or between those who break the precepts and those who
    have deep evil karma.

If only people convert their minds and recite the Nembutsu
    many times,
They are transformed, as if rubble were turned into gold.
I make an announcement to the assembly here:
Those who share the same connection with Amida and
    seek to go to the Pure Land should ask each other—

Question: Where should we aspire to go to?
Answer: To Amida's Pure Land.

Question: By what cause can we attain birth there?
Answer: Nembutsu recitation naturally brings you there.

Question: We have much karmic hindrance in this life;
    How can we possibly enter the Pure Land?
Answer: By calling the Name, you can rid yourself of your
    karmic evil,
As when a shining lamp enters a dark room.

Question: Can ordinary people attain birth there?
    How is it possible that one recitation brightens the dark-
    ness?
Answer: If you remove doubt and recite the Nembutsu
    many times,
Amida naturally comes close to you in person.

It is stated in the hymns by Fa-chao based on the *Sutra on
Contemplation of Amitāyus (Contemplation Sutra)*:

Foolish beings who have committed the ten evil acts and
    the five grave offenses
Have been drowning in samsara for eternally long *kalpa*s,
    covered with the dust of evil passions.
When they reach Amida's land by calling his Name even
    once,
They will become one with the Dharma-nature body.

Master Kyeong-heung says:[26]

The Tathāgata Śākyamuni's detailed exposition of the *Larger Sutra* is divided into two parts. First, he fully expounds the [cause and] result of the Tathāgata Amida's Pure Land, namely, his practices and his accomplishments. Next, he fully expounds the cause and result of sentient beings' birth in the Pure Land, namely, Amida's embrace and the benefit to be gained.

He also says:

It is stated in the *Sutra on the Lotus of Compassion*, "Chapter on Giving Predictions to Bodhisattvas":

At that time, the Tathāgata Treasure Store praised the wheel-turning monarch, saying, "Very well, very well.... Great king, in the western direction, after passing a thousand million *koṭi*s of Buddha lands, there is a world called August, Good, and Undefiled. In that land there is a Buddha named August Sound King.... He is at present preaching the Right Dharma to bodhisattvas.... It is the land of the genuine Mahayana, pure and unadulterated. Sentient beings are born there transformed in the same form. There are no women, not even the word for woman. The merit of that Buddha land is manifested as pure adornments. All are exactly the same as the great king vowed, showing no difference at all.... Now your name shall be changed to Infinite Purity."

It is stated in the *Teaching Assembly of the Tathāgata of Infinite Life:*

Amida established such extensive, great universal vows and has already fulfilled them all. They are rare in the world. Having made these vows, Amida dwelled peacefully in truth and accomplished various merits, with which he brought to perfection his vast and pure Buddha land of majestic glory.

It is also stated:[27]

Since Amida has accomplished the two adornments of merit and wisdom, he equally endows sentient beings with the merit of practice. Since he benefits sentient beings with the merit of his own practice, he realizes accomplishment of his merit in them.

It is also stated:[28]

Through good causes provided for us over eons of time, we can encounter the Buddha and rejoice to hear the Dharma.

It is also stated:[29]

The people in the Pure Land are sages, and the land is exquisite. Who would not exert themselves to go there? Aspire for birth by doing good. The cause of birth having already been accomplished, how can the result not be obtained spontaneously? Hence, "naturally." Regardless of whether you are noble or base, you are enabled to attain birth. Hence, "no discrimination between high or low."

It is also stated:[30]

"The land is easy to reach, but very few actually go there. It rejects nobody, but naturally and unfailingly attracts beings."[31] By performing the causal practice, all can attain birth. Without performing it, very few attain birth. Anyone who seeks birth by performing the causal practice is not rejected; hence, "easy to go to."

It is also stated:[32]

"Because of the Primal Vow-Power" means that through the Vow-Power one attains birth. "Because of the perfectly fulfilled vow" means that his vows are complete and there is nothing lacking. "Because of the clear and manifest vow" means that what Amida sought to attain was unfailingly realized. "Because of the firm vow" means that his vows cannot be destroyed by any influence from outside. "Because of the accomplished vow" means that his vows were bound to be fulfilled.

It is also stated:[33]

In general, in order to make ordinary and inferior beings increase their desire for birth, one should reveal the excellent qualities of that land.

It is also stated:[34]

There is a statement, "In this world they performed bodhisattva practices." From this we know that King Areṇemi once lived in this world. So did Samudrareṇu.

It is also stated:[35]

By hearing of the vastness of the Buddha's majestic virtue, one reaches the stage of non-retrogression.

It is stated in the *Collection of Passages on the Land of Bliss* (*Le-pang wen-lei*):

The general officer in charge of military affairs, Chang-lun, says:

596a

The Name of the Buddha is very easy to hold, and the Pure Land is very easy to reach. Among the eighty-four thousand teaching gates, there is none that is superior to this quick way to liberation. By setting aside a little time in the early morning, you should by all means store merit for the indestructible provision that will last for eternal *kalpa*s. That is to say, with slight effort one gains inexhaustible merit. What affliction do sentient beings suffer that keeps them from taking up the Name? Ah, all is a dream or illusion, and is unreal. Life is ephemeral and difficult to maintain for long. The moment one breath is not followed by another, the next life begins. Once human life is lost, it will not be regained even in ten thousand *kalpa*s. Unless we attain realization this time, what

can the Buddha do to save us? May all of you deeply
reflect on impermanence and be careful not to regret in
vain! Thus I, Chang-lun, the Layman of Pure Bliss, urge
those with whom I am karmically related.

Dharma Master Ch'ing-wen of Shan-yin, master of the T'ien-
t'ai school, says:

> Because the Buddha's Name manifests from his true body
> of recompense, because it arises from the oceanlike com-
> passion, because it arises from the oceanlike vow, from the
> oceanlike wisdom, and from the oceanlike Dharma gates, to
> call exclusively the Name of this Buddha is to call the names
> of all Buddhas. Because it contains immeasurable merit, it
> destroys the hindrances of our karmic evil, thereby enabling
> us to be born in the Pure Land. Why should there be any
> doubt about this?

Yüan-chao, master of the Vinaya school, says:

> With great compassion the Buddha revealed the Pure Land
> teaching and benevolently recommended this in many
> Mahayana scriptures. There are people who doubt and slan-
> der this after seeing and hearing it; immersed in self-com-
> placency, they do not seek spiritual transcendent attainment.
> The Tathāgata considered such people to be pitiable beings.
> They do not accept this because they do not realize that this
> teaching is indeed extraordinary. It does not choose between
> wise and foolish, monks and laypeople; it does not question
> whether one has practiced for a long time or not, nor whether
> one's karmic offense is heavy or light. It only requires firm
> faith as the cause of birth in the Pure Land.

He further says:

> In various Pure Land sutras there is no mention whatsoever of
> devils' hindrances; hence, we know that in this teaching there
> is no devils' hindrance. This matter is discussed in great detail

in the *Dharma Gate of True Faith* (*Cheng hsin fa men*) by Master Ch'ing-wen of Shan-yin. Let us quote the discussion in full:

> *Question:* Some say, "It may happen that at the time of death one beholds the Buddha and bodhisattvas coming in radiant light and bringing a lotus seat and, accompanied by heavenly music and wonderful fragrance, one is welcomed to attain birth. This is all devils' work." I wonder if this assertion is true.

> *Answer:* When one practices *samādhi* in accordance with the *Śūraṅgama Samādhi Sutra* (*Sutra of the Samādhi of Heroic Advance*), devils of the five aggregates may appear. When one practices *samādhi* in accordance with the *Treatise on the Mahayana* (*Mahāyana-śraddhotpāda-śāstra**)[36] external devils may appear. When one practices *samādhi* in accordance with the *Discourse on Cessation and Contemplation* (*Chih kuan lun,* i.e., *Mo he chih kuan*), "time spirits" may appear. All of these appear when different kinds of devils' hindrances, which are determined by the different natures of self-power of meditation practitioners, are stimulated by meditative practices. If you clearly realize this and apply the proper remedy, these hindrances are immediately removed. If, however, you assume that you are already a sage, you will suffer from devils' hindrances. (The above shows that practice to realize enlightenment in this world may give rise to devils' hindrances.)
> Concerning the Nembutsu *samādhi* that we now practice, we rely on the Buddha's power. It is just as those who are close to the king are free of any danger of assault. It is because Amida Buddha has the power of great compassion, the power of great vows, the power of great wisdom, the power of great *samādhi,* the great majestic power, the great power to destroy evils, the great power to subdue devils, the power of the divine eye to see far, the power of the divine ear to hear at distance, the power to know others' thoughts,

and the power of universally shining light with which he embraces sentient beings. Amida has all these inconceivable powers. How could he not protect persons of the Nembutsu and keep them from hindrances until death? If he could not protect them, what would be the use of his power of compassion? If he could not remove devils' hindrances, what would be the use of his power of wisdom, power of *samādhi*, majestic power, power to destroy evils, and power to subdue devils? If he could not perceive beforehand and allowed devils to inflict hindrances upon the practitioner, what would be the use of his power of divine eye to see far, power of divine ear to hear at distance, and power to know others' thoughts? The [*Contemplation*] *Sutra* states:

> The rays of light that issue from Amida Buddha's physical characteristics and minor marks illumine all the worlds of the ten directions, embracing and not forsaking sentient beings of the Nembutsu.

If one who recites the Nembutsu suffered devils' hindrances at the time of death, what would be the use of Amida's power of universally shining light with which he embraces sentient beings? Moreover, many sutras describe how people of the Nembutsu perceive miraculous signs at the time of death. These are all the Buddha's words. How could you belittle them and say that those signs belong to the devils' sphere of actions? I have thus corrected and cleared wrong thoughts and doubts. You should awaken the true faith.

(The above is the quotation from [Master Ch'ing-wen].)

He also says:[37]

The ultimate teachings of the One Vehicle all point to the Land of Bliss as the last refuge. The Name of Amida's Buddhahood is most distinguished as the embodiment of the perfect virtues of myriad practices. Amida in his causal state of a bodhisattva established the vows. Holding fast to his aspiration, he accomplished practices. He entertained compassion to save beings for "dust-motes" *kalpas*. There is no place, even as small as a mustard seed, where he did not abandon his life for their sake. He embraced and guided all, without exception, with the six perfections of compassion and wisdom. He never failed to respond to the need of the people by giving away his possessions and his own self. When conditions matured, his practices were fulfilled and his virtues were perfected; and thus he all at once perfectly realized the three Buddha bodies, and the myriad merits manifest themselves in the four characters (*A-mi-da-butsu*).

He also says:

What is more, our Buddha Amida encompasses beings with his Name. And so, as we hear it with the ears and recite it with the lips, boundless exalted merits enter into our hearts and become the seeds of Buddhahood forever; they instantaneously remove heavy karmic evil that would entail transmigration for a hundred million *kalpas*, thereby making us realize highest enlightenment. We truly know that the Name possesses much merit, not little good.

He also says:

Concerning right mindfulness, when ordinary people are about to die they have no control over their consciousness. So all kinds of karmic seeds, both good and evil, manifest themselves. Some give rise to wicked thoughts, some wrong views, some loving attachment, and others manifest devilish features of insanity. Do we not say that all of these are caused by perverted thoughts? But those who had previously recited the Buddha's Name had their karmic evil destroyed and karmic hindrances removed. Emitting the fragrance of pure karma within and embraced by the light of compassion, they are instantly delivered from suffering and attain the pleasures [of the Pure Land]. A passage of the sutra below urges us to seek birth, because there is such a benefit.

596c

[He also says:]

Master Tz'u-yün explains:

> Only the pure act for birth in the Land of Peace and Provision is the quick way to truth. Therefore, you should practice it. Any one of the four groups of Buddhists (i.e., monks, nuns, laymen, and laywomen) who seeks to destroy ignorance quickly and remove forever karmic evils, such as the five grave offenses and the ten evil acts, both heavy and light, should perform this practice. Those who wish to maintain pure observance of the Mahayana or Hinayana precepts for a long time, attain the Nembutsu *samādhi,* and accomplish the bodhisattva's [six] perfections, should learn this method. Those who wish to be free of fear at the time of death, attain peace and comfort of mind and body, see hosts of sages appear and extend their hands to welcome them, so that they may be rid of defiling afflictions for the first time and immediately reach the stage of non-retrogression, thereby realizing the non-arising of all *dharma*s without passing long *kalpa*s—they should learn this method.

Why do you not follow the Dharma words of this ancient sage? In the above five sections, I have briefly presented the essentials [of the *Contemplation Sutra*]. I will not discuss more here. A detailed exposition will be given in the explanatory section.

According to the *Catalog of Scriptures (K'ai-yüan shih chiao lu)* compiled in the K'ai-yüan era, there were two translations of this [*Contemplation*] *Sutra.* The earlier version has been lost. The one that exists was translated by Kālayaśas. The *Biographies of Monks (Kao-seng ch'uan)* has this note: "Kālayaśas' name is translated as 'Time-praise'; he came to the capital in the beginning of the Yüan-chia era of the Sung dynasty, during the reign of Emperor Wen."

Tz'u-yün praises in a hymn:

This is the supreme teaching of all the teachings that fully
explain the truth;
This is the highest teaching of all the teachings that lead
quickly to perfect enlightenment.

Tai-chih praises in a hymn:

This is the One Vehicle teaching that leads quickly to
perfect enlightenment;
It is pure and unadulterated.

Chieh-tu of the Vinaya school says:

The Buddha's Name contains practices performed for many
kalpas; myriad virtues accumulated by them are manifested
in the four-character Name. Therefore, anyone who recites
it gains no small benefit.

Yung-ch'in of the Vinaya school says:

If you recite and contemplate the auspicious Name of the
Buddha with your mouth and mind, you will unfailingly be
endowed with the immeasurable merits he accumulated from
his causal state to his Buddhahood.

He also says:

All the Buddhas have realized ultimate reality after practicing for "dust-motes" *kalpas* and yet they grasp nothing.
Hence, they made formless great vows; they performed excellent practices of no-abode; they realized ungraspable enlightenment; they dwell in the lands of no-adornment; they manifest transcendent powers of no-transcendent powers; they
display eloquent tongues covering the whole universe to
preach speechless speech. For this reason, they urge us to
accept this [*Amida*] *Sutra* in faith. How could we conceive of
this or discuss it? In my humble opinion, the inconceivable

virtues of the Buddhas are at once comprised in Amida's two kinds of recompensed glorious adornments. Concerning the practice of holding the Name, the Buddhas [who urge this] should include Amida.

Master Chia-hsiang of the Three Discourse school says:[38]

Question: How can the Nembutsu *samādhi* eliminate so much karmic evil?

Answer: My interpretation is this: the Buddha possesses immeasurable merits. By being mindful of his immeasurable merits, one can have one's immeasurable karmic evil destroyed.

Master Bob-wi of the Consciousness Only school says:[39]

All Buddhas invest their virtues in their names. To call their names is to glorify their virtues. Virtues destroy karmic evil and produce merits. So do the names. If one believes in a Buddha's name, it is certain and without doubt that it produces good and destroys evil. Why should there be any doubt about birth in the Pure Land through recitation of the Name?

597a

Fei-hsi of the Zen school says:[40]

The Nembutsu *samādhi* is the best of all good [practices]. Because it is the foremost of myriad practices, it is called "the king of *samādhi*s."

It is stated in the *Collection of Essential Passages Concerning Birth (Ōjōyōshū)*:

(Second,) although the acts to be performed by the three groups of aspirants presented in the *Two-fascicle Sutra*[41] are distinguished into different levels in depth, they have this common element: "singleminded and exclusive mindfulness of the Buddha of Infinite Life." Third, among the Forty-eight Vows Amida made a special vow concerning the Nembutsu teaching, declaring, "If the beings who repeat the Nembutsu even ten times would not be born, may I not attain perfect enlightenment." Fourth, the *Contemplation Sutra* states, "For those with extremely heavy karmic evil there is no other way of salvation. They can attain birth in the Land of Utmost Bliss only through recitation of Amida's Name."

It is also stated in the same work:

We should rely on the six kinds of virtue [of the Buddha] presented in the *Sutra on Contemplation of the Mind-base* (*Hsin ti kuan ching*): 1) the supreme, great field of virtues, 2) the supreme, great benevolence, 3) the most honored of all beings, whether they have no legs, two legs, or many legs, 4) the one who is as extremely rare to encounter as an *uḍumbara* blossom, 5) the only one who appears in the universe of a thousand million worlds, and 6) the one who fully possesses all the worldly and supramundane merits. With these six kinds of virtues, the Buddha continuously benefits all sentient beings.

With reference to these six kinds of virtues, Master Genshin says:

1. Practice the Nembutsu! All who say *"Namo butsu"* even once have already attained the Buddhist path. Hence, I take refuge in and worship the supreme field of virtues.

2. Practice the Nembutsu! The Buddha looks upon sentient beings with compassionate eyes without discrimination, as though each of them were his only child. Hence, I take refuge in and worship the mother of greatest compassion.

3. Practice the Nembutsu! All great beings of the ten directions revere and worship Amida, the Holy One. Hence, I take refuge in and worship the most honored one among the beings who have two legs.

4. Practice the Nembutsu! Hearing the Buddha's Name even once is rarer than encountering an *uḍumbara* blossom. Hence, I take refuge and worship the one most difficult to encounter.

5. Practice the Nembutsu! No two Honored Ones simultaneously appear in the one hundred *koṭis* of worlds. Hence,
I take refuge and worship the great Dharma King who rarely
appears in the world.

6. Practice the Nembutsu! The sea of virtues of the
Buddha, Dharma, and Sangha is of one entity throughout
the three periods of time (i.e., past, present, and future).
Hence, I take refuge and worship the honored one who fully
possesses myriad perfect virtues.

He also says:

If a robe is perfumed with flowers of a *pārijāta* tree even for a
single day, its fragrance far surpasses the scent perfumed with
flowers of *campaka* and *vārṣika* trees for a thousand years.

He also says:

It is like a pound of "stone-liquid" transforming a thousand
pounds of copper into gold. In the Himalayas grows an herb
called "enduring." If a cow eats it, *maṇḍa* is produced. If the
śirīṣa tree faces the constellation Kṛttikā, it bears fruit.   597b

It is stated in the *Collection of Passages on the Nembutsu Chosen in the Original Vow (Senchaku Hongan Nembutsu Shū)* compiled by Genkū:

Namu amida butsu: The fundamental act for the attainment
of birth is the Nembutsu.

It also states:

If you wish to free yourself from birth and death quickly, you
should, of the two superior teachings, lay aside the path of
sages and choose to enter the Pure Land path. If you wish to
enter the Pure Land path, you should, of the two practices,
right and sundry, abandon all sundry practices and choose
to rely on right practices. If you wish to perform right practices, you should, of the two kinds of acts, the act of right

assurance and auxiliary acts, set aside auxiliary acts and take up and exclusively practice the act of right assurance. The act of right assurance is to call the Buddha's Name. Recitation of the Name certainly enables one to attain birth, because it is based on the Buddha's Primal Vow.

[The Benefit of the Nembutsu Practice]

We now clearly know (from the above quotations) that the Nembutsu is not a self-power practice performed by ordinary people or sages; hence, it is called "practice not to be transferred [toward the Buddha]." Mahayana and Hinayana sages as well as people with karmic evil, whether heavy or light, should all equally take refuge in the great treasure-sea of the selected Primal Vow and attain Buddhahood through the Nembutsu.

Hereupon, the *Commentary on Vasubandhu's Discourse on the Pure Land* states:

> In the Land of Peace and Bliss there is no one who is not born transformed from within the pure flower of Amida Tathā-gata's enlightenment. [They are so born] by one and the same path of the Nembutsu, and not by other paths.

Thus, those who have received true practice and faith have much joy in their minds; hence this state is called the "stage of joy." It is compared to the first fruit [of Hinayana sagehood], because sages of the first fruit will not be subject to the twenty-ninth state of existence, even if they become slumberous and indolent. Even more certain of liberation are the multitudes of beings of the ten directions who rely on this practice and faith, for they are embraced and never forsaken. For this reason, this Buddha is called "Amida." This [saving activity] is called Other-Power. Hereupon, Mahāsattva Nāgārjuna says,[42] "They immediately enter the stage of definite assurance." Master T'an-luan says,[43] "They join those who are rightly established in the Mahayana path." We should respectfully trust in and exclusively follow this practice.

[The Cause and Condition of Birth]

We truly know that if it were not for the compassionate father of the virtuous Name, there would be no active cause of birth; if it were not for the compassionate mother of Light, there would be no passive cause of birth. Even if the active and passive causes are united, without the karma-consciousness of entrusting heart, one would not reach the Land of [Infinite] Light. The karma-consciousness of true entrusting heart is the internal cause, and the father of Name and the mother of Light are the external conditions. When the internal cause and the external condition are united, one realizes the body of truth in the Recompensed Land.

Therefore, Master [Shan-tao] says,[44] "With the Light and the Name, Amida embraces and benefits all beings throughout the ten directions, guiding them to realize faith." [Fa-chao says,[45] "Attaining Buddhahood through the Nembutsu is the true teaching of the Way." [Shan-tao] also says,[46] "The true teaching of the Way is difficult to encounter." We should discern this well.

[The Significance of One Utterance of the Nembutsu]

Concerning the practice and faith transferred to us in the phase of going forth, there is in practice "one utterance," and there is in faith "one thought." The one utterance of practice reveals, with regard to the number of Nembutsu recitations, the ultimate point of the easy practice of the selected Primal Vow.

Therefore, the *Larger Sutra* states:

> The Buddha said to Maitreya, "If there are people who hear the Name of that Buddha, rejoice so greatly as to dance, and call it even once, then you should know that they have gained great benefit by receiving the unsurpassed virtue."

597c

The Master of Kuang-ming Temple says:[47] "down to one utterance," also[48] "one pronouncing, one utterance," and also[49] "exclusive thought, exclusive utterance."

In the *Collection of Liturgical Passages from Various Scriptures,* fascicle two, Master Chih-sheng quotes [a passage from Shantao's work]:[50]

> Deep mind is true entrusting heart. It is to accept in faith that one is an ordinary person full of evil passions, with few roots of good, and, unable to escape from this "burning house," transmigrating in the three worlds. It is also to believe, without a single thought of doubt, that Amida's original Universal Vow enables anyone who calls the Name even down to ten times or hears it to attain birth without fail. Hence, it is called "deep mind."

In the [*Larger*] *Sutra* the term "even (down to)" is used; in the *Commentary*[51] "down to" is used. These terms are different but their meaning is the same. Further, "even (down to)" can include both once and many times. "Great benefit" is contrasted to small benefit. "Unsurpassed" is contrasted to surpassable. We truly know that the unsurpassed great benefit is the true benefit of the One Vehicle. Small benefit that is surpassable refers to the eighty-four thousand provisional teaching gates.

"Exclusive thought" in the *Commentary*[52] means singlemindedness; it describes the absence of "double-mindedness." "Exclusive utterance" is the single practice; it describes the absence of a second practice.

"Calling the Name once" transmitted to Maitreya is the single pronouncing. The single pronouncing is the single utterance. The single utterance is the single practice. The single practice is the right practice. The right practice is the right act. The right act is the right mindfulness. The right mindfulness is the Nembutsu; this is *Namu amida butsu.*

When we board the ship of the vow of great compassion and sail out on the vast sea of light, the breezes of the utmost virtue blow softly and the waves of our karmic evil turn into merit. Thus, the darkness of ignorance being broken, we shall quickly reach the Land of Infinite Light and realize great nirvana. Then we shall act in accord with the virtue of Samantabhadra. This we should know.

The *Collection of Passages on the Land of Peace and Bliss* states:

> "Repeating the Nembutsu ten times" is simply an indication of the number by the Sage (Śākyamuni). When one repeatedly utters the Nembutsu and focuses one's thought on it, without being distracted by other matters, one's act for attainment of birth is accomplished and nothing more is needed. Why do we take the trouble of keeping count of the number of our Nembutsu recitations? There is another piece of advice: those who practice the Nembutsu for a long time should, in many cases, follow this way. Beginners, however, could very well count the number, for there is a scriptural reference to support this.

These passages quoted above are clear testimony that reveals the true practice. We truly know that this is [the practice of] the selected Primal Vow, the supreme practice which is unequaled and rare, the Right Dharma which is all-complete and truly excellent, and the ultimate and unhindered great practice. This we should know.

[Other-Power]

Other-Power is the Tathāgata's Primal Vow-Power. 598a

The *Commentary*[53] says:

> "The Primal Vow-Power" shows that great bodhisattvas with their Dharma bodies always dwell in *samādhi* and yet manifest various bodies, employ various transcendent powers, and proclaim various teachings through their Primal Vow-Power; it is like an *asura*'s harp which spontaneously produces music even though there is no one playing it. This is called the feature of the fifth merit in the stage of teaching others.
>
> "Bodhisattvas accomplish the practice for their own benefit with the four gates in the phase of 'going in.' One

should realize the implication of this." "To accomplish" means to fulfill for one's own benefit. "One should realize the implication of this" means that one should realize that by accomplishing self-benefit one is able to benefit others; one cannot benefit others without first benefiting oneself.

"Through the fifth gate of going out bodhisattvas accomplish the practice of benefiting others by merit transference. One should realize the implication of this." "To accomplish" means to attain the fruition of the stage of teaching others as the result of merit transference to them. One can benefit others, whether in the stage of cause or in the stage of effect. "One should realize the implication of this" means that one should realize that by accomplishing self-benefit one is able to benefit others; one cannot benefit oneself without being able to benefit others.

Thus, by performing the five mindful practices, bodhisattvas accomplish both self-benefit and benefit for others, and so quickly attain *anuttara-samyak-saṃbodhi*. The Dharma that the Buddha has attained is called "*anuttara-samyak-saṃbodhi*," and because he has realized this "*bodhi*," he is called Buddha. "Quickly attain *anuttara-samyak-saṃbodhi*" means "quickly become a Buddha." "*A*" means "not"; "*(n)uttara*," "above"; "*samyak*," "right'; "*saṃ*," "universal"; and "*bodhi*," "way." Together, the term is translated "the highest, right, and universal Way." "Highest" means that this Way (*bodhi*) has probed the principle of reality to the depths and thoroughly investigated the ultimate nature of existence and so there is nothing that surpasses it. The reason for its being [the highest] is that it is "right." "Right" implies sacred wisdom. Because it knows all that exists just as they are, this is called "right wisdom." Because the ultimate nature of existence is noncharacteristic, the sacred wisdom is unknowing. "Universal" has two meanings: 1) the sacred mind universally knows all things; 2) the Dharma body universally pervades the Dharma realm; neither body nor mind is limited in pervasiveness. "Way" means the path of nonhindrance. The [*Garland*] *Sutra* says, "The Unhindered Ones throughout the ten directions transcend birth and death by the single path." "The single path" means the single path of nonhindrance. "Nonhindrance" implies the realization that birth and death is identical with nirvana; such a teaching of insight into nonduality has the characteristic of nonhindrance.

Question: For what reason is it said, "quickly attain *anuttara-samyak-saṃbodhi*"?

Answer: Because, as it is said in the *Discourse on the Pure Land,* "by performing the five mindful practices, [bodhisattvas] accomplish both self-benefit and benefit for others." When we deeply probe into the roots, we find that Amida Tathāgata provides the predominant condition. There is a difference between "benefit by the Other" and "benefit for others." Speaking from the Buddha's viewpoint, one should say "benefit for others." Speaking from the viewpoint of sentient beings, one should say "benefit by the Other." Since the Buddha's power is under discussion, one should say, "benefit for others." One should realize this implication.

598b

Generally speaking, attainment of birth in the Pure Land and the various practices performed by the bodhisattvas and human and heavenly beings living there are brought about by the Primal Vow-Power of Amida Tathāgata. The reason for saying so is that if it were not for the Buddha's power, the Forty-eight Vows would have been made in vain. Now I (T'an-luan) will select three vows to demonstrate the import of this.

The [Eighteenth] Vow says:

If, when I attain Buddhahood, the sentient beings of the lands of the ten directions who sincerely and joyfully entrust themselves to me, desire to be born in my land, and call my Name even ten times should not be born there, may I not attain perfect enlightenment. Excluded, however, are those who commit the five grave offenses and abuse the Right Dharma.

Due to the Buddha's Vow-Power, one attains birth by invoking the Name ten times. Since one attains birth, one is freed from transmigration in the three worlds. Since one thus attains deliverance from transmigration, this is the first proof for the rapid attainment [of *anuttara-samyak-sambodhi*].

The [Eleventh] Vow says:

If, when I attain Buddhahood, humans and *deva*s in my land should not dwell in the definitely assured stage and unfailingly reach nirvana, may I not attain perfect enlightenment.

Due to the Buddha's Vow-Power, one dwells in the rightly established stage. Because one dwells in the rightly established stage, one unfailingly reaches nirvana. Once one has reached nirvana, there will be no more suffering of transmigration. Hence, this is the second proof for the rapid attainment [of *anuttara-samyak-sambodhi*].

The [Twenty-second] Vow says:

If, when I attain Buddhahood, bodhisattvas in the Buddha lands of the other directions who visit my land should not ultimately and unfailingly reach the stage of becoming a Buddha after one more life, may I not attain perfect enlightenment. Excepted are those who wish to teach and guide sentient beings in accordance with their original vows. For they wear the armor of great vows, accumulate merit, deliver all beings from birth and death, visit Buddha lands to perform the bodhisattva practices, make offerings to Buddha Tathāgatas throughout the ten directions, enlighten countless sentient beings as numerous as the sands of the Ganges River, and establish them in highest, perfect enlightenment. Such bodhisattvas transcend the course of practice of ordinary bodhisattvas, manifest the practices of all the bodhisattva stages, and cultivate the virtues of Samantabhadra.

Due to the Buddha's Vow-Power, one transcends the practices of ordinary bodhisattvas, manifests the practices of all the bodhisattva stages, and cultivates the virtues of Samantabhadra. Since one thus transcends the ordinary bodhisattva stages, this is the third proof for the rapid attainment [of *anuttara-samyak-saṃbodhi*].

   When we ponder Other-Power, it is the predominant condition [for our rapid attainment of *anuttara-samyak-saṃbodhi*]. How can it be otherwise?

   I will present another illustration to show the distinctive features of "self-power" and "Other-Power." One observes the precepts out of fear of the three painful states of existence. Because one observes the precepts, one is able to practice meditation. By practicing meditation, one cultivates transcendent powers. With transcendent powers one is able to travel freely in the four [great] continents. This is called "self-power." Though a man of little virtue who rides a donkey cannot fly, if he were to follow the procession of a wheel-turning monarch he could fly in the air and travel in the four [great] continents without any hindrance. This is called   598c
"Other-Power." How foolish are scholars of these latter days! Having heard that Other-Power is to be trusted in, they should accept it in faith and not entertain restricted views.

Master Yüan-chao says:[54]

The way of destroying delusion and realizing true suchness in this world, which is based on one's self-power, is expounded in various Mahayana and Hinayana sutras. The way of realizing enlightenment after going to another land and hearing the Dharma there is necessarily dependent on the Other-Power, and so birth in the Pure Land is taught. Although these two ways are different, they are both means for making us realize our minds [as they are].

[The Ocean of the One Vehicle]

Concerning "the ocean of the One Vehicle,"[55] the One Vehicle is the Great Vehicle. The Great Vehicle is the Buddha vehicle. To attain the One Vehicle is to attain highest, perfect enlightenment. Highest enlightenment is the realm of nirvana. The realm of nirvana is the ultimate Dharma body. To attain the ultimate Dharma body is to reach the ultimate end of the One Vehicle. There is no other Tathāgata; there is no other Dharma body. Tathāgata is the Dharma body. To reach the ultimate end of the One Vehicle is to realize boundless and endless [enlightenment]. In the One Vehicle there are no two vehicles or three vehicles. The two vehicles and three vehicles are established to lead us to the One Vehicle. The One Vehicle is the vehicle of the highest truth. It refers solely to the One Buddha Vehicle of the Vow.

The *Nirvana Sutra* states:[56]

> Sons of good families, true reality is called the Great Vehicle; the principles outside the Great Vehicle are not called true reality. Sons of good families, true reality is the Buddha's exposition, not the devil's. If this is the devil's exposition, not the Buddha's, it cannot be called true reality. Sons of good families, true reality is the single way, pure and nondual.

This sutra also states:[57]

> How do bodhisattvas follow one reality? They provide means of leading all sentient beings to the single way. The single way is the Great Vehicle. Buddhas and bodhisattvas divide it into three for the sake of sentient beings. Thus bodhisattvas follow it without running counter to it.

This sutra also states:[58]

> Sons of good families, there are two kinds of "ultimate": the ultimate that glorifies Buddhahood and the ultimate that has been consummated; the former is the ultimate in the worldly

realm, and the latter is the ultimate in the supramundane realm. The ultimate that glorifies Buddhahood refers to the six perfections; the ultimate that has been consummated refers to the One Vehicle which all sentient beings will realize. The One Vehicle is called Buddha-nature. For this reason, I proclaim that each and every sentient being possesses Buddha-nature. All sentient beings possess the One Vehicle. Because it is covered over by their ignorance, they cannot see it.

This sutra also states:[59]

Why do you expound "one"? Because all sentient beings, without exception, possess the One Vehicle. Why do you expound "not one"? Because the three vehicles are established. Why do you expound "neither one nor not one"? Because [the absolute truth] is beyond the scope of reckoning.

599a

The *Garland Sutra* states:[60]

The Dharma realized by Mañjuśrī (i.e., the Nembutsu
    samādhi) is eternally unchangeable;
To the Dharma King [Amida] belongs only this one Dharma.
All the [Buddhas] who have realized the principle of
    unhinderedness
Have liberated themselves from birth and death by the
    single way.

The bodies of all the Buddhas
Are only one Dharma body;
They possess one and the same mind and wisdom;
Their [ten] powers and [four] fearlessnesses are equally
    the same.

Now, we see that the spiritual attainment described above is all the great benefit to be gained in the Pure Land of Peace and Provision and the inconceivable, ultimate virtues actualized by the Buddha's [Primal] Vow.

[The Meaning of "Ocean"]

"Ocean"[61] has the following meaning: all the waters of the rivers of sundry practices and sundry good acts that ordinary people and sages have performed since the beginningless past, and the waters of the ocean of evil passions, numerous as the sands of the Ganges River, of those who have committed the five grave offenses, those who have abused the Dharma, and those devoid of good roots, are transformed into the waters of the great treasure-ocean of myriad true virtues, as numerous as the sands of the Ganges River, actualized by the great compassion and wisdom of the Primal Vow. Hence, the metaphor of "ocean." Here we truly know the import of a sutra, which states, "The ice of evil passions melts and becomes the water of virtue."

The ocean of the Vow does not keep the corpses of sundry good acts performed by the middle and lower sages of the two vehicles [without changing them into Amida's virtues]. How then does it keep the corpses of false and perverted good acts and poisoned and mixed thoughts of humans and gods?

Thus, the *Larger Sutra* states:

> Neither *śrāvaka*s nor bodhisattvas are able to know
> The Sage's mind exhaustively;
> They are like those who are born blind
> And yet wish to guide others.
>
> The ocean of the Tathāgata's wisdom
> Is deep, vast, and boundless.
> Even sages of the Hinayana cannot fathom it;
> Only the Buddha clearly knows it.

[The *Commentary on Vasubandhu's*] *Discourse on the Pure Land* states:

> What is the accomplishment of the glorious merit of the unfailing sustenance? It is said in the verse:

When I observe the Buddha's Primal Vow-Power,
I find that those who meet with it do not pass it in vain.
They are enabled to quickly gain
The great sea of the treasure of merit.

Accomplishment of the merit of the unfailing sustenance is said of Amida Tathāgata's Primal Vow-Power. I shall briefly present some [examples of] vain provisions which do not support [one's life] and thereby reveal the meaning of "unfailing sustenance."

"Unfailing sustenance" results from the original Forty-eight Vows of Dharmākara Bodhisattva and is maintained by the transcendent power that Amida Tathāgata can freely use now. His vows gave rise to the power; the power fulfills the vows. The vows have not been vain; the power is not empty. The power and vows work in complete harmony, and are not in the least discordant with each other; hence, "accomplishment."

It also states:

The word "ocean" describes the Buddha's omniscience; it is limitless in depth and breadth and does not hold impure merits of the two vehicles; it does not retain the "corpses" of the middling and inferior [vehicles]; hence, this is compared to an ocean. For this reason, it is stated:

Heavenly and human beings, unshakable [in their
    spiritual attainments],
Are born out of the ocean of pure wisdom.

"Unshakable" means that the heavenly and human beings in his land have acquired the root of the Mahayana, and so their minds cannot be shaken by anything.

The Master of Kuang-ming Temple says:[62]

I rely on the bodhisattva-*piṭaka*,

The teaching for sudden liberation, the ocean of the One
Vehicle.

He also says:[63]

In the *Ornament Sutra* (*P'u-sa ying-lo ching*) the teaching
for gradual liberation is expounded.
One reaches the stage of non-retrogression after performing practices for ten thousand *kalpas*.

599b
The teachings expounded in the *Contemplation Sutra* and
the *Amida Sutra*
Are those for sudden liberation, the bodhi[sattva]-*piṭaka*.

In the *Collection of Passages on the Land of Bliss*, Tsung-hsiao
says:

One grain of elixir transforms iron into gold; one word of truth
transforms evil karma into good.

[Comparisons between the Nembutsu and Other Practices]

Now, when I compare the Nembutsu with various good practices
in regard to the teaching, there are the following comparisons:
1. Easy over difficult;
2. Sudden over gradual;
3. Crosswise over vertical;
4. Transcending over traversing;
5. Harmonizing with [the Vow] over discordant;
6. Great over small;
7. Much over little;
8. Superior over inferior;
9. Intimate over alien;
10. Near over far;
11. Deep over shallow;
12. Strong over weak;
13. Weighty over light;

14. Wide over narrow;

15. Unadulterated over mixed;

16. Short way over long way;

17. Quick over slow;

18. Special over ordinary;

19. Non-retrogressive over retrogressive;

20. Straightforwardly expounded over expounded with hidden intentions;

21. Recitation of the Name over meditative and non-meditative practices;

22. Exhaustive exposition of truth over partial exposition of truth;

23. Encouraged [by Buddhas] over not encouraged;

24. Uninterrupted over interrupted;

25. Unceasing over ceasing;

26. Continuing over not continuing;

27. Unsurpassed over surpassable;

28. Highest of the high over lowest of the low;

29. Inconceivable over conceivable;

30. Virtue of the fruition stage over causal practices;

31. Exposition on the Buddha's own initiative over exposition on others' request;

32. Not to be transferred [to the Buddha] over to be transferred;

33. Protected [by Buddhas] over not protected;

34. Verified [by Buddhas] over not verified;

35. Praised [by Buddhas] over not praised;

36. Transmitted [to Maitreya] over not transmitted;

37. Perfect teaching over imperfect teaching;

38. Practicable over not practicable;

39. Selected [by Amida] over not selected;

40. True over temporary;

41. Not seeing the Buddha's passing into nirvana over seeing the Buddha's passing into nirvana;

42. Beneficial even in the Age of the Extinct Dharma over not beneficial;

43. [Practice of] the Other-Power over [practices of] self-power;

44. Conforming to the Vow over not conforming to the Vow;
45. [Practitioners are] embraced over not embraced;
46. Leading to the stage of definitely assured over not leading to it;
47. Leading to birth in the Recompensed Land over leading to birth in the Transformed Land.

Such are the comparisons. However, when I ponder the ocean of the One Vehicle of the Primal Vow, I see that it is the all-merging, perfect, unhindered, absolute, and unparalleled teaching that brings about the quickest effect.

[Comparisons between Nembutsu Practitioners and Others]

Next, making a comparison with regard to practitioners, there are the following comparisons:
1. Entrusting over doubting;
2. Good over evil;
3. Right over perverse;
4. Right over wrong;
5. Truthful over vain;
6. True over false;
7. Pure over defiled;
8. Wise over dull;
9. Quick over slow;
10. Noble over mean;
11. Bright over dark.

Such are the comparisons. However, when I ponder the receptacle of the ocean of the One Vehicle, I see that adamantine faith is the absolute and unparalleled receptacle.

[Praise of the One-Vehicle Teaching]

Respectfully I proclaim to all aspirants of birth: The ocean of the One Vehicle of the Universal Vow is consummated with the utmost virtues that are unhindered, boundless, supreme, wonderful, ineffable, unspeakable, and inconceivable. Why is this so? Because the Vow is inconceivable.

The compassionate Vow is: 1) like great space because its excellent virtues are vast and boundless; 2) like a great vehicle because it carries all ordinary people and sages; 3) like a wonderful lotus flower because it cannot be defiled by anything in the world; 4) like Sudarśana, the king of medicine, because it cures all illnesses of evil passions; 5) like a sharp sword because it cuts the armor of all arrogance; 6) like the banner of the Heroic General (Indra) because it subdues all the devils' armies; 7) like a sharp saw because it cuts all the trees of ignorance; 8) like a sharp ax because it chops 599c down all the branches of suffering; 9) like a good teacher because it frees us from all bondage of birth and death; 10) like a leader because it shows the essential way of liberation for ordinary people; 11) like a spring because it inexhaustibly supplies the water of wisdom; 12) like a lotus flower because it is not defiled by any karmic evil; 13) like a swift wind because it disperses the fog of all hindrances; 14) like sweet nectar because it completely possesses the taste of all virtues; 15) like the right path because it leads multitudes of beings into the castle of wisdom; 16) like a magnet because it draws beings to the cause [of birth] of the Primal Vow; 17) like Jambūnada gold because it outshines all the good acts of the conditioned world; 18) like a hidden storehouse because it stores all the teachings of the Buddhas; 19) like the great earth because all the Tathāgatas of the past, present, and future throughout the ten directions arise from it; 20) like the light of the sun because it dispels the darkness of ignorance of all ordinary people and awakens joyful faith in them; 21) like a king because it surpasses [the teachings of] all sages of the higher vehicles (i.e., Buddhas); 22) like a strict father because it guides all ordinary people and sages; 23) like a compassionate mother because it nurtures the true cause of birth in the Recompensed Land; 24) like a nursing mother because it fosters and protects all the aspirants of birth, whether good or evil; 25) like the great earth because it sustains all those who are to be born; 26) like the great floods because it washes off all the grime of evil passions; 27) like the great fire because it burns the wood of all wrong views; and 28) like the great wind because it goes everywhere in the world without hindrance.

[The compassionate Vow] leads beings out of the three worlds, the castle of fetters, and closes the gates of the twenty-five states of existence. It enables us to reach the True Recompensed Land, and distinguishes the right path from wrong ways. It dries up the ocean of ignorance and carries us into the ocean of the Vow. It enables us to board the ship of omniscience and to float in the ocean of multitudes of beings. It fills the storehouse of merit and wisdom and opens the storehouse of expediency. Indeed, we should reverently receive and uphold it.

[Conclusion]

Now, with regard to the vows, there are [vows of] true practice and faith, and also there are [vows of] expedient practice and faith. The vow of true practice is the vow that the Name shall be praised by all the Buddhas. The vow of true faith is the vow of sincere mind and joyful faith. These are the practice and faith of the selected Primal Vow. Those who receive and practice them are all good and evil beings, the sages of the Mahayana and the Hinayana, and ordinary, foolish people. The kind of birth they attain is the inconceivable birth. The Buddha and the land are the Recompensed Buddha and the Recompensed Land. All of this is the accomplishment of the inconceivable vow, the ocean of one reality, or true suchness. This is the ultimate teaching of the *Larger Sutra on the Buddha of Infinite Life* and the right purport of the true teaching of Other-Power.

Hereupon, acknowledging the Buddha's benevolence and wishing to repay it, I have perused Master [T'an-luan's] *Commentary [on Vasubandhu's Discourse on the Pure Land]* and found the following passage:

A bodhisattva submits to the Buddha just as a dutiful son obeys his parents or a loyal subject serves his sovereign,

600a

whether king or queen, with actions not motivated by his desires but always in compliance with the wishes of the sovereign. Since he is appreciative of the Buddha's benevolence and eager to repay it, he naturally addresses the Buddha first. Furthermore, he has taken weighty vows. Without the support of the Tathāgata's supernatural power, how could he fulfill them? Here [Vasubandhu] entreats the Buddha to support him with his supernatural power, and so respectfully addresses the Buddha.

[Hymn of True Faith and Nembutsu]

Thus, having taken refuge in the true words of the Great Sage and perused the commentaries of the great masters, I have realized the profundity of the Buddha's benevolence. And so I have composed the *Hymn of True Faith and Nembutsu (Shōshin nembutsu ge)*.

I take refuge in the Tathāgata of Infinite Life;
I take refuge in the Buddha of Inconceivable Light.
Bodhisattva Dharmākara, in his causal stage,
Was in the presence of Lokeśvararāja, the Enlightened One.

He saw the pure lands of many Buddhas, observed how
    they had been established,
And examined everything, good and bad, about the
    humans and gods inhabiting them.
He then brought forth the unsurpassed and most excellent
    vows,
The great vows, immeasurable in scope and depth, which
    the world had never known.

Dharmākara chose and cherished his vows after
    contemplation for five *kalpa*s.
He further vowed that his Name would be heard
    throughout the ten directions.
Amida sends forth universally the immeasurable and
    boundless light,

The unimpeded, incomparable, and majestically flaming
   light,

The pure light, the light of joy, the light of wisdom,
The unceasing, inconceivable, and ineffable light,
And the light outshining the sun and the moon; with this
   light he illuminates the innumerable worlds.
All sentient beings are illuminated by his light.

The Name promised in the Primal Vow is the act of right
   assurance;
The vow of sincere mind and joyful faith provides the cause
   of our birth;
To attain the state next to the Buddha and realize great
   nirvana
Is due to the fulfillment of the Vow that assures our
   unfailing attainment of nirvana.

The reason for the Buddha's appearance in the world
Is, above all, to expound the Primal Vow of Amida, broad
   and deep as the ocean.
All beings in the evil age of the five defilements
Should believe in the truth of the Buddha's words.

If the single thought of joy and gratitude is awakened in us,
We shall realize nirvana without severing our blind passions.
When ordinary people and sages as well as those who
   commit the [five] grave offenses and abusers of the
   [Right] Dharma are taken into the Vow,
They become one in spiritual attainment, just as many
   rivers become of one taste upon entering the sea.

The light of all-embracing compassion always illuminates
   and protects us;
The darkness of ignorance has already been destroyed by it.
But still the clouds and mists of greed, desire, anger, and
   enmity
Continually cover the sky of true faith;

Yet, just as the sunlight is obstructed by clouds or mists,
Below them it is light and there is no darkness.
When we receive faith, regard and revere the Dharma, and
    attain great joy,
We immediately transcend the five evil realms.

If ordinary people, whether good or evil,
Hear the Dharma and trust Amida's Universal Vow,
Śākyamuni praises them as "humans of great and superior
    understanding";
Such people are called "white lotus flowers."

The Nembutsu promised in the Primal Vow of Amida
    Buddha
Is difficult for evil people who have wrong views and are
    arrogant
To receive and retain with joyful faith;
Of all difficulties nothing is more difficult than that.

The discourse writers of India, the land in the west,
And noble masters of China and Japan
Revealed the true purpose of the Great Sage's appearance
And clarified that Amida's Primal Vow responds to our need.   600b

Śākyamuni, the Tathāgata, while dwelling on Mount Laṅkā,
Prophesied to the assembly of monks that in Southern India
A great being named Nāgārjuna would appear in the world
And destroy all wrong views on "existence" and
    "nonexistence."

Proclaiming the unsurpassed teaching of the Mahayana,
He would reach the stage of joy and attain birth in the
    Land of Peace and Bliss.
He taught that the difficult practices are toilsome like
    traveling by land,
And urged us to believe that the easy practice is pleasant
    like sailing on water.

When a thought of mindfulness of Amida's Primal Vow
    arises,
At that instant we spontaneously enter the stage of
    [definite] assurance.
Always reciting only the Name of the Tathāgata,
We should seek to repay our indebtedness to his great
    compassion.

Bodhisattva Vasubandhu composed a discourse, in which
    he professed
That he took refuge in the Tathāgata of Unhindered Light;
In accordance with the sutras he expounded the true merits,
And clarified that the great Vow enables us to leap over
    [samsara] crosswise.

He revealed One Mind in order to emancipate multitudes
    of beings
Through Amida's merit transference by the power of
    his Primal Vow.
Upon entering the great treasure-ocean of merits,
We will unfailingly join the great assembly.

Upon reaching the Lotus-store world,
We will realize true suchness and attain the Dharma body.
Then, playing in the forests of evil passions, we will display
    supernatural powers;
Entering samsaric states, we will manifest accommodated
    and transformed bodies to save beings.

Master T'an-luan was venerated by the Emperor of Liang;
Facing toward his place, the king worshiped him as a
    bodhisattva.
When Bodhiruci, the Tripiṭaka master, gave him a Pure
    Land scripture,
T'an-luan burned his Taoist texts and took refuge in the
    Land of Bliss.

He wrote a commentary on Bodhisattva Vasubandhu's
  Discourse, explaining in it:
Both the cause and the effect of our birth in the Land of
  Recompense come from Amida's vows;
The karmic energy for our birth and returning to this
  world originates from Other-Power.
The cause of attaining the stage of definite assurance is
  faith alone.

When faith is awakened in the minds of deluded and
  defiled ordinary people,
They are made aware that birth and death is nirvana.
After they unfailingly reach the Land of Infinite Light,
They will save sentient beings everywhere, so says T'an-luan.

Master Tao-ch'o determined that by the path of sages
  enlightenment is difficult to attain
And clearly presented the Pure Land path as the only way
  of salvation.
He disparaged practicing thousands of acts of merit with
  self-power
And urged us to recite exclusively the Name of perfect
  virtues.

He kindly taught the three aspects of imperfect faith and
  those of right faith.
He compassionately guided those of the Ages of the
  Semblance Dharma, the Decadent Dharma, and the
  Extinct Dharma alike.
Whatever evils we may commit throughout our lives, if we
  encounter the Universal Vow,
We shall reach the Land of Peace and Provision and realize
  the supreme fruition.

Shan-tao alone clarified the true intent of Buddha
  Śākyamuni.

Out of compassion for those who practice meditative or
non-meditative good as well as those who commit the
five grave offenses and the ten evil acts,
He clarified that the Light and the Name are the cause
and condition for birth in the Pure Land.
When aspirants are led into the sea of great wisdom of the
Primal Vow,

They are endowed with adamantine faith;
After attaining a single thought of joy of oneness with
Amida,
They obtain the three insights, as did Vaidehī,
And will realize the eternal bliss of Dharma-nature.

Genshin widely expounded the Buddha's lifetime
teachings;
While he devoutly sought refuge in the Land of Peace and
Provision, he urged all to follow him.
He distinguished between deep faith in practicing the
Nembutsu exclusively and shallow faith in practicing
miscellaneous acts of merit,
And so clarified the different states of attainment: birth
in the Land of Recompense and birth in the
Transformed Land.

Those with extremely heavy evil karma should only recite
the Buddha's Name.

Although I, too, am in Amida's embracing light,
My evil passions hinder me from perceiving it,
But his light of great compassion never ceases to shine on
me untiringly.

Genku, the master of our school, was well versed in
Buddhism;
He was compassionately mindful of both good and wicked
ordinary people.

Disseminating the teaching of the True Way throughout
 Japan,
He spread the selected Primal Vow in this evil world.

Transmigration in the house of samsara
Is definitely caused by the fault of doubt;
Quick entry into the capital of tranquility and non-action
Is necessarily realized by faith.

The bodhisattvas and masters of this school who spread
 the teaching of the Pure Land sutras
Have saved innumerable beings, totally defiled and evil.
People of the present age, both priests and laypeople,
 should with one accord
Only accept in faith the teachings of those virtuous masters.

Here ends the *Hymn,* one hundred and twenty lines in sixty
verses.

End of Chapter II: Revealing the True Practice

Chapter III

Revealing the True Faith

Preface

When I deeply contemplate matters, I find that attainment of joyful faith arises from the Tathāgata's mind in which the Primal Vow was selected and embraced, and that the awakening of true faith occurs through the compassionate skillful means of the Great Sage. However, monks and laypeople of this latter age and the masters of these days, drowned in the concepts of "one's self-nature [being identical with Buddha]" and "[all that exists is in] one's mind," despise true enlightenment in the Pure Land; or, deluded by self-power efforts to perform meditative and non-meditative good practices, they are ignorant of the adamantine true faith.

Now I, Gutoku Shinran, disciple of Śākyamuni, have sincerely accepted the true teaching of the Buddhas and Tathāgatas and studied the doctrines of the discourse writers and commentators. Guided by the beneficial revelation of the three [Pure Land] sutras, I will elucidate, in particular, the "flower passage" concerning One Mind [by Vasubandhu]. In so doing, I will present some questions and later give answers to them by citing clear evidence.

Being appreciative of the Buddha's deep benevolence, I am not afraid of people's abuse. Those who aspire for the Pure Land and those who abhor this defiled world are requested not to slander this teaching, even though they may choose to accept or discard it.

[Presentation of the Great Faith]   601a

When I humbly contemplate the "going forth" aspect of Amida's

merit transference, I find that there is great faith. Great faith is
the divine prescription for a long life without death; the wonderful way of aspiring for the Pure Land and abhorring the defiled
world; the direct mind endowed through the selected Primal Vow;
the deep and vast joyful faith endowed by Other-Power; the true
adamantine faith; the pure faith for easy attainment of birth in
the Pure Land which, nevertheless, very few gain; the One Mind
embraced and protected by the light that issues forth from Amida's
mind; the great entrusting heart that is rare and supreme; the
quick way that is difficult for the people of the world to trust; the
true cause of realizing great nirvana; the white path that leads to
quick attainment of all-complete virtues; and the ocean of faith
that contains true suchness and ultimate reality.

This mind arises from the vow of attaining birth through the
Nembutsu. This great vow is called the selected Primal Vow, also
called the vow of the three minds of the Primal Vow, the vow of
sincere mind and joyful faith, and the vow of faith for our going
forth [to the Pure Land].

For ordinary foolish people who are eternally immersed in samsara, the multitudes of beings who are floundering in transmigration, the supreme wonderful fruition of enlightenment is not
difficult to realize; it is true joyful faith that is, indeed, difficult to
realize. Why is this so? Because it is attained through the endow-
ment of the Tathāgata's power; because it arises through the power
of great compassion and universal wisdom. If one, by rare chance,
obtains pure faith, this mind is not perverted nor vain. On attaining faith, sentient beings of extremely heavy and grave karmic
evil will have great joy in their hearts and receive the protection
and loving care of all the Holy Ones.

The passage of the vow of sincere mind and joyful faith in the
Larger Sutra states:

> If, when I attain Buddhahood, sentient beings in the lands
> of the ten directions who sincerely and joyfully entrust them-
> selves to me, desire to be born in my land, and call my Name

even ten times should not be born there, may I not attain perfect enlightenment. Excluded, however, are those who commit the five grave offenses and abuse the Right Dharma.

The *Teaching Assembly of the Tathāgata of Infinite Life* states:

If, when I realize the highest enlightenment, living beings in other Buddha lands who, having heard my Name, transfer all their roots of good to my land in every thought, desire to be born in my land, and call my Name even ten times should not be born there, may I not attain enlightenment. Excepted, however, are those who commit evil acts that would consign them to the Avīci hell and those who abuse the Right Dharma and the sages.

The passage on the fulfillment of the Primal Vow in the [*Larger*] *Sutra* states:

All sentient beings who have heard his Name, rejoice in faith, and think of him even once—through his sincere merit transference; aspiring to be born there, they immediately become assured of birth and dwell in the stage of non-retrogression. But excluded are those who have commited the five grave offenses and abused the Right Dharma.   601b

The *Teaching Assembly of the Tathāgata of Infinite Life,* translated by Bodhiruci, states:

All living beings in the Buddha lands of other directions, having heard the Name of the Tathāgata of Infinite Life, awaken a single thought of pure faith, rejoice, and enjoy Amida's transference of all the roots of good to them, thereby wishing to be born in the Land of Infinite Life. All will then be born there in accordance with their wishes, attain the stage of non-retrogression, and, finally, realize highest, perfect enlightenment. Excluded, however, are those who commit the five evil acts that would consign them to the Avīci hell (i.e., the five grave offenses), who abuse the Right Dharma, and who slander the sages.

It is also stated:[64]

If you have heard the Dharma and do not forget it
But regard and revere it with great joy,
You are my good friend. For this reason,
You should awaken aspiration for birth.

It is also stated:[65]

Such people are those endowed with great, majestic virtue. They will be born in the land consummated with the distinguished virtues of the boundless Buddha-Dharma.

It is stated in the same sutra:

The Tathāgata's virtues are known only to Buddhas;
The World-honored One alone can reveal them.
They are beyond the knowledge of gods, dragons, and
    yakṣas,
And the two vehicles themselves have no words to describe
    them.
Even if all living beings became Buddhas,
With their practices surpassing Samantabhadra, and,
    having reached the other shore,
Sought to expound one Buddha's virtues
During the period of many inconceivable kalpas,
And even passing the period in which they enter nirvana,
They would not be able to fathom the Buddha's supreme
    wisdom.
For this reason—if those who have faith, hear much
    teaching
And receive favors of good friends,
Are able to hear this profound and excellent Dharma—
They will receive the protection and loving care of all the
    Holy Ones.

Only Buddhas thoroughly know the Tathāgata's supreme
wisdom
And the meanings of the teaching that reach throughout
space.
Hence, having heard much about [Amida's] land of various
wisdoms,
Accept in faith the true words of my teaching.
It is extremely difficult to receive human existence;
It is also difficult to encounter a Tathāgata's appearance in
the world.
It is rare indeed to obtain the wisdom of faith.
Hence, the practitioner should pursue the Way with
diligence.
If you hear this wonderful Dharma,
All the Buddhas will always rejoice.

The *Commentary on Vasubandhu's Discourse on the Pure Land*
states:

[Vasubandhu says,] "One calls the Name of that Tathāgata
which describes his light, the embodiment of wisdom, wishing to practice in accord with the Dharma, that is, in agreement with the significance of the Name."

"To call the Name of that Tathāgata" means to call the
Name of the Tathāgata of Unhindered Light; "describes his
light, the embodiment of wisdom of that Tathāgata" shows
that the Buddha's light is the embodiment of wisdom. This
light is unhindered in illuminating all the worlds of the ten
directions. Its activity of removing the darkness of ignorance
of all sentient beings throughout the universe cannot be compared with the light of the sun and moon or with the brilliance of the [maṇi-]gem, which can only remove the darkness of a hollow or cave. Next, "wishing to practice in accord
with the Dharma, that is, in agreement with the significance
of the Name," shows that the Name of the Tathāgata of
Unhindered Light is capable of removing the darkness of

ignorance of sentient beings and of fulfilling all their aspirations.

If, however, he who calls the Name and thinks of [Amida] finds ignorance still persisting in his mind and, consequently, his aspiration has not yet been fulfilled, it is because he has not been practicing in accord with the Dharma, that is, in agreement with the significance of the Name.

What is the cause of not practicing in accord with the Dharma, or in agreement with the significance of the Name?

It is due to failure to understand that the Tathāgata [Amida] is a body of reality and also a body for the sake of living beings. It is also due to the three incorrect faiths:

1. One's faith is not sincere; at one time it exists and at another it does not;

2. One's faith is not singlehearted, because it is not firm;

3. One's faith is not constant, because it is mingled with other thoughts.

These three are mutually related, each becoming the cause of the next. Thus, because one's faith is not sincere, it is not firm. Because it is not firm, one's thought [of Amida] is not continuous. Because one's thought is not continuous, one cannot attain firm faith. Because one's faith is not firm, it is not sincere. If these incorrect faiths are eliminated, one can practice in accord with the Dharma. Therefore, the author of the *Discourse* says at the beginning, "with singleness of mind, I...."

It is stated in the *Hymns in Praise of Amida Buddha* (*Tsan a mi t'o fo chieh*) [composed by Master T'an-luan]:

All beings, having heard Amida's virtuous Name,
Attain joyful faith, rejoice in what they hear,
And call his Name even once. The person of sincerity, Amida,
Endows merit to them. All who aspire for birth attain birth.
Excluded are those who commit the five grave offenses and
    abuse the Right Dharma.

Hence, I prostrate myself to worship him and aspire to be
born there.

It is stated in the *Commentary on the Contemplation Sutra*
(*Kuan ching shu*)[66] by the Master of Kuang-ming Temple:

"According to one's wishes"[67] has two meanings: first, Amida
saves all sentient beings according to their wishes; second,
according to Amida's wishes, he observes beings to be saved
with the five kinds of perfectly illuminating eyes and, freely
exercising the six supernatural powers, approaches them, in
body and mind, simultaneously in a single moment; he then
enlightens them with three kinds of acts. The ways in which
he benefits them are different for each individual.

He also says:[68]

The beings in the six realms all experience the five defilements
and the five kinds of suffering, and none can ever be free of
them. They are constantly tormented by them. Anyone who
does not receive such afflictions cannot be counted among
ordinary beings.

He also says:[69]

The passage from "What are the three?" to "will unfailingly
be born in his land" distinguishes the three minds and clarifies
that they are the true cause of birth. This passage is divided
into two: 1) it is shown that the World-honored One has profound and unfathomable intent in endowing benefits to the
beings in accordance with their capacities, and so unless the
Buddha himself raised the question and revealed the point,
there would be no way of understanding his intent; 2) it is
shown that the Tathāgata himself gave the answer, explaining the three minds mentioned before.

The [*Contemplation*] *Sutra* states: "First, sincere mind
(*shijōshin*)": "*shi*" means true, and "*jō*" means sincere. [Amida]
here wishes to show clearly that both the understanding and

the practice to be cultivated by all sentient beings with their acts of body, speech, and mind ought to come from what [Amida] accomplished with a true and sincere mind. We should not show outwardly how wise, virtuous, and diligent we are, because, inwardly, we entertain deceitfulness. Being possessed of all kinds of greed, anger, falsity, and crookedness, we can hardly remove our evil nature; we are indeed like snakes or scorpions. Even if we perform practices with acts of body, speech, and mind, they are called "poisoned good acts" and also "false practices"; they are not called "true practices." Practices performed in such a state of mind are all called "poisoned good acts," even if we painstakingly strive, mind and body, throughout the twelve periods of the day and night, running up and down, as if to sweep fire off our heads. It is completely wrong to seek birth in that Buddha's Pure Land by transferring [the merits of] such poisoned practices there. Why? The reason is that, when Amida Buddha in his causal state performed bodhisattva practices, all his acts of body, speech, and mind were done with a true and sincere mind at all times, even every thought-moment or instant.

602a

What is given [by Amida] constitutes what we aspire for. All that is given is true. There are two kinds of true and sincere mind: of self-benefit and of other's benefit.... Regarding the three kinds of acts that are not good, we should discard what Amida discarded with a true and sincere mind. When we practice three kinds of good acts, we should practice what Amida practiced with a true and sincere mind. Thus we uphold [Amida's] true and sincere mind, whether dealing with matters inside or outside, bright or dark. Hence, "sincere mind."

"Second, deep mind": deep mind is deep entrusting faith. It has two aspects. First, to believe deeply and unwaveringly that we are actually ordinary beings of karmic evil subject to birth and death, ever sinking and ever transmigrating in samsara since innumerable *kalpas* ago without a chance to escape from it. Second, to believe deeply and unwaveringly that the Forty-eight Vows of Amida Buddha enfold sentient beings, enabling them to board his Vow-Power and attain birth. It is also to believe deeply and unwaveringly that Śākyamuni Buddha expounds in the *Contemplation Sutra* the three meritorious acts, the nine grades of aspirants, and the two kinds of good, that is, meditative and non-meditative, and also bears witness to and praises the primary and dependent rewards, that is, the Buddha's body and land, with a view to making people aspire for the Pure Land. It is also to believe deeply and unwaveringly that in the *Amida Sutra* Buddhas of the ten directions, as numerous as the sands of the Ganges River, present themselves as witnesses and urge all ordinary beings to attain birth unfailingly.

May all practitioners of deep mind singleheartedly accept the Buddha's words and hold fast to the [Nembutsu] practice, even at the risk of their lives. Let them give up what the Buddha urges them to give up and practice what he urges them to practice. Let them abandon what he urges them to abandon. To practice this way is called "to follow the Buddha's teaching and to accord with the Buddha's intent." This is also called "to accord with the Buddha's vows." Such practitioners are called "true disciples of the Buddha."

Further, all practitioners who perform practices with deep faith in accordance with this [*Contemplation*] *Sutra* are able to guide other beings without mistakes. Why? Because the Buddha is a person of perfect compassion, and also his words are words of truth. Those who haven't yet attained Buddhahood are imperfect in wisdom and practice; being still in the stage of training, they have not yet completely removed their evil passions and their residues, and so their aspiration for Buddhahood has not yet been fulfilled. Such sages and ordinary people cannot decisively know the Buddhas' intent however hard they may try to fathom it. Even if they are able to understand it correctly, they ought to request the Buddha's testimony as the final authority. If one's interpretation agrees with the Buddha's intent, he approves of it, saying, "So it is, so it is." If not, he will say, "Your exposition is incorrect." The words not approved by the Buddha are unauthentic, without benefit, and useless, but those approved by the Buddha are in accord with his right teaching. Every word and exposition of the Buddha is the right teaching, the right principle, the right practice, the right understanding, the right act, and the right wisdom. How could any bodhisattva, human, or *deva* determine whether the Buddha's words are correct or not, no matter how long or short they may be? The Buddha's exposition is the teaching that fully clarifies the truth, while expositions by bodhisattvas or others are all teachings that do not fully clarify the truth. We should reflect on this.

For this reason, I now respectfully urge all aspirants for the Pure Land who have close ties with us to accept the Buddha's words with deep faith and hold them with utmost care. Do not believe in the unauthentic teachings of bodhisattvas and others, and do not entertain doubts and delusions or confuse yourself, thereby losing the great benefit of attaining birth....

Śākyamuni urges all ordinary beings to practice the Nembutsu singleheartedly throughout their lives; when they die, they will definitely be born in that land. All the Buddhas of the ten directions, without exception, praise and recommend this teaching and give testimony to its truth. Why do they do so? Because their great compassion arises from the same essence. One Buddha's teaching is the teaching of all the Buddhas; all the Buddhas' teachings are one Buddha's teaching. Hence, it is stated in the *Amida Sutra:*

> Śākyamuni praises various adornments of the Land of Utmost Bliss, and also urges ordinary people to focus their thoughts on Amida's Name for one to seven days, thus leading them to attain birth there.

It is further stated in the passage that follows:

In each of the ten directions there are Buddhas as numerous as the sands of the Ganges River who praise Śākyamuni for appearing in the evil age of the five defilements, in the evil world when evil beings, wrong views, evil passions, evil acts, and disbelief prevail, glorifying Amida's Name and urging sentient beings to call it so that they unfailingly attain birth.

This is the testimony. Further, the Buddhas of the ten directions, fearing that sentient beings might not accept the teaching of one Buddha, Śākyamuni, extended their tongues with one accord and covered with them the universe of a thousand million worlds; they then spoke the following true and sincere words:

Sentient beings, you should accept in faith Śākyamuni's teaching, his words of praise, and his testimony. All ordinary people, regardless of the amount of their karmic evil and merit or of the length of time of their practice, should singlemindedly concentrate on Amida's Name, even up to the end of their lives of a hundred years and down to one to seven days. There is no doubt that they will unfailingly attain birth.

Thus, one Buddha's teaching is testified to by all the Buddhas. This is called "establishing faith in the persons (i.e., Buddhas)...."

Next, the right practice is again divided into two: first, one concentrates on Amida's Name singleheartedly, being mindful of it every moment, whether walking, standing, sitting, or lying down, and regardless of the length of time of one's practice; this is called "the act of right assurance" because 602c it is in accord with the Buddha's [Eighteenth] Vow. [Second,] if one performs acts such as worshiping and chanting sutras, these are called "auxiliary acts." All good acts other than these two kinds of acts are called "sundry practices...." They are called "loose and mixed practices." Deep mind is so called for the above reasons.

"Third, the mind of aspiring for birth by merit transference": Those who wish to attain birth by developing aspiration and transferring merit should, without fail, be definitely sure to make use of [Amida's] aspiration to transfer his merit [to sentient beings] with true and sincere mind and so dwell in the thought of attaining birth. Since this mind of deep entrusting is [indestructible] like a diamond, it is not shaken or destroyed by people of other views, other teachings, different understandings, or different practices. You should firmly and resolutely hold [to the Vow] singleheartedly and take the path straightforwardly, without heeding the remarks of others. For if you are indecisive as to whether to go forward, or if you retreat and look back apprehensively, you will stray from the path and fail to gain the great benefit of birth in the Pure Land.

Question: People of wrong and miscellaneous practices with different understandings and pursuits may come up to you and confuse you by putting forward troublesome questions and declaring, "You will not attain birth." Or they may say, "To all beings, whether ordinary people or sages, you, sentient beings, have, from distant *kalpas* ago up to this present life, committed the ten evil acts, the five grave offenses, and the four major prohibitions, also abused the Dharma, destroyed the seed of Buddhahood, violated the precepts, destroyed the right view, and so forth; yet, you have not been able to eliminate this evil karma. Such evil karma will bind you to the evil realms in the three worlds. How is it possible that by performing meritorious deeds and practicing the Nembutsu only for one lifetime you reach the undefiled land of no-birth and attain the stage of non-retrogression forever?"

Answer: The teachings and practices taught by the Buddhas are more numerous than the number of particles or grains of sand. Favorable conditions for realizing enlightenment that fit the propensities of people are diverse. To give an illustration, people of the world do not doubt what they see with their eyes: light disperses darkness, space enfolds, the earth bears and nurtures, water moistens and grows, and fire ripens and destroys. These are relative things that can be observed with the eye. They are distinct in myriad ways. In how much more multifarious ways does the inconceivable power of the Buddha-Dharma not benefit us?

To go out from one [Dharma] gate is to go out from a gate of evil passions; to enter one [Dharma] gate is to enter a gate of liberation wisdom. Thus, we should undertake any practice in accordance with given conditions and seek liberation. Why do you disturb me with a practice that is not the essential practice suitable to my condition? What I like to hold on to is the practice suitable to my conditions; it is not what you seek. What you like to hold on to is the practice suitable to your conditions, which is not what I seek. By performing practices in accordance with each person's desire, one can without fail quickly attain liberation.

Practitioners, you should know that if you wish to gain knowledge of Buddhism you can learn, without hindrance, all about ordinary beings and sages, even about the Buddha's fruition. But if you wish to undertake practice, never fail to follow the method of practice suitable to your conditions. For you will gain much benefit by making a small effort. 603a

[The Parable of Two Rivers and the White Path]

I wish to say to all aspirants for birth: I will now present a parable for practitioners in order to protect their faith and guard it against attacks by those who have wrong, perverted, and unauthentic views. What is the parable?

Suppose a man is traveling a hundred thousand *li* toward the west. On the way, he suddenly comes upon two rivers: a river of fire that extends southward, and a river of water that extends north-ward. The two rivers are each a hundred paces wide and unfath-omably deep, extending endlessly to the north and south. Where they meet there is a white path, four or five inches wide. This path is a hundred paces long from the east bank to the west. The waves of the water splash upon the path, and the flames of the fire burn the path. The waves and flames alternate without ceasing.

This traveler has already journeyed far into the open, deserted plain. Suddenly, there appear many bandits and vicious beasts. Seeing him alone, they approach, vying with each other to kill him. Afraid of death, the man at once runs to the west. When he suddenly comes upon the great river, he says to himself, "This river extends endlessly to the south and to the north. I see a white path in the middle, but it is extremely narrow. Although the two banks are close to each other, how can I get across? Undoubtedly, I shall die this day. When I turn around to go back, I see bandits and vicious beasts coming closer and closer. If I try to run to the south or north, I see vicious beasts and poisonous insects vying with each other to attack me. If I take the path to the west, I will certainly fall into one of the two rivers of water and fire."

His horror at this moment is beyond words. So he thinks to himself, "If I turn back now, I shall die; if I stay, I shall die; if I go forward, I shall die, too. Since I cannot escape death in any way, I would rather follow this path. Because there is a path, it must be possible to cross the rivers."

When this thought occurs to him, he suddenly hears a voice from the eastern bank urging him, "Take this path with firm res-olution. There is no danger of death. If you stay there, you will die." Then he hears another voice from the western bank calling to him, "Come at once singleheartedly with right mindfulness. I will protect you. Do not fear that you may fall into the calamities of water or fire." Since the traveler hears this voice urging him from the bank and the calling from the other, resolute in body and mind he takes the path and proceeds at once without doubt or apprehension.

As he takes a few steps, he hears the voices of the bandits on the eastern bank, saying "Come back! That path is treacherous. You cannot cross it. Undoubtedly, you are sure to die. We have no evil intentions in pursuing you." Though he hears the voices calling, the traveler does not look back. He proceeds straight on the path singleheartedly, quickly reaches the western bank, and is now free from all danger. There he meets his good friend and his joy knows no end. This is the parable.

The meaning of the parable is as follows. "The eastern bank" is the burning house of this Sahā world. "The western bank" is the Treasure Country of Utmost Bliss. The bandits and vicious beasts calling with feigned friendship refer to sentient beings' six sense organs, six sense consciousnesses, six sense bases, five aggregates, and four elements. "The open deserted plain" refers to always consorting with evil friends without having a chance to meet a true good teacher. The "two rivers of water and fire" describes sentient beings' greed and lust, which are like water, and their anger and hatred, which are like fire. The white path in the middle, four or five inches wide, shows that a pure aspiration for birth arises from within sentient beings' evil passions of greed and anger. Since greed and anger are intense, they are compared to water and fire. Since the good mind is faint, it is compared to a white path. Further, "waves always splash upon the path" describes that greed always arises and defiles one's good mind, and "flames always burn the path" shows that anger and hatred burn the Dharma treasure of virtue. "The man at once takes the path westward" shows that he immediately proceeds westward, turning aside various practices. "Hearing a voice from the eastern bank urging him to proceed, he immediately takes the path to the west" shows that even though Śākyamuni has already [passed on from the world] and people cannot see him, his teaching still exists and can be followed; the teaching is compared to the voice. "As he takes a few steps, bandits call him to return" shows that people of different understandings, different practices, and wrong views confuse him with their false views, saying, "You will commit evil karma and

603b

97

fall back from the path." "There is a man on the western bank calling to him" refers to the purport of Amida's Vow. "He quickly reaches the western bank and rejoices at seeing his good friend" shows that sentient beings, who have long been immersed in the ocean of birth and death, transmigrating from the eternal past, deluded and bound by their own karma from which they cannot free themselves, are now urged by Śākyamuni to go to the west and are also summoned by Amida's compassion. Faithfully following the wishes of the two sages, they take the path of Vow-Power with constant mindfulness, unafraid of the two rivers of water and fire; after death, they will be born in his land, where with boundless joy they will see the Buddha.

Since all practitioners always have this understanding and thought in performing practices in the three modes of action, whether walking, standing, sitting, or lying down, regardless of time, whether day or night, we call such a state of mind the "mind of aspiring for birth by merit transference." Also "merit transference" (literally, "turning and facing toward") means that after we have been born in that land we awaken great compassion, with which we turn toward and enter [the cycle of] birth and death to teach and guide sentient beings. This is also called "merit transference."

If one possesses the three minds, there is no practice that will not be accomplished. It does not stand to reason that even though one already has aspiration and practice one cannot attain birth. It is to be noted that these three minds also apply to meditative good.

603c

[Shan-tao] also says:[70]

> Reverently I say to all my fellow practitioners for Pure Land birth: You should be deeply grateful. Śākyamuni Tathāgata is truly our compassionate father and mother. He awakens the unsurpassed faith in us by various means.

The *Newly Compiled Catalog of Scriptures in the Chen-yüan Era* (*Chen-yüan hsin ting shih chiao mu-lu*), fascicle eleven, states:

> The *Collection of Liturgical Passages from Various Scriptures,*

two fascicles, was compiled by Chih-sheng, a monk of West Ch'ung-fu Temple during the T'ang dynasty. By imperial order, dated the twenty-third day of the tenth month, fifteenth year of Chen-yüan (800 C.E.), it was newly included in the Tripiṭaka. When Chih-sheng compiled the first fascicle of the liturgies from various sutras, he quoted the hymns for the midday chant from Shan-tao's *Hymns of Birth in the Pure Land* in presenting the liturgy for the *Contemplation Sutra*. The second fascicle bears the title, "Collected by Monk Shan-tao."

In the important passages from the *Collection of Liturgical Passages from Various Scriptures* it is stated:

> Second is deep mind. It is true entrusting heart. We realize that we are ordinary beings full of evil passions, with little stock of good, subject to transmigration in the three worlds, and unable to escape this burning house. We also realize, without so much as a thought of doubt, that the original Universal Vow of Amida definitely enables those who recite the Name even ten times or hear it to attain birth. For this reason, this mind is called "deep mind.... "

> Those who have heard
> The Name of Amida Buddha,
> Rejoicing as they attain a single thought of faith,
> Will all be born in that land.

It is stated in the *Collection of Essential Passages Concerning Birth:*

> We read in the "Chapter on Entry into the Dharma Realm" [in the *Garland Sutra*]:

> > If a man obtains a medicine that renders him indestructible, his enemies and adversaries will not be able to find the opportunity to harm him. So it is with bodhisattva *mahāsattva*s. If they obtain the Dharma medicine for securing the indestructible *bodhi*-mind, no evil passions,

devils, or adversaries will be able to destroy them. Again, if a man obtains a *maṇi*-gem from the ocean and makes it his ornament, he will not drown in deep waters. Likewise, if [bodhisattvas] obtain the *maṇi*-gem of *bodhi*-mind, they will not drown in the sea of birth and death. It is also like the *vajra* that does not decay even if immersed in water for a hundred thousand *kalpas*. *Bodhi*-mind will not perish or become damaged even if it is submerged in the karma of evil passions in birth and death for immeasurable *kalpas*.

It is also stated in the same work:

Even though I am in Amida's embrace, my evil passions obstruct my sight and so I cannot see [the light]; however, great compassion always shines on me untiringly.

Thus, there is nothing, whether practice or faith, that has not been transferred to us by Amida Tathāgata out of his pure vow-mind. It is not that there is no cause [for birth] or that there is a cause other than this. This we should remember.

604a

[The Three Minds and One Mind]

Question: In the Primal Vow, the Tathāgata already made the vow of sincere mind, joyful faith, and desire for birth. Why does the author of the *Discourse,* Vasubandhu, profess "One Mind"?

Answer: In order to make ignorant sentient beings understand more easily. Amida Tathāgata made [the vow of] three minds, but the true cause of nirvana is faith only. For this reason, it seems that the author of the *Discourse* puts the three together into one.

When I consider the literal meaning of the three minds, the three should be one. The reason is as follows: with regard to sincere mind (*shishin*), "*shi*" means true, real, and sincere; "*shin*" means seed and fruit. With regard to joyful faith (*shingyō*), "*shin*" means true, real, sincere, full, utmost, accomplished, function, heavy, discerning, test, expounding, and loyal; *"gyō"* means desire, aspiration, appreciation, rejoicing, delight, joy, gladness, and happiness. With regard to desire for birth (*yokushō*), *"yoku"* means vow, aspiration, awakening, and realization; *"shō"* means accomplishing, making, doing, and raising.

We clearly realize as follows. Sincere mind is the mind of true, real, and genuine [wisdom] and of the seed [of Buddhahood]; hence, it is not mixed with doubt. Joyful faith is the mind full of truth and sincerity, the mind of utmost trust and reverence, the mind of clear perception [of Amida's salvific power] and steadfastness, the mind of aspiration and appreciation, and the mind of joy and delight; hence, it is not mixed with doubt. Desire for birth is the mind of certainty and assurance [of birth], the desire to become [a Buddha] and perform [altruistic activities], and the mind endowed by great compassion; hence, it is not mixed with doubt.

When I consider the meanings of the characters that make up the words for the three minds, they are the true mind not mixed with delusion and the sincere mind not mixed with falsehood. I truly realize that it is the mind not mixed with doubt; hence, it is called joyful faith. Joyful faith is One Mind; One Mind is true entrusting heart. For this reason, the author of the *Discourse* professed "One Mind" at the outset [of the *Discourse*]. This we should realize.

Question: From the above explanation of the meanings of the characters, I see that it is reasonable for the author of the *Discourse* to combine the three into one. But how can we conceive of the vow of three minds that Amida Tathāgata made for the benefit of ignorant and evil sentient beings?

Answer: The Buddha's intention is difficult to fathom. I will, however, venture to surmise his intent. From the beginningless past to this day and up to this moment, the oceanlike multitudes of beings have been defiled and evil and lacking pure mind; they have been deluded and deceitful and lacking true mind. Consequently, when the Tathāgata awakened compassion for all suffering oceanlike sentient beings and performed the bodhisattva practices for inconceivable millions and billions of *kalpa*s, his practices in the three modes of action have never been impure or untrue, even for a thought-moment or an instant. With a pure, true, and sincere mind, the Tathāgata perfected the complete, all-merging, unhindered, inconceivable, indescribable, and ineffable supreme virtue. The Tathāgata endows his sincere mind to the oceanlike multitudes of beings who are full of evil passions, evil karma, and perverted wisdom. This is the true and sincere mind endowed by him to benefit such beings; hence, it is not mixed with doubt. The basis for the sincere mind is the sacred Name of the supreme virtue.

604b

Thus, we read in the *Larger Sutra:*

> He (Dharmākara Bodhisattva) did not harbor any thought of greed, hatred, or cruelty; nor did he allow any ideas of greed, hatred, or cruelty to arise. He was unattached to any form, sound, smell, taste, touch, or idea. Possessed of the power to persevere, he did not avoid undergoing various afflictions. Having little desire for his own sake, he knew contentment. Without any impure thought, enmity, or stupidity, he dwelled continually in tranquil *samādhi*. His wisdom was unobstructible and his mind free of falsehood and deceitfulness. With expressions of tenderness on his face and with kindness in his speech, he spoke to others in consonance with their inner thoughts. Courageous and diligent, strong-willed and untiring, he devoted himself solely to the pursuit of the pure Dharma, thereby benefiting multitudes of beings. He revered the Three Treasures, respected his teachers and elders, and thus adorned his practices with a great store of merits. By so doing, he enabled sentient beings to partake of them.

The *Teaching Assembly of the Tathāgata of Infinite Life* states:

> The Buddha said to Ānanda, "Bhikṣu Dharmākara widely proclaimed those great, universal vows before Lokeśvararāja Tathāgata, gods, humans, devils, Brahmā, monks, and brahmans. He has already fulfilled the vows. Having proclaimed

those vows, which were rare in the world, he dwelled firmly in the realization of them. He obtained various merits with which he adorned the pure Buddha land of extensive majestic virtues. The time that elapsed while he performed such bodhisattva practices was immeasurable, innumerable, inconceivable, unequaled *koṭi*s of *nayuta*s of a hundred thousand *kalpa*s. During that time, he did not harbor in his mind a single thought of greed, anger, or ignorance (i.e., the three poisons), nor conceive any idea of greed, cruelty, or anger. He never had an attached thought of form, sound, smell, taste, or touch. For all sentient beings he embraced a feeling of love and respect as he would do for his relatives.... He had a docile and friendly nature and never resorted to violence. He always maintained a heart of compassion and patience for all living beings, and was never deceitful or flattering. Neither was he indolent or slothful. He encouraged all to do good acts and led them to seek the pure Dharma. For the sake of all beings, he courageously remained steadfast in his resolve and never retreated. Thus he benefited the whole world and fulfilled his great vows."

The Master of Kuang-ming Temple says:[71]

It is completely wrong to seek birth in that Buddha's Pure Land by transferring [the merits of] such poisoned practices there. Why? The reason is that when Amida Buddha in his causal state performed bodhisattva practices, all his acts of body, speech, and mind were done with a true and sincere mind at all times, even every thought-moment or instant. What is given [by Amida] constitutes that for which we aspire. All that is given is true. There are two kinds of true and sincere mind: of self-benefit and of benefit for others.... Regarding the three kinds of acts that are not good, we should discard what Amida discarded with a true and sincere mind. 604c When we practice three kinds of good acts, we should practice what Amida practiced with a true and sincere mind. Thus we uphold [Amida's] true and sincere mind whether dealing with matters inside or outside, bright or dark. Hence, "sincere mind."

From the true words of the Great Sage and the explanation of the master of this school (Shan-tao), we truly realize that this mind is the true and sincere mind endowed by the Buddha for our benefit through the inconceivable, indescribable, and ineffable oceanlike vow of great wisdom of the One Vehicle. This is called "sincere mind."

In the above passage we find the word "true." Concerning "true," the *Nirvana Sutra* states:[72]

> True reality is the single path of purity that does not presuppose a second path. True reality is none other than Tathāgata; Tathāgata is none other than true reality. True reality is none other than space; space is none other than true reality. True reality is none other than Buddha-nature; Buddha-nature is none other than true reality.

[Shan-tao's] *Commentary* says "whether dealing with matters inside or outside, bright or dark."

In the phrase "inside or outside," "inside" refers to the supramundane and "outside" refers to the worldly. In the phrase "bright or dark," "bright" refers to the supramundane and "dark" refers to the worldly. Further, "bright" refers to wisdom and "dark" refers to ignorance. The *Nirvana Sutra* states:[73]

> Darkness refers to the worldly and brightness refers to the supramundane. Darkness refers to ignorance and brightness refers to wisdom.

Next, joyful faith is the oceanlike faith, complete, all-merging, and unhindered, consummated with the Tathāgata's great compassion. For this reason, it is not mixed with doubt. Hence, it is called joyful faith. The basis for joyful faith is sincere mind endowed by Other-Power.

However, all the oceanlike multitudinous beings, since the

beginningless past, have been transmigrating in the sea of ignorance, drowning in the cycle of birth and death, bound to samsara,
and lacking pure joyful faith. As a natural consequence they have
no true joyful faith. Therefore, it is difficult for them to meet the
highest virtue and attain the supreme pure faith. All ordinary
beings of limited capacities, at all times, constantly defile their
good minds with greed and lust, and their anger and hatred continuously burn the treasure of Dharma. Even if they act and practice as busily as though they were sweeping fire off their heads,
their practices are called "poisoned and mixed good" and also
"deluded and deceitful practices," and are not called "true acts."
To seek to attain birth in the Land of Infinite Light with these
deluded and poisoned good [acts] would be in vain. Why? Because
when the Tathāgata [Amida] performed the bodhisattva practices,
his three modes of action were not mingled with doubt even for a   605a
thought-moment or an instant. Because this mind (joyful faith) is
the Tathāgata's great compassion, it necessarily becomes the decisive cause of birth in the Land of Recompense. The Tathāgata, out
of compassion toward the suffering multitudes, endowed the unhindered, great pure faith to the ocean of beings. This is called true
entrusting heart of Other-Power.

The passage of fulfillment of the vow of faith, the Primal Vow,
reads as follows:

> All sentient beings, having heard his Name, rejoice in faith
> and think of him even once.

It is also stated:[74]

> All sentient beings in the Buddha lands of other directions,
> having heard the Name of the Tathāgata of Infinite Life,
> awaken a single thought of pure faith and rejoice.

We read in the *Nirvana Sutra*:[75]

> Sons of good families, great compassion and great benevolence
> are called Buddha-nature. Why? Because great compassion

105

and great benevolence accompany bodhisattvas just as shadows accompany objects. All sentient beings will ultimately and surely realize great compassion and great benevolence. For this reason, I make this remark, "All sentient beings have Buddha-nature." Great compassion and great benevolence are called Buddha-nature. Buddha-nature is called Tathāgata. Great joy and great abandonment are called Buddha-nature. Why? Because if bodhisattva *mahāsattva*s were unable to abandon the twenty-five states of existence, they would not be able to realize highest, perfect enlightenment. Because all sentient beings ultimately and surely attain it, I say that "All sentient beings have Buddha-nature." Great joy and great abandonment are Buddha-nature. Buddha-nature is Tathāgata. Buddha-nature is great faith. Why? Because it is through faith that bodhisattva *mahāsattva*s have accomplished all the practices of the perfections, from charity (*dāna*) to wisdom (*prajñā*). Because all sentient beings ultimately and surely attain great faith, I say, "All sentient beings have Buddha-nature." Great faith is Buddha-nature. Buddha-nature is Tathāgata. Buddha-nature is called the "one-child stage" (i.e., the stage in which one regards each being as one's only child). Why? Because through attainment of the "one-child stage" bodhisattvas have realized the mind of equality with regard to all sentient beings. Because all sentient beings ultimately and surely attain the "one-child stage," I make this remark, "All sentient beings have Buddha-nature." The "one-child stage" is Buddha-nature. Buddha-nature is Tathāgata.

It is also stated:[76]

Concerning highest, perfect enlightenment, faith is its cause. Although there are innumerable causes of enlightenment, if faith is presented they are exhaustively included in it.

It is also stated:[77]

There are two kinds of faith: one arises from hearing, and

the other arises from thinking. This person's faith arises from hearing, and not from thinking. Hence, it is called incomplete faith. There are another two kinds of faith: one is to believe that there is the path to enlightenment, and the other is to believe that there are people who have attained it. This person believes only that there is the path to enlightenment, but does not believe that there are people who have attained it. This type of faith is called incomplete faith. 605b

It is stated in the *Garland Sutra:*[78]

Those who hear this teaching, rejoice
In faith, and entertain no doubt
Quickly realize supreme enlightenment;
They are equal to the Tathāgatas.

It is also stated in the same sutra:[79]

The Tathāgata removes forever
The doubts of all sentient beings,
And fulfills their aspirations
According to their wishes.

The same sutra also states:[80]

Faith is the source of enlightenment and the mother of
    virtues;
It nurtures all kinds of good.
It renders the net of doubt and leads us away from the
    currents of desires;
It opens up the highest path of nirvana.

Faith is free of defiled mind and is pure;
It destroys arrogance and is the root of reverence;
It is the foremost treasure of the Dharma storehouse;
It is the hand of purity that receives various practices.

Faith performs charity ungrudgingly;
Faith rejoicingly enters the Buddha-Dharma;

107

Faith augments wisdom and virtues;
Faith unfailingly reaches the stage of the Tathāgata.

Faith purifies the sense organs and makes them clear and
   sharp;
Since faith-power is firm and strong, nothing can destroy it.
Faith destroys forever the root of evil passions;
Faith solely leads one to the Buddha's virtues.

Faith knows no attachment to the external world;
It avoids all adverse conditions and secures safety from them;
Faith transcends devils' paths
And manifests the highest path of liberation.

Faith keeps the seeds of virtues from decay;
Faith grows the tree of enlightenment.
Faith augments the supreme wisdom.
Faith causes all Buddhas to appear.

For this reason, if we explain in the order of performing
   practices,
Foremost is joyful faith, which is extremely difficult to
   attain. . . .

If one constantly reveres Buddhas with faith,
This means making great offerings.
If one makes great offerings,
One comes to accept in faith the Buddha's inconceivable
   working.

If one constantly upholds the sacred Dharma,
One never tires of hearing the Buddha's teaching;
If one never tires of hearing the Buddha's teaching,
One comes to accept in faith the Dharma's inconceivable
   power.

If one reverently serves pure monks,
One's faith will not retrogress;

If one attains non-retrogressive faith,
One's power of faith becomes immovable.

If one gains the power of faith that is immovable,
One's sense organs become pure, clear, and sharp;
If one attains pure, clear, and sharp sense organs,
One can approach good teachers.

If one approaches good teachers,
One can practice and accumulate extensive good;
If one practices and accumulates extensive good,
One acquires the great causal power [for attaining
    Buddhahood].

If one acquires the great causal power,
One gains the excellent, decisive understanding;
If one gains the excellent, decisive understanding,
One is protected by all the Buddhas.

If one is protected by all the Buddhas,
One awakens *bodhi*-mind;
If one awakens *bodhi*-mind,
One learns the virtues of the Buddhas.

If one cultivates the virtues of the Buddhas,   605c
One is born in the Tathāgata's family;
If one is born in the Tathāgata's family,
One learns skillful means.

If one learns skillful means,
One can attain pure joyful faith;
If one attains pure joyful faith,
One realizes the distinguished supreme mind.

If one realizes the distinguished supreme mind,
One constantly performs the practice of the perfections;
If one constantly performs the practice of the perfections,
One accomplishes the Mahayana.

If one accomplishes the Mahayana,
One makes offerings to Buddhas as prescribed;
If one makes offerings to Buddhas as prescribed,
One's mindfulness of the Buddha does not waver.

If one's mindfulness of the Buddha does not waver,
One always sees innumerable Buddhas;
If one always sees innumerable Buddhas,
One sees that the quintessence of the Tathāgata is eternal.

If one sees that the quintessence of the Tathāgata is eternal,
One realizes that the Dharma is imperishable;
If one realizes that the Dharma is imperishable,
One attains unhinderedness in acquiring intellectual powers.

If one attains unhindered intellectual powers,
One can expound boundless teachings;
If one expounds boundless teachings,
One saves sentient beings with a compassionate heart.

If one saves sentient beings with a compassionate heart,
One attains the firm mind of great compassion;
If one attains the firm mind of great compassion,
One rejoices in the profound Dharma.

If one rejoices in the profound Dharma,
One removes the faults of the conditioned world;
If one removes the faults of the conditioned world,
One frees oneself from arrogance and unruliness.

If one frees oneself from arrogance and unruliness,
One can benefit all beings without exception;
If one benefits all beings without exception,
One can dwell in birth and death without feeling fatigued.

It is stated in the *Commentary on Vasubandhu's Discourse on the Pure Land:*

[O]ne can practice in accord with the Dharma. Therefore, the author of the *Discourse* says at the beginning, "with single-ness of mind, I. ... "

It is also stated in the same work:

At the beginning of a sutra it is stated, "Thus [have I heard]"; this indicates the faith with which one is led [into the teaching].

Next, desire for birth is the Tathāgata's command calling the multitudes of beings to come to his land. The basis for desire for birth is true joyful faith. Indeed, this is not a desire of transferring one's merit with self-power as harbored by Mahayanists or Hinayanists, ordinary people or sages, or those who practice meditative or non-meditative good. Hence, it is called "not transferring one's merit."

The sentient beings of the worlds, numerous as dust particles, floundering in the sea of evil passions, and drifting in the sea of birth and death, lack the true or pure desire to transfer merit. For this reason, the Tathāgata [Amida] awakened compassion for all suffering beings and performed the bodhisattva practices; at that time, all his practices in the three modes of action were carried out, every thought-moment or instant, with transference of his merit as his principal concern, thereby fulfilling the great compassion. And so, to the ocean of all beings he endows true desire for birth that benefits others. Desire for birth is [the Buddha's] 606a desire to transfer his merit [to sentient beings]. This is the mind of great compassion; hence, it is not mingled with doubt.

Here, we find that the passage of fulfillment of the vow with regard to desire for birth is stated in the [*Larger*] *Sutra* as follows:

[All sentient beings ...]through his sincere merit transfer-ence; aspiring to be born there, they immediately become assured of birth and dwell in the stage of non-retrogression. But excluded are those who have committed the five grave offenses and abused the Right Dharma.

It is also stated:[81]

If they appreciate [Amida's] transference of the roots of good
and aspire to be born in the Land of Infinite Life, they shall
all be born there according to their wishes and attain the
stage of non-retrogression and, finally, realize highest, perfect enlightenment. Excluded, however, are those who commit the five evil acts that would consign them to the Avīci
hell, abuse the Right Dharma, and slander the sages.

The [*Commentary on*] *Vasubandhu's Discourse on the Pure
Land* states:

"How does one transfer [the merit of the practice]? One does
not forsake suffering beings but constantly resolves in one's
mind to perfect the great compassion by putting merit transference above anything else." Merit transference has two
aspects: the "going" aspect, and the "returning" aspect. The
"going" aspect is that one turns one's merit over to all sentient beings with the aspiration that all will be born together
into Amida Tathāgata's Pure Land of Peace and Bliss. The
"returning" aspect is that, after having been born in his land,
one acquires the fruit of cessation and contemplation practices and attains the power of employing expedient means,
whereby one reenters the dense forest of birth and death and
leads all sentient beings into the Buddhist path. Whether
"going" or "returning," one seeks to deliver sentient beings
from the sea of birth and death. For this reason, Vasubandhu
says, "[P]erfect the great compassion by putting merit transference above anything else."

It is also stated in the [*Commentary*]:

'The pure [manifestation] entering into the vow-mind" is as
follows: "I (Vasubandhu) have explained above the contemplation of accomplishment of the glorious merits of the Buddha
land, the Buddha, and the bodhisattvas. These three kinds
of accomplishment are adorned with the vow-mind. One
should realize the implication of this." "One should realize

the implication of this" means that one should realize that the three kinds of glorious accomplishment are, in their origin, [Dharmākara's] adornment with the pure vow-mind through the Forty-eight Vows, and so on. Since the cause is pure, the result is equally pure. They are not what has come into existence without any cause or by some other cause.

It is also stated in the [*Commentary*]:

"The fifth gate in the phase of 'going out'" is to observe with great compassion all suffering beings, manifest accommodated and transformed bodies, and enter the garden of birth and death and the forest of evil passions, where [bodhisattvas] play about, exercising transcendent powers; they thus dwell in the stage of teaching others through merit transference by their Primal Vow-Power. This is called the fifth gate in the phase of "going out."

The Master of Kuang-ming Temple says:[82]

Again, those who transfer merit aspiring to be born in the Pure Land should unfailingly avail themselves of the Vow that Amida transfers with decisive and true and sincere mind and dwell in the thought of attaining birth. Since this mind is a deep, adamantine faith, it is not liable to be disturbed or destroyed by people of different views, different teachings, other understandings, or other practices. You should decisively and singlemindedly hold fast to the Vow and proceed straightforwardly without giving heed to what others say. If you waver between going forward and retreating and look back with cowardly apprehension, you will stray from the path and lose the great benefit of attaining birth.

606b

Truly we realize that in the parable of the two rivers [and the white path], "the white path four or five inches wide" has the following meaning: "white" in "the white path" is contrasted to "black"; "white" refers to the white act selected and adopted [in the Vow], that is, the pure karmic act endowed to us for our going forth. "Black" refers to the black (evil) actions of our ignorance and evil passions and also to the miscellaneous good deeds done by the followers of the two vehicles, humans, and gods. "Path" is contrasted to "lane"; the path refers to the straight path of the truth of the Primal Vow— the supreme great path leading to great and complete nirvana. "Lane" refers to the small passages of the teachings of the two vehicles and the three vehicles and of myriad good deeds and various practices. "Four or five inches wide" refers to the four elements and the five aggregates that constitute sentient beings. "A pure aspiration for birth arises" means attainment of the adamantine true faith; since it is the ocean of great faith endowed by the Primal Vow-Power, it is indestructible; hence, it is compared to a diamond.

It is stated in the commentary on the *Contemplation Sutra*:[83]

> People of the present, both monks and laypeople, have all
>   awakened the highest aspiration,
> But birth and death is extremely difficult to abhor and the
>   Buddha-Dharma hard to seek.
>
> Together you should make the adamantine aspiration and
>   leap over the four violent streams;...
> Those who have received the adamantine mind, coming
>   into accord with [the Vow] in a flash of thought,
> Shall realize the fruition of nirvana.

It is also stated:[84]

> Having thoroughly attained true faith, you should abhor this Sahā world of pain, aspire for the happiness of non-action, and enter forever the state of eternal bliss. But it is not easy to enter straightaway the realm of non-action; nor is it easy to escape readily from the Sahā world of afflictions. Unless you awaken the adamantine aspiration, how can you eradicate forever the roots of birth and death? If you do not closely follow the Compassionate One, how can you free yourselves from the long sorrow?

It is also stated:[85]

"Adamantine" indicates undefiled [wisdom].

Hence, we truly realize that although sincere mind, joyful faith, and desire for birth are different terms, their significance is the same. Why is this so? Because the three minds are not mingled with doubt, and so they are the true One Mind. This is called adamantine true faith. Adamantine true faith is called true entrusting heart. True entrusting heart is necessarily accompanied by [recitation of] the Name. [Recitation of] the Name, however, is not always accompanied by the entrusting heart of the Vow-Power. For this reason, the author of the *Discourse,* Vasubandhu, declares at its beginning, "I, with One Mind," and also says "wishing to practice in accord with the Dharma, that is, in agreement with the significance of the Name."

[Concluding Remarks Praising Great Faith]

When I contemplate the ocean of great faith, I see that it does not discriminate between nobles and commoners, monks and laypeople, men and women, old and young. The amount of karmic evil committed is not questioned nor is the length of practice considered. It is neither practice nor good acts; neither sudden attainment nor gradual attainment; neither meditative practice nor non-meditative practice; neither right contemplation nor wrong contemplation; neither contemplation of form nor contemplation of no-form; neither in everyday life nor at the end of life; neither many recitations nor a single recitation. It is solely joyful faith that is inconceivable, indescribable, and ineffable. It is like the *agada* medicine that destroys all poisons. The medicine of the Tathāgata's Vow removes the poisons of our wisdom and stupidity.

606c

[Faith is the *Bodhi*-Mind]

With regard to the *bodhi*-mind, there are two kinds [of teachings]: vertical and crosswise. The vertical [teaching] is again divided into

115

two groups: vertical transcendence and vertical going out. Vertical transcendence and vertical going out refer to various teachings—accommodated and real, exoteric and esoteric, Mahayana and Hinayana. The *bodhi*-mind in these teachings is the mind set on attaining *bodhi* by the roundabout way of practice for many *kalpas*; it is the adamantine mind of self-power, that is, the great mind of the bodhisattva.

The crosswise [teaching] is again divided into two groups: crosswise transcendence and crosswise going out. Crosswise going out is the *bodhi*-mind of self-power within the Other-Power teaching, set on performing practices—right and miscellaneous, meditative and non-meditative. Crosswise transcendence refers to joyful faith endowed to us by the Vow-Power; it is called the aspiration to attain Buddhahood. The aspiration to attain Buddhahood is the great *bodhi*-mind for crosswise [transcendence]. This is called the adamantine mind of crosswise transcendence.

Concerning the *bodhi*-mind, whether crosswise or vertical, the same word is used with different meanings. The essential point, however, is entry into truth, and the true and sincere mind is fundamental. It is wrong to follow perverted and mixed practices, and it is a loss to entertain doubt.

Those who aspire for the Pure Land, both monks and laypeople, should deeply understand the golden words concerning "imperfect faith" and so become free of the wrong concept with "imperfect hearing."

The *Commentary on Vasubandhu's Discourse on the Pure Land* states:

> In the *Sutra on the Buddha of Infinite Life* preached at Rājagṛha, I find in the section on the three groups of aspirants that although their practices differ according to their superior or inferior qualities, they all, without fail, awaken aspiration for highest *bodhi* (*bodhicitta*). Aspiration for highest *bodhi* is the resolve to attain Buddhahood. The aspiration to attain Buddhahood is the resolve to save all sentient

beings. The aspiration to save sentient beings is the resolve to embrace sentient beings and lead them to attain birth in a Buddha land. It follows that those who wish to be born in the Pure Land of Peace and Bliss should awaken aspiration for highest *bodhi*. If there is anyone who does not awaken aspiration for highest *bodhi* but, having heard of the endless pleasures to be enjoyed in that land, desires to be born there simply because of such pleasures, he will not attain birth [there]. And so it is said, "they do not seek to enjoy the pleasures for their own sustenance" but "to remove the suffering of all sentient beings." "The pleasures for their own sustenance" means that the Pure Land of Peace and Bliss has been produced and maintained by Amida Tathāgata's Primal Vow-Power, and so there is no end to the pleasures to be enjoyed. The meaning of "merit transference" is that one transfers the merits one has accumulated to all sentient beings so that they, too, will follow the Buddha's Way.

607a

Master Yüan-chao says:[86]

It is extremely difficult because no other [Buddha] could do [just as Śākyamuni did]; it is rare because the world has never seen this.

He also says:

The Nembutsu teaching does not discriminate between fools and the wise, rich and poor; it does not question the length of your practice or whether your practice is good or bad. So long as you are resolute and unwavering in your faith, you will attain birth with ten utterances of the Nembutsu, even if sinister signs may appear at the end your life. It is the Dharma by which ordinary and foolish beings bound by evil passions, those in the lower levels of society, such as hunters and traders, can instantly transcend birth and death and attain Buddhahood. This is called "[the Dharma] which is the most difficult thing in the world to accept in faith."

He further says:

> It is difficult to perform practices and attain Buddhahood in
> this evil world. A second difficulty is to expound this teach-
> ing for the sake of all sentient beings. These two difficulties
> serve to clarify that the Buddhas' praise [of Śākyamuni] is
> not vain. Sentient beings are led to hear and accept the teach-
> ing in faith.

Yung-ch'in of the Vinaya school says:

> Concerning the difficulty of accepting this Dharma in faith,
> to transform ordinary people into sages through this Dharma
> is actually as easy as turning one's palms—so easy that many
> people with shallow wisdom are skeptical about this. Thus
> the *Larger Sutra* states, "[The Pure Land] is easy to reach
> but very few actually go there." Hence, we know that this
> Dharma is difficult to accept in faith.

It is stated in the *Notes for Memory* (*Wen ch'ih chi*) [to Yüan-
chao's *Commentary on the Amida Sutra* (*A mi t'o ching i shu*)]:[87]

> "Not to discriminate between fools and the wise" is said
> because there are different human capacities, such as sharp
> and dull. "Not to discriminate between rich and poor" is said
> because there are different karmic rewards, such as strong
> and weak. "Not to question the length of your practice" is
> said because there are different effects of practice, such as
> deep and shallow. "Not to question whether your practice is
> good or bad" is said because there are different natures of
> practice, such as agreeable and disagreeable. "So long as you
> are resolute and unwavering in your faith...even if sinister
> signs may appear at the end your life" is said because the
> *Contemplation Sutra,* in the section of the middle level of the
> lowest grade, states, "the flames of hell suddenly close in on
> him," and so forth. "Ordinary and foolish beings bound by
> evil passions" is said because they are possessed of two kinds

of delusion. "Those in the lower levels of society, such as hunters and traders, can instantly transcend birth and death and attain Buddhahood. This is called [the Dharma] which is the most difficult in the world to accept in faith" means that such evil persons as hunters and wine dealers can transcend samsara and attain birth through ten utterances of the Nembutsu, and so is not this teaching difficult to accept in faith?

Amida Tathāgata is called the True Illumination, the Equally Enlightened One, the Inconceivable One, the Ultimate Resort, Great Arhat, Great Consolation, the One Equal to the Unequaled, and the Inconceivable Light.

In the postscript to the *Collection of Passages on the Land of Bliss* it is stated:

There are always many who practice the Pure Land teaching, but very few reach its gate and enter it straightaway. There are always many who discuss the Pure Land teaching, but very few grasp its essentials and directly expound them to others. But I have never heard of anyone who presents his view while having hindrances and obscurities within himself. I present my view since I have understood the teaching. Of all hindrances, nothing is stronger than greed; of all obscurities, nothing surpasses doubt. In the Pure Land teaching, these two elements, greed and doubt, eventually cease to cause any hindrance. They are never left alone; Amida's Universal Vow always and spontaneously enfolds them. This is its natural working.

[The Single Thought of Faith]

When I contemplate true joyful faith, there is in it a single thought. The single thought reveals the very first moment joyful faith is awakened in us, and also expresses the great and inconceivable joy [of receiving faith].

The *Larger Sutra* states:

607b

> All sentient beings who have heard his Name, rejoice in faith, and think of him even once—through his sincere merit transference; aspiring to be born there, they immediately become assured of birth and dwell in the stage of non-retrogression.

Further it is stated:[88]

> All sentient beings in the Buddha lands of the other directions, having heard the Name of the Tathāgata of Infinite Life, awaken a single thought of pure faith and rejoice.

Also it is stated:[89]

> By the power of that Buddha's Original Vows,
> All who hear his Name and desire birth
> Will, without exception, be born in his land. . . .

Again, it is stated:[90]

> They hear the Buddha's virtuous Name.

It is stated in the *Nirvana Sutra*:[91]

> What is called "imperfect hearing"? To accept only half of the twelve divisions of the scriptures expounded by the Tathāgata and reject the other half—this is called "imperfect hearing." Also, even if one upholds these six divisions of the scriptures one cannot recite them, and so one's exposition of the scriptures cannot benefit others; this is called "imperfect hearing." Further, having received the six divisions of the scriptures, one upholds, recites, and expounds them for the sake of disputation, in order to defeat others in discussions, to gain profit, or for secular purposes; this is called "imperfect hearing.'

The Master of Kuang-ming Temple says,[92] "singlehearted practice of the Nembutsu" and also "wholehearted practice of the Nembutsu."

[Ten Benefits of Faith in This Life]

When the *Larger Sutra* says "hear,"[93] it means that sentient beings, having heard how the Buddha made and fulfilled the vow, entertain no doubt. This is what is meant by "hear." "Faith" [in "rejoice in faith"] refers to the faith endowed by the Primal Vow-Power. "Rejoice" shows the state of joy in body and mind. "Even [once]" is the term that comprises both many and few. "A single thought" means that one's faith is free of double-mindedness; hence, it is called "a single thought." This is what [Vasubandhu] calls "One Mind." The One Mind is the true cause of birth in the Pure Land of Recompense.

When we acquire adamantine true faith, we transcend crosswise the five evil realms and the eight adverse conditions, and unfailingly gain ten benefits in this life. What are the ten?

1. The benefit of being protected by unseen divine beings;
2. The benefit of attaining utmost virtues;
3. The benefit of our karmic evil being transformed into good;
4. The benefit of being protected and remembered by all the Buddhas;
5. The benefit of being praised by all the Buddhas;
6. The benefit of being protected constantly by the light of Amida's heart;
7. The benefit of having much joy in our hearts;
8. The benefit of acknowledging Amida's benevolence and repaying our debt of gratitude for his virtues;
9. The benefit of constantly practicing great compassion;
10. The benefit of entering the rightly established stage.

[Implications of the Single Thought of Faith]

The word "exclusive practice of the Nembutsu" mentioned by Master [Shan-tao] is the sole practice. "Singleness of mind" refers to the One Mind. Hence, "a single thought" in the passage of fulfillment [of the Eighteenth Vow] refers to singlemindedness. Singlemindedness

607c is deep mind. Deep mind is deep faith. Deep faith is steadfast deep faith. Steadfast deep faith is decisive mind. Decisive mind is supreme mind. Supreme mind is true faith. True faith is enduring mind. Enduring mind is sincere mind. Sincere mind is mindfulness. Mindfulness is the true One Mind. The true One Mind is great joy. Great joy is the true entrusting heart. The true entrusting heart is adamantine faith. Adamantine faith is the aspiration for Buddhahood. The aspiration for Buddhahood is the desire to save sentient beings. The desire to save sentient beings is the desire to embrace sentient beings and bring them to the Pure Land of Peace and Bliss. This desire is the great *bodhi*-mind. This mind is the great compassion, for it arises from the wisdom of infinite light. The oceanlike vow is without discrimination; hence, aspiration for *bodhi* is without discrimination. Since aspiration for *bodhi* is without discrimination, the wisdom of the path is also without discrimination. Since the wisdom of the path is without discrimination, great compassion is without discrimination. Great compassion is the right cause of the Buddha's enlightenment.

It is stated in the *Commentary on Vasubandhu's Discourse on the Pure Land:*

> Those who wish to be born in the Pure Land of Peace and Bliss should awaken the aspiration for highest *bodhi*.

It is also stated in the same [text]:

> "That mind itself produces Buddhas" [in the *Contemplation Sutra*] means that the [meditating] mind (i.c., faith) becomes Buddha. "That mind is itself the Buddha" means that there is no Buddha apart from the [meditating] mind. It is just as fire comes from wood but is not separate from the wood. Because it is not separate from the wood, it burns the wood. The wood becomes fire, which burns the wood and turns it, too, into fire.

The [Master of] Kuang-ming [Temple] says:[94]

> This mind becomes Buddha. This mind is itself Buddha. There is no Buddha apart from this mind.

Hence we realize that the One Mind is described as "to practice in accord with the Dharma." This is the right teaching, the right meaning, the right practice, the right understanding, the right act, and the right wisdom.

The three minds are the One Mind; the One Mind is the adamantine true mind. I have given the answer concerning this matter in the above passages. Reflect on this.

The *Discourse on Cessation and Contemplation* states:

> "*Bodhi*" is an Indian word; here [in China] it is translated as "Way." "*Chih-to*" (*citta*) represents an Indian sound; here it is translated as "mind." Mind means discerning.

[Crosswise Transcendence]

"Transcending crosswise and cutting off the four streams"[95] means: "crosswise" contrasts with vertical transcendence and vertical going out. "Transcendence" is the word that contrasts with indirect journeying. "Vertical transcendence" refers to the true Mahayana teachings. "Vertical going out" refers to the provisional Mahayana teachings, that is, the teachings of the two vehicles and the three vehicles that provide indirect approaches.

"Crosswise transcendence" refers to the absolute and all-complete true teaching actualized by the fulfillment of the [Eighteenth] Vow, that is, the true essence [of the Pure Land Way]. There is also "crosswise going out," which refers to the meditative and nonmeditative teachings applicable for the three groups of aspirants and the nine grades of beings; that is, the acts of virtue for roundabout approaches leading to the Transformed Land or the realm of sloth and pride. In the Pure Recompensed Land produced by the great vow, there is no distinction of grades and stages. In an instantaneous thought-moment one quickly realizes highest, perfect, true enlightenment. Hence, we say "crosswise transcendence." 608a

The *Larger Sutra* says, "[Dharmākara made the] supreme, unsurpassed vows."

It also says:

I have made vows, unrivaled in all the world;
I shall certainly reach the unsurpassed Way....

My Name shall be heard throughout the ten directions;
Should there be any place where it is not heard,
May I not attain perfect enlightenment.

It also says:

Strive to escape from samsara and be born in the Land of
Peace and Provision. Then, the causes of the five evil realms,
having been destroyed, they will naturally cease to be and so
you will progress unhindered in your pursuit of the Way. The
Pure Land is easy to reach but very few actually go there. It
rejects no one but naturally and unfailingly attracts beings.

It is stated in the *Larger Sutra on Amida:*[96]

Strive to escape from samsara. When you are born in the
[Pure] Land of Amida Buddha the five evil realms will be
instantly destroyed and those realms will naturally cease to
be. You will progress unhindered in your pursuit of the Way.
The Pure Land is easy to reach but very few actually go there.
It rejects no one but naturally and unfailingly attracts beings.

"Cutting off" [the four streams] means that since you have
awakened the One Mind for going forth, there are no more states
of existence that you must undergo, no more realms [of samsara]
for which you are destined. Both the causes and results of the six
realms and the four modes of birth will be destroyed. You will
immediately sever birth and death in the three worlds. Hence, we
say "cutting off." "The four streams" are the four violent streams;
they also refer to birth, old age, sickness, and death.

The *Larger Sutra* states:

Then you will surely enter the Buddha's enlightenment
And everywhere deliver beings from the river of birth and
death.

It is also stated:[97]

You will surely become World-honored Ones
And deliver all beings from birth, old age, and death.

The *Nirvana Sutra* states:[98]

Nirvana is called an island. For what reason? Because the four violent streams cannot wash it away. What are the four violent streams? First, desire; second, existence; third, wrong views; and fourth, ignorance. For this reason, nirvana is called an island.

The Master of Kuang-ming Temple says:[99]

I say to all practitioners: Abhor birth and death, [the fate of] ordinary beings, and do not cling to it; aspire for Amida's Pure Land, do not think lightly of it. If you abhor the Sahā world you will forever part from it; if you aspire for the Pure Land you will eternally dwell in it. If you part from the Sahā world the causes of the six realms will cease to be and the resultant states of transmigration will spontaneously perish. If the causes and the results cease to be, the forms and names [of samsaric states] will be immediately annihilated.

He also says:[100]

My respectful wish is this: All aspirants for birth should reflect on their abilities. Those who aspire in this life to be born in that land should never fail to strive, body and mind, whether walking, standing, sitting, or lying down, and never cease continuous practice day and night. It may seem somewhat painful to continue to practice throughout your life until death, but the moment your life ends you will in the next 608b moment be born in that land, where you will enjoy the Dharma pleasure of non-action for eternally long *kalpas*. Until you become a Buddha, you will not be bound to any more birth and death. Is this not joy? Reflect on this.

[The True Disciple of the Buddha]

The true disciple of the Buddha means this: "true" contrasts with false and provisional. "Disciple" means a disciple of Śākyamuni and other Buddhas, namely, the practitioner who has attained adamantine faith. Because one certainly realizes great nirvana with this faith and practice, one is called a true disciple of the Buddha.

It is stated in the *Larger Sutra:*

> If, when I attain Buddhahood, sentient beings in the immeasurable and inconceivable Buddha lands of the ten directions who have been touched by my light should not feel peace and happiness in their bodies and minds surpassing those of humans and *deva*s, may I not attain perfect enlightenment.
>
> If, when I attain Buddhahood, sentient beings in the immeasurable and inconceivable Buddha lands of the ten directions who have heard my Name should not gain the bodhisattva's insight into the non-arising of all *dharma*s and should not acquire various profound *dhāraṇī*s, may I not attain perfect enlightenment.

It is stated in the *Teaching Assembly of the Tathāgata of Infinite Life:*

> If, when I attain Buddhahood, sentient beings in the immeasurable, boundless, inconceivable, and unequaled worlds throughout the ten directions, who have received the Buddha's glory and have been illumined and touched by its light, should not feel peace and happiness in their bodies and minds surpassing those of humans and gods, may I not attain perfect enlightenment.

It is also stated in the *Larger Sutra:*

> If you have heard the Dharma and do not forget it
> But regard and revere it with great joy,
> You are my good friend.

It is further stated in the same [text]: "Anyone who sincerely desires birth in the Land of Peace and Bliss is able to attain purity of wisdom and supremacy in virtue."

It is stated,[101] "those who have attained vast and superior understanding."

It is also stated, "Such people, those who have attained great, majestic virtue, will enter the distinguished gateway of the vast Dharma."

It is stated:[102] "You should know that all who are mindful of that Buddha are like white lotus flowers among humankind."

We read in the *Collection of Passages on the Land of Peace and Bliss:*

> I will explain the prescribed method of preaching and hearing the Dharma according to various Mahayana sutras. The *Great Assembly Sutra (Mahāvaipulyamahāsaṃnipāta-sūtra)* says:
>
>> The preacher of the Dharma should think of himself as the physician king intent on eliminating pains; he should consider the Dharma preached to be nectar or *maṇḍa.* Those who hear the Dharma should seek to attain superior understanding and be cured of their illnesses. If such is the preacher and the listener, they are able to make the Buddha-Dharma flourish. They will always dwell in the presence of the Buddha.

We read in the *Nirvana Sutra:*

> The Buddha said, "If a person sincerely practices the Nembutsu *samādhi,* the Buddhas of the ten directions will always watch over him, just as if they were actually in front of him."

Hence, the *Nirvana Sutra* states:

> The Buddha said to Bodhisattva Kāśyapa, "If there are sons or daughters of good families who always sincerely perform 608c

the exclusive practice of the Nembutsu, whether they dwell in mountain forests or in villages, whether they practice it in the daytime or at night, and whether they do so while sitting or lying down, Buddhas and World-honored Ones always watch over them just as if they were before their eyes, and are ready to accept their offerings and endow merits to them."

According to the *Commentary on the Perfection of Great Wisdom Sutra (Mahāprajñāpāramitā-upadeśa*)*, there are three explanations of this. First, the Buddha is the supreme Dharma King, and bodhisattvas are the Dharma vassals. The only person we should venerate and revere is the Buddha, the World-honored One. For this reason, we should always be mindful of the Buddha.

Second, there are many bodhisattvas who profess, "Since innumerable *kalpas* ago the World-honored One has nurtured our Dharma bodies, wisdom bodies, and bodies of great compassion. Through the Buddha's aid we have been able to accomplish meditation, wisdom, and immeasurable practices and vows. In order to repay our indebtedness to his benevolence, we desire to be near him and serve him always, just as the ministers who have received the king's grace are always mindful of him."

Third, there are many bodhisattvas who also make this remark, "When we were in the causal stage of discipline, we met bad teachers, and so abused *prajñā* and consequently fell into the evil realms. During the passage of immeasurable *kalpas* we performed other practices without being able to attain liberation. Later, one day when we were with a good teacher, he taught us the Nembutsu *samādhi*, which eliminated various hindrances and enabled us to attain liberation. Because of this great benefit we wish that we shall not be separated from the Buddha."

The *Larger Sutra* states [in effect]:

If you wish to be born in the Pure Land, the basic requirement is to awaken the *bodhi*-mind. The reason is that *bodhi* is a name for the supreme path. If you have awakened the aspiration for Buddhahood, this aspiration is so vast as to pervade the Dharma realm. This aspiration is everlasting, reaching the limit of the future age. It is free of all the hindrances of the two vehicles. If you have awakened this aspiration even once, the beginningless cycle of birth and death will be destroyed.

The *Great Compassion Sutra (Mahākaruṇā-sūtra)* has this to say:

What is "great compassion"? If you exclusively and continuously practice the Nembutsu, you will definitely be born in the Land of Peace and Bliss when your life ends. Those who in their turn encourage others to practice the Nembutsu are called those who practice great compassion.

The Master of Kuang-ming Temple says:[103]

How regrettable it is that my fellow beings doubt what
    should not be doubted!
The Pure Land is before your eyes; it should not be denied.
Do not argue whether Amida embraces you or not;
What is essential is whether or not you singlemindedly
    direct your thoughts [toward the Pure Land].

They say [to each other] that from now until the time
    they attain Buddhahood,
They will repay the Buddha's benevolence by praising him
    for a long *kalpa*.
If not blessed by the great power of Amida's vow,
When and in which *kalpa* would we be able to escape from
    this Sahā world?

How can you expect to reach the Treasure Land now?
It is indeed due to the power of the great master of the
    Sahā world.
Without the exhortation of the great master and good friend,
How can you enter the Pure Land of Amida?

He also says:[104]

It is extremely difficult to encounter an age in which a
    Buddha appears in the world;
It is also difficult for the people to realize the wisdom of faith.
To be able to hear the rare Dharma
Is among the most difficult.
To accept it in faith and teach others to believe in it
Is the difficulty among all the difficulties.
To spread great compassion everywhere and guide others
Is truly to repay the Buddha's benevolence.

609a

He also says in the same work:

The color of Amida's body is like the golden mountain;
The rays of light of his physical characteristics and marks
    illumine the ten directions;
Only those who recite the Nembutsu are enfolded in the
    light;
Realize that the Primal Vow has the strongest power.

The Tathāgatas of the ten directions extend their tongues
    and give witness:
Through exclusive recitation of the Name, you reach the
    Western Land;
Mounting the lotus seat, you will hear the excellent
    Dharma;
You will see the vows and practices of the ten bodhisattva
    stages manifest themselves spontaneously.

He also says:[105]

Should there be sentient beings who are exclusively mindful
of Amida Buddha, the light of the Buddha's heart always
shines on them, protecting and never forsaking them. It is
not stated that the light shines on practitioners of various
other acts and embraces them. This is also the strong condition of protection in the present life.

Again he says:[106]

"They will rejoice and attain insight" shows that when the pure light of Amida Buddha's land suddenly appears before one's eyes, what a joy it would be! Out of this joy, one attains insight into the non-arising of all *dharmas*. This is also called "perception of joy," "perception of awakening," and "perception of faith." Since this remark is made long before [the exposition of the main part of the sutra], it has not yet been clarified when Queen [Vaidehī] actually attained this insight. [The Buddha] wanted her to seek this benefit wholeheartedly. This means that when one courageously and singleheartedly desires to visualize [Amida], one attains insight. This is mainly the insight realized in the ten stages of understanding, not the one realized in or above the stages of dwelling and practice.

He also says:[107]

The passage from "those who are mindful of the Buddha" to "will be born into the family of the Buddhas" clarifies that the merit of the Nembutsu *samādhi* surpasses anything else; it cannot be compared with merit of various good acts. This passage is divided into five sections: First, exclusive recitation of Amida Buddha's Name is presented. Second, the persons who recite the Name are praised. Third, those who continuously practice the Nembutsu are described as extremely rare; nothing can be compared with them, and so *puṇḍarīka* (lotus flower) is used as an analogy. *Puṇḍarīka* is called the "excellent flower" among human beings; it is also called the "rare flower"; also "the very best flower"; and it is also called the "wonderful, excellent flower" among human beings. This flower has traditionally been called "auspicious flower."

Practitioners of the Nembutsu are "excellent people" among human beings, "wonderful, excellent people" among human beings, "the very best people" among human beings, "rare people" among human beings, and "the most excellent people" among human beings.

Fourth, when you singlemindedly recite Amida's Name, Avalokiteśvara and Mahāsthāmaprāpta will always follow you and protect you, just as shadows follow objects. They are like your close friends and teachers.

Fifth, already in this life you receive such benefit. At the end of your life you will enter the family of the Buddhas, that is, the Pure Land. After you have arrived there, you will hear the Dharma for a long time and visit other Buddha lands to make offerings to the Buddhas. Thus the cause and result of Buddhahood are accomplished. How can the seat of enlightenment be far away?

Wang Jih-hsiu says:[108]

609b

I read in the *Sutra on the Buddha of Infinite Life,* "All sentient beings who having heard his Name rejoice in faith and are mindful of him even once, aspiring to be born there, will attain birth and dwell in the stage of non-retrogression." "The stage of non-retrogression" is *avaivartika* in Sanskrit. The *Lotus Sutra (Saddharmapuṇḍarīka-sūtra)* says "[it is] the stage of reward attained by Bodhisattva Maitreya." Those who attain birth through a single thought of mindfulness are the same as Maitreya. The Buddha's words are not spoken in vain. The *Sutra on the Buddha of Infinite Life* is truly the shortest way to birth, the divine method of eliminating suffering. All should accept it in faith.

The *Larger Sutra* says:

[The Buddha said to Maitreya,] "Sixty-seven *koṭis* of non-retrogressive bodhisattvas from this world will be born there. Each of these bodhisattvas has previously made offerings to innumerable Buddhas [and is next to Buddhahood like Maitreya]."

Further it is stated:[109]

> The Buddha said to Maitreya, "There are seventy-two *koṭi*s
> of bodhisattvas in this Buddha land (i.e., the Sahā world).
> They have planted various roots of good at the place of a hun-
> dred thousand immeasurable *koṭi*s of *nayuta*s of Buddhas,
> and so have attained the stage of non-retrogression. They
> will be born in that land."

Yung-ch'in of the Vinaya school says:

> In the profundity of the teaching, nothing surpasses the ulti-
> mate doctrine of the *Garland Sutra* or the excellent message
> of the *Lotus Sutra*. But we have never seen in those sutras
> the prediction of Buddhahood given to all sentient beings. It
> is due to the benefit of [Amida's] inconceivable virtue that
> all sentient beings receive in the present life the prediction
> of attaining highest, perfect enlightenment.

[Those Who Have Faith
Are Equal to Maitreya]

We truly realize: Because Mahāsattva Maitreya has attained the
adamantine mind of equal enlightenment, he will reach the stage
of highest enlightenment under a dragonflower tree, where he will
give three sermons; whereas, because the followers of the Nembutsu have acquired the adamantine mind of crosswise transcendence, they will realize the great *parinirvāṇa* on the eve of the
moment they die. Hence, it is said, "[like Maitreya]."

Moreover, those who have attained admantine faith gain the
perception of joy, awakening, and faith as did Vaidehī. This is
because the true faith endowed to them for their going forth has
penetrated their hearts and also because the inconceivable Primal
Vow has been working on them.

Chih-chüeh of the Ch'an school says in praise of the followers
of the Nembutsu:[110]

How wonderful! The Buddha's power is inconceivable; there has not been anything like this in all ages.

Master Yüan-chao of the Vinaya school says:[111]

As for the clear understanding of the doctrine and contemplation, who excels Chih-che (i.e., Chih-i)? Near the end of his life he upheld the *Contemplation Sutra;* after glorifying the Pure Land, he passed away.

As for the insight into the Dharma realm, who is equal to Tu-shun? He urged all four groups of Buddhists to be mindful of the Buddha; after perceiving the miraculous signs, he passed away to the west.

As for practicing meditation and seeing Buddha-nature, who surpasses Kao-yü and Chih-chüeh? They formed societies for contemplating the Buddha and both attained the highest grade of birth.

As for deep learning in Confucian studies, who can match Liu, Lei, Liu Tzu-hou, and Po Lo-t'ien? They all took up the brush and wrote sincere words, aspiring to be born in that land.

609c

[Provisional and False Disciples of the Buddha]

"Provisional" [disciples] refer to practitioners of the path of sages and those who practice meditative or non-meditative good of the Pure Land Way.

Thus, the Master of Kuang-ming Temple says:[112]

The Buddha's teaching has many gates, numbering
  eighty-four thousand,
Precisely because the capacities of beings are different.

He also says:[113]

Provisional gateways of expedience are the same and not different [in their objective].

134

He also says:[114]

Teaching gates that differ from each other are called the "gradual teaching";
One must perform painful practices for tens of thousands of *kalpa*s before realizing the non-arising of all *dharma*s.

"False" [disciples] refers to the adherents of the sixty-two views and the followers of the ninety-five wrong paths.
The *Nirvana Sutra* states:[115]

The World-honored One always preached, "All non-Buddhists learn the ninety-five [wrong teachings] and fall into the evil realms."

The Master of Kuang-ming Temple says:[116]

The ninety-five [wrong teachings] all defile the world;
Only the Buddha's single path is pure and tranquil.

I deeply realize: How sad it is that I, Gutoku Shinran, immersed in the vast sea of attachment and desire and lost in the great mountain of fame and profit, do not rejoice at joining the group of the rightly established stage, nor do I enjoy coming nearer the realization of true enlightenment. How shameful, how grievous it is!

[Salvation of Evil Beings]

Concerning beings with incorrigible illnesses, the Buddha said in the *Nirvana Sutra:*[117]

Kāśyapa, there are three kinds of people in the world whose illnesses are hard to cure: first, those who slander the Mahayana; second, those who commit the five grave offenses; and third, those devoid of the seed of good (*icchantikas*). These three illnesses are the most serious in the world and cannot be cured by *śrāvakas, pratyekabuddhas,* or bodhisattvas. Sons of good families, suppose a person is stricken with a fatal illness but there is no cure; yet, appropriate treatment and medicine specially prescribed by a doctor are given to this person. Without them, his illness could not be cured and there is no doubt that he would die. Sons of good families, these three kinds of people are like this. Having heard the Dharma from the Buddha or a bodhisattva, their illnesses are cured and so they can awaken aspiration for highest, perfect enlightenment. But *śrāvaka*s, *pratyekabuddha*s, or bodhisattvas, whether they preach the Dharma or not, cannot bring such people to awaken aspiration for highest, perfect enlightenment.

It is also said in the same sutra:[118]

At that time, there was in the great town of Rājagṛha [a person called] Ajātaśatru. Being of vicious nature, he often engaged in killing. Committing four evils in speech, he was possessed of greed, anger, and ignorance, and his heart raged furiously.

Through his association with evil people he became attached to the worldly pleasures of the five desires, which led him to commit the outrageous act of murdering his innocent father, King Bimbisāra, [and ascend the throne]. Because of this, he developed a fever of remorse. Because of the fever of remorse in his heart, scabs formed all over his body. Their foul stench and filth kept people away. He thought to himself, "I have already received in this present body the retribution of my evil act. The karmic retribution of hell must be drawing near."

At that time, his mother, Queen Vaidehī, applied various ointments to his body, but the scabs spread and showed no sign of alleviation. King Ajātaśatru said to his mother, "These scabs are caused by the mind, they are not the product of the four material elements. If someone says he can cure them it is contrary to reason that he can do so."

At that time, there was a minister named Candrayaśas. He went to see the king. Standing to one side, he said to the king, "Great king, why are you sorrowful and emaciated and why does your countenance look unhappy? Do you have pain in body or mind?" Ajātaśatru replied to the minister, "How should I not have pain in mind and body? I committed the outrageous act of murdering my innocent father. I once heard from a wise man that there are in the world five kinds of people who cannot escape falling into hell; they are people who have committed the five grave offenses. I have already committed immeasurable, boundless, and incalculable karmic evils. How could I not have pain in body and mind? There is no excellent physician who can cure me."

The minister said to the king, "Do not grieve so much." He then remarked in verse:

> If one is sorrowful all the time,
> The sorrow grows and multiplies.
> It is just as sleep indulged in
> Grows and becomes intense.
> So it is with craving lust
> And drinking wine.

"The king has said that there are in the world five kinds of people who cannot escape falling into hell. Who has been to hell and, after coming back, reported to you? Hell is simply talked about in the world by many so-called wise men. You also say that there is no excellent physician who can cure your illness of mind and body. There is a great doctor named Pūraṇa-kāśyapa. He has complete knowledge of everything and has attained freedom in exercising power. Having thoroughly practiced the pure and sacred acts, he now always expounds the path to the supreme nirvana to immeasurable and boundless sentient beings. He teaches thus to his disciples:

> There is no black karma, nor retribution for black karma;
> There is no white karma, nor reward for white karma.

There is no black or white karma, nor their retribution
   or reward.
There is no superior act nor inferior act.

"This master is now in Rājagṛha. I pray, great king, that
you condescend to pay a visit to him and let him treat your
mind and body."

The king replied, "If he could unmistakably get rid of my
karmic evil I would certainly go to him for refuge."

Again, there was another minister named Prāptagarbha.
He approached Ajātaśatru and said, "Great king, why are
you so emaciated, with your lips dried up and your voice fee-
ble? What affliction torments your body and mind?" The king
replied, "How should I not have pain in mind and body? I am
ignorant and blind, having no eyes of wisdom. I made friends
with many evil people. In particular, following the advice of
Devadatta, the evil person, I outrageously murdered my father
who was devoted to the Right Dharma. Once I heard a wise
man recite this verse:

> If you entertain ill thoughts
> And commit evil acts
> To your father or mother,
610b To the Buddha or his disciple,
> The retribution will be
> Falling into the Avīci hell.

"Because of this, I tremble with fear and am greatly tormented. I fear there is no treatment, even by an excellent
physician."

The minister continued, "Great king, please do not be so
fear-stricken. There are two kinds of law: one is for those who
have renounced the world and the other is for kings. The law
for kings recognizes the case in which one becomes a king by
killing one's father. Although such an act is a high treason,
it does not actually constitute a crime. It is like the *karāla*

worm; it necessarily tears through its mother's womb to be born. This is the law of birth for the worm. Even though it tears through its mother's womb, this does not form any crime. It is also like a mule with foal. The law of statesmen is like this. Even if one kills one's father or brother, this is not actually a crime. The law of those who have renounced the world stipulates that to kill even a mosquito or an ant is a crime. You say that there is no excellent physician in the world who can cure your illness in mind and body. There is a great master named Maskarī-gośālīputra. He has attained omniscience and has compassion for sentient beings as if they were his own children. He has freed himself from his evil passions and is able to extract the sharp arrows of the three poisons from sentient beings. This master is now in the great city of Rājagṛha. I pray, great king, that you condescend to pay a visit to him. If you see him, your karmic evils will be destroyed."

The king replied, "If he could unmistakably get rid of my karmic evil I would certainly go to him for refuge."

There was another minister named Tattvalabdha. He approached the king and spoke in verse:

> Great king, why have you
> Cast off your bodily ornaments?
> Why is your hair so disheveled?
> What is this all about?
> Does your mind or your body ache?

Ajātaśatru replied, "How should I not have pain in mind and body? My father, the late king, was benevolent and tender-hearted. He looked on people with loving-kindness. He was really free of fault. He went to see a soothsayer, who said, 'When born, this child will certainly kill his father.' Even after hearing this, he cared for me and raised me. Once I heard a wise man make this remark: If there is a person who commits incest with his mother, violates a nun, steals from the sangha, kills one who has awakened aspiration for highest *bodhi,* or murders his own father, such a person will definitely fall into the Avīci hell. How should I not have pain in mind and body?"

The minister said, "Great king, you should not grieve and suffer so much.... All sentient beings have residues of their karma. Due to karmic conditions, they repeatedly undergo birth and death. Since the late king had a residue of karma for which he received the retribution of being killed by you, you are not to blame. I pray, great king, that you be at ease and do not grieve. For it is said:

> If one is sorrowful all the time,
> The sorrow grows and multiplies.
> It is just as sleep indulged in
> Grows and becomes intense.
> So it is with craving lust
> And drinking wine.

610c [There is a master named Sañjayī-vairaṭīputra....]

Again, there was a minister named Sarvārthajña. He approached Ajātaśatru and said.... The king replied, "How should I not have pain in mind and body?... I committed the outrageous act of killing the late king, though he was innocent. Once I heard a wise man say, 'If one kills one's father, one will undergo great torment for immeasurable and uncountable *kalpas.*' There is no doubt that I will fall into hell before long. There is no excellent physician who can cure my illness of karmic evil." The minister said, "I pray, great king, that you give up sorrow and affliction. Have you not heard that a long time ago, there was a king named Rāma. He killed his father and ascended the throne. Great King Bhadrīka, King Virūchin, King Nahuṣa, King Kathika, King Viśākha, King Candraprabha, King Sūryaprabha, King Kāma, and King Bahujanadhāra—these kings all killed their fathers and ascended the throne. But not one of them has gone to hell. At present, King Virūḍhaka, King Udayana,

King Caṇḍa, King Mūṣaka, and King Padma all killed their fathers but none of them suffer from sorrow and affliction. Although people speak of hell, the realm of the hungry ghosts, and the heavenly realm, who has ever seen [these places]? Great king, there are only two states of existence: the state of humans and that of animals. Although there are these two states, one is not born through causes and conditions, neither does one die through causes and conditions. If there are neither causes nor conditions, what is good and what is evil? I pray, great king, that you do not entertain grief and fear, for it is said:

> If one is sorrowful all the time,
> The sorrow grows and multiplies.
> It is just as sleep indulged in
> Grows and becomes intense.
> So it is with craving lust
> And drinking wine.

[There is a master named] Ajitakeśakambala. . . .

Again, there was a minister named Maṅgala. . . . "What is the meaning of hell [naraka]? Let me explain it. 'Nara' means earth, and 'ka' means to break. Breaking hell without having any karmic retribution; this is called hell. Again, 'nara' means human, and 'ka' means divine. By killing one's father one reaches the human or heavenly realm. For this reason, the ascetic Vasu proclaims, 'By killing sheep, one gains the pleasure of the human or heavenly realm.' This is called hell. Again, 'nara' means life, and 'ka' means long. By killing beings, one gains long life. This is called hell.

"Great king, for this reason, hell does not actually exist. Great king, it is just as one sows wheat and reaps wheat; also just as one sows rice and reaps rice. By destroying hell, one attains hell. By killing people, one gains human life.

"Great king, if you listen to my explanation, you will see that there is actually no killing. If there is a real ego, one cannot kill it. If there is no ego, one cannot kill it, either. Why? Because if ego exists, it does not undergo any change; since it is eternally abiding, one cannot kill it. It cannot be broken, destroyed, bound, nor does it get angry or rejoice; [it is] like empty space. How would there be the crime of killing? If there is no ego, then all things are impermanent. Because they are impermanent, they perish every moment. Because they perish every moment, the killer and the killed also perish every moment. If they perish every moment, who is to blame?

"Great king, it is like fire, which is innocent of burning wood; it is also like an ax, which is innocent of cutting down a tree; it is also like a scythe, which is innocent of cutting grass. Suppose a sword kills a man—it is not a person, and so it is innocent, nor is the person to blame. When poison kills a man, it is not a person, and so the poison is not to blame. How can there be a crime? So it is with all the myriad things; there cannot actually be killing, so how can there be a crime? I pray, great king, that you do not allow yourself to give rise to sorrow and affliction, for it is said:

> If one is sorrowful all the time,
> The sorrow grows and multiplies.
> It is just as sleep indulged in
> Grows and becomes intense.
> So it is with craving lust
> And drinking wine.

"Now there is a great master named Kakuda-kātyāyana."

Again, there was a minister named Abhaya.... "Now there is a great master named Nirgrantha-jñātiputra.... "

At that time there was a great physician named Jīvaka. He approached Ajātaśatru and said, "Can you sleep well?" The king answered in verse.... "Jīvaka, my illness is very serious. I committed the outrageous act of killing the king who was devoted to the Right Dharma. There is no excellent physician, medicine, spell, or careful nursing that can cure my incorrigible illness. Why? Because I outrageously killed my father, the late king, who followed the law of justice in ruling the state and was blameless in his conduct. I feel as if I were a fish on the ground.... A long time ago, I heard a wise man say, 'If a man's acts of body, speech, and mind are not pure, you may be sure that he will definitely fall into hell.' This is exactly what I am. How could I sleep peacefully? There would not be an excellent physician, unrivaled in the world, whose medicine of the Dharma could remove my pain of illness."

Jīvaka replied, "It is wonderful that even though you committed a crime you have profound remorse in your heart and are full of shame and repentance. Great king, Buddhas and World-honored Ones always teach as follows:

> There are two good acts that save sentient beings. One is shame and the other is repentance. Shame keeps one from committing evil acts, and repentance leads others to refrain from committing evil acts. Again, shame is shamefulness felt within oneself, and repentance is confession of one's evil acts to others. Further, shame is feeling shame before other people, and repentance is feeling shame before gods. These are called shame and repentance. Those without shame and repentance are not worthy of humans; they are called animals. Because you feel shame and repentance, you respect your parents and teachers. Because you feel shame and repentance, you can maintain harmony   611b
> with your parents, brothers, and sisters.

"It is wonderful, great king, that you are filled with shame and repentance....

"You say that there is no one who can cure your illness. You ought to know, great king, that the son of King Śuddhodana of Kapilavastu—his family name is Gautama and his given name Siddhārtha—naturally attained awakening without a teacher and realized highest, perfect enlightenment.... He is the Buddha, the World-honored One. Possessed of adamantine wisdom, he can destroy all the karmic evil of sentient beings. It would be wrong to say that he could not.... Great king, the Tathāgata has a cousin named Devadatta, who caused disunity in the sangha, hurt the Buddha's body, and killed the nun Lotus. He thus committed three of the [five] grave offenses. By expounding to him various essentials of the Dharma, the Tathāgata lessened his heavy karmic evil. Thus the Tathāgata is regarded as a great, distinguished physician. He is unlike the six masters.... "

[The deceased King Bimbisāra's voice is heard in the air.] "Great king, by committing one grave offense, one fully receives retribution for that. By committing two grave offenses, one receives two times as much retribution. By committing all five grave offenses, one receives five times as much retribution. Great king, you certainly know that you cannot escape retribution for your evil acts. I pray, great king, that you quickly go to see the Buddha. People other than the Buddha, the World-honored One, cannot possibly save you. As I feel pity for you, I, too, urge you to take my advice."

Hearing these words, Ajātaśatru was filled with fear and his whole body shook with terror. The five parts of his body violently trembled like a plantain tree [in a storm]. He looked upward and replied, "Who is in heaven? No form is seen; only a voice is heard."

"Great king, I am your father, Bimbisāra. You ought to follow Jīvaka's advice. Do not follow the words of the six ministers who have wrong views."

Hearing this, the king fainted and fell on the ground. The scabs on his body spread more and grew in intensity, and their stench became even worse. Cooling medicine was applied to the scabs, but they gave forth vapor and their poisonous fever rose ever higher, showing no sign of alleviation.

(The six ministers were: Great Minister Candrayaśas, Prāptagarbha, a minister named Tattvalabdha, a minister named

Sarvārthajña, Great Minister Maṅgala, and Abhaya. The six masters were: Pūraṇa-kāśyapa, Maskarī-gośālīputra, Sañjayī-vairaṭīputra, Ajitakeśakambala, Kakuda-kātyāyana, and Nirgrantha-
jñātiputra.)

It is also stated in the same sutra:[119]

> [The Buddha said:] "Sons of good families, as I have declared,
> for the sake of King Ajātaśatru, I will not enter nirvana. You
> may not understand the profound meaning of this. The rea-
> son for this is: 'for the sake of' means for all ordinary beings.
> 'King Ajātaśatru' means all those who commit the five grave
> offenses. Also, 'for the sake of' means for all beings subject to
> conditioned states of existence. I do not dwell in the world for
> the sake of beings who have attained the stage of non-action.
> Why? Because one who has attained the unconditioned stage
> is no longer a sentient being. 'Ajātaśatru' refers to those pos-
> sessed of evil passions. Further, 'for the sake of' is for sentient
> beings who have not yet seen Buddha-nature. I do not dwell
> long in the world for those who have seen Buddha-nature.
> Why? Because one who has seen Buddha-nature is no longer
> a sentient being. 'Ajātaśatru' refers to all those who have not
> yet awakened aspiration for highest, perfect enlightenment....
> Again, 'for the sake of' is said of Buddha-nature. 'Ajāta' means
> not produced. 'Śatru' means enemy. Because one does not pro-
> duce Buddha-nature one gives rise to the enemy, that is, the
> evil passions. Because one gives rise to the enemy, evil pas-
> sions, one does not see Buddha-nature. When one does not
> give rise to evil passions one sees Buddha-nature. Because one
> sees Buddha-nature, one can firmly dwell in the great and
> complete nirvana. This is what is meant by 'not produced.'
> Hence, the name 'Ajātaśatru.'
>
> "Sons of good families, 'ajāta' means not produced; what
> is not produced is nirvana. 'Śatru' refers to worldly matters.
> 'For the sake of' means not defiled. Because [the Buddha] is
> not defiled by any of the eight kinds of worldly concerns, he

does not enter nirvana for immeasurable, boundless, and countless *kalpa*s. For this reason, I say, 'For the sake of Ajātaśatru,
I will not enter nirvana for countless *koṭi*s of *kalpa*s.'

"Sons of good families, the Tathāgata's mystic words are
inconceivable. The Buddha, Dharma, and Sangha are also
inconceivable. Bodhisattva *mahāsattva*s too are inconceivable. The *Great Nirvana Sutra (Mahāparinirvāṇa-sūtra)* is
equally inconceivable."

Then the World-honored One, the Great Compassionate
Guide, entered the *samādhi* of moonlight love for the sake
of King Ajātaśatru. Having entered the *samādhi* the Buddha
emitted a great flood of light. The light, which was pure and
refreshing, reached the king and shone upon his body. Then
the scabs were instantly healed....

Ajātaśatru said to Jīvaka, "He is the foremost of the [five
kinds of] gods. For what reason does he emit this light?"

"Great king, it seems to me that this auspicious sign is
for your sake. Because you said that there was no excellent
physician who could cure your body and mind, he first emits
this light to heal your body, and then your mind."

612a   The king said to Jīvaka, "Does the Tathāgata, the World-
honored One, deign to think of me?"

Jīvaka replied, "Suppose a man has seven children. When
one of them becomes ill, the parents' hearts lean heavily toward
this sick child, though their hearts are not biased. Great king,
so it is with the Tathāgata. Although he is equally compassionate for all sentient beings, he is especially concerned about
those who have karmic evil. The Buddha's compassionate
thought is on indolent and unruly persons; he pays little attention to diligent persons. Who are diligent persons? They are
the bodhisattvas of the first six stages. Great king, various
Buddhas, World-honored Ones, do not perceive sentient beings'
family origin, age, wealth, auspicious times, astrological ref-
erences, craftsmanship, low social status, or status as man or
maidservant. They perceive only those sentient beings who

possess the good mind. If they have the good mind, the Buddhas' compassionate thought is on them. Great king, you should realize that this auspicious sign is the light the Tathāgata sends forth as he enters the *samādhi* of moonlight love."

The king then asked, "What is the *samādhi* of moonlight love?"

Jīvaka replied, "Just as moonlight causes all the blue lotuses to bloom in clear brilliance, the *samādhi* of moonlight love causes sentient beings to open up the good mind. Hence, it is called 'the *samādhi* of moonlight love.' Great king, just as moonlight produces joy in the hearts of travelers, this *samādhi* produces joy in the hearts of those who practice the path of nirvana. Hence, it is called 'the *samādhi* of moonlight love.... ' It is the king of all good; it is the nectar. It is what all sentient beings love and adore. Hence, it is called 'the *samādhi* of moonlight love.... '"

Then the Buddha said to the whole assembly, "Among the causes and conditions that bring all sentient beings closer to highest, perfect enlightenment, nothing is more important than good friends. For, King Ajātaśatru, if you did not follow Jīvaka's advice, you would certainly die on the seventh day of next month and fall into the Avīci hell. Hence, with the approach of the day of death nothing is more important than a good friend."

On the way [to see the Buddha], King Ajātaśatru had heard that King Virūḍhaka of Śrāvastī burned to death while cruising in a boat and that Bhikṣu Kokālika fell alive into the Avīci hell through a cleft that suddenly appeared in the earth. Sunakṣatra, on the other hand, committed various evil acts but all his karmic evil was destroyed when he visited the Buddha. Having heard these stories, Ajātaśatru said to Jīvaka, "I have heard these two kinds of stories but I still have anxiety. Since you have come to see me, Jīvaka, I want to ride on the same elephant with you. When I am about to fall into the Avīci hell, hold me tight and keep me from falling.

For I have heard in the past that one who has attained the Way never falls into hell. ... "

[The Buddha said,] "Why do you say that you will certainly fall into hell? Great king, all the karmic evil committed by sentient beings is of two kinds: light and heavy. The evil committed with the mind and speech is light. The evil committed with body, speech, and mind is heavy. Great king, when you have committed evil with the mind and speech but not with the body, the retribution you will receive is light. Great king, in the past you did not verbally command that [your father] be killed, you simply ordered that his legs be cut off. Great king, if you had ordered your vassals to behead him, they would have beheaded him straightaway while he was standing. If they had executed him while he was sitting, you would be innocent. How much less innocent you are, since you did not give such an order.

"Great king, if you are guilty, all Buddhas, World-honored Ones, are also guilty. The reason is that your father, the former king Bimbisāra, always planted roots of good [by making offerings] to the Buddhas. For this reason, he was able to secure the throne in this life. If the Buddhas had not accepted the offerings he would not have become king. If he had not become king, you would not have killed him in order to seize the kingdom. So if you are guilty of committing evil by killing your father, we Buddhas are equally guilty. If the Buddhas, the World-honored Ones, are not guilty, how can you alone be guilty?

"Great king, Bimbisāra formerly conceived an evil thought. He went to Mount Vipula; he traversed the moor hunting deer but shot no game at all. He happened to meet a hermit who had acquired the five transcendent powers. Having seen him, the king conceived enmity and an evil thought: 'I have been hunting. The reason I have been unable to shoot any game must surely be that this man has driven the animals away.' He then ordered his attendants to kill the hermit.

148

"At the time of death the hermit became enraged; because of an evil thought he had conceived, he lost his transcendent powers. He vowed, 'I am completely innocent. With your thought and words you have outrageously ordered my execution. In the next life, I will execute you in the same manner with thought and word.' Hearing this, the king became remorseful and conducted a burial service for the dead man.

"The former king thus received light retribution and escaped falling into hell. How would you, great king, receive the retribution of tortures in hell when you have not done such an act? The former king committed evil and himself received the retribution. How should you be guilty of killing him? You say that your father, the king, was innocent, but was he really innocent? Since he committed evil he received retribution. If he had not committed evil he would not have received retribution. If your father, the former king, was innocent, how could there be retribution? In this world, Bimbisāra received both good and evil recompense. So the recompense he received was actually indeterminate. Because his recompense was indeterminate, your act of killing is also indeterminate. If so, how can it be determined that you will fall into hell?

"Great king, the insanity of sentient beings is of four kinds: 1) the insanity induced by greed, 2) the insanity caused by intoxicating substances, 3) the insanity caused by spells, and 4) the insanity caused by one's karmic conditions from the past. Great king, these four kinds of insanity are found among my disciples. Even though such disciples commit much evil I have never declared that they have broken the precepts. Their acts will not lead them into the three evil realms. If they regain their senses, I do not tell them that they have violated the precepts. Great king, you originally killed your father out of greed for the kingdom. It was in the state of insanity induced by greed that you did this. How is it possible that you are guilty of committing evil? Great king, it is like a man who kills his mother while drunk but is full of remorse when he becomes sober. You should realize that such an act does not produce retribution. Great king, you were intoxicated with greed. You did not commit that act in the normal state of mind. If it was not committed in the normal state of mind, how could you be guilty?

"Great king, an illustration of a magician may be presented here. At the crossroad he magically creates various forms of people, elephants, horses, ornaments, and robes. Foolish people take these images as real, but the wise know that they are not. So it is with killing. Ordinary people take it as real but Buddhas, the World-honored Ones, know that it is not.

"Great king, it is also like the echo of a voice in the mountain valleys. Foolish people take this as a real voice but the wise know that it is not. So it is with killing. Ordinary people take it as real, but Buddhas, the World-honored Ones, know that it is not.

"Great king, it is also like a person who entertains malicious intent but approaches you with feigned friendship. Ignorant people take this as true friendliness but the wise, knowing thoroughly, realize that it is empty pretense. So it is with killing. Ordinary people take it as real but Buddhas, the World-honored Ones, know that it is not.

"Great king, it is like taking up a mirror and looking at one's image in it. Ignorant people take the reflection as real but the wise, knowing thoroughly, realize that it is not. So it is with killing. Ordinary people take it as real but Buddhas, the World-honored Ones, know that it is not.

"Great king, it is like the shimmering of a mirage. Ignorant people take it as water but the wise, knowing thoroughly, realize that it is not. So it is with killing. Ordinary people take it as real but Buddhas, the World-honored Ones, know that it is not. . . .

"Great king, it is like enjoying the pleasures of the five

sensual desires in a dream. Ignorant people take these pleasures as real but the wise, knowing thoroughly, realize that they are not. So it is with killing. Ordinary people take it as real but Buddhas, the World-honored Ones, know that it is not.

"Great king, I have attained thorough understanding concerning the way of killing, the act of killing, the one who kills, and the consequences of killing, and also freedom from the consequences, but this does not mean that I am guilty of killing. Great king, even if you know about killing, how can this make you guilty? Great king, it is like a man in charge of wine; he knows much about wine but he does not become drunk unless he drinks.   613a

"Again, one who knows about fire does not burn. In the same way, great king, you know about killing but how can that make you guilty? Great king, sentient beings commit various crimes in the daylight and also commit theft in the moonlight, but they do not commit any crime when there is no sun or moon in the sky. It is true that because of the sun and the moon crimes are committed, but they are not really guilty. So it is with killing. . . .

"Great king, just as nirvana is neither existent nor nonexistent and yet it is existent, so it is with killing. Although it is neither existent nor nonexistent and yet it is existent, it is not existent for one who is repentant and is not nonexistent for one who is not repentant. For one who receives retribution of killing, it is existent. For one who realizes emptiness, killing is considered nonexistent. For one who sees [inherent] entity in each thing, killing is not nonexistent. For one who clings to the view of existence, killing is existent, because such a person receives retribution. One who rejects the view of existence receives no retribution. For one who realizes the eternal presence of nirvana, killing is not existent. For one who does not, it is not nonexistent. One who clings to the eternal presence of nirvana cannot see killing as nonexistent, because such a person receives retribution for evil acts. Thus one who clings to the eternal presence of nirvana cannot see killing as nonexistent. For this reason, although killing is neither existent nor nonexistent, it is described as existent. Great king, sentient beings are so termed as long as they exhale and inhale breath. When the exhalation and inhalation of breath is cut off, this is called killing. The Buddhas speak of killing in accordance with the common practice in the world. . . . "

[Ajātaśatru said,] "O World-honored One, as I observe things in the world, I see that from a seed of the *eraṇḍa* grows an *eraṇḍa* tree. I do not see that from a seed of the *eraṇḍa* grows a sandalwood tree. I now see for the first time that from a seed of the *eraṇḍa* grows a sandalwood tree. I mean that the *eraṇḍa* seed is myself and the sandalwood tree is faith that has no root in my heart. By 'having no root' I mean that formerly I did not know what it was to revere the Tathā-gata, and did not believe in the Dharma and Sangha (i.e., the Three Treasures) either. I describe this as 'having no root.' World-honored One, had I not encountered the Tathāgata, the World-honored One, I would undergo immeasurable suffering in the Avīci hell for immeasurable and countless *kalpa*s. I have now met the Buddha. Having observed the Buddha's virtue, I will destroy with it the evil passions and evil thoughts of sentient beings."

The Buddha said, "Great king, very good. I now realize that you will unfailingly destroy the evil thoughts of sentient beings."

"World-honored One, so long as I can surely destroy evil thoughts of sentient beings, even if I were to dwell in the Avīci hell, undergoing pain for immeasurable *kalpa*s for the sake of sentient beings, I would not regard such pain as unbearable."

At that time, innumerable people of Magadha all awak-ened aspiration for highest, perfect enlightenment. Because those innumerable people awakened the great aspiration,

613b

King Ajātaśatru's heavy evil karma became slight. The king, queen, consorts, and court ladies all awakened aspiration for highest, perfect enlightenment.

At that time, King Ajātaśatru said to Jīvaka, "Jīvaka, even before my death I have already attained the pure heavenly body. Abandoning the short life, I have acquired long life; casting aside the impermanent body, I have gained a body of eternity. I will lead sentient beings to awaken aspiration for highest, perfect enlightenment.... "

Having uttered these words, the disciple of the Buddhas (i.e., Ajātaśatru) [made offerings to the Buddha] with various jeweled banners...and praised him with a verse:

Your words of truth are exceedingly subtle and
     wonderful,
Skillful in guidance and in the use of expression;
They are a treasury of profound mystic truths.
For the sake of the multitude,
You display extensive words to explain the principles;
For the sake of the multitudes, you present short
     explanations.
Being possessed of such words,
You cure the illnesses of sentient beings.
If there are sentient beings
Who are able to hear these words,
Whether they accept them in faith or not,
They will surely come to know the Buddha's teaching.
The Buddhas always speak in gentle words,
But for some people, they expound in rough words.
Their words, both gentle and rough,
Are grounded in the highest truth.
For this reason, I now
Take refuge in the World-honored One.
The Tathāgata's words are of one taste,
Like the waters of the great ocean.

This we call the highest truth.
Hence, there are no meaningless words;
What the Tathāgata now teaches—
The various innumerable teachings—
Men and women, old and young, hear
And are equally led to the highest truth.
[Nirvana] is without cause and without effect,
Non-arising and non-perishing.
So it is called great nirvana.
Those who hear the Dharma can have their bonds
    destroyed.
The Tathāgata, for the sake of all beings,
Always becomes one's father or mother.
Know that all sentient beings
Are the Tathāgata's children.
The World-honored One of great compassion
Performed painful practices for the sake of the
    multitudes,
Like a person possessed by spirits
Running about wildly in a frenzy.
I have now been able to meet the Buddha
And acquired good through the three modes of action;
May I transfer the merit accruing from this
Toward attainment of the supreme *bodhi*.
I now make offerings

613c

To the Buddha, Dharma, and Sangha;
May I, with the merit of this,
Ensure the presence of the Three Treasures in the
    world.
I have now acquired
Various merits;
May I, with such merits, defeat
The four devils of sentient beings.
Having met with evil friends, I have committed
    offenses

Which bring retribution in the past, present, and
future.
These offenses I now repent before the Buddha.
May I never commit such evils again.
May all sentient beings alike
Awaken aspiration for *bodhi*
And with concentrated thought always
Be mindful of all the Buddhas of the ten directions.
May all sentient beings
Destroy their evil passions forever
And clearly see Buddha-nature
As Mañjuśrī does.

Then the World-honored One praised King Ajātaśatru,
"Very good, very good! It should be known that if a person
awakens the *bodhi*-mind, he adorns assemblies of Buddhas.
In the past, great king, you have already awakened aspiration for highest, perfect enlightenment for the first time in
the presence of Buddha Vipaśyin. From that time until my
appearance in the world you have never fallen into hell and
undergone suffering there. You should know, great king, that
the *bodhi*-mind produces immeasurable rewards like this.
Great king, from now on be careful to cultivate the *bodhi*-
mind. The reason is that by doing so you will be able to extinguish immeasurable karmic evil."

Then King Ajātaśatru and all the people in Magadha rose
from their seats, circumambulated the Buddha three times,
took their leave, and returned to the palace city.

It is also stated:[120]

[The Buddha said:] "Sons of good families, King Bimbisāra
of Rājagṛha had a son named Sudarśana, who under the
influence of previous karma gave rise to atrocious thoughts;
he tried to kill his father but had no chance. At that time, a
wicked man, Devadatta, equally under the influence of some

karmic cause from the past, produced evil thoughts against me and tried to kill me. Having acquired the five transcendent powers he soon succeeded in establishing a friendly relationship with Prince Sudarśana.

"Devadatta demonstrated various miracles to the prince: he disappeared from where there was no exit and reappeared through the gate, or went out through the gate and reappeared from where there was no gate. On another occasion, he manifested an elephant, a horse, an ox, a sheep, a man, and a woman. Having seen these, Prince Sudarśana entertained thoughts of friendship, joy, and respect. Thereupon, he had various things prepared and offered them to Devadatta.

614a
"The prince next said, 'Great Master, the Saint, I wish to see *māndārava* blossoms.' Then Devadatta immediately ascended to the Heaven of Thirty-three Gods and tried to obtain blossoms from the gods. But since his merit had already been exhausted, none of the gods gave him blossoms. Failing to obtain the blossoms, he thought, '*Māndārava* blossoms have no sense of "I" or "mine," so no crime will be committed even if I pick them.' As soon as he tried to pick the blossoms he lost his transcendent powers. He then found himself in Rājagṛha. Full of shame, he was not able to see Prince Sudarśana.

"He further thought, 'I will now go to the Tathāgata and ask him to grant me his sangha. If the Buddha agrees, I will be able to give instructions as I please and order about Śāriputra and others.'

"Then Devadatta came to me and said, 'I request you, Tathāgata, to leave the leadership of the sangha to me. I will expound various teachings to them and transform and train them.' I replied to this foolish man, 'Śāriputra and others, having learned the great wisdom, are trusted and respected by the world. Nevertheless, I do not transfer leadership of the sangha to them. How much less would I leave it to the care of a fool like you who deserves to be spat upon!'

"Thereupon, as Devadatta's evil thoughts increased, he

said, 'Gautama, even though you now control the sangha, its power will not last long. It will perish before my eyes.'

"As soon as he uttered these words, the earth shook six times. As Devadatta fell to the ground, a violent wind arose about his body, blowing up dust and covering and soiling his body with it. Seeing this bad omen, Devadatta made this remark, 'If I am doomed to fall into the Avīci hell in this present life, I will take revenge of the great evil done to me.'

"Then Devadatta stood up and went to see Prince Sudarśana. Seeing him, Sudarśana asked the master, 'Why do you look so emaciated and sorrowful?'

"Devadatta replied, 'I am always like this. Did you not know?' Sudarśana said, 'Please explain the reason. What is the cause of this?' Devadatta said, 'I have become your close friend. Those outside the palace abuse you, saying you are in the wrong. When I hear this, why should I not feel sorrow?'

"Prince Sudarśana further said, 'How do the people of the kingdom abuse and insult me?' Devadatta replied, 'They abuse you, calling you "Unborn Enemy."' Sudarśana asked, 'Why do they call me "Unborn Enemy"? Who made this name?'

"Devadatta answered, 'Before you were born all the soothsayers predicted, "This child, when born, will surely kill its father." For this reason, people outside the palace all called you "Unborn Enemy." Those inside the palace, however, called 614b you "Sudarśana" in order to spare your feelings. Having heard the soothsayers' words, Queen Vaidehī, after the delivery, dropped you from the top of the tower. When you hit the ground one of your fingers was broken. For this reason, people also called you "Broken-Fingered." When I heard this, I was so full of sorrow and resentment that I could not tell this to you.'

"Devadatta, relating this and other pernicious stories to the prince, instigated him to kill his father. He said, 'If you kill your father I will kill the mendicant Gautama.'

"Thereupon, Prince Sudarśana asked a minister named Varṣakāra, 'Why did the great king give me the name "Unborn

Enemy"?' In reply the minister told him all that had happened, which was the same as Devadatta's explanation. On hearing this, Sudarśana together with the minister seized his father, King Bimbisāra, confined him in a place outside the palace, and ordered the four kinds of soldiers to guard it. Hearing this, Queen Vaidehī immediately went to see the king. But the guards under strict order of the king intercepted her and did not allow her to enter. Angered by this, the queen rebuked them.

"Then the guards reported to the prince, 'The wife of the great king wishes to see your father the king. Should we allow her in or not?' Hearing this, Sudarśana became enraged. He immediately went to his mother, grasped her by the hair, drew his sword, and was about to kill her.

"Then Jīvaka said to the great king, 'Since the founding of this kingdom, no woman has ever been executed, however serious her offenses may be. How would you kill the woman who gave birth to you?'

"Sudarśana, hearing this, followed Jīvaka's advice and let go of his mother. But he stopped supplying the great king with clothing, bedding, food, drink, and medicine. Seven days passed, and the king's life ended.

"Seeing his father's death, Prince Sudarśana became remorseful. Minister Varṣakāra taught him various evil views, saying, 'Great king, all kinds of acts are blameless. Why are you remorseful?' Jīvaka further said, 'Great king, you must know that this act of yours involves a twofold evil: one is killing your father and the other is killing a stream-winner. Apart from the Buddha there is no one who can remove your evil.' King Sudarśana said, 'The Tathāgata is pure and free of defilement. How would he see such an evil man as me?'

"Sons of good families, I was aware of this happening. I said to Ānanda, 'After three months I will enter nirvana.' Hearing of this, Sudarśana immediately came to see me. As

I expounded the Dharma to him, his heavy karmic evil became slight and he attained the faith that has no root in him.

"Sons of good families, having heard my words my disciples failed to understand my intent and said, 'The Tathāgata has declared that he would enter complete nirvana.' Sons of good families, there are two kinds of bodhisattvas: bodhisattvas in the true sense and those in provisional name only. Bodhisattvas in provisional name only, on hearing that I would enter nirvana in three months, all fell into regressive thoughts, saying, 'If the Tathāgata is subject to impermanence and will not dwell in the world [forever], what should we do? In order to resolve this matter [of impermanence] we have undergone great pain for countless lifetimes. The Tathāgata, the World-honored One, has perfected and is possessed of immeasurable merit; still, he cannot destroy the devil of death. How then could we ever destroy it?'

"Sons of good families, for the sake of such bodhisattvas I declare, 'The Tathāgata is eternally abiding and immutable.' If my disciples, hearing this, fail to understand my intent they will say, 'The Tathāgata will ultimately never enter nirvana.'"

From the words of truth of the Great Sage, we see that when the three kinds of people who are difficult to save, or those with the three kinds of illness that are difficult to cure, entrust themselves to the Universal Vow of great compassion and take refuge in the ocean of faith of Other-Power, the Buddha arouses compassion for them and cures their illness; in other words, he takes pity on them and heals their sickness. It is like the excellent medicine of *maṇḍa* that cures all illnesses. Beings of the defiled world, the multitudes full of depravity and evil, should seek to attain true adamantine faith. They should hold fast to the Primal Vow, the excellent medicine of *maṇḍa*. This one should realize.

In various Mahayana sutras, beings who are difficult to save are mentioned. The *Larger Sutra* says, "Excluded are those who commit the five grave offenses and abuse the Right Dharma." It is also said,[121] "Excepted are those who commit the evil acts that would consign them to the Avīci hell and those who abuse the Right Dharma and the sages." The *Contemplation Sutra* clarifies that those who commit the five grave offenses can attain birth but does not state that those who abuse the [Right] Dharma can. The *Nirvana Sutra* speaks of the beings who are difficult to save and the illnesses that are difficult to cure. How should we understand [different expositions in] these teachings of truth?

It is stated in the *Commentary on Vasubandhu's Discourse on the Pure Land:*

> *Question:* The *Larger Sutra* says, "Aspirants for birth [in the Pure Land] will all attain birth, except those who have committed the five grave offenses and abused the Right Dharma." The *Contemplation Sutra* says, "Those who have committed the five grave offenses and the ten evil acts as well as various other evils will also attain birth." How do you harmonize these [differing] descriptions in the two sutras?

> *Answer:* The *[Larger] Sutra* mentions the commission of the two gravest evils, namely, the five grave offenses and abuse of the Right Dharma. Since one has committed those two kinds of evils one is not able to attain birth. The other sutra mentions only the commission of the ten evil acts and the five grave offenses; it does not mention abuse of the Right Dharma. Since one has not abused the Right Dharma one is able to attain birth.

> *Question:* If there is a man who has committed the five grave offenses but not abused the Right Dharma, he will, according to the *[Contemplation] Sutra,* be able to obtain birth. Suppose there is a man who has abused the Right Dharma but has not committed the five grave offenses. If he desires birth in the Pure Land, will he be able to attain it?

> *Answer:* He who has committed the transgression of abusing the Right Dharma will not be able to attain birth, even though

he has not committed any other evils. For what reason? The [*Perfection of Great Wisdom*] *Sutra* (*Mahāprajñāpāramitā-sūtra*) says:

> Those who have committed the five grave offenses will fall into the great Avīci hell, where they will receive retributions of the grave evils in various ways for one *kalpa*. Those who have abused the Right Dharma will also fall into the great Avīci hell. When the period of one *kalpa* comes to an end, they will be sent to the great Avīci hell of another world. In this way, such evildoers will consecutively pass through a hundred thousand great Avīci hells.

The Buddha thus did not mention the time of their release [from the Avīci hells]. This is because the transgression of abusing the Right Dharma is extremely grave.

Further, the Right Dharma refers to the Buddha-Dharma. Such ignorant persons have abused it; therefore, does it stand to reason that they should seek birth in a Buddha land? If they seek birth merely from a desire to enjoy pleasures, it is as if they sought to attain ice that is not made from water or fire that does not produce smoke. Is it not contrary to reason that they would be able to attain birth?

Question: What is the act of abusing the Right Dharma?

Answer: If one says, "There is no Buddha," "There is no Buddha-Dharma," "There is no bodhisattva," or "There is no Dharma for bodhisattvas," such views, held firmly in the mind by one's own reasoning or by listening to others' teachings, are called "abusing the Right Dharma."

Question: The fault of holding such views belongs only to those who hold them. What suffering does it cause to other beings which makes it more serious than the five grave offenses?

Answer: If there were no Buddhas or bodhisattvas who edify living beings by teaching them ways of both worldly and supramundane good, how could they know about [the Confucian moral virtues, namely,] benevolence, righteousness, propriety, knowledge, and sincerity? The result would be that all worldly good, such as those virtues, would perish and there would be no wise men and holy sages [who practice the way of supramundane good]. You only know of the gravity of the five grave offenses. You are not aware that they arise from the absence of the Right Dharma. For this reason, abusing the Right Dharma is the gravest of all evils.

Question: Sutras explaining the law of karma state that it is like a balance; a heavier object pulls it down. According to the *Contemplation Sutra,* those who have committed the five grave offenses and the ten evil acts as well as various other evils will fall into the evil realms, where they will pass many *kalpa*s undergoing immeasurable suffering. If, however, at their death they meet a good friend who urges them to recite the Name, "Homage to the Buddha of Infinite Life," and accordingly they repeat it ten times continuously with sincere heart, then they will obtain birth in the Pure Land of Peace and Bliss. There they will join those who are rightly established in the Mahayana path. Thus, they will not retrogress [from the attainment of enlightenment] and will forever be free from various suffering in the three evil realms. How do you explain this in the light of [the law of karma according to which a heavier karma] pulls one down? Furthermore, from the beginningless past, sentient beings have been given to acts of various defilements, and so they are tied to the three worlds. If, as you say, they can attain liberation from the three worlds by mere mindfulness of Amida Buddha with ten repetitions of his Name, what will become of the bondage of karma?

Answer: You consider the bondage of karma, such as the five grave offenses and the ten evil acts, as heavy, and the ten repetitions of the Name by a person of the lowest level of the lowest grade as light. And so you contend that such an evildoer will first fall into hell owing to his evildoing and thus be tied to the three worlds. Now let us examine the weight of karmic evils in the light of Buddhist principles. 615b

It is dependent on 1) state of mind, 2) the object, and 3) the degree of concentration, and not by length of time.

1. State of mind: The evildoer in question has committed evils in his false and perverted state of mind, whereas the ten repetitions of the Name arise when he hears the teaching of true reality from a good friend who consoles him by various skillful means. One is truthful and the other false. How can they be compared with each other? Suppose there is a room that has been dark for a thousand years. If a light is cast into the room even for only a short while, the room will instantly become bright. How could the darkness refuse to leave because it has been there for a thousand years? This is what is meant by "state of mind."

2. The object: The evildoer with deluded thoughts has committed evils against other sentient beings who have also come into existence as the result of evil passions and deluded thoughts. The ten repetitions of the Name arise from the unsurpassed faith by taking as object the Name of Amida Tathāgata of a glorious body of skillful means that comprises immeasurable merits that are true and pure. Suppose a man is hit by a poisoned arrow that has pierced his sinews and broken a bone. If he hears the sound of a drum treated with a special antidote, the arrow will instantly come out and the poison will be removed. It is stated in the *Śūraṅgama [Samādhi] Sutra:*[122]

A parable may be given to a medicine called Remover. If, in the battlefield, it is applied to a drum, those who hear the sound of the drum will have the arrows extracted and the poison removed. So it is with bodhisattva *mahāsattva*s.

If they dwell in the *śūraṅgama samādhi* or hear its name, the arrows of the three poisons will spontaneously come out.

How could the arrow stuck in the body be too deep to come out when the sound of the drum is heard? Also, how could the poison be too strong to be removed? This is what is meant by "the object."

3. The degree of concentration: The evildoer has committed transgressions with a thought that anticipates the result and is, therefore, mixed with other thoughts. The ten repetitions of the Name are based on a state of mind which does not anticipate results and is, therefore, not mixed with other thoughts. This is what is meant by "degree of concentration."

From the above examination of these three matters, it is clear that the ten repetitions of the Name are stronger [than the five grave offenses or the ten evil acts] and so this "stronger" karma prevails, enabling the evildoer to escape from the three [painful] states of existence. Thus there is no discrepancy between the two sutras.

Question: How long is "one thought"?

Answer: There are a hundred and one arisings and perishings [of a *dharma*] in one moment; there are sixty such moments in one thought-moment. The term "thought" under discussion does not have this temporal meaning. The ten repetitions of the Name are ten consecutive thoughts of Amida Buddha not mingled with other thoughts, whether they arise from contemplation of his entire body or part of it, depending on the conditions. [Ten] repetitions of the Name should be interpreted in the same way.

Question: If our thoughts settle on some other thing [than Amida], we can collect and redirect them [to him]. We can, in this way, count the number of the Nembutsu thoughts. But when the number of repetitions of the Name is knowable, they cannot arise one after another without interruption. When we concentrate and focus our thoughts [on the Name], how can we count the number of them?

Answer: When the [*Contemplation*] *Sutra* speaks of "ten times," it simply means to show that the karmic force necessary for birth in the Pure Land is accomplished [by this act]. We do not need to know the [exact] number of [repetitions]. As it is said, the summer cicada has no knowledge of spring or autumn. How could this insect know it is summertime? Those who know this speak like that. Likewise, only those who have transcendent faculties can tell that the karmic force necessary for birth in the Pure Land is accomplished by ten repetitions of the Name. We have only to remember Amida continuously, thought after thought, without thinking of other things. Why is it necessary to know the number of repetitions of the Name? But if you must know it there is a method. Follow the method that has been transmitted orally [from master to disciple]. This method should not be written down.

615c

The Master of Kuang-ming Temple says:[123]

Question: According to the Forty-eight Vows, only those who commit the five grave offenses and those who abuse the Right Dharma are excluded from attainment of birth. Here, in the passage of the *Contemplation Sutra* on the lowest grade of the lowest class, it is disclosed that those who abuse the [Right] Dharma are rejected but those who commit the five grave offenses are saved. What is the implication of this?

Answer: This matter is to be understood as a teaching to prevent us from doing evil. In the Forty-eight Vows those who abuse the [Right] Dharma and those who commit the five grave offenses are excluded from salvation, for these two kinds of evil are the gravest of all karmic hindrances. If sentient beings commit them, they will at once fall into the Avīci hell, where they are tormented for many *kalpas* without any chance of escape. Fearing that we would commit these two kinds of offenses, the Tathāgata, through skillful means, forbids us to commit them, saying that offenders will not attain birth. This does not mean that they are not really saved and embraced.

When it is disclosed in the passage on the lowest grade of the lowest class that those who commit the five grave offenses are saved but those who abuse the [Right] Dharma are excluded, it is because the beings of this group have already committed the five grave offenses and so they should not be abandoned and left to revolve in transmigration. Thus Amida, awakening great compassion, enfolds them and brings them to the Pure Land. Since, in this case, the offense of abusing the [Right] Dharma has not yet been committed, in order to prevent them from doing so, it is stated that if one abuses the [Right] Dharma, one will not attain birth. This is said of the karmic evil that has not yet been committed. If one has committed this offense, one is still enfolded by Amida and brought to the Pure Land. Although such an offender is able to attain birth there, he will be enclosed in a lotus bud and pass many *kalpa*s in that state.

While these offenders stay in the lotus buds they have three obstructions: first, they cannot see Buddhas and a host of sages; second, they cannot hear the Right Dharma; third, they cannot visit Buddha lands to make offerings to the Buddhas. Apart from these obstructions they are free of various suffering, as it is said in the sutras, "they are like monks who have entered the pleasure of the third meditation heaven." One should know that although they are enclosed in the lotus buds for many *kalpa*s, is this not far better than undergoing various torments in the Avīci hell for many *kalpa*s? This matter has been explained as a teaching to prevent us from doing evil.

He also says:[124]

The Pure Land is forever free of abusive language and hatred; all are equal and there is no sorrow or affliction. Humans and gods, whether good or evil, can all go to be born there. Upon reaching that land their distinctions no longer exist. Being the same in their spiritual attainment, they dwell in the stage of non-retrogression. What made this so? When Amida was in his causal stage, under the guidance of Buddha Lokeśvararāja, he abandoned the throne and left his home. He then awakened the mind of compassion and wisdom and widely proclaimed the Forty-eight Vows. Through the Buddha's Vow-Power, those who have committed the five grave offenses and the ten transgressions can have their karmic evil removed and attain birth. Whether they are those who have abused the [Right] Dharma or those lacking the seed of Buddhahood (*icchantika*s), all attain birth if they convert their minds.

The five grave offenses are explained as follows:[125]

According to Tzu-chou, there are two traditions concerning the five grave offenses. One is the five grave offenses in the tradition of the three vehicles: 1) intentionally killing one's father; 2) intentionally killing one's mother; 3) intentionally killing an arhat; 4) destroying the harmony of the sangha with perverted views; and 5) with evil intent causing blood to flow from the Buddha's body. These are called "grave" [literally, "going against"] because they go against the field of benevolence and the field of merits. Those who commit these grave offenses, when their bodies perish and their life ends, definitely fall into the Avīci hell where they undergo pain without interruption for one great *kalpa*. Hence, these offenses are called "the karma bringing about uninterrupted pain."

The *Abhidharma-kośa* mentions the five acts that bring about uninterrupted pain as equivalents to those above. A verse reads:

616a

> Violating one's mother or a nun of the stage of no more
>   learning [equivalent to the offense of killing one's mother],
> Killing a bodhisattva who abides in meditation
>   [equivalent to the offense of killing one's father],

Killing a sage of the stage of learning or no more learning
[equivalent to the offense of killing an arhat],
Destroying the cause of harmony of the sangha
[equivalent to the offense of destroying the sangha],
Destroying stupas [equivalent to causing blood to flow
from the body of the Buddha].

The second tradition is the five grave offenses of the Mahayana,
as stated in the *Sutra Expounded by Mahāsatyanirgrantha* (*Mahā-
satya-nirgrantha-nirdeśa**):

1) Destroying pagodas, burning sutra repositories, or stealing properties of the Three Treasures; 2) slandering the teaching of the three vehicles by saying that it is not the sacred
teaching of the Buddha, obstructing and depreciating it, or
hiding it; 3) beating and rebuking those who have renounced
the world (i.e., monks and nuns), whether they observe the
precepts, have received no precepts, or have broken them;
enumerating their transgressions, confining them, sending
them back to secular life, forcing them to do menial work,
enforcing tax duties on them, or putting them to death; 4)
killing one's father, killing one's mother, causing blood to
flow from the body of a Buddha, destroying the harmony of
the sangha, or killing an arhat; 5) rejecting the law of causation and constantly performing the ten transgressions
throughout life.

It is stated in the sutra:[126]

1) Killing a *pratyekabuddha* with evil intent—this is the
offense of killing; 2) violating an arhat nun—this is an
immoral act; 3) stealing or destroying offerings made to the
Three Treasures—this is an act of stealing; 4) destroying the
harmony of the sangha with perverted views—this is an act
of speaking false words.

End of Chapter III: Revealing the True Faith

Chapter IV

Revealing the True Enlightenment

[Presentation of the True Enlightenment]

If I am to reveal, with respect, the true enlightenment, it is the supreme state of perfect accomplishment realized by Other-Power, that is, the ultimate fruition of unsurpassed nirvana. It originates from the vow of unfailing attainment of nirvana, which is also called the vow of realization of great nirvana.

When we, ordinary people filled with evil passions, the multitudes defiled by karmic evil and subject to birth and death, attain the faith and practice transferred by Amida for our going forth, we will immediately join the Mahayana group of the rightly established stage. Because we dwell in the rightly established stage, we unfailingly reach nirvana. Unfailing attainment of nirvana is [attainment of] eternal bliss. Eternal bliss is the ultimate state of tranquility and extinction. Tranquility and extinction is the supreme nirvana. Supreme nirvana is the Dharma body of non-action. The Dharma body of non-action is true reality. True reality is Dharma-nature. Dharma-nature is true suchness. True suchness is Oneness. We note that Amida Tathāgata comes from thusness and manifests various forms of recompensed, accommodated, and transformed bodies.

The passage of the vow of unfailing attainment of nirvana in the *Larger Sutra* reads:

> If, when I attain Buddhahood, humans and *deva*s in my land should not dwell in the definitely assured stage and unfailingly reach nirvana, may I not attain perfect enlightenment.

It is stated in the *Teaching Assembly of the Tathāgata of Infinite Life:*

> If, when I become Buddha, the sentient beings in my land should not decidedly attain the stage equal to perfect enlightenment and realize great nirvana, may I not attain *bodhi.*

The passage of the fulfillment of this vow in the [*Larger*] *Sutra* reads:

> Sentient beings who are born in that Buddha land all reside among those assured of nirvana. The reason is that in that land there are neither beings who are destined to adverse conditions nor those whose destinies are uncertain.

It is also stated in the same sutra:

> That Buddha land, like the realm of unconditioned nirvana, is pure and serene, resplendent and blissful. The *śrāvakas*, bodhisattvas, heavenly beings, and humans there have lofty and brilliant wisdom and are masters of the supernatural powers. They are all of one form, without any differences, but are called "heavenly beings" and "humans" simply by analogy with states of existence in other worlds. They are of noble and majestic countenance, unequaled in all the worlds, and their appearance is superb, unmatched by any being, heavenly or human. They are all endowed with bodies of naturalness, emptiness, and infinity.

It is also stated:[127]

> Sentient beings of that land and those to be born there will fully realize supreme *bodhi* and reach the nirvanic state. For what reason? Because those who are in the wrongly established stage and those who are not in the definitely established stage are unable to understand that the cause [of birth] has been established [by the Buddha].

The [*Commentary on Vasubandhu's*] *Discourse on the Pure Land* states:

> Accomplishment of the glorious merit of the wonderful Name is described in the verse as:
>
>> The sacred Name enlightens people far and wide;
>> It is subtle and wonderful and is heard everywhere in
>>   the ten directions.
>
> Why is this inconceivable? A sutra says that those who only hear of the purity and blissfulness of that land and wholeheartedly desire to be born there and those who have attained birth all enter the rightly established stage. This shows that the name of the land performs the work of the Buddha. How can we conceive of this?
>
> Accomplishment of the glorious merit of the Lord Buddha is described in the verse as:
>
>> [The Pure Land] is firmly upheld by Amida,
>> The Enlightened One, the Dharma King.
>
> Why is this inconceivable? Amida, the Enlightened One, is inconceivable. The Pure Land of Peace and Bliss is firmly upheld (*jūji*) by the merit power of Amida, the Enlightened One, and so how can we conceive of this?
>
> "*Jū*" means not to change or perish; "*ji*" means to keep something from dispersing or being lost. It is like applying antidotal treatment to seeds. The seeds thus processed will not be destroyed by water or fire. When favorable conditions arise, the seeds will sprout. How is this possible? It is due to the power of the antidotal treatment. Once a human being is born in the Pure Land of Peace and Bliss, if he afterward desires to be reborn in the three worlds to teach and guide sentient beings, he is able to terminate his life in the Pure Land and be reborn therein according to his wishes. Although

616c

he is reborn in the "water" and "fire" of various states of the three worlds, the seed of supreme *bodhi* is never subject to decay. How is this possible? It is due to the power of Amida, the Enlightened One, which firmly supports and maintains [the Pure Land and the beings born there].

Accomplishment of the glorious merit of kinsmen is described in the verse as:

> The hosts of sages in the likeness of pure flowers
>   surrounding the Tathāgata
> Are born there, transformed from within the flower of
>   enlightenment.

Why is this inconceivable? In the realms of various births, whether from a womb, from an egg, from moisture, or by metamorphosis (i.e., the four modes of birth), one's kinsmen are many and there are tens of thousands of varieties of pleasure and pain resulting from the inhabitants' different acts [in the past]. In the Land of Peace and Bliss there is no one who is not born transformed from within the pure flower of Amida Tathāgata's enlightenment. [They are so born] by one and the same path of the Nembutsu, and not by other paths. Within the four seas, all [Nembutsu practitioners], even those living in the remotest places, are their kinfolk. Hence, their kinfolk are innumerable. How can we conceive of this?

It is also stated in the same work, fascicle two:

> Those who wish to be born in the Pure Land are originally divided into nine classes, but [after they have been born there] there are no differences, just as the waters of the Tzu River and the Sheng River become of one taste [upon entering the sea]. How can we conceive of this?

It is also stated in the same work:

> Accomplishment of the glorious merit of purity is described in the verse as:

When I contemplate the nature of that land
I find that it surpasses all states of existence in the
three worlds.

Why is this inconceivable? When ordinary human beings
full of evil passions attain birth in the Pure Land, the karmic
bonds of the three worlds will no longer affect them. Even
without severing evil passions they will attain the state of
nirvana. How can we conceive of this?

It is stated in the *Collection of Passages on the Land of Peace
and Bliss:*

The supernatural powers of the two Buddhas (Amida and
Śākyamuni) are equal. Be that as it may, Śākyamuni Tathāgata does not speak of his own capacities but especially reveals
Amida's distinguished capacities, out of his desire to make
all sentient beings equally take refuge in Amida. For this
reason, in many sutras Śākyamuni praises Amida and urges
beings to take refuge in him. We ought to be aware of the
Buddha's intent. Master T'an-luan's true intention was to
turn to [the Western Land] for refuge, so he composed hymns
of praise in the spirit of the *Larger Sutra:*

The *śrāvaka*s and bodhisattvas in the Land of Peace
and Bliss
As well as humans and gods, too, all thoroughly attain
wisdom;
Their bodily appearance and adornments are the same.
Different names are applied to them simply in
accordance with customs in other worlds.
Their countenances are noble and beautiful and
beyond compare;
Their delicate and subtle bodies are unlike those of
humans and gods.
They are of the substance of emptiness and bound-
lessness.

For this reason, I prostrate myself and worship the One
Possessed of the Power of Equality.

We read in the commentary of the Master of Kuang-ming
Temple:[128]

617a

The Universal Vow is presented in the *Larger Sutra*. All good
and evil ordinary beings will not attain birth without recourse
to the karmic power of Amida Buddha's great vow as the
supreme aid. Furthermore, the Buddha's hidden intent is
vast and profound, and so his teachings are difficult to understand. Even those in the three stages of wisdom and the ten
stages cannot fathom it; how can we, petty fools outside the
[ten stages of] understanding, know its significance?

As I reverently contemplate matters, Śākyamuni, on this
shore, urges us to go to the [Western Land], while Amida
from that land comes to welcome us. In the midst of the calling voice from there and the voice of exhortation from here,
how could we refuse to go westward? We should sincerely
devote ourselves to this teaching until the end of our life and,
after abandoning our defiled bodies, realize the eternal bliss
of Dharma-nature.

He also says:[129]

The capital of tranquility and non-action in the West
Is ultimately free and blissful, above existence and
    nonexistence.
With a heart imbued with great compassion, one freely
    plays in the Dharma realm;
Transforming oneself into various forms, one benefits
    beings equally and without discrimination.

Exercising supernatural powers, one expounds the
    Dharma;
One manifests glorious physical characteristics and marks,
    and then enters nirvana without remainder.

Apparitional adornments are produced according to
    one's wishes;
The multitudes who see them have all their karmic evil
    removed.

I also praise in hymns:

Let us return home!
We should not stay in our native land of devils.
Since innumerable *kalpas* ago, we have been transmigrating
In the six realms, taking up our abodes everywhere.

Nowhere have we seen any pleasure;
We only hear the voices of samsaric pain.
After the end of this life,
Let us enter the capital of nirvana.

[Conclusion to the Aspect of Going Forth]

When I contemplate the teaching, practice, faith, and enlightenment of the Pure Land Way, I realize that they are the benefit
endowed through the Tathāgata's great compassion. Whether cause
or effect, there is nothing that has not been accomplished through
the merit transference by the Tathāgata's pure vow-mind. Because
the cause is pure, the effect is also pure. This we should know.

[The Aspect of Returning]

Second is the aspect of returning of merit transference. This is the
benefit we receive for the activity in the stage of benefiting and
teaching others. It originates from the vow of unfailing attainment
of the rank next to Buddha. It is also called the vow of attainment
of Buddhahood after one lifetime. It can also be called the vow of
merit transference for our return to this world. Since this vow
appears in the *Commentary on Vasubandhu's Discourse on the
Pure Land,* I will not quote it here. Refer to the *Commentary.*
    It is stated in the *Discourse on the Pure Land:*

The fifth gate in the phase of "going out" is to observe with great compassion all suffering beings, manifest accommodated and transformed bodies, and enter the garden of birth and death and the forest of evil passions, where [bodhisattvas] play about, exercising supernatural powers; they thus dwell in the stage of teaching others through merit transference by their Primal Vow-Power. This is called the fifth gate in the phase of "going out."

It is stated in the *Commentary on Vasubandhu's Discourse on the Pure Land:*

The "returning aspect" is that after having been born in his land one acquires the fruit of the cessation and contemplation practices and attains the power of employing expedient means, whereby one reenters the dense forest of birth and death and leads all sentient beings onto the Buddhist path. Whether "going" or "returning," one seeks to deliver sentient beings from the sea of birth and death. For this reason, [Vasubandhu] says, "perfect the great compassion by putting merit transference above anything else."

It is also stated in the same work:

[Vasubandhu] says, "When bodhisattvas who have not yet attained the pure mind see the Buddha, they will finally be able to realize the Dharma body of equality and will eventually be equal to bodhisattvas of pure mind and those of the upper stages in the realization of tranquility and equality."

617b

'The Dharma body of equality" is said of a bodhisattva of the eighth stage or above, who has a body manifested from the Dharma-nature.

"Tranquility and equality" is the principle of tranquility and equality realized by such a Dharma-body bodhisattva. Because he realizes the principle of tranquility and equality, he is called [a bodhisattva of] the "Dharma body of equality";

because this principle is realized by a bodhisattva of Dharma body of equality, it is called "the principle of tranquility and equality."

Such a bodhisattva attains the *samādhi* called "produced from the fruit." With the supernatural power of this *samādhi*, he can, while remaining in one place, instantaneously and simultaneously manifest himself in any or every land throughout the ten directions. He can then make offerings in many ways to all Buddhas and their assemblies of sages. He can also manifest himself in various forms anywhere in innumerable worlds where there are no Buddhas, no Buddhist teachings, or no assemblies of Buddhist practitioners, and teach and save all the sentient beings there. Although he always performs such Buddhist activities, he has, from the beginning, no thought of going and coming, of making offerings, or of saving beings. For this reason, the body [of such a bodhisattva] is called "the Dharma body of equality," and the Dharma he has realized is called "the principle of tranquility and equality."

"Bodhisattvas who have not yet attained the pure mind" are bodhisattvas in the first to the seventh stages. They can also manifest their bodies in a hundred worlds where no Buddhas live, or a thousand, ten thousand, a *koṭi*, or a billion *koṭi*s of worlds where they perform the Buddha's work. But in order to do so, they must make conscious efforts to enter that *samādhi*. Without making effort they cannot enter it. Because they still require conscious effort, they are called "those who have not yet attained the pure mind." If those bodhisattvas desire to be born in the Pure Land of Peace and Bliss, they can see Amida Buddha there. Having seen the Buddha, they eventually attain the same bodies and the same realization as bodhisattvas in the higher stages. It is exactly for this reason that such bodhisattvas as Nāgārjuna and Vasubandhu aspired for birth in Amida's land.

Question: In the *Sutra on the Ten Stages (Daśabhūmika-sūtra)* we read that bodhisattvas rise through stages as they accumulate immeasurable merit by practicing for many *kalpa*s. How could it be that when one sees Amida Buddha one will eventually attain the same body and the same realization as bodhisattvas of the higher stages?

Answer: [The *Discourse*] says "eventually ... equal" and not "instantly ... equal." Simply because one eventually attains the same [body, and so on], [the *Discourse*] says "equal."

Question: If one does not instantly become equal [to a bodhisattva in a higher stage], why is it not said [in the *Discourse*] that when a bodhisattva reaches the first stage he will gradually rise through the stages until he spontaneously becomes equal to a Buddha? Why is it said that he will be equal to a bodhisattva in a higher stage?

Answer: When a bodhisattva has attained great tranquility in the seventh stage, he no longer envisions Buddhas to whom he should strive to become equal, nor does he see sentient beings whom he should save. Thus he is tempted to abandon the Buddhist Way and enter the [Hinayana] realization of true reality. At that time, if Buddhas of the ten directions do not admonish him with their divine power, he will pass into extinction and be like a Hinayana [sage]. If, however, a bodhisattva goes to the Land of Peace and Bliss and sees Amida Buddha there, he will not have this problem. For this reason, one should say "eventually ... equal [to a bodhisattva in a higher stage]."

617c

Further, in the *Larger Sutra,* one of Amida Tathāgata's Primal Vows reads:

If, when I attain Buddhahood, bodhisattvas in the Buddha lands of the other directions who visit my land should not ultimately and unfailingly reach the stage of becoming a

Buddha after one more life, may I not attain perfect enlightenment. Excepted are those who wish to teach and guide sentient beings in accordance with their original vows. For they will wear the armor of great vows, accumulate merit, deliver all beings from birth and death, visit Buddha lands to perform the bodhisattva practices, make offerings to Buddha Tathāgatas throughout the ten directions, enlighten countless sentient beings as numerous as the sands of the Ganges River, and establish them in highest, perfect enlightenment. Such bodhisattvas transcend the course of practice of ordinary bodhisattvas, manifest the practices of all the bodhisattva stages, and cultivate the virtues of Samantabhadra.

Reading this sutra, one may assume that bodhisattvas in that land do not rise from one stage to the next. The ten-stage system appears to be a method of guidance provided by Śākyamuni Tathāgata for the inhabitants of Jambudvīpa. Why should other pure lands necessarily be the same? Among the five inconceivables, the Buddha-Dharma is the most inconceivable.

If you assume that bodhisattvas must necessarily rise from one stage to the next and that there is no way of transcending stages, you are not yet completely familiar with the teaching. I will show you by the analogy of a tree called "Very Strong." This tree grows underground for a hundred years. It then grows above ground one thousand feet in height each day, and keeps growing at the same rate. If one calculates the height the tree will reach after a hundred years, how can such a tree be compared with tall pine trees? Pine trees grow no more than an inch a day. How can one believe in such a tree? One will argue: "When one hears that Śākyamuni Tathāgata enlightened [Śāriputra] to arhatship at one session or that he made people realize the insight into the non-arising of all *dharma*s in the brief time before breakfast, he will think that these are words of expedient means to guide people to Buddhism and are not the literal truth." So, hearing the present discussion, a person will not believe it. Extraordinary words do not reach the ears of ordinary people. So we must expect such a question as "How is this possible?"

[Vasubandhu] says, "I have briefly explained the eight aspects [of the Buddha's activity], demonstrating that the Tathāgata's glorious merits for his own benefit and that of others have been accomplished in due order. You should realize the implication of this."

What is this order? The seventeen aspects mentioned before were about accomplishment of the glorious merit of the [Pure] Land. Having seen the land's aspects, we should know the lord of the land. Therefore, we contemplate the Buddha's merit. How is he adorned and where does he sit? This question leads us first to visualize the seat. Having seen that, we envision the lord who sits there. Next, we contemplate the Buddha's glorious body. Having seen that, we contemplate his voice and name. Hence, we next concentrate on the Buddha's glorious speech. Having realized how widespread his Name is, we should consider how he acquired that Name. And so we next contemplate the Buddha's glorious mind. Having realized that he has attained accomplishment of the three kinds of karma, we should distinguish who deserves to be taught by this great master of humans and gods. Therefore, we should next contemplate the merits of the congregation. Having seen that the congregation has immeasurable merits, we should know who is the head [of that congregation]. Hence, we contemplate the head, who is the Buddha [Amida]. Since we may perhaps consider him simply as the most senior member, we should next contemplate his lordship. Having visualized his lordship, we should realize his superior virtue; so we next contemplate the glorious merit of his unfailing sustenance. In this way, the eight aspects are presented in due order.

618a

180

Concerning "contemplation of the bodhisattvas," [Vasu-
bandhu] says, "What is the contemplation of accomplishment
of the glorious merits of the bodhisattvas? It is to contemplate the bodhisattvas, in whom we find accomplishment of
the merits in performing the four right practices. You should
realize the implication of this."

True suchness is the very substance of all existence. Since
[the bodhisattvas of the Pure Land] perform practices while
realizing that their essence is suchness, their practices are,
in fact, non-practice. To perform practices while aware that
they are non-practice is called "practice in accord with the
Dharma." Although their essence is one, this is divided into
four according to the distinct meanings that are implied. For
this reason, the four practices are all described as "right."

[Vasubandhu] says, "What are the four? First, while
dwelling motionless in a Buddha land, [bodhisattvas] display
various transformed bodies throughout the ten directions,
manifest performance of practices in accord with the Dharma,
and engage constantly in the Buddha's work. The verse says:

The Land of Peace and Bliss is pure and serene;
[The Buddha] always turns the undefiled wheel
    [of the Dharma].
Transformed Buddhas and bodhisattvas [illuminate
    the whole world] like the sun,
[While remaining motionless] like Mount Sumeru.
For they seek to enable sentient beings to bloom like
    lotuses in a muddy pool.

Bodhisattvas in and above the eighth stage always dwell
in *samādhi*. Without leaving their abodes, by the power of
samādhi they can reach all the worlds of the ten directions,
where they make offerings to the Buddhas and teach sentient beings. "The undefiled wheel [of the Dharma]" is part
of the virtue of Buddhahood, which is free of the defilements
of evil passions and their residues. The Buddha always turns

the wheel of the Dharma for the sake of bodhisattvas, and various great bodhisattvas also turn the same wheel of the Dharma, without resting even for a short while, in order to awaken and guide all living beings; hence, "always turns."

The Dharma body is like the sun, whose rays of light, in the form of accommodated and transformed bodies, pervade all the worlds in the ten directions. "Like the sun" is not really an adequate description. Since it is brilliant and motionless, it is also described as "like Mount Sumeru." Regarding "lotuses in a muddy pool," it is said in the [*Vimalakīrtinirdeśa*]-*sūtra:* "Lotuses do not grow on high land; they grow in low and muddy pools." This metaphor shows that ordinary beings, while submerged in the mud of evil passions, are still able to produce the flower of enlightenment through the guidance of bodhisattvas. Indeed, [bodhisattvas in the Pure Land] endeavor to inherit and exalt the Three Treasures and always ensure their continuance in the world.

[Vasubandhu] says, "Second, at any time they choose, their accommodated and transformed bodies emit great light and reach all worlds in the ten directions simultaneously and in a flash of thought in order to teach and guide sentient beings; for they seek to remove the suffering of all sentient beings by various expedient means, practices, and acts. The verse says:

> The pure, glorious light [of the bodhisattvas],
> In a flash of thought and simultaneously,
> Illuminates each and every Buddha's assembly
> And gives benefit to multitudes of beings."

When it is said above, "while dwelling motionless, they can reach [all the worlds in the ten directions]," this could mean that there is a lapse of time between their actions. For this reason, it is said here that all their actions take place in a flash of thought and simultaneously, without any time intervening.

[Vasubandhu] says, "Third, having reached all the worlds without exception, they illuminate each and every Buddha's

618b

assembly. On such a vast and immense scale, they make offerings to the Buddha Tathāgatas, pay homage to them, and praise their virtues. The verse says:

> They shower heavenly musical instruments, flowers, robes,
> Fine incense, and so forth, with which they worship the Buddhas;
> They praise and extol the merits of the Buddhas
> Without discriminative thoughts."

"Without exception" shows that they reach all the worlds and the great assemblies of all the Buddhas, without leaving any world or any Buddha's assembly unvisited. Seng-chao says:

> The Dharma body has no form of its own and yet manifests various forms, corresponding to [the conditions and capacities of sentient beings]. The sound of the ultimate truth has no words and yet extensively unfolds scriptures of profound teachings. The unfathomable expediency has no planning and yet works in agreement with things.

This is, indeed, the implication here.

[Vasubandhu] says, "Fourth, they visit places in all the worlds in the ten directions where the Three Treasures do not exist. Establishing and glorifying the oceanlike merit of the treasures of the Buddha, Dharma, and Sangha, they display and explain the correct practices to all. The verse says:

> If there is any world in the universe
> Without the treasure of merit of the Buddha-Dharma,
> I resolve to be born there
> And to preach the Dharma as does a Buddha."

The first three passages speak of [the bodhisattvas'] visits to all [the worlds] but these are all lands where Buddhas dwell. Without this [fourth] passage, one might suppose that for the Dharma body there are places where the Dharma does not reach and that the supreme good [of the bodhisattvas] contains parts that are not good. Here ends the chapter on the objects of contemplation.

The following is the fourth chapter of the "Commentary" section, called "The Pure [Manifestation] Entering into the Vow-Mind." It is as follows.

[Vasubandhu] says: "I have explained above the contemplation of accomplishment of the glorious merits of the Buddha land, the Buddha, and the bodhisattvas. These three kinds of accomplishment are adorned with the vow-mind. One should realize the implications of this."

"One should realize the implications of this" means that one should realize that the three kinds of glorious accomplishment are, in their origin, [Dharmākara's] adornment with the pure vow-mind through the Forty-eight Vows, and so on. Since the cause is pure, the result is equally pure. They are not what has come into existence without any cause or by some other cause.

[Vasubandhu] says: "Presented in brief, they enter into the one Dharma principle."

The seventeen aspects of the adornments of the [Pure] Land, the eight aspects of the adornments of the Tathāgata, and the four aspects of the adornments of bodhisattvas are the extensive manifestation. "Entering into the one Dharma principle" is the all-inclusive principle.

Why is it shown that the extensive manifestation and the all-inclusive principle enter into each other? The reason is that Buddhas and bodhisattvas have two Dharma bodies: the Dharma body of Dharma-nature, and the Dharma body of expediency. From the Dharma body of Dharma-nature originates the Dharma body of expediency; through the Dharma bodies of expediency the Dharma body of Dharma-nature is revealed. These two Dharma bodies are different but inseparable; they are one but not the same. For this reason, the extensive manifestation and the all-inclusive principle enter into each other. Those two are comprised in the Dharma [body]. If bodhisattvas did not realize interpenetration of the two ways of presentation, they would not be able to benefit both themselves and others.

[Vasubandhu] says, "The one Dharma principle is the purity principle; the purity principle is the Dharma body of non-action that is to be realized through true wisdom."

These three phrases enter into each other, the previous one leading to the next. For what reason is [the ultimate principle] called "the [one] Dharma [principle]"? Because it is the purity [principle]. For what reason is it called "the purity [principle]"? Because it is the Dharma body of non-action realized by true wisdom. "True wisdom" is the wisdom of realizing true reality. Because true reality is without forms, true wisdom is unknowing. "The Dharma body of non-action" is the body of Dharma-nature. Because Dharma-nature is nirvanic, the Dharma body is formless. Because it is formless, there is no form that it cannot manifest. Therefore, [the body] adorned with the marks of excellence is itself the Dharma body. Because it is unknowing, there is nothing it does not know. For this reason, the wisdom of knowing all forms of existence is true wisdom. The reason why "wisdom" is described as "true" is in order to show that it is neither free of mental effort nor non-effort. The reason why "Dharma body" is described as "non-action" is in order to show that the Dharma body is neither possessed of form nor without form. When a negation is negated, how can a double negation be a [simple] affirmation? Indeed, absence of negation is called affirmation. If an affirmation exists by itself without opposition, it is no longer an affirmation. [The ultimate principle] is neither an affirmation nor a negation; it is beyond description even by a hundred negations. Hence, "purity." Purity refers to the Dharma body of non-action that is to be realized with true wisdom.

[Vasubandhu] says, "Purity is distinguished into two kinds. One should realize this."

618c

Concerning these [three] principles, each leading up to the next, by penetrating the [one] Dharma [principle], one enters into the purity [principle]; by penetrating the purity [principle], one enters into the Dharma body. Now, two kinds of purity are to be distinguished. And so, it is said, "One should realize this."

[Vasubandhu] says, "What are the two kinds? First, purity of the land as the receptacle; and second, purity of its inhabitants. Purity of the land refers to the accomplishment of the seventeen kinds of adornment of that Buddha land; these are called the purity of the land. Purity of the inhabitants refers to the eight kinds of adornment of the Buddha and the four kinds of adornment of bodhisattvas; these are called the purity of the inhabitants. Thus the one Dharma principle contains these two kinds of purity. One should realize the implication of this."

The inhabitants have come into being as the primary reward for their individual karma, while the land is the derivative reward which is enjoyed and shared by those who have common karma. The primary reward and the derivative one are not the same. And so, it is said, "One should realize the implication of this."

It is to be noted that all things are [transformations of] mind; nothing exists outside of mind. The inhabitants and the land are neither different nor the same. Since they are not the same, they are distinguishable according to their different characteristics. Also, since they are not different, they are both pure.

"Land as the receptacle" is that which is to be used. The Pure Land is the realm which is used by its pure inhabitants. Hence, it is called a "receptacle." If a dirty container is used for clean food, the food becomes contaminated because of the dirty container. If a clean container is used for dirty food, the container becomes contaminated because of the dirty food. Both must necessarily be clean before they can be described as clean. For this reason, the word "purity" necessarily covers these two kinds.

Question: When you say that the purity of the inhabitants means that of the Buddha and the bodhisattvas, are the human and heavenly beings [born in the Pure Land] excluded?   619a

Answer: No, they can also be described as "pure," although they are not yet really pure. For example, sages who have renounced the world are called *"bhikṣus"* (monks) because they have "killed" the enemy of evil passions. Ordinary people who have renounced the world, whether they observe the precepts or not, are also called *"bhikṣus."* It is like a crown prince; at birth he is possessed of the thirty-two physical marks of excellence and is one to whom the seven treasures will belong. Even though he is not yet able to rule as a wheel-turning monarch, he is called "wheel-turning monarch" because he will surely become one. So it is with those human and heavenly beings. Since they all join those who are rightly established in the Mahayana path, they will surely acquire the pure Dharma body. Because they are sure to attain it, they can be described as "pure."

Concerning "converting beings by skillful means," [Vasubandhu] says, "bodhisattvas thus practice cessation concerning the all-inclusive principle and contemplation on the extensive manifestation, and so attain the pliant mind."

"The pliant mind" is the nondual mind attained by performing the harmonious practice of tranquilization concerning the all-inclusive principle and of contemplation on the extensive manifestation, just as an object is perfectly reflected in water when the water is both clear and calm.

[Vasubandhu] says, "They truly realize both the extensive manifestations and the all-inclusive principle."

"To realize truly" means "to know in accord with true reality." Neither the twenty-nine aspects of the extensive manifestations nor the all-inclusive principle is in disagreement with true reality.

[Vasubandhu] says, "Thus they accomplish merit transference by skillful means."

"Thus" means that both the extensive manifestation mentioned earlier and the all-inclusive principle mentioned later are in accord with true reality. When they realize true reality, they see the perverse and false nature of the sentient beings in the three worlds. When they see the perverse and false nature of sentient beings, true compassion arises. When they realize the true Dharma body, true devotion arises. Compassion, devotion, and skillful means are explained below.

[Vasubandhu] says, "What is the bodhisattvas' merit transference by skillful means? The bodhisattvas' merit transference by skillful means is that they turn over all the merits and roots of good accumulated by performing the five kinds of practice, such as worship, to all sentient beings to remove their suffering, for they do not seek to enjoy the pleasures for their own sustenance but wish to embrace all sentient beings and help them attain birth in that Buddha Land of Peace and Bliss together with themselves. This is called 'the bodhisattvas' accomplishment of merit transference by skillful means.'"

In the *Sutra on the Buddha of Infinite Life* preached at Rājagṛha, I find in the section on the three grades of aspirants that although their practices differ according to their superior or inferior qualities, they all, without fail, awaken aspiration for highest *bodhi* (*bodhicitta*). This aspiration is the resolve to become a Buddha. The aspiration to become a Buddha is the resolve to save all sentient beings. The aspiration to save sentient beings is the resolve to embrace sentient beings and lead them to attain birth in a Buddha land. It follows that those who wish to be born in the Pure Land of Peace and Bliss should awaken aspiration for highest *bodhi*. If there is anyone who does not awaken aspiration for highest *bodhi* but, having heard of the endless pleasures to be enjoyed in that land, desires to be born there simply because of such pleasures, he will not attain birth [there]. And so, it is said, "they do not seek to enjoy the pleasures for their own suste- 619b nance" but "to remove the suffering of all sentient beings."

"The pleasures for their own sustenance" means that the Pure Land of Peace and Bliss has been produced and maintained by Amida Tathāgata's Primal Vow-Power, and so there is no end to the pleasures to be enjoyed.

The meaning of "merit transference" is that one transfers the merits one has accumulated to all sentient beings so that they, too, will follow the Buddhist path.

"Skillful means" is the bodhisattvas' desire to burn with the fire of their own wisdom the grasses and trees of the evil passions of all sentient beings. They resolve, "While there remains even one sentient being who has not yet attained Buddhahood, I will not become a Buddha." Even though all sentient beings have not yet become Buddhas, bodhisattvas do attain Buddhahood. This is like trying to burn grasses and trees with a wooden firebrand. Before all the grasses and trees are consumed by fire, the firebrand itself will burn out. In the same way, the bodhisattva attains enlightenment before other sentient beings do, even though he places their liberation above his own. Hence, this is called "skillful means."

"Means" here implies that the bodhisattva resolves to embrace all sentient beings and lead them to birth in that Buddha Land of Peace and Bliss. That Buddha land is the path to ultimate realization of Buddhahood, the unsurpassed means of guidance.

Concerning "eliminating hindrances to *bodhi,*" [Vasubandhu] says, "Having mastered the method of accomplishing merit transferenceŏ, bodhisattvas can now eliminate the three hindrances to *bodhi*. What are the three? First, by entering the gate of wisdom (*chi-e*), they do not seek their own pleasure, and thus they eliminate any thought of self-attachment."

"*Chi*" means to know how to advance [toward *bodhi*] and keep oneself from any relapse into [the Hinayana stages]; "*e*" means to realize emptiness and egolessness. Because of *chi,* they do not seek their own pleasure; and because of *e,* they eliminate any thought of self-attachment.

[Vasubandhu] says, "Second, by entering the gate of compassion (*ji-hi*), they remove the suffering of all sentient beings and eliminate disinclination to give them peace."

"*Ji*" means to remove suffering; "*hi*" means to give pleasure. Through *ji,* they remove the sufferings of all sentient beings; through *hi,* they eliminate disinclination to bring peace to them.

[Vasubandhu] says, "Third, by entering the gate of expedient means (*hō-ben*), they attain compassion for all sentient beings and thus eliminate any thought of seeking veneration and respect from others."

"*Hō*" means righteous; "*ben*" means to disregard oneself. Through righteousness, they attain compassion for all sentient beings; by disregarding themselves, they eliminate any thought of seeking veneration and respect from others. [Vasubandhu] says, "These are called elimination of the three kinds of hindrances to *bodhi.*"

Concerning "coming into accord with *bodhi,*" [Vasubandhu] says, "Having thus eliminated the three kinds of hindrances to *bodhi,* bodhisattvas can now completely attain the three minds that are in accord with *bodhi.* What are these? First, the undefiled pure mind: [they attain this mind] because they do not seek their own pleasure."

Bodhi is the state of undefiled purity. If bodhisattvas sought pleasures for their own sake they would run counter to *bodhi.* For this reason, the undefiled pure mind accords with *bodhi.*

619c

[Vasubandhu] says, "Second, the peaceful pure mind: [bodhisattvas attain this mind] because they seek to remove the suffering of all sentient beings."

Bodhi is the state of purity in which all sentient beings are led to dwell in peace. If bodhisattvas did not endeavor to remove the suffering of all sentient beings they would run counter to *bodhi.* For this reason, [the mind] to remove the suffering of all sentient beings accords with *bodhi.*

[Vasubandhu] says, "Third, the blissful pure mind: [bodhisattvas attain this mind] because they enable all sentient beings to reach great *bodhi,* and [for this purpose] they receive sentient beings and lead them to attain birth in that [Pure] Land."

Bodhi is the state of ultimate, eternal bliss. If bodhisattvas did not seek to lead all sentient beings to ultimate, eternal bliss they would run counter to *bodhi.* How can beings attain ultimate, eternal bliss? It is through the gate of the Mahayana. The gate of the Mahayana is the Buddha Land of Peace and Bliss. For this reason, [Vasubandhu] says, "receive sentient beings and lead them to attain birth in that [Pure] Land," and also "these are called 'completely attaining the three minds that are in accord with *bodhi.*' One should realize the implication of this."

Concerning "correspondence between [key] terms," [Vasubandhu] says, "The three gates mentioned above—wisdom, compassion, and skillful means—contain *prajñā; prajñā* contains skillful means. One should realize the implication of this."

"Prajñā" is the insight of penetrating to suchness (*e*); "skillful means" is the wisdom of knowing provisional means (*chi*). If one reaches suchness, one's mental acts become tranquil; if one becomes conversant with provisional means, one knows all about sentient beings. The wisdom of knowing all about sentient beings arises in response to their needs and yet it is unknowing. Insight into nirvanic tranquility is unknowing and yet it sees through beings. Thus *prajñā* and skillful means work cooperatively; while interacting, they are tranquil. Because of the working of wisdom, one does not lose tranquility while active; because of the power of skillful means, one does not cease to be active while absorbed in tranquility. And so, [it is said] "wisdom, compassion, and skillful means contain *prajñā; prajñā* contains skillful means."

"The implication" is that wisdom and skillful means are the parents of a bodhisattva. Unless he depends on wisdom and skillful means, the duties of the bodhisattva are not fulfilled. The reason is that if the bodhisattva seeks to perform his duties for the sake of sentient beings without having wisdom, he will fall into erroneous views. If he contemplates the Dharma-nature without having recourse to skillful means, he will merely attain [Hinayana] true reality. Hence, it is said, "One should realize the implication of this."

[Vasubandhu] says, "The three eliminations mentioned above—elimination of any thought of self-attachment, elimination of disinclination to give peace to sentient beings, and elimination of any thought of seeking veneration and respect from others—are the ways of removing hindrances to *bodhi*. One should realize the implication of this."

All existing things create hindrances to each other, like wind disturbing calm, earth obstructing [the movement of] water, water extinguishing fire, the five transgressions and the ten evil [acts] preventing rebirth as a human or heavenly being, and the four erroneous views hindering the attainment of the *śrāvaka*'s goal. If these three kinds of thought are not eliminated they will prevent the realization of *bodhi*.

"The implication" is that if one wishes to be free of hindrances [to *bodhi*], one should eliminate those three kinds of hindrances.

[Vasubandhu] says, "The three minds mentioned above— undefiled pure mind, peaceful pure mind, and blissful pure mind—are combined to form 'the supreme, blissful, unsurpassed, and true mind.' One should realize the implication of this."

620a

Concerning "blissful," three kinds of bliss or pleasure are distinguished: 1) external pleasure, or pleasure arising from the five sense perceptions; 2) internal pleasure, or pleasure arising from consciousness absorbed in the first, second, and third meditations [in the world of form]; and 3) the pleasure of Dharma music, or bliss arising from wisdom; it arises from love of the Buddha's merit.

When the three states of mind—the mind free of any thought of self-attachment, the mind free of disinclination to give peace to sentient beings, and the mind free of any thought of seeking veneration and respect from others—grow pure and strong, they are together called "the supreme, blissful, unsurpassed, and true mind." The word "supreme" means excellent, for this bliss arises from contact with the Buddha. The word "unsurpassed" means transcending pleasures in the three worlds. The word "true" means not false and not deluded.

Concerning "fulfillment of the vow and the acts," [Vasubandhu] says, "In this way the bodhisattvas' mind of wisdom, mind of expediency, mind of nonhindrance, and unsurpassed and true mind bring about birth in the Buddha's Pure Land. One should realize the implication of this."

"One should realize the implication of this" means that one should know that with those four kinds of pure virtue one can be born in the Buddha's Pure Land, and not under other conditions.

[Vasubandhu] says, "This is called 'accomplishing the acts of the bodhisattvas and *mahāsattvas* as they desire through the five Dharma gates.' The acts of body, speech, mind; wisdom; and skillful means as mentioned above are the Dharma gates that conform to the way of birth in the Pure Land."

"As they desire" means that with those five kinds of merit power one can be born in the Buddha's Pure Land, where one attains complete freedom in action. "The act of body" refers to worship; "the act of speech," to praise; "the act of mind," to aspiration; "the act of wisdom," to contemplation; and "the act of wisdom of skillful means," to merit transference. What is meant here is that when those five acts are united they constitute the Dharma gates that conform to the way of birth in the Pure Land and so enable one to attain complete freedom of action.

Concerning "accomplishment of the beneficial acts," [Vasubandhu] says, "Again, there are five gates, which in order produce five kinds of merit. One should realize the implication of this. What are the five gates? They are: 1) the gate of approaching, 2) the gate of the great assembly, 3) the gate of the residence, 4) the gate of the chamber, and 5) the gate of the playing ground."

Those five gates show the way of "going in" and "going out." First, in the phase of "going in," reaching the Pure Land is the aspect of "approaching," for when one enters the rightly established stage of the Mahayana, one approaches highest, perfect enlightenment. When one has reached the Pure Land, one enters the Tathāgata's "great assembly." Having joined the assembly, one reaches the "residence" through the practice of calming one's mind. Having entered the residence, one proceeds to the "chamber" through contemplation practice. Having accomplished these practices, one reaches the stage of teaching others. The stage of teaching others is the stage of the bodhisattvas' playing for their enjoyment; for this reason, the phase of "going out" is called "the gate of the playing ground."

620b   [Vasubandhu] says, "Of those five gates, the first four produce merit in the phase of 'going in' and the fifth produces merit in the phase of 'going out.'"

What is the merit in the phases of "going in" and "going out"? It is stated in the *Discourse:*

The first gate in the phase of "going in" is to worship Amida Buddha in order to be born in his land; by this one attains birth in the Land of Peace and Bliss, and so it is called the first gate in the phase of "going in."

To worship the Buddha with an aspiration to be born in the Buddha land is the feature of the first merit.

[Vasubandhu] says, "The second gate in the phase of 'going in' is to praise Amida Buddha, while reciting his Name in compliance with its meaning and practicing in compliance with his light of wisdom; by this, one joins the great assembly. This is called the second gate in the phase of 'going in.'"

To praise in compliance with the meaning of the Tathāgata's Name is the feature of the second merit.

[Vasubandhu] says, "The third gate in the phase of 'going in' is to aspire singlemindedly and wholeheartedly to be born there and to perform the practice of the *samādhi* of cessation and tranquility; by this one can reach the Land of the Lotus Treasury. This is called the third gate in the phase of 'going in.'"

To aspire singlemindedly to be born in that land by performing the practice [of the *samādhi* of] cessation of thought is the feature of the third merit.

[Vasubandhu] says, "The fourth gate in the phase of 'going in' is to contemplate wholeheartedly those glorious adornments and so practice contemplation; by this one can reach that land, where one will enjoy various flavors of the Dharma. This is called the fourth gate of 'going in.'"

"Various flavors of the Dharma" means that by practicing concentration one enjoys innumerable flavors of the Buddhist path related to the glorious adornments [of the Pure Land], such as the flavor of contemplating the purity of the Buddha land, the flavor of the Mahayana that embraces sentient beings, the flavor of everlasting sustenance [of those born in the Pure Land], and the flavor of the [bodhisattvas'] practices and vows to establish Buddha lands in response to the needs of sentient beings. Hence, "various." This is the feature of the fourth merit.

[Vasubandhu] says, "The fifth gate in the phase of 'going out' is to observe with great compassion all suffering beings, manifest accommodated and transformed bodies, and enter the garden of birth and death and the forest of evil passions, where [bodhisattvas] play about, exercising supernatural powers; they thus dwell in the stage of teaching others through merit transference by [Amida's] Primal Vow-Power. This is called the fifth gate in the phase of 'going out.'"

"To manifest accommodated and transformed bodies" describes the manifestation mentioned in the "Chapter on the Universal Gate" in the *Lotus Sutra*. "To play" has two meanings: "freedom of action," for bodhisattvas save sentient beings as easily as a lion hunts a deer, or as if one is playing; and "saving without seeing the saved," for when bodhisattvas observe sentient beings they see them as ultimately nonexistent; even though they save innumerable beings, they realize that not even one has really entered nirvana. The way they save sentient beings is like playing. "The Primal Vow-Power" shows that great bodhisattvas with their Dharma bodies always dwell in *samādhi* and yet manifest various bodies, employ various supernatural powers, and proclaim various teachings through [Amida's] Primal Vow-Power; it is like an *asura*'s harp that spontaneously produces music even though no one is playing it. This is called the feature of the fifth merit in the stage of teaching others.

620c

[Concluding Remarks Praising the Two Aspects of Merit Transference]

Hereupon, from the Great Sage's words of truth, I truly realize that it is through the merit transference by the Vow-Power that we attain the great nirvana. The beneficial acts in the phase of returning express the true intent of Other-Power. Accordingly, the author of the *Discourse,* Vasubandhu, proclaims the vast and unimpeded One Mind, thereby universally guiding the multitudes of this Sahā world which is defiled by evil passions. Master T'an-luan clarifies the going and returning aspects of merit transference that arise from great compassion, and also carefully expounds the profound meaning of "other's benefit" and "benefiting others." We should respectfully uphold this teaching and, above all, accept it in faith.

End of Chapter IV: Revealing the True Enlightenment

Chapter V

Revealing the True Buddha and Land

[Presentation of the True Buddha and Land]

When I reverently contemplate the true Buddha and land, I find that the Buddha is the Tathāgata of Inconceivable Light and his land is the Land of Immeasurable Light. They are called the True Recompensed Buddha and Land because they have been rewarded for the vows of great compassion. Amida already made the vows, that is, the vows of light and life.

The *Larger Sutra* states:

> If, when I attain Buddhahood, my light should be limited, illuminating even a hundred thousand *koṭi*s of *nayuta*s of Buddha lands, may I not attain perfect enlightenment.

Again it is stated in the same sutra:

> If, when I attain Buddhahood, my lifespan should be limited, even to the extent of a hundred thousand *koṭi*s of *nayuta*s of *kalpa*s, may I not attain perfect enlightenment.

The passage of fulfillment of these vows reads:[130]

> The Buddha said to Ānanda, "The majestic light of [the Buddha of Infinite Life] is the most exalted. No other Buddha's light can match his.... For this reason, the Buddha of Infinite Life is called by the following names: the Buddha of Infinite Light, the Buddha of Boundless Light, the Buddha of Unhindered Light, the Buddha of Incomparable Light, the Buddha of the Light of the King of Flame, the Buddha of Pure Light,

the Buddha of the Light of Joy, the Buddha of the Light of Wisdom, the Buddha of Unceasing Light, the Buddha of Inconceivable Light, the Buddha of Ineffable Light, and the Buddha of the Light Outshining the Sun and the Moon.

"If sentient beings encounter his light, their three defilements are removed; they feel tenderness, joy, and pleasure; and good thoughts arise. If sentient beings in the three realms of suffering see his light they will all be relieved and freed from affliction. At the end of their lives, they all reach liberation.

"The light of [the Buddha of Infinite Life] shines brilliantly, illuminating all the Buddha lands of the ten directions. There is no place where it is not perceived. I am not the only one who now praises his light. All the Buddhas, *śrāvaka*s, *pratyekabuddha*s, and bodhisattvas praise and glorify it in the same way. If sentient beings, having heard of the majestic virtue of his light, glorify it continually, day and night, with sincerity of heart, they will be able to attain birth in his land as they wish. Then the multitudes of bodhisattvas and *śrāvaka*s will praise their excellent virtue. Later, when they attain Buddhahood, all the Buddhas and bodhisattvas in the ten directions will praise their light, just as I now praise the light of [the Buddha of Infinite Life]."

The Buddha continued, "The majestic glory of the light of [the Buddha of Infinite Life] could not be exhaustively described even if I praised it continually, day and night, for one *kalpa*."

The Buddha said to Ānanda, "The lifespan of [the Buddha of Infinite Life] is so long that it is impossible for anyone to calculate it. To give an illustration, let us suppose that all the innumerable sentient beings in the worlds of the ten directions were reborn in human form and that every one became a *śrāvaka* or *pratyekabuddha*. Even if they assembled in one place, concentrated their thoughts, and exercised the power of their wisdom to the utmost to reckon the length of the

Buddha's lifespan by the number of *kalpa*s, even after a thousand million *kalpa*s they could still not reach its limit."

It is stated in the *Teaching Assembly of the Tathāgata of Infinite Life*:

Ānanda, for this reason, the Buddha of Infinite Life has the following different names: Immeasurable Light, Boundless Light, Light Free of Attachment, Unhindered Light, King of the Brilliance of Light, Majestic Light, Pleasant Light, Light of Joy, Light Which Deserves to be Seen, Inconceivable Light, Incomparable Light, Ineffable Light, Light Outshining the Sun, Light Outshining the Moon, and Light Outshining the Sun and Moon. His light is pure and immense and gives pleasure and happiness to the bodies and minds of sentient beings. It also gives joy and delight to gods, dragons, *yakṣa*s, *asura*s, and others in all the other Buddha lands.

It is stated in the *Sutra on the Immeasurably Pure and Equal Enlightenment:*

Going beyond samsara swiftly,
You should reach the Land of Peace and Bliss;
Having attained the Land of Immeasurable Light,
You will make offerings to innumerable Buddhas.

It is stated in the *Sutra on the Way of Salvation of Humans by Amida, the Perfectly Enlightened One, That Transcends All Buddhas,* translated by Chih-ch'ien:

The Buddha said, "Amida's light is most august and peerless. No other Buddha's light can compare with it. Of all the countless Buddhas of the eight directions, zenith, and nadir, there are some who emit light from their heads that extends seventy feet; some others who emit light that extends a *li*. ... There are still some others who emit light from their heads that shines over two million Buddha lands."

The Buddha continued, "Such is the extent reached by

the light from the heads of countless Buddhas of the eight directions, zenith, and nadir. The light from the head of Amida Buddha shines over ten million Buddha lands. The reason why there are such differences in the distance covered by the light of these Buddhas is that when they were seeking the Way as bodhisattvas in their previous lives, their merits, which they vowed to attain, were naturally different in scale. On attaining Buddhahood, they acquired what they had vowed. This accounts for the difference in the extent of these Buddhas' lights. The majesty of the Buddhas, however, is certainly the same. Their vows, based on their free will, and their acts are not predetermined. The extent of Amida's light is the greatest. The other Buddhas lights do not match his."

The Buddha praised the supreme quality of Amida Buddha's light, saying, "Amida Buddha's light is of the finest quality; it is the most excellent of all that is good; it is pleasing beyond compare; it is superb and unparalleled. Amida Buddha's light is pure, serene, and unblemished, and lacks nothing. Amida Buddha's light is incomparably excellent, shining a thousand million *koṭi*s times more brilliantly than the sun and moon. It is the brightest of all the Buddhas' lights. It is the most excellent of all lights, the strongest of all lights, and the finest of all lights. It is the king of all Buddhas, the most august of all lights, and the most brilliant of all lights. Since it illuminates all the dark and murky places in countless worlds, they are always radiant. Of all humans, and even the insects that hop and the worms that crawl, there is none that does not see Amida's light. Of all beings that see it, there is none that does not rejoice with the mind of compassion. Of all beings who are possessed of greed, anger, and delusion, there is none who, upon seeing Amida's light, does not come to perform good acts. If those suffering in the realms of hell, animals, hungry ghosts, or *asura*s see Amida's light, there is none that does not gain respite and, though not delivered at once, attain liberation from sorrow and pain after death.

Amida Buddha makes his light and name heard throughout the boundless, limitless, and countless Buddha lands in the eight directions, zenith, and nadir, so there is none among gods and humans who does not hear or perceive them. Of those who hear or perceive them, there is none who does not attain liberation."

The Buddha said, "I am not the only one who praises the light of Amida Buddha. Countless Buddhas, *pratyekabuddhas*, bodhisattvas, and arhats of the eight directions, zenith, and nadir all praise Amida as I do."

The Buddha further said, "If there are people, good men and good women, who, having heard Amida Buddha's voice, praise his light and always extoll his glorious features sincerely, morning and evening without interruption, they will attain birth in the [Pure] Land of Amida Buddha as they wish."

It is stated in the *Sutra on Amoghapāśa's Divine Manifestation and Mantra (Amoghapāśakalpa-rāja)*:

The realm where you will be born is Amida Buddha's Pure 621c Recompensed Land. Born transformed from a lotus flower, you will see Buddhas all the time and realize various insights concerning *dharmas*. Your lifespan will be immeasurable, extending to a hundred thousand *kalpas*. You will at once reach highest, perfect *bodhi,* from which you will never fall back. I will always protect you.

The *Nirvana Sutra* states:[131]

Again, liberation is called emptiness; emptiness is liberation. Liberation is Tathāgata; Tathāgata is emptiness; it is the activity of non-action.... True liberation is non-arising and non-perishing. For this reason, liberation is indeed Tathāgata. So is Tathāgata—non-arising and non-perishing, neither aging nor dying, neither subject to destruction nor decay. It is not a conditioned *dharma*. For this reason, it is said: the Tathāgata enters great nirvana....

Further, liberation is called unsurpassed supremacy....
Unsurpassed supremacy is true liberation; true liberation is
Tathāgata.... When one has realized highest, perfect enlightenment, one becomes free of attachment and doubt. Being free
of attachment and doubt is true liberation; true liberation is
Tathāgata.... Tathāgata is nirvana; nirvana is the inexhaustible; the inexhaustible is Buddha-nature; Buddha-nature
is certainty; certainty is highest, perfect enlightenment.

Bodhisattva Kāśyapa said to the Buddha, "World-honored One, if nirvana, Buddha-nature, certainty, and Tathāgata are terms that have the same meaning, why do you teach
the Three Refuges?"

The Buddha replied to Kāśyapa, "Son of good family, all
sentient beings seek the Three Refuges because they fear
samsara. Through the Three Refuges they come to know of
Buddha-nature, certainty, and nirvana. Son of good family,
there are some Dharma terms that are called by the same
name but have different meanings; there are other Dharma
terms whose names and meanings are different. Concerning
the same name used with different meanings, that which is
eternal is Buddha, Dharma, and Sangha; nirvana and space
are both eternal. These are examples of the same name used
with different meanings. Concerning different names used
with different meanings, Buddha is termed enlightenment,
Dharma is termed non-enlightenment, and Sangha is termed
harmony; nirvana is termed liberation; and space is termed
non-good and unimpeded. These are examples of different
names used with different meanings. Son of good family, the
same applies to the Three Refuges."

It is also stated:[132]

Light is called undecaying; what is undecaying is called Tathāgata. Again, light is called wisdom.

It is also stated:[133]

Sons of good families, all conditioned things are impermanent. Space is unconditioned, and so it is eternal. Buddha-
nature is unconditioned, and so it is eternal. Space is Buddha-
nature; Buddha-nature is Tathāgata; Tathāgata is
unconditioned; the unconditioned is eternal. The eternal is   622a
Dharma; Dharma is Sangha; Sangha is unconditioned; the
unconditioned is eternal. . . .

Sons of good families, I will give you an illustration: milk
is produced from a cow, cream from the milk, curdled milk
from the cream, butter from the curdled milk, and *maṇḍa* is
produced from the butter. *Maṇḍa* is the finest. If one takes
it, one's illnesses are all cured, for all kinds of medicine are
contained in it.

Sons of good families, so it is with the Buddha. The
Buddha sets forth the twelve-divisioned scriptures; from the
twelve-divisioned scriptures arise the sutras; from the sutras
arise the Extensive sutras (Vaipulya sutras); from the Extensive sutras arise the Perfection of Wisdom sutras (Prajñā-
pāramitā sutras); from the Perfection of Wisdom sutras arises
the *Great Nirvana Sutra,* just as *maṇḍa* is obtained last of
all. Buddha-nature is compared to *maṇḍa;* Buddha-nature is
Tathāgata.

Sons of good families, for this reason, it is taught that
the merit possessed by the Tathāgata is immeasurable, boundless, and uncountable.

It is also stated:[134]

Sons of good families, the path is divided into two kinds, eternal and temporary. The characteristics of bodhisattvas are of
two kinds, eternal and temporary. So is nirvana. Non-Buddhist
paths are described as temporary, whereas the Buddhist path
is described as eternal. The *bodhi* that *śrāvaka*s and *pratyekabuddha*s attain is described as temporary, whereas the *bodhi*
that bodhisattvas and Buddhas attain is described as eternal.

The liberation of the non-Buddhist paths is described as temporary, whereas Buddhist liberation is described as eternal.

Sons of good families, the path, *bodhi,* and nirvana are all described as eternal. All sentient beings, however, are unable to see them because they are constantly covered by immeasurable evil passions and so they lack the eye of wisdom. Hence, desirous of seeing them, sentient beings observe the precepts (*śīla*), practice meditation (*samādhi*), and cultivate wisdom (*prajñā*). Through these practices, they can see the path, *bodhi,* and nirvana. This is called bodhisattvas' attainment of the path, *bodhi,* and nirvana. The nature and characteristics of the path are indeed non-arising and non-perishing. Hence, they cannot be grasped.... Although the path is formless one can see it and conceive of it as actually possessing efficacy.... Further, the mind of a sentient being is not a material thing, neither long nor short, neither rough nor fine, neither bound nor liberated, nor is it visible. However, as a *dharma,* it is an existing thing.

It is also stated:[135]

Sons of good families, because nirvana possesses great pleasure, it is called great nirvana. Nirvana is the state of non-pleasure. Because it possesses four kinds of pleasure, it is called great nirvana. What are the four? The first is destruction of all pleasures. Non-destruction of pleasures is called pain. If pain exists, nirvana is not called great pleasure. Since pleasure is destroyed, pain ceases to exist. Nonexistence of pleasure and pain is called great pleasure. The nature of nirvana is nonexistence of pleasure and pain. Hence, nirvana is called great pleasure. For this reason, it is called great nirvana.

622b

Next, sons of good families, there are two kinds of pleasure: the pleasure of ordinary people and that of Buddhas. The pleasure of ordinary people is temporary and subject to decay, and so it is non-pleasure. The Buddhas' pleasure is eternal pleasure; since it is not subject to change, it is called great pleasure.

Next, sons of good families, there are three kinds of sensation: painful sensation, pleasant sensation, and sensation of neither pain nor pleasure. Neither pain nor pleasure is also classified as pain. Nirvana, too, is neither pain nor pleasure, but is called great pleasure. Since it is great pleasure, nirvana is called great nirvana.

Second, because nirvana is great tranquility, it is called great pleasure. The nature of nirvana is great tranquility, because it is free of all that disturbs and torments the mind and body. Because nirvana is great tranquility, it is called great nirvana.

Third, because nirvana is omniscient, it is called great pleasure. That which is not omniscient is not called great pleasure. All Buddha Tathāgatas are omniscient, and so they are said to be [possessed of] great pleasure. Because it is great pleasure, it is called great nirvana.

Fourth, because [in nirvana] the indestructible body is attained, it is called great pleasure. If the body is subject to decay, it is not described as possessing pleasure. The Tathāgata's body is diamondlike and undecaying. Because it is not a body of evil passions or impermanence, it is called great pleasure. Because it is great pleasure, it is called great nirvana.

It is also stated:[136]

Because nirvana is inexplicable and inconceivable, it can be called *mahāparinirvāṇa*. Because it is genuinely pure, it is called great nirvana. In what way is it genuinely pure? There are four kinds of purity. What are they? First, the twenty-five states of existence are described as impure. Since they are forever destroyed, it can be called pure. That which is pure is nirvana. Nirvana such as this can be called an existence, but nirvana is not really an existence. In accordance with worldly practice, Buddha Tathāgatas teach that nirvana is an existence, just as people of the world call someone who is not one's father "father," call someone who is not one's mother "mother," or call those who are not one's parents "parents." So it is with nirvana; in accordance with worldly practice, it is taught that Buddhas are existent and are great nirvana.

Second, because of karmic purity. The karmas of all ordinary people are impure, and so they are not nirvana. The karmas of Buddha Tathāgatas are pure, and so they are called great purity. Because it is great purity, it is called great nirvana.

Third, because of the purity of the body. If the body is impermanent, it is described as impure. Since the Tathāgata's body is eternal, it is called great purity. Because it is great purity, it is called great nirvana.

Fourth, because of purity of the mind. If the mind is defiled, it is called impure. The Buddha's mind is undefiled, and so it is called great purity. Because it is great purity, it is called great nirvana. Sons of good families, those [who practice the teaching of the *Nirvana Sutra*] are called sons and daughters of good families.

It is also stated:[137]

622c   Sons of good families, Buddha Tathāgatas do not give rise to evil passions. This state is called nirvana. The wisdom they possess is unimpeded in penetrating *dharma*s; so they are called Tathāgatas. Tathāgatas are not ordinary beings, *śrāvaka*s, *pratyekabuddha*s, or bodhisattvas; so they are called Buddha-nature. The Tathāgata's body, mind, and wisdom pervade, without hindrance, the immeasurable, boundless, and uncountable lands; so it is called space. Since Tathāgatas are eternal and are not subject to change, they are called true reality. Thus Tathāgatas do not remain in the ultimate nirvanic state; such beings as those are called bodhisattvas.

It is also stated:[138]

Bodhisattva Kāśyapa said, "World-honored One, Buddha-nature is eternal, like space. Why does the Tathāgata explain

206

that it belongs to the future? Tathāgata, when you say that *icchantika*s do not possess any [roots of] good, does this mean that they do not have any thought of love toward their fellow disciples, their teachers, parents, relatives, wives, or children? If they have such a thought, is this not good?"

The Buddha replied, "Very good, son of a good family, it is gratifying to me that you have asked me this question. Buddha-nature is like space, belonging neither to past nor future nor present. All sentient beings have three kinds of bodies: past, future, and present bodies. In the future they will attain glorious pure bodies and be able to see Buddha-nature. For this reason, I say that Buddha-nature belongs to the future. Sons of good families, for the sake of sentient beings, at one time I present a cause as an effect, and at another I present an effect as a cause. In this sutra, therefore, I present life (effect) as nourishment (cause), and also present form (effect) as the tactile sensation (cause). Because one attains a pure body in the future, I refer to Buddha-nature as belonging to the future."

"World-honored One, if such is the Buddha's exposition, why do you declare that all sentient beings have Buddha-nature?"

"Sons of good families, even if sentient beings have no Buddha-nature now, you should not consider Buddha-nature as nonexistent. It is like space. Although its nature is emptiness, you cannot consider it as nonexistent at present. Again, although all sentient beings are impermanent, their Buddha-nature is eternal and is not subject to change. For this reason, I declare in this sutra that sentient beings' Buddha-nature is neither within nor without, like space. It is neither within nor without, like space, and yet it is existent. That which is within and without is space, but we do not consider it one or eternal. Nor can we consider it omnipresent. Further, space is neither within nor without but all sentient beings possess it. So it is with Buddha-nature.

"Concerning the *icchantika*s you speak of, they perform such acts as bodily acts, verbal acts, mental acts, acts of grasping, desiring, giving, and understanding, but they are all wrong acts. For what reason? Because they do not seek proper causation. Sons of good families, it is like the *harītakī*'s roots, stalk, branches, leaves, flowers, and fruits, which are all bitter. The acts of *icchantika*s are like this."

623a

It is also stated:[139]

Sons of good families, the Tathāgata possesses the power of knowing the capacities of beings. Hence, discerning the superior, average, or inferior capacities of beings, he, with thorough knowledge of particular persons, changes them from inferior to average; also, with thorough knowledge of other persons, the Tathāgata changes them from average to superior; again, with thorough knowledge of still other persons, the Tathāgata changes them from superior to average; further, with thorough knowledge of different persons, the Tathāgata changes them from average to inferior. Thus one should know that the capacities of sentient beings are not fixed. Since they are not fixed, their roots of good can be destroyed; after they have been destroyed, they may arise again. If the capacities of sentient beings were fixed, after they have been destroyed they would not arise again. Again, we could not say that the *icchantika*s' lifespan in hell is one *kalpa*. For this reason, sons of good families, the Tathāgata teaches that *dharma*s have no fixed natures.

Kāśyapa Bodhisattva said to the Buddha, "World-honored One, the Tathāgata must have known, with his power of knowing people's capacities, that Sunakṣatra would destroy his roots of good. Why did you allow him to leave home to join the sangha?"

The Buddha replied, "Sons of good families, a long time ago, when I became a mendicant, my [half-]brother Nanda, my cousins Ānanda and Devadatta, and my son Rāhula all followed me, renounced the world, and practiced the Way. If I had not allowed Sunakṣatra to leave home he would have succeeded to the throne. If so, he would have employed his power as he pleased and destroyed the Buddha-Dharma. For this reason, I allowed him to leave home and engage in the practice of the Way. Sons of good families, if Sunakṣatra had not become a mendicant he would have destroyed his roots of good. In that case, he would have been bereft of benefit for immeasurable lives. Now, after joining the sangha, he destroyed his roots of good but still he observed the precepts and paid homage to and revered elders, seniors, and virtuous people. He also practiced the first through the fourth meditations. These are good causes. Such good causes produce good things. When good things are produced, he would engage in the practice of the Way. When he practiced the Way, he would realize highest, perfect enlightenment. For this reason, I allowed Sunakṣatra to leave home and join the sangha. Sons of good families, if I had not allowed Bhikṣu Sunakṣatra to renounce the world and receive the precepts, I would not have deserved to be called the Tathāgata possessed of the ten powers.... Sons of good families, the Tathāgata knows well the superior, average, and inferior capacities of sentient beings. Therefore, the Buddha is called one who possesses the power of knowing people's capacities."

Bodhisattva Kāśyapa said to the Buddha, "World-honored One, the Tathāgata possesses the power of knowing people's capacities. Thus, knowing well the distinct capacities of all sentient beings, such as superior, average, and inferior, and also sharp and dull, the Tathāgata acts in response to the people, their intentions, and the time. Hence, the Tathāgata is called one who possesses the power of knowing people's capacities.... At times he teaches that those who violate the four major prohibitions, those who commit the five grave offenses, and *icchantikas* all have Buddha-nature.... "

[The Buddha replied,] "The Tathāgata, the World-honored

One, explains one thing in two ways in response to the conditions of the place, to the times, to others' use of words, to the needs of the people, and to their various capacities; namely, he uses innumerable names for one thing, he uses innumerable names that have one and the same meaning, and he uses innumerable names for innumerable meanings.

"What is 'using innumerable names for one thing'? 'Nirvana' may be presented as an example. It is called 'nirvana,' also 'non-arising,' 'non-emerging,' 'non-action,' 'unconditioned,' 'taking refuge,' 'cave shelter,' 'liberation,' 'light,' 'torch,' 'the other shore,' 'fearlessness,' 'non-retrogression,' 'place of peaceful rest,' 'tranquility,' 'formlessness,' 'nonduality,' 'single practice,' 'coolness,' 'no darkness,' 'nonhindrance,' 'no dispute,' 'nondefilement,' 'vastness,' 'nectar,' and also 'auspiciousness.' This is an example of 'using innumerable names for one thing.'

"What is 'using innumerable names that have one and the same meaning'? Śakra may be presented as an example. . . .

"What is "using innumerable names for innumerable meanings'? 'Buddha' and 'Tathagata' are examples of this. 'Tathāgata' is a different name with different meaning, so is 'arhat,' also *samyaksambuddha,* 'helmsman,' 'leader,' 'enlightened one,' 'possessed of wisdom and practice,' 'great king of lions,' 'mendicant,' 'brahman,' 'tranquil one,' 'donor,' 'gone to the other shore,' 'great physician king,' 'great elephant king,' 'great dragon king,' 'giver of the eye,' 'possessed of great power,' 'great fearlessness,' 'mass of jewels,' 'caravan leader,' 'one who has attained liberation,' 'great man,' 'teacher of gods and humans,' 'great *puṇḍarīka,*' 'solitary and peerless one,' 'great field of merit,' 'great wisdom sea,' 'no characteristics,' and also 'one possessed of eight wisdoms.' These are all different names with different meanings. Sons of good families, this is 'using innumerable names for innumerable meanings.'

"Further, there are cases in which the Tathāgata uses innumerable names with one meaning. An example of this is 'aggregates.' It is called 'aggregates,' also 'perversion,' '[Four Noble] Truths,' 'four bases of mindfulness,' 'four kinds of nourishment,' 'four bases of consciousness,' 'existence,' 'path,' 'time,' 'sentient beings,' 'world,' 'highest truth,' 'three practices,' namely, body, precepts, and mind, also 'causality,' 'evil passions,' 'liberation,' 'twelve causations,' also '*śrāvaka*s, *pratyeka-* 623c *buddha*s, and Buddhas,' also 'hell, hungry ghosts, animals, humans, and gods,' also 'past, present, and future.' These are examples of 'using innumerable names with one meaning.'

"Sons of good families, the Tathāgata, the World-honored One, for the sake of sentient beings, presents a brief meaning while expounding extensively, and also presents extensive [names and meanings] while giving a short one. He also explains highest truth in terms of worldly truth, and explains worldly truth in terms of highest truth."

It is also stated:[140]

Kāśyapa said, "World-honored One, the highest truth is also called 'path,' also '*bodhi*,' and also 'nirvana'.... "

It is also stated:[141]

Sons of good families, I have stated in this sutra that the Tathāgata's body is distinguished into two: one is the physical body and the other is the Dharma body. The physical body is the accommodated or transformed body manifested by skillful means. This body is subject to birth, old age, sickness, and death, and can be described as long or short, black or white, this or that; and also it may or may not require learning. If my disciples hear this but fail to understand my intention, they will say, "The Tathāgata has decisively stated that the Buddha body is a conditioned *dharma*."

The Dharma body is eternal, blissful, almighty, and pure. It is forever free of birth, old age, sickness, and death, and is neither white nor black, neither long nor short, neither this nor that, and neither requiring learning nor not requiring it.

Whether or not the Buddha appears in the world, he is constantly unmoving and undergoes no change. Sons of good families, if my disciples hear this but fail to understand my intention, they will say, "The Tathāgata has decisively stated that the Buddha body is an unconditioned *dharma*."

It is also stated:[142]

As I have explained in the twelve divisions of scriptures, some are the teachings that are in accord with my intention, some are those that are in accord with others' intention, and some are those that are in accord with both my intention and [that of] others'....

Sons of good families, when I said that bodhisattvas in the tenth stage see a little of Buddha-nature, this is the teaching that is in accord with others' intention. Why did I say "see a little"? Bodhisattvas in the tenth stage have attained such *samādhi*s as the "heroic advance" (*śūraṅgama*) and also the three thousand Dharma gates; hence, [they are] clearly aware of the fact that they will attain highest, perfect *bodhi,* but [they] do not see that all sentient beings will definitely attain highest, perfect *bodhi.* For this reason, I say that bodhisattvas in the tenth stage see a little of Buddha-nature.

Sons of good families, I always declare that all sentient beings have Buddha-nature; this is the teaching that is in accord with my own intention. That all sentient beings are unceasing and unperishing and that they eventually attain highest, perfect *bodhi*—this is the teaching that is in accord with my own intention. Although they all have Buddha-nature they cannot see it because it is covered over by evil passions—this is my teaching and also yours; this is called the teaching that is in accord with my and others' intention. Sons of good families, the Tathāgata sometimes expounds innumerable teachings in order to present one teaching.

624a   It is also stated:[143]

One who is awakened to all things is called [one who possesses] Buddha-nature. Bodhisattvas in the tenth stage cannot be called all-awakened ones; even if they see Buddha-nature, they cannot see it clearly. Sons of good families, there are two kinds of seeing: seeing with the eyes and seeing through hearing. All Buddhas, World-honored Ones, see Buddha-nature with their eyes as clearly as if they were looking at a mango in the palm of their hand. Bodhisattvas in the tenth stage see Buddha-nature through hearing but not very clearly. Bodhisattvas in the tenth stage only know that they will definitely attain highest, perfect *bodhi* but do not know that all sentient beings have Buddha-nature.

Sons of good families, those who see it with the eyes are Buddha Tathāgatas. Bodhisattvas in the tenth stage see Buddha-nature with the eyes and also see it through hearing. All sentient beings up to bodhisattvas in the ninth stage see Buddha-nature through hearing. Even when bodhisattvas hear that all sentient beings have Buddha-nature, if they cannot believe this, we do not say that they see it through hearing. . . .

Bodhisattva Mahāsattva Lion's Roar said, "World-honored One, all sentient beings are incapable of knowing the Tathāgata's mind. How can they observe and know it?"

"Sons of good families, all sentient beings are indeed incapable of knowing the Tathāgata's mind. If they want to observe and know it, there are two ways: one is seeing with the eyes and the other is seeing through hearing. If they see the Tathāgata's bodily acts and know that this is the Tathāgata, it can be said that they see him with the eyes. If they see the Tathāgata's verbal acts and know that this is the Tathāgata, it can be said that they see him through hearing. If they see the Tathāgata's countenance, which is unequaled among all sentient beings, and know that this is the Tathāgata, it can be said that they see him with the eyes. If they hear his subtle and supreme voice, which is unequaled among the voices of all sentient beings, and know that this is the Tathāgata, it can be said that they see him through hearing. If they see the transcendent power displayed by the Tathāgata, they may wonder whether it is for the sake of sentient beings or for his own benefit; then they realize that it is for the sake of sentient beings and not for his own benefit and that this is what the Tathāgata is. To realize thus is seeing him with the eyes. If they see the Tathāgata observing sentient beings with the wisdom of knowing others' thoughts, they may wonder whether it is for the sake of his own benefit or for the sake of sentient beings; then they realize that it is for the benefit of sentient beings and not for his own benefit and that this is what the Tathāgata is. To realize thus is seeing him through hearing."

The *Discourse on the Pure Land* says:

O World-honored One, with singleness of mind, I
Take refuge in the Tathāgata of Unhindered Light
Shining throughout the ten directions,
And aspire to be born in the Land of Peace and Bliss.

When I contemplate the nature of that land,
I find that it surpasses all states of existence in the
    three worlds.
It is ultimately like space,
Vast and without bounds.

It is stated in the *Commentary on Vasubandhu's Discourse on the Pure Land:*

Accomplishment of the glorious merit of purity is described in the verse as:

When I contemplate the nature of that land
I find that it surpasses all states of existence in the
    three worlds.

Why is this inconceivable? When ordinary men full of evil passions attain birth in the Pure Land, the karmic bonds

624b

of the three worlds will not affect them any more. Even without severing evil passions, they will attain the state of nirvana. How can we conceive of this?

It is also stated in the same work:

> Out of the great compassion of the right path
> And from the root of supramundane good has it arisen.

These two lines show what is called "accomplishment of the glorious merit of essential nature. . . . "

"Nature" means "base." This means to say, the Pure Land complies with Dharma-nature and is not in conflict with the Dharma base. It originates in the same way as explained in the *Garland Sutra,* in the "Chapter on the Origination of the Tathāgata from the Dharma-nature Just as Treasure is Produced from *Maṇi,* the King of Gems."

Another meaning is that repeated practice becomes the essential nature. That is to say, Bodhisattva Dharmākara repeatedly performed the practices of perfection (*pāramitā*s), thereby producing [the supreme nature of the Pure Land].

Again, "essential nature" refers to the sages' family. Formerly, in the presence of Lokeśvararāja Buddha, Bodhisattva Dharmākara attained insight into the non-arising of all *dharma*s. This stage is called the sages' family. While dwelling there, he made the Forty-eight Great Vows, whereby he was able to establish his land called the "Pure Land of Peace and Bliss." This means that this land is the result of that cause. Here the cause is explained in the result; hence, [Vasubandhu] calls it "essential nature."

Further, "essential nature" has the meaning of "being so of necessity" and "inalterable." [The essential nature of the Pure Land is] like the nature of the ocean, which has one taste; upon flowing into it, all river water "necessarily" acquires that one taste, and the taste of the ocean is "not altered" by that of the river water. It is also like the nature

of the body which is impure; when things beautiful to look
at, sweet-smelling, and of wholesome taste are taken into it,
they all become defiled. Those born in the Pure Land of Peace
and Bliss are free of the impurity of body and mind; they will
ultimately attain the Dharma body of purity, equality, and
non-action. This is because the Land of Peace and Bliss is perfected with the nature of purity.

> Out of the great compassion of the right path
> And from the root of the supramundane good
> has it arisen.

["The right path"] means the great path of universal
equality. The reason why the great path of universal equality is called "the right path" is that universal equality is the
essence of all *dharmas*. Since all *dharmas* are equal [in
essence], the *bodhi*-mind [which Dharmākara awakened upon
realizing the essence of *dharmas*] is universally equal. Since
the *bodhi*-mind is universally equal, the path [to enlightenment that he followed] is universally equal. Since the path
is universally equal, the great compassion [that attended it]
is also universally equal. Great compassion is indeed the right
cause of the Buddhist path. Hence, it is said: "[Out of] the
great compassion of the right path."

There are three kinds of objects for which [three kinds
of] compassion are aroused: first, that which takes sentient
beings as its object is called small compassion; second, that
which takes *dharmas* as its object is called medium compassion; and third, that which takes emptiness as its object is
called great compassion. Great compassion is the supramundane good. Since the Pure Land of Peace and Bliss has
been produced by this great compassion, it is regarded as the
origin of the Pure Land. Hence, it is said: "And from the root
of the supramundane good has it arisen."

It is also stated in the same work:

Question: When we read Bodhisattva Dharmākara's vows and Bodhisattva Nāgārjuna's [verses of] praise, we find that they mention the existence of many *śrāvaka*s as if it were something marvelous. Why is this so?

Answer: *Śrāvaka*s regard ultimate reality as the [final] enlightenment. It is presumed that they cannot produce the seed of aspiration for enlightenment of the Buddha. But, with the inconceivable divine power of his Primal Vow, the Buddha embraces them and enables them to be born in the Pure Land. With his divine power he will certainly make them awaken aspiration for the highest *bodhi*. It is just as a *chin* bird kills fish and shellfish when it enters the water, but the dead fish are all revived when a rhinoceros enters the water. Just so, [the Buddha enables *śrāvaka*s to] awaken [the *bodhi*-mind that they] cannot achieve [by their own power]. This is indeed a marvelous thing. Moreover, of the five inconceivables, the Buddha-Dharma is most inconceivable. That the Buddha [Amida] enables *śrāvaka*s to awaken aspiration for the highest *bodhi* is indeed difficult to conceive.

624c

It is also stated in the same work:

By "inconceivable power" is meant that the power of the seventeen kinds of glorious merit of the Buddha land is beyond comprehension. According to various sutras, there are five inconceivables: first, the number of sentient beings [which neither increases nor decreases]; second, karma-power; third, the dragons' power [to cause rain to fall]; fourth, meditation power [to produce miracles, and so on]; and fifth, the power of the Buddha-Dharma. Regarding the inconceivability of the Buddha land, there are two powers: first, karma-power, namely, [the power] produced by Bodhisattva Dharmākara's supramundane goodness and the karma-power of his great vow; and second, the power of Amida, the Enlightened King of the Dharma, that maintains [the Pure Land].

It is also stated in the same work:

Concerning "manifestation of the perfection of self-benefit and benefiting of others," [Vasubandhu says in the *Discourse*]:

I have briefly explained the seventeen kinds of glorious merits of Amida Buddha's land, which manifest the Tathāgata's perfection of both the great merit power for his own benefit and the merit for benefiting others.

"Briefly" implies that the merits of the land are of innumerable kinds and not limited to seventeen. It is said that Mount Sumeru is contained in a mustard seed and one pore of the skin holds the great ocean. Is this because of the miraculous power of the mountain or the ocean, or because of the power of the mustard seed or the pore? It is simply because the miraculous power of the [bodhisattva] is capable of it.

It is also stated in the same work:

What is the accomplishment of the glorious merit of the unfailing sustenance? It is said in the verse:

When I observe the Buddha's Primal Vow-Power,
I find that those who meet with it do not pass it
    in vain.
They are enabled to gain quickly
The great sea of the treasure of merit.

The accomplishment of the merit of the unfailing sustenance describes Amida Tathāgata's Primal Vow-Power. . . . "Unfailing sustenance" results from the original Forty-eight Vows of Bodhisattva Dharmākara and is maintained by the transcendent power that Amida Tathāgata can freely use now. His vows gave rise to the power; the power fulfills the vows. The vows have not been vain; the power is not empty. The power and vows work in complete harmony and are not in the least discordant with each other; hence, it is said "accomplishment."

The *Hymns in Praise of Amida Buddha* composed by Master T'an-luan say:

> *Namu amida butsu*
>
> Explaining this, we call him "Infinite Life"; I give my praise in accompaniment to the sutra; he is also called "Peaceful Sustenance."

Since Amida attained Buddhahood, ten *kalpa*s have
    passed;
His lifespan is indeed beyond measure.
The halo of his Dharma body pervades the Dharma realm,
Shining on the blind and ignorant of the world; hence, I
    prostrate myself and worship him.   625a

His light of wisdom cannot be measured;
Therefore, the Buddha is also called "Infinite Light."
All those with limited dimensions are benefited by the
    light that dawns in their minds;
Hence, I pay homage to the True Illumination.

His halo of liberation is without bounds;
For this reason, he is also called "Boundless Light."
Those touched by the light are freed of ideas of "being"
    and "non-being."
Hence, I bow in worship to the Equally Enlightened One.

His light-cluster is unhindered like space.
For this reason, the Buddha is also called "Unhindered
    Light."
All those with hindrances receive the light's benefit.
Hence, I prostrate myself and worship the Inconceivable
    One.

His light of purity is incomparable.
For this reason, the Buddha is also called "Incomparable
    Light."

Those who encounter his light are rid of their karmic bonds.
Hence, I bow in worship to the Ultimate Refuge.

The Buddha's light shines forth most brilliantly.
For this reason, the Buddha is also called the "King of
    Blazing Light."
The darkness of the three lowest realms is dissipated by
    the light.
Hence, I prostrate myself and worship the Great Arhat.

His light of enlightenment is brilliant and its color is superb.
For this reason, the Buddha is also called "Light of Purity."
Once shone upon by the light, we are freed of our karmic
    defilements,
And all attain liberation. Hence, I prostrate myself and
    worship him.

Sending forth the light of compassion far and wide, he
    bestows happiness.
For this reason, the Buddha is also called "Light of Joy."
Wherever the light reaches, it enables us to attain joy of
    the Dharma.
Hence, I bow and prostrate myself to worship the Provider
    of Great Consolation.

The Buddha's light destroys the darkness of ignorance.
For this reason, the Buddha is also called "Light of
    Wisdom."
All Buddhas and sages of the three vehicles
Together praise and extoll him. Hence, I bow in worship
    to him.

His light shines everywhere at all times.
For this reason, the Buddha is also called "Unceasing
    Light."
By accepting in faith the power of his light, with
    continuous mindfulness,

We all attain birth. Hence, I prostrate myself and
  worship him.

His light cannot be fathomed, except by Buddhas.
For this reason, the Buddha is also called "Inconceivable
  Light."
Buddhas of the ten directions praise our birth
And extoll Amida's virtue. Hence, I bow in worship to him.

His majestic light is above all distinctive features and so
  cannot be described in words.
For this reason, the Buddha is also called "Ineffable Light."
Amida became a Buddha through the vow of light; his
  light illumines blazingly.
It is praised by all Buddhas. Hence, I prostrate myself
  and worship him.

His light shines brilliantly, surpassing the sun and moon.
For this reason, the Buddha is also called "Light
  Outshining the Sun and Moon."
Even Śākyamuni Buddha could not praise him
  exhaustively.
Hence, I bow and worship the Unequaled One....

Our master, Nāgārjuna Mahāsattva,
Appeared at the beginning of the Age of the Semblance
  Dharma and corrected degenerate teachings.
He closed wrong paths and opened the right way.
He is the eye for all beings in this Jambudvīpa continent.

Reverently accepting the words of the Honored One, he
  reached the stage of joy;
He took refuge in Amida and attained birth in the
  Land of Peace and Bliss.

From the beginningless past, I have wandered about
  in the three worlds,

Subject to transmigration caused by false and deluded
thoughts.
The karma I commit every moment, every instant,
Binds me to the six realms and keeps me in the three
painful states of existence.

May Amida protect me with the light of compassion,
And ensure that I do not lose my *bodhi*-mind.
I praise the Name of the Buddha's wisdom and virtue.
May all beings of the ten directions who are closely related
to Amida hear this teaching

And may all who aspire for birth in the Land of Peace
and Bliss
Realize their desire without hindrance.
I will transfer all my merits, whether great or small,
To all beings, so that all may be born there together.

625b   I entrust myself to the Inconceivable Light,
Singleheartedly take refuge in him, bow and worship him.

Those with infinite wisdom of the three times throughout
the ten directions,
Having equally practiced in accord with Oneness, have
become "perfectly enlightened."
Their two kinds of wisdom are fully perfected and their
enlightenment is the same.
Their salvific activity, which is in keeping with the
conditions of beings, is truly immense.

My taking refuge in Amida's Pure Land
Is taking refuge in all Buddha lands.
I praise one Buddha singleheartedly.
May my praise extend to the Unhindered Ones
throughout the ten directions.

To each one of the immeasurable Buddhas of the
ten directions,

I sincerely prostrate myself and pay homage.

The Master of Kuang-ming Temple says:[144]

Question: Is Amida's Pure Land a Recompensed Land or a Transformed Land?

Answer: It is a Recompensed Land, not a Transformed Land. How do you know this? The *Mahayana Sutra on the Equal Nature (Mahāyāna-samasvabhāva-sūtra*)* says:

> The Western Land of Peace and Bliss and Amida Buddha are a Recompensed Land and a Recompensed Buddha.

It is also stated in the *Sutra on the Buddha of Infinite Life:*

> When Bhikṣu Dharmākara was performing the bodhisattva practices under Lokeśvararāja Buddha, he made the Forty-eight Vows. In each vow, he promised to the following effect:

> > If, when I become a Buddha, the sentient beings of the ten directions, aspiring to be born in my land, call my Name even ten times but fail to attain birth, may I not attain perfect enlightenment.

He has already become a Buddha. This means that he is a body of reward for his causal vows. Furthermore, in the *Contemplation Sutra* it is stated that when the three classes of aspirants of the highest grade are about to die, Amida Buddha together with his transformed bodies come to welcome them. In this case, the recompensed body together with transformed bodies come and extend their hands to them; hence, the sutra says "together with." From this testimonial passage we know that Amida is a recompensed body.

It is to be noted that "recompensed body" and "accommodated body" are synonyms, like "eye" and "visual organ." In the earlier translation [of the *Summary of the Great Vehicle (Mahāyāna-saṃgraha)*] "recompensed" was rendered "accommodated," but in the later translation "accommodated" was rendered "recompensed." Basically, "recompensed" means that the causal practice is not futile but necessarily brings about its result in the future. The result corresponds to the cause. Hence, we say "recompensed." Again, the myriad practices performed during three uncountable *kalpa*s necessarily bring *bodhi*. Now, enlightenment has already been realized; this is the accommodated body. Concerning the Buddhas of the past and present, three bodies are distinguished. There is no other body apart from them. Even though the eight major events [of a Buddha's life] have infinite variations and the Buddhas' names are as numerous as grains of sand and dust motes, viewed from the perspective of their essential nature all [manifestations of the Buddhas] are contained in transformed bodies. Amida is actually a recompensed body.

Question: Speaking of "recompensed body," it is eternally abiding, neither arising nor perishing. For what reason is it stated in the *Sutra on the Prediction of Avalokiteśvara's Buddhahood (Avalokiteśvara-bodhisattva-vyākaraṇa-sūtra*)* that there is a time when Amida Buddha enters nirvana? How do you interpret this?

Answer: Whether or not a Buddha enters nirvana is a matter that belongs to the realm of Buddhas, of which sages of the three vehicles are unable even to have a glimpse with their shallow wisdom. How much less so with us, petty and ordinary people! We cannot possibly know the reason. If, however, you insist on knowing this, I will draw upon a sutra for clear evidence. It is stated in the *Perfection of Great Wisdom Sutra*, the "Chapter on Nirvana Being not Illusory":

> The Buddha said to Subhūti, "What do you think: if an illusory man creates an illusory man, is the latter of real substance or not, is it empty or not?"
>
> Subhūti replied, "World-honored One, it is not."

625c

The Buddha said to Subhūti, "Form is illusion; sensation, conception, volition, and consciousness are illusion. All things up to all-knowing wisdom are illusion."

Subhūti said to the Buddha, "World-honored One, are worldly *dharma*s illusion? Are supramundane *dharma*s also illusion? The four bases of mindfulness, the four correct strivings, the four bases of supernatural knowledge, the five faculties, the five powers, the seven factors of enlightenment, the Noble Eightfold Path, and the three gates of liberation; the Buddha's ten powers, the four fearlessnesses, the four unhindered wisdoms, the eighteen special qualities; the results of various practices, and those in the stage of sagacity and the sages, namely, stream-winners (*srota-āpanna*), once-returners (*sakṛdāgā-min*), non-returners (*anāgāmin*), arhats, *pratyeka-buddha*s, bodhisattvas, *mahāsattva*s, and Buddhas, World-honored Ones—are they all illusion?"

The Buddha replied to Subhūti, "All *dharma*s are illusion. Among these *dharma*s there are illusory *dharma*s for *śrāvaka*s, those for *pratyekabuddha*s, those for bodhisattvas, those for Buddhas; also there are illusory dharmas based on evil passions, and those based on karmic causation. For this reason, Subhūti, all *dharma*s are illusion."

Subhūti said to the Buddha, "World-honored One, in various stages of the destruction of evil passions, such as the fruit of the stream-winner, the fruit of the once-returner, the fruit of the non-returner, the fruit of the arhat, and the path of the *pratyekabuddha,* practitioners destroy the residue of evil passions. Are these all illusion?"

The Buddha said to Subhūti, "All *dharma*s that have the aspect of arising and perishing are illusion."

Subhūti said, "World-honored One, what *dharma* is not illusion?"

The Buddha said, "The *dharma* that neither arises nor perishes is not illusion."

Subhūti said, "What *dharma* neither arises nor perishes and so is not illusion?"

The Buddha said, "Nirvana which is free of falsity is the *dharma* that is not illusion."

"World-honored One, you the Buddha have taught that all *dharma*s are equal and that they have not been created by *śrāvaka*s, *pratyekabuddha*s, bodhisattvas, *mahāsattva*s, or by Buddhas. Whether a Buddha appears in the world or not, the essential nature of all *dharma*s is always emptiness. Emptiness of their essential nature is nirvana. Why is this *dharma*, nirvana, not illusion?"

The Buddha said to Subhūti, "So it is. All *dharma*s are equal; they have not been created by *śrāvaka*s, and so on. Emptiness of their essential nature is nirvana. If bodhisattvas who have a newly awakened aspiration for *bodhi* hear that all *dharma*s are ultimately empty in their essential nature and that even nirvana is illusion, their hearts will become agitated and fear-ridden. For the sake of those initiate bodhisattvas, I deliberately make a distinction, saying that all *dharma*s that arise and perish are illusion and those that neither arise nor perish are not illusion."

From this scripture we clearly know that Amida is definitely a recompensed body. This does not preclude Amida from entering nirvana in the future. The wise should realize this.

Question: If, as you say, the Buddha and his land are a recompensed body and land, they are too high and subtle for lesser sages. How could ordinary people with defilements and hindrances enter there?

Answer: Considering sentient beings' defilements and hindrances, they cannot possibly hope to attain birth there. But

626a

when they entrust themselves to the Buddha's Vow, it becomes the strong cause enabling those of the five vehicles equally to enter Amida's land.

He also says:[145]

The passage [in the *Contemplation Sutra*] beginning with "I wish to be born in [the Pure Land of Amida]" shows that Queen [Vaidehī] especially chose the land where she desired to be born. This refers to Amida's land. Each of the Forty-eight Vows gave rise to the supreme cause; through the cause the excellent practice was performed; through the practice the excellent result was attained; through the result the excellent recompense was accomplished; through the recompense the Land of Peace and Bliss was manifested; through the Land of Bliss the compassionate salvific activity was revealed; through the compassionate salvific activity the gate of wisdom was opened. The compassionate mind is inexhaustible; so is wisdom. Through the joint practice of compassion and wisdom, the nectar of the Dharma has been made available everywhere. Thus the nourishment of the Dharma benefits multitudes of beings universally. Many other sutras encourage us to follow this sutra. Many sages join their hearts in urging us to take this path. For this reason, the Tathāgata secretly led the queen to choose birth in Amida's land.

He also says:[146]

The capital of tranquility and non-action in the
  Western Land
Is ultimately free and peaceful, transcending existence
  and nonexistence.
With the mind imbued with great compassion, one plays
  in the Dharma realm.
Manifesting bodies of incarnation, one benefits beings
  equally without discrimination.

Let us return home! We should not stay
In this realm of devils. Since innumerable *kalpa*s ago
We have been transmigrating
In all the states of the six realms.

Nowhere has there been any pleasure;
We only hear the voices of samsaric pain.
At the end of this life,
Let us enter the capital of nirvana!

It is also stated:[147]

The Land of Utmost Bliss is the nirvana realm of
    non-action;
I fear those who perform sundry practices following given
    conditions are perhaps unable to be born there.
Hence, the Tathāgata Śākyamuni selected the essential
    teaching,
And taught us to be mindful of Amida singleheartedly.

It is also stated:[148]

Following the Buddha, one effortlessly returns to
    naturalness;
Naturalness is Amida's land.
Free of defilements and non-arising, it is originally
    the realm of truth.
Whether going or returning, advancing or stopping,
    one always follows the Buddha;
One realizes there the body of Dharma-nature of
    non-action.

It is also stated:[149]

Amida's excellent fruit of enlightenment is called supreme
nirvana.

Master Kyeong-heung says:[150]

"Buddha of Infinite Light"—because the light is beyond cal-
culation. "Buddha of Boundless Light"—because there is nothing it does not shine upon. "Buddha of Unhindered Light"—
because it is not hindered by anyone or anything. "Buddha of
Incomparable Light"—because bodhisattvas' [lights] cannot
be compared with it. "Buddha of the Light of the King of
Flame"—because the light is unrestricted in its activity and
nothing surpasses it. "Buddha of Pure Light"—because it has
arisen from the roots of good free of greed and also because it
removes the defilements of greed from the minds of sentient
beings; the light is pure because it is free of the defilements
of greed. "Buddha of the Light of Joy"—because it has arisen
from the roots of good free of anger and also because it removes
fierce anger from the minds of sentient beings. "Buddha of
the Light of Wisdom"—because it has arisen from the roots
of goodness free of ignorance and also because it removes sentient beings' mental activities related to ignorance. "Buddha
of Unceasing Light"—because the Buddha's constant light
always illumines and benefits beings. "Buddha of Inconceivable Light"—because sages of the two vehicles cannot fathom
it. "Buddha of Ineffable Light"—because those of other vehicles [than that of the Buddha vehicle] are unable to evaluate
it. "Buddha of the Light Outshining the Sun and the Moon"—   626b
because the sun cannot shine universally but Amida's light
illumines this Sahā world pervasively. That all beings receive
the light's brilliance on their bodies is due to the vow of making the bodies and minds of sentient beings soft and gentle
(the Thirty-third Vow).

[Concluding Remarks]

We clearly know from the Tathāgata's teaching of truth and the
masters' commentaries that the Pure Land of Peace and Provision
is the True Land of Recompense. Sentient beings with delusion and
defilements cannot see Buddha-nature here, because it is covered

over by evil passions. The [*Nirvana*] *Sutra*[151] says, "I say that bodhi-sattvas of the tenth stage see a little of Buddha-nature." Hence, we know that when we reach the Buddha Land of Peace and Bliss, Buddha-nature will certainly be revealed to us—through the merit transference by the Primal Vow-Power. It is also stated in the [*Nirvana*] *Sutra:*[152] "Sentient beings will, in the future, attain and glorify bodies of purity and be able to see Buddha-nature."

It is stated in the *Discourse on the Awakening of Faith* [*in the Mahayana*] (*Mahāyāna-śraddhotpāda-śāstra**):[153]

> To realize that even though there is an exposition there is no one who expounds it, and that [even though there is thinking] there is no one who thinks—this is called "being in accord with reality." To become free of thought is to enter [*samādhi*].

[Fei-hsi's explanation:] "To enter" means to enter the *samādhi* of true suchness. It is to be noted that the state of no-thought is that of wonderful enlightenment. It is to realize how the first arising of mind takes place. To realize the first arising of mind is no-thought; even bodhisattvas in the tenth stage cannot know it. Since people of today have not yet reached the ten stages of understanding, why should they not rely on Aśvaghoṣa Mahāsattva? He says, "From speech one enters no-speech; from thought one enters no-thought."

[True and Provisional Recompense]

When I contemplate "recompense," I find that the accomplished land has resulted as the recompense for the Tathāgata's oceanlike vow. Hence, "recompensed." Concerning the oceanlike vow, there is true and provisional. For this reason, concerning the Buddha land, too, there is true and provisional.

By the right cause, the selected Primal Vow, the true Buddha land has been established.

Concerning the true Buddha, the *Larger Sutra* says, "the

Buddha of Boundless Light, the Buddha of Unhindered Light"; also,[154] "The king of all Buddhas, the most august of all lights." The *Discourse on the Pure Land* says, "Homage to the Tathāgata of Unhindered Light Shining throughout the Ten Directions."

Concerning the true land, the *Larger Sutra*[155] says "the Land of Infinite Light"; also it says[156] "the Land of Wisdoms." The *Discourse on the Pure Land* describes it as "ultimately like space, vast and without bounds."

Concerning birth in the Pure Land, the *Larger Sutra* says, "They are all endowed with bodies of naturalness, emptiness, and infinity." The *Discourse on the Pure Land* states, "The hosts of sages in the likeness of pure flowers surrounding the Tathāgata are born there, transformed from within the flower of enlightenment." Also the *Commentary on Vasubandhu's Discourse on the Pure Land* says, "[They are so born] by one and the same path of the Nembutsu, and not by other paths." Also it is said,[157] "Inconceivable birth."

Provisional Buddhas and lands are discussed below.

Both the true and provisional [Buddhas and lands] have been recompensed for the oceanlike vow of great compassion. Hence, we know that they are Recompensed Buddhas and Lands. Since there are thousands of different karmic causes for birth in the provisional Buddha lands, there are thousands of different Buddha lands. They are called provisional Transformed Buddhas and Lands. Those who are ignorant of the distinction between true and provisional [Buddhas and lands] fail to acknowledge the great benevolence of the Tathāgata.

626c

Accordingly, I have disclosed the true Buddha and true land. These are the very objective that the true essence of the Pure Land Way seeks to clarify. Respectfully revere and accept in faith the right teaching of Śākyamuni, the master who preached the sutras, and the writers of the discourses and the expositions by the Pure Land masters. You should particularly uphold them. You should be well aware of this.

End of Chapter V: Revealing the True Buddha and Land

Chapter VI

Revealing the Transformed Buddhas and Lands

[General Exposition]

I reverently present the Transformed Buddhas and Lands: the Buddhas are like the one taught in the *Contemplation Sutra,* that is, the Buddha described in the contemplation of the true Buddha body. The lands are the various forms of the Pure Land specified in the *Contemplation Sutra* and also the land presented in the *Sutra on the Bodhisattvas Dwelling in the Womb (P'u sa ch'u t'ai ching),* that is, the realm of sloth and pride. They are also described in the *Larger Sutra* as the castle of doubt and the womb palace.

[The Nineteenth Vow Teaching]

Here we find that even if the multitudes of this defiled world, the depraved and evil sentient beings, have departed from the ninety-five wrong paths and entered the Dharma gates, such as the imperfect and perfect, provisional and true, it is extremely difficult to find true followers and rare indeed to meet real ones; false practitioners are numerous and nominal ones are innumerable. Thereupon, Śākyamuni Buddha guides the multitudes of beings by disclosing the store of merit, and Amida Tathāgata made the Vow through which he saves sentient beings.

We already have the compassionate Vow, which is called "the vow of performing meritorious acts," "the vow of Amida's appearance at one's deathbed," "the vow of Amida's appearance at one's death to guide one to birth in the Pure Land," and "the vow of

233

Amida's coming to receive the aspirant"; it can also be called "the vow of sincere mind and aspiration."

Here the [Nineteenth] Vow says in the *Larger Sutra:*

> If, when I attain Buddhahood, sentient beings in the lands of the ten directions who awaken aspiration for enlightenment, do various meritorious deeds, and sincerely desire to be born in my land, should not, at their death, see me appear before them surrounded by a multitude of sages, may I not attain perfect enlightenment.

It is stated in the *Sutra of the Lotus of Compassion,* "Chapter on Great Charity":[158]

627a

> When I have realized highest, perfect *bodhi,* those sentient beings in the immeasurable, uncountable, and innumerable Buddha lands who awaken aspiration for highest, perfect *bodhi* and cultivate roots of goodness, desiring to be born in my land, will see me appear before them at their death, surrounded by a host of sages. Seeing me, they will, in my presence, attain joy in their hearts. By virtue of the merit of seeing me they will be freed of all hindrances and, after death, will be born in my land.

The statement concerning fulfillment of this [Nineteenth] Vow is found in the passage on the three grades of aspirants[159] and the passages from the *Contemplation Sutra* on the meditative good and the non-meditative good in the nine levels of aspirants.

The *Larger Sutra* states:

> Again, the *bodhi* tree of the Buddha of Infinite Life is four million *li* in height and five thousand *yojanas* in circumference at its base. Its branches spread two hundred thousand *li* in each of the four directions. It is a natural cluster of all kinds of precious stones and is adorned with the kings of jewels, namely, moonbright *maṇi*-gems and ocean-supporting wheel gems. ...

Ānanda, when humans and *deva*s of that land see the *bodhi* tree, they will attain three insights: first, insight into reality through hearing the sacred sounds; second, insight into reality by being in accord with it; and third, insight into the non-arising of all *dharma*s. These benefits are all bestowed by the majestic power of [the Buddha of Infinite Life], the power of his Original Vow, his perfectly fulfilled vow, his clear and manifest vow, his firm vow, and his accomplished vow....

Again, the halls, monasteries, palaces, and pavilions are spontaneous apparitions, all adorned with the seven kinds of jewels and hung with curtains of various other jewels, such as pearls and moonbright *maṇi*-gems.

Inside and out, to right and left, are bathing ponds. Some of them are ten *yojana*s in length, breadth, and depth; some are twenty *yojana*s; others, thirty; and so on, until we come to those measuring a hundred thousand *yojana*s in length, breadth, and depth. They are full to the brim with the water that possesses the eight excellent qualities, clear, fragrant, and tasting like nectar.

It is also stated in the same sutra:

Those in the embryonic state dwell in palaces as high as a hundred *yojana*s or five hundred *yojana*s, where they spontaneously enjoy pleasures as do those in the Heaven of the Thirty-three Gods.

Then Bodhisattva Maitreya said to the Buddha, "World-honored One, for what reason are some of the inhabitants of that land in the embryonic state and the others born by transformation?"

The Buddha replied, "Maitreya, if there are sentient beings who do various meritorious deeds, aspiring for birth in that land while still entertaining doubt, such beings are unable to comprehend the Buddha wisdom, inconceivable wisdom, ineffable wisdom, boundless Mahayana wisdom, and incomparable, unequaled, and unsurpassed supreme wisdom.

Although they doubt these wisdoms, they still believe in retribution for evil and reward for virtue and so cultivate a store of merit, aspiring for birth in that land. Such beings are born in a palace, where they dwell for five hundred years without being able to behold the Buddha, hear his exposition of the Dharma, or see the hosts of bodhisattvas and *śrāvaka*s. For this reason, that type of birth in the Pure Land is called the "embryonic state".... Maitreya, you should know that those born by transformation are possessed of supreme wisdom, while those in the embryonic state lack that wisdom.... "

627b

The Buddha said to Maitreya, "Let us suppose that a wheel-turning monarch has a special chamber that is adorned with the seven kinds of jewels and provided with curtained couches and silken banners hanging from the ceiling. If princes have committed an offense against the king, they are taken to that chamber and fettered with gold chains.... "

The Buddha said to Maitreya, "Those beings born within the lotus buds are like that. Because of their doubt of the Buddha's wisdom, they have been born in palaces.... If those beings become aware of the faults committed in their former lives and deeply repent, they can, as they wish, leave [there].... Maitreya, you should know that the bodhisattvas who allow doubt to arise lose great benefits."

It is stated in the *Teaching Assembly of the Tathāgata of Infinite Life:*

The Buddha said to Maitreya, "Suppose there are sentient beings who, while harboring doubt, accumulate roots of good and seek to realize the Buddha wisdom, the all-pervasive wisdom, the inconceivable wisdom, the unequaled wisdom, the majestic wisdom, and the vast and extensive wisdom. They are unable to establish faith in their roots of good. For this reason, they dwell within the palace for five hundred years.... Ajita, as you observe those of excellent wisdom, you will see them born transformed in lotus flowers through the power

of vast wisdom and sitting with their legs crossed. When you
observe the inferior aspirants . . . , you will find that they cannot practice various meritorious acts. Hence, they will not be
able to serve the Buddha of Infinite Life. These people have
become so because of the faults of doubt in the past. . . . "

The Buddha said to Maitreya, "So it is, so it is. They plant
roots of good while harboring doubt, and seek to realize various wisdoms, from the Buddha wisdom to the vast and extensive wisdom. They are unable to establish faith in their own
roots of good. Since they have awakened faith through hearing the Buddha's Name, even though born in his land they
will be enclosed in the lotus buds and will not emerge from
there. These beings dwell in the lotus matrix, feeling as if
they were in a garden or palace."

The *Larger Sutra* states:

> [B]odhisattvas of lesser practices and those who have per-
> formed small acts of merit, whose number is beyond calcu-
> lation, will all be born there.

It is also stated:[160]

> How much more incalculable are other bodhisattvas who are
> born there with small roots of good!

The Master of Kuang-ming Temple says in his *Commentary*:[161]

> Some of them are enclosed within the lotus buds, unable to
> emerge from there; some are born in the borderland, and oth-
> ers fall into the womb palace.

Master Kyeong-heung says:[162]

> Because of doubting the Buddha wisdom, although they are
> born in that land they stay in the borderland and are not
> benefited by the Buddha's guidance. If you receive birth in
> the embryonic state, you must, by all means, reject it.

In the *Collection of Essential Passages Concerning Birth* by the Master of Shuryōgon-in (Genshin), the following passage is quoted from Master Huai-kan's *Discourse:*[163]

627c

> *Question:* The *Sutra on the Bodhisattvas Dwelling in the Womb,* fascicle two, says,

>> In the western direction, twelve *koṭi*s of *nayuta*s from this Jambudvīpa, is the realm of sloth and pride.... Sentient beings who have awakened aspiration for birth in the land of Amida Buddha are all deeply attached to this realm, and so are unable to advance to the land of Amida Buddha. Only rarely, one out of *koṭi*s of millions of people can attain birth in the land of Amida Buddha.

> A question arises regarding the statement of this sutra: Is there any possibility of attaining birth there?

> *Answer:* In the *Discourse Clearing Doubts about the Pure Land Teaching (Shih ching t'u ch'ün i lun)*, Huai-kan quotes again the passage of Master Shan-tao, which has been quoted before, to answer this question, and he further adds:

>> The sutra says below, "For what reason? Because they are indolent and complacent and so their resolution is not firm." Hence, we know that those who engage in sundry practices are people of weak resolution. For this reason, they are born in the realm of sloth and pride. If you solely perform this act (reciting the Nembutsu), without engaging in sundry practices, your resolution is firm, and so you will definitely be born in the Land of Utmost Bliss....
>> Again, those who are born in the Pure Land of Recompense are very few, and those who are born in the Transformed Pure Land are not few. Thus the different exposition in this sutra does not diverge from the teaching of the [three Pure Land] sutras.

> Thereupon, when I contemplate the exposition of the Master

238

of Shuryōgon-in (i.e., the *Collection of Essential Passages Concerning Birth*), I find that in the "Chapter on Verification of the Nembutsu," he clarifies the Eighteenth Vow as the special vow of all special vows. He urges those who engage in meditative and non-meditative good as taught in the *Contemplation Sutra* to realize that they are people of extremely heavy evil karma and simply to recite Amida's Name. Monks and laypeople of this defiled world should reflect on their own capacities. This one should know.

[Explicit and Implicit Teachings of the Three Pure Land Sutras]

Question: Are the three minds in the *Larger Sutra* and those in the *Contemplation Sutra* the same or different?

Answer: When I carefully read the *Sutra on the Contemplation of the Buddha of Infinite Life* according to the intent of the commentator (Shan-tao), I find that there is an explicit meaning and an implicit, hidden, and concealed meaning.

In its "explicit" aspect, [the sutra] presents the meditative and non-meditative good acts and sets forth the three levels of aspirants and the three minds. The two kinds of good acts and the three meritorious acts, however, are not the true cause for birth in the Recompensed Land. The three minds held by various types of aspirants are based on their self-power and are individually different, and so they are not the same as the One Mind of Other-Power. [The good acts] are the provisional means that the Tathāgata especially provided and the roots of good with which one adoringly aspires for the Pure Land. This is the sutra's message—its explicit meaning.

In its "implicit" aspect, [the sutra] discloses the Tathāgata's Universal Vow and reveals the One Mind of Other-Power which ensures birth for all beings. Through the outrageous acts of Devadatta and Ajātaśatru, Śākyamuni disclosed, with a smile, his original intention. Through Vaidehī's selection of [Amida's land] in particular, Amida's Primal Vow of great compassion was revealed. This is the implicit meaning of the sutra.

Hereupon, when the [*Contemplation*] *Sutra* says, "I entreat you, O sunlike Buddha, to teach me how to visualize a land of pure karmic perfection," the "land of pure karmic perfection" is the Land of Recompense established by the Primal Vow. "[T]each me how to contemplate" is the provisional means; "teach me how to attain *samādhi*" refers to adamantine true faith. When the sutra says, "Fix your thoughts upon and contemplate the person of pure karmic perfection in that Buddha land," it teaches us to contemplate the Tathāgata of Unhindered Light shining throughout the ten directions which has come into existence through the Primal

628a Vow. "I shall describe it to you in detail with various illustrations" refers to the thirteen contemplations. "You are unenlightened and so your spiritual powers are weak and obscured" shows that [Vaidehī] is one of the evil persons suited for the teaching of birth in the Pure Land. "The Buddha Tathāgatas have special ways [to enable you to see afar]" shows that various meditative and non-meditative good acts are provisional teachings. "[T]hrough the Buddha's power, even I have now been able to see the land" implies Other-Power. "[A]fter the Buddha's passing sentient beings... " shows that sentient beings of the future are precisely the beings to be led to birth in the Pure Land. "[If your perception agrees with the sutra], it is called the attainment of the general perception of the Land of Utmost Bliss" indicates that the meditative practice is difficult to accomplish. "While in this life, you will attain the Nembutsu *samādhi*" shows that the benefit of accomplishing the meditative practice is the attainment of the Nembutsu *samādhi*. This indicates that the meditation course is a provisional teaching. "Those who have these three kinds of faith (i.e., the three minds) will certainly be born there" and "there are three other kinds of sentient beings who also attain birth" show that three kinds of three minds and two kinds of birth are distinguished for the three levels of aspirants.

I truly know that this [*Contemplation*] *Sutra* has both the explicit and the implicit, hidden, and concealed meanings.

I will now discuss the similarities and differences between the three minds of the two sutras; this matter requires careful consideration. The message of the *Larger Sutra* and that of the *Contemplation Sutra* are different in their explicit meaning, but the same in their implicit meaning. This we should know.

Hereupon, the Master of Kuang-ming Temple says:[164]

> The Lord Preacher of this Sahā world, responding to [Vaidehī's] request, opened widely the essential gate to the Pure Land, and the Capable One of the Land of Peace and Bliss revealed the Universal Vow that manifests his special intent. The essential gate refers to the two courses of meditative and non-meditative good acts. Meditative practice consists in stopping wandering thought and concentrating the mind; non-meditative practice lies in ceasing to do evil and performing good. Aspirants are taught to aspire for birth by transferring the merit of these two practices [to that end]. The Universal Vow is set forth in the *Larger Sutra*.

He also says:[165]

> The *Contemplation Sutra* has the Buddha-contemplation *samādhi* as its essence; it also has the Nembutsu *samādhi* as its essence. Its basic theme is to attain birth in the Pure Land by singlemindedly making aspiration for birth and transferring the merit of one's practice to it.
>
> *Question:* Concerning whether its teaching is Mahayana or Hinayana, in which of the two *piṭaka*s is this sutra included and in which of the two teachings is it contained?
>
> *Answer:* The *Contemplation Sutra* is included in the bodhi-sattva-*piṭaka* and contained in the sudden teaching.

He also says:[166]

> "Thus [have I heard]" implies the teachings, that is, the meditative and non-meditative teachings. "Thus" is the word

indicating something definitely. Those who perform practices definitely gain benefit. This shows that the Tathāgata's words are unerring. Hence, "thus."

Further, "thus" means "as sentient beings wish." In accordance with their wishes, the Buddha saves them. The correspondence between the beings and the teaching is indicated by "thus." Hence, "thus."

Further, "thus" shows the way the Tathāgata expounds the Dharma. He expounds the gradual teaching as such; he expounds the sudden teaching as such; he expounds forms as such; he expounds emptiness as such; he expounds the teaching for humans as such; he expounds the teaching for *deva*s as such; he expounds the Hinayana as such; he expounds the Mahayana as such; he expounds the nature of ordinary beings as such; he expounds the nature of sages as such; he expounds cause as such; he expounds result as such; he expounds pain as such; he expounds pleasure as such; he expounds things far as such; he expounds things near as such; he expounds sameness as such; he expounds difference as such; he expounds purity as such; he expounds defilement as such; he expounds all *dharma*s in millions of different ways. The Tathāgata's insightful observation is clear and manifest. He performs practices in accord with his wishes, benefiting the beings in different ways. The results of his acts agree with the nature of the Dharma and are free of errors. This is described as "thus." Hence, "thus."

628b

He also says:[167]

The passage from "whoever wishes to be born in his land" to "[these three] are called the pure karma" urges people to practice the three meritorious acts. This shows that the capacities of all sentient beings are divided into two kinds: one is meditative and the other is non-meditative. If only the meditative practice were set forth, it would not be applicable to all beings. For this reason, the Tathāgata, out of skillful means, provided the three meritorious acts to accommodate those who have distracted minds.

He also says:[168]

There are two kinds of true and sincere [acts]: one is true and sincere [acts] for self-benefit and the other is true and sincere [acts] for benefiting others. True and sincere [acts] for self-benefit are further distinguished into two; first is to stop one's own and others' evil acts and abandon this defiled world with the true and sincere mind, and also seek to do as all bodhisattvas do to stop all evils, whether walking, standing, sitting, or lying down. Second is to promote, with the true and sincere mind, good acts for oneself and others, whether ordinary people or sages. As for the verbal act to be performed with the true and sincere mind, one praises Amida Buddha and his two fruits of reward—beings and lands. Further, as the verbal act to be performed with the true and sincere mind, one speaks disapprovingly of the pain and evil of one's own and others' two kinds of recompense—beings and environment—such as the three worlds and the six realms of existence. Again, one praises good acts performed by all sentient beings in their three modes of action. If their acts are not good, one should respectfully keep distant from them and not rejoice in such acts. Further, as the bodily act to be performed with the true and sincere mind, one worships and reveres with joined hands Amida Buddha and his two fruits of reward—beings and lands—and makes offerings to them with the four kinds of gifts. Also, as the bodily act to be performed with the true and sincere mind, one loathes and shuns one's own and others' two kinds of recompense—beings and environment—such as the three worlds of samsara. Again, as the mental act to be performed with the true and sincere mind, one contemplates, observes, and is mindful of Amida and his two fruits of reward—beings and lands—feeling as if they were before one's eyes. Also, as the mental act to be performed with the true and sincere mind, one loathes and shuns one's own and others' two kinds of recompense—beings and environment—such as the three worlds of samsara. . . .

Further, one deeply and decisively believes that Śākyamuni Buddha expounds in the *Contemplation Sutra* the three meritorious acts, nine grades of aspirants, and two kinds of good—meditative and non-meditative—and verifies and praises Amida Buddha's two fruits of reward—beings and lands—in order to lead people to adore and aspire for the Pure Land. . . .

Further, deep faith with deep mind is to establish one's belief resolutely on a firm basis, thereby practicing in accord with the teaching, removing doubt forever, and remaining steadfast and unmoved by all different understandings, different practices, other teachings, other views, and biases. . . .

628c

Next, concerning establishing one's belief about practice, there are two kinds of practice: one is right practice and the other is sundry practices. Right practice is to engage solely in the practices as prescribed in the sutras that teach the way to birth in the Pure Land. What is this practice? It is to chant singlemindedly only the *Contemplation Sutra,* the *Amida Sutra,* and the *Sutra on the Buddha of Infinite Life* (i.e., the three Pure Land sutras). It is also to concentrate on, think of, observe, and be mindful of the twofold glorious reward of the Pure Land. When one worships, one should singlemindedly worship Amida Buddha alone. When one recites a name, one should singlemindedly recite Amida's Name alone. When one praises and makes offerings, one should singlemindedly praise and make offerings [to Amida] alone. This is right practice.

Further, right practice is divided into two. One is to recite Amida's Name singlemindedly, whether walking, standing, sitting, or lying down, with uninterrupted, continuous thought and without regard to the length of practice. This is called the act of right assurance, for it is in accord with the Buddha's vow. If one engages in worship, chanting, and so forth, these are called auxiliary acts. Other forms of good than these two kinds of practice are all called sundry practices.

When one performs the act of right assurance and auxiliary acts, one feels close to Amida and one's mindfulness continues without interruption; hence, they are called "uninterrupted [practices]." If one engages in sundry practices, one's thought is constantly interrupted. Although birth can be attained through merit transference [toward the Pure Land], they are all called "alienated" practices.

For the above reasons, this mind is called deep mind.

The third is the mind of aspiring for birth by merit transference. This mind is to aspire for birth in that land by rejoicing in the worldly and supramundane roots of good cultivated with one's acts of body, speech, and mind of past and present lives, and the worldly and supramundane roots of good cultivated with the acts of body, speech, and mind of all ordinary beings and sages, and transferring all the roots of good cultivated by oneself and others to the land with the mind of true deep faith. For this reason, this mind is called the mind of aspiring for birth by merit transference.

He also says:[169]

The meditative good is a means to contemplation [of the faith of Other-Power].

He also says:[170]

The non-meditative good is a means to practice [of the Nembutsu].

He also says:[171]

The essential [gateway] to the Pure Land is difficult to encounter.

He also says:[172]

As stated in the *Contemplation Sutra,* if, first of all, you possess the three minds you will certainly attain birth. What are the three? First, sincere mind: with the act of the body, one worships Amida Buddha; with the act of speech, one praises and extols the Buddha; with the act of mind, one is mindful of the Buddha and contemplates him. Whenever one gives rise to any of the three acts, one unfailingly makes sure that true and sincere mind accompanies it; hence, "sincere mind...." Third, the mind of aspiring for birth by merit transference: one aspires for birth in the Pure Land by transferring to it all the roots of good one has performed. Hence, we call this the mind of aspiring for birth by merit transference. By possessing these three minds, one can definitely attain birth. If any of the three is lacking, one cannot attain birth. The detailed explanation of this is given in the *Contemplation Sutra;* this one should know.

629a

Bodhisattvas who have already freed themselves from birth and death seek to attain the fruit of Buddhahood by transferring to it all the merits of good acts they perform. This is self-benefit. [At the same time,] they teach and guide sentient beings through all future ages. This is benefiting others.

All sentient beings of the present age, being fettered by evil passions, are unable to become liberated from the pain of birth and death in the evil realms. But under favorable conditions they perform practices and aspire to be born in the land of Amida Buddha by transferring quickly all the roots of good toward it. Once they have reached that land, they have no fear. The four kinds of practice mentioned before are naturally and effortlessly performed and both self-benefit and benefiting others are necessarily accomplished. This one should know.

He also says:[173]

Of those who abandon the sole practice [of the Nembutsu] and seek to perform sundry acts, very rarely, one or two out of a hundred or, very rarely, three or five out of a thousand, will attain birth. Why? For the following reasons: miscellaneous conditions confuse their minds and so they lose right mindfulness; they are not in accord with the Buddha's Primal Vow; they run counter to the Buddha's teaching; they do not follow the Buddha's words; their concentration does not continue; their mindfulness is interrupted; their merit transference and aspiration are not sincere and truthful; evil passions, such as greed, anger, and wrong views, arise and disturb their concentration; and they lack the feeling of shame and repentance.

There are three grades of repentance:...high, middle, and low. The high grade of repentance is to shed blood from the pores of one's body and also to shed blood from one's eyes. The middle grade of repentance is to shed hot sweat from the pores of one's whole body and also to shed blood from one's eyes. The low grade of repentance is to feel feverish all over the body and also to shed tears from one's eyes. These three grades of repentance are different from each other, but they can all be carried out by those who have long cultivated the roots of good in the stage leading to liberation. If people in this life revere the Dharma, pay respect to preachers, practice without regard for their lives, and repent even small transgressions, then their repentance will penetrate to their bones and marrow. If repentance is performed in this way, their heavy hindrances, whether accumulated for a long or short time, will instantly dissappear. Unless done in this way, any assiduous practice that one may perform throughout the twelve periods of the day and night will not yield any benefit. Those who do not repent in the proper way should know this. Even though one is unable to shed tears and blood, one will get the same result described above if one thoroughly attains the true faith.

He also says:[174]

It is not stated that [Amida's Light] illuminates and encompasses practitioners of sundry acts other than [the Nembutsu].

He also says:[175]

> The Tathāgata, appearing in the world of the five
> defilements,
> Guides the multitudes of beings appropriately by
> skillful means.
> At times, he teaches that one attains liberation through
> much hearing;
> At times, he teaches that one attains the three
> supernatural faculties through a little understanding.
>
> He also teaches that a joint practice of meritorious acts
> and cultivation of wisdom removes hindrances,
> And that one should be mindful, practicing meditation
> and contemplation while sitting.
> The various Dharma gates all lead to liberation.

He also says:[176]

> Meritorious practices for tens of thousands of *kalpa*s
> are indeed difficult to perform;
> Even for a short time, a hundred thousand evil passions
> intervene.
> If you seek to realize insight into [the non-arising of] all
> *dharma*s in this Sahā world,
> Such a time will never come—even in *kalpa*s as numerous
> as the sands of the Ganges River—while transmigrating
> in the six realms.
>
> Teaching gates that vary according to the practitioners
> are called the "gradual teaching";
> One must perform painful practices for tens of thousands
> of *kalpa*s before realizing the non-arising of all *dharma*s.
> Until the end of your life, you should exclusively recite
> the Nembutsu,

629b

248

As soon as your life ends, the Buddha will come to
  welcome you.

Even in such a short time as taking a meal, [evil passions]
  intervene;
How then can you keep greed and anger from arising for
  tens of thousands of *kalpas*?
Greed and anger are the hindrances to the path leading
  to the reward of heavenly and human beings.
They cause one to dwell in the three evil realms or the
  four realms.

He also says:[177]

Enter the Treasure Land by transferring both the
  meditative and non-meditative good acts toward it.
These are indeed the Tathāgata's special means of
  salvation.
Vaidehī was none other than a woman
At the stage of an ordinary person full of greed and anger.

It is stated in the *Commentary on Vasubandhu's Discourse on
the Pure Land:*

There are two kinds of merit. One is the merit that accrues
from the activity of a defiled mind and is not in accordance
with the Dharma-nature. Such merit arises from the various
good acts of ordinary persons and heavenly beings. It also
refers to the reward of human and heavenly states of existence. Both the cause and effect of such good acts are inverted
and false; hence, they are called "false merit."

It is stated in the *Collection of Passages on the Land of Peace
and Bliss:*

The following passage is quoted from the Moon Matrix section of the *Great Assembly Sutra:*

During the Age of the Decadent Dharma billions of

sentient beings will set out to practice the Way, but not even one will attain the end.

The present age is that of the Decadent Dharma and the world is an evil one with the five defilements. Only the Pure Land gate is open for us to pass through.

It is also stated in the same work:

Before the length of practice reaches ten thousand *kalpas* one cannot escape from the burning house of samsara, because one's thought is inverted and one's practice is subject to regression. Whatever great effort one may make, the reward one acquires is deceptive.

In the *Larger Sutra* the true and provisional vows are established. In the *Contemplation Sutra* the true and provisional teachings are revealed. In the *Smaller Sutra* only the true gate is presented and no provisional good acts are provided. Thus we realize that the true message of the three Pure Land sutras is the selected Primal Vow, which is their essence. The provisional teaching of the three Pure Land sutras is the practice of various good acts, which is their essential message.

Hereupon, when I contemplate the provisional vow (the Nineteenth Vow), I find that there are the true and temporary aspects; also there are practice and faith. This vow is the vow of Amida's appearance at one's deathbed. The practice refers to the good of various meritorious acts. The faith refers to sincere mind, aspiration, and desire for birth. Through the practice and faith of this vow, the essential gate of the Pure Land Way, that is, its provisional and temporary teaching, is revealed.

From this essential gate three types of acts are disclosed: right, auxiliary, and sundry. Within the right and auxiliary acts, exclusive and mixed practices are distinguished. Concerning the practitioners, there are two kinds: practitioners of meditation and those of non-meditation.

There are also two kinds of three minds and two kinds of birth. The two kinds of three minds are meditative three minds and non-meditative three minds. The meditative and non-meditative minds are minds of self-power that are different in each practitioner. The two kinds of birth are immediate birth and provisional birth. Provisional birth is birth in an embryonic state, and borderland; it is birth beneath the twin *śāla* trees. Immediate birth refers to birth by sudden transformation into the Recompensed Land.

In this [*Contemplation*] *Sutra* there is the true aspect, which is the disclosure of adamantine true faith and Amida's embracing and never forsaking. Thus Śākyamuni, the Well-Gone One, who guides beings of this defiled world, proclaimed the vow of sincere mind and joyful faith, because the true cause for birth in the Recompensed Land is joyful faith. Hence, the *Larger Sutra* says "joyfully entrust themselves to me." Entrusting oneself to the Tathāgata's vow and having no doubt about it is called faith. The *Contemplation Sutra* describes this as deep mind—"deep" because it is contrasted with the shallow faith of other practitioners. The *Smaller Sutra* says "singleheartedly"—"single" because no two practices intermingle. Concerning singleheartedness, there are deep and shallow aspects. The deep aspect of it refers to the true faith for benefiting others; the shallow aspect refers to the mind of self-benefit to practice meditative or non-meditative good.

Master [Shan-tao's] intent seems to be as follows. He says,[178]

> The number of the gateways of the excellent practices provided for different capacities of people is eighty-four thousand and more. Gradual and sudden teachings are suited to their capacities. Those who follow favorable conditions all attain liberation.

We note, however, that ordinary and ignorant people, who are constantly immersed in the sea of birth and death, find it hard to cultivate a meditative mind, because this requires the cessation of thought and concentration of the mind. A non-meditative mind is also hard to cultivate, because it requires abolishing evil and practicing good. For this reason, visualizing forms and fixing the mind on them are hard to accomplish; hence, Shan-tao says:[179]

> Even if one dedicates a lifetime of a thousand years, the Dharma eye will not be opened.

How much more difficult it is for practitioners to attain formlessness and no-thought! Therefore, he says:

> The Tathāgata knew beforehand that ordinary people of the latter age defiled by karmic evil would not be able to accomplish even the practice of visualizing forms and concentrating on them—to say nothing of seeking realization without visualizing forms. It would be like building a house in the air without magical means.

Concerning the sentence, "gateways... and more," "gateways" refers to the eighty-four thousand provisional teaching gates, and "more" refers to the oceanlike One-Vehicle teaching of the Primal Vow.

Of all the Buddha's lifetime teachings, those that provide the means of entering sagehood and realizing enlightenment in this world are [collectively] called the path of sages, which is also described as the path of difficult practice. Within this path, there are such teachings as the Mahayana and the Hinayana; gradual and sudden; One Vehicle, two vehicles, and three vehicles; expedient and true; exoteric and esoteric; vertical going out and vertical transcendence. These are self-power teachings, the expedient and provisional ways prescribed by [the bodhisattvas of] the stage of benefiting and teaching others.

Entering sagehood and realizing enlightenment in the Pure Land of Peace and Provision is called the Pure Land path, which is described as the path of easy practice. Within this path, there are such teachings as crosswise going out and crosswise transcendence; temporary and true; gradual and sudden; auxiliary acts, right acts, and sundry acts; and mixed and exclusive performances.

Right acts refer to the five kinds of right acts. Auxiliary acts refer to the five kinds of acts except recitation of the Name. Sundry acts refer to all the various acts other than the right and auxiliary acts; they are the temporary gates of self-power teachings, such as crosswise going out, gradual teaching, meditative and non-meditative [practices], the three kinds of meritorious conduct, and teachings for the three groups of practitioners and the nine levels of aspirants.

Crosswise transcendence is the way of removing the mind of self-power through mindfulness of the Primal Vow; this is called the Other-Power teaching for crosswise transcendence. This is the most exclusive of all the exclusive practices, the most distinguished of all the sudden teachings, the truest of all the true teachings, and the ultimate One-Vehicle teaching of all the One-Vehicle teachings. This is the true essence [of the Pure Land Way], which I have already clarified in the chapter on "Revealing the True Practice." 630a

"Sundry practices" and "mixed performances" contain the same character ("zō," "mixed") but their meanings are different. The character "zō" encompasses thousands of practices. As opposed to the five right acts, there are five sundry acts. The character "zō" implies that understandings and practices of humans, *devas*, and bodhisattvas are mixed up. They are not originally the cause for birth in the Pure Land, but are the good acts which require turning over the mind and transferring their merit; hence, they are called sundry practices of the Pure Land Way. Concerning sundry practices, exclusive practice and exclusive thought are distinguished; also mixed practices and mixed thoughts are distinguished. Exclusive practice is to practice only one good act. Exclusive thought is the mind focused on transferring the merit of practice. Mixed practices with mixed thoughts are mixed practices of various good acts; hence, they are called sundry acts. Mixed thoughts are so called because meditative and non-meditative minds intermingle.

With regard to right and auxiliary acts, exclusive practice and mixed practice are distinguished. Within mixed practices, there are exclusive mind and mixed minds. Exclusive practice is further distinguished into two: recitation of the Buddha's Name only, and five exclusive practices. With regard to these practices, exclusive mind and mixed minds are distinguished. The five exclusive practices are: 1) exclusive worshiping, 2) exclusive chanting [of the Pure Land sutras], 3) exclusive contemplation [of Amida and the Pure Land], 4) exclusive recitation [of the Name], and 5) exclusive praising [of Amida]. These are called the five exclusive practices. Although the same phrase "exclusive practices" is used, it implies different meanings, that is, meditative exclusive practice and non-meditative exclusive practice.

Exclusive mind is the mind concentrated on practicing the five right acts without other thoughts mingled with it; hence, it is called "exclusive mind." This includes both meditative exclusive mind and non-meditative exclusive mind.

Mixed practice is so called because both right and auxiliary acts are jointly practiced. Mixed minds are so called because meditative and non-meditative minds intermingle. This one should discern.

Speaking of all the various practices, Master Tao-ch'o says "myriad practices," Master Shan-tao says "sundry practices," and Master Huai-kan says "various practices." Master Genshin used the same term as Master Huai-kan (various practices), and Master Genkū followed Master Shan-tao (sundry practices). When I examine Master [Shan-tao's] commentaries based on the sutras' exposition, I find that there are within "sundry practices" the following: sundry practice performed with mixed minds, sundry practice with exclusive mind, and exclusive practice with mixed minds; also within "right acts" there are exclusive practice with exclusive mind, exclusive practice with mixed minds, and mixed practices with mixed minds. These are all the karmic causes for birth in the borderland, the womb palace, and the realm of sloth and pride. Therefore, even though one is born in the Land of Utmost Bliss, one is unable to see the Three Treasures, for the light of the Buddha's mind does not illuminate and embrace practitioners of other miscellaneous acts. How meaningful is the [Nineteenth] Vow for temporary guidance! The teaching of the temporary gate and [Shan-tao's] exposition that makes people aspire for the Pure Land have hereby become even clearer.

The two kinds of the three minds in the two sutras are different in their explicit meaning, but one and the same in their implicit meaning. I have thus answered the question concerning the sameness and differences of the two kinds of the three minds.

Question: Are the three minds in the *Larger Sutra,* those in the *Contemplation Sutra,* and the One Mind in the *Smaller Sutra* the same or different?

Answer: With regard to the vow of the true gate (the Twentieth Vow), which is provided as an expedient means, there is practice and faith; also there are the true and the provisional aspects.   630b

This vow is known as the vow of planting roots of virtue. The practice is of two kinds: the roots of good and the roots of virtue. The faith refers to sincere mind, the mind aspiring to merit transference, and desire for birth.

Practitioners are of two kinds: meditative and non-meditative. The birth [they attain] is the incomprehensible birth. The Buddha [who appears before them] is a transformed body. The land [where they are born] is the castle of doubt and the womb palace.

From the example of the *Contemplation Sutra* we can presume that this [*Smaller*] *Sutra,* too, has an explicit meaning and an implicit, hidden, and concealed meaning. In its explicit meaning, the preacher of the sutra abhors and despises the lesser good of all the various practices and sets forth the true gate of roots of good and roots of virtue, thereby encouraging [the Nembutsu practice with] One Mind for self-benefit and urging us to seek the incomprehensible birth. Thus, the sutra says, "[Recitation of the Name is] the cause of the many roots of good, much virtue, and many merits." A commentary says,[180] "The nine levels of aspirants should transfer their merits toward the Pure Land and attain the stage of non-retrogression." It also says:

> Nothing surpasses birth in the Western Land through
>   the Nembutsu;
> The Buddha comes to welcome those who recite the Name
>   even three or five times.

This shows the explicit meaning of the [*Smaller*] *Sutra*. This is the expedient means within the true gate.

In its implicit meaning, the sutra brings forth the true message which is hard to receive in faith. It is meant to reveal the oceanlike inconceivable vow and lead us to the oceanlike unhindered great faith. Since we are urged [to accept this teaching] by Buddhas countless as the sands of the Ganges River, our faith is the faith awakened by the encouragement of Buddhas as countless as the sands of the Ganges River; hence, the sutra says, "the most difficult in the world to accept in faith." The commentary says:[181]

> Amida's Universal Vow has the strong power,
> Enabling ordinary people who recite the Name to attain
>   birth immediately.

This shows the implicit meaning. The [*Smaller*] *Sutra* says "*shūji*" ("hold fast" to [the Name]) and "*isshin*" ("one mind"). "*Shū*" means that the mind is steadfast and unmoving; "*ji*" means that the mind is not distracted or lost. "*Ichi*" (one) means nondual; "*shin*" means true and sincere.

This [*Smaller*] *Sutra* is a Mahayana sutra that the Buddha expounded of his own accord without awaiting questions. Thus, the reason for the Tathāgata's appearance in the world, as evidenced by the witness and protection of Buddhas as countless as the sands of the Ganges River, is solely to present this sutra. Thereupon, the great beings [Nāgārjuna and Vasubandhu], who were among the four dependable sages and who promulgated the sutras, as well as the masters of the Pure Land Way in the three countries, revealed the Nembutsu of the true teaching and so guided the wrong-viewed and deceitful people of the defiled world.

Although in the three Pure Land sutras there are the explicit meaning and the implicit, hidden, and concealed meaning, their essential message is to disclose faith as the cause of entry [into enlightenment]. For this reason, each sutra begins with the remark, "Thus [have I heard]." This opening remark signifies deep faith. When I carefully read the three Pure Land sutras, I find that adamantine true faith is the most essential part. True faith is great faith; great faith is rare, most excellent, truly wonderful, and pure. Why? Because the sea of great faith is extremely difficult to enter, because it arises through the Buddha's power. Conversely, the True Land of Bliss is extremely easy to go to, because one can attain birth there through the Vow-Power.

I have discussed the sameness and differences of the One Mind [of the *Smaller Sutra* and the three minds of the other two sutras]. I hope I have clarified this problem.

I have thus answered the question about the One Mind in the three Pure Land sutras.

[The Twentieth Vow Teaching] 630c

Monks and laypeople of this defiled world should quickly enter the true gate of complete practice of the utmost virtues and aspire for the incomprehensible birth. In the provisional teaching of the true gate there are roots of good and roots of virtue, and also the meditative exclusive mind, the non-meditative exclusive mind, and the meditative and non-meditative mixed mind.

"Mixed mind" means that all good and evil beings, whether of the Mahayana or Hinayana, ordinary people or sages, recite the Name with the thought of performing the right and auxiliary acts in a mixed way. Thus the teaching being followed is that of sudden attainment, but the practitioners who follow it are suited for the teaching of gradual attainment. Although they perform the exclusive practice, their minds are mixed. Hence, this is called "mixed mind."

"Meditative and non-meditative exclusive mind" is the mind that approaches the Primal Vow-Power with the belief in the reward for good acts and retribution for evil ones; this is called the "exclusive mind of self-power."

"Roots of good" refers to the Tathāgata's auspicious Name. Since it fully contains thousands of good acts, it is the root of all good; hence, it is called the root of good. "Roots of virtue," too, refers to the Tathāgata's virtuous Name. When we recite this virtuous Name even once, it fills us with the utmost virtue and transforms all our karmic evil. Since it is the root of the virtuous names of the Buddhas of the three periods throughout the ten directions, it is called the root of virtue.

Hereupon, Śākyamuni Buddha opens the store of virtue and guides beings of the defiled worlds of the ten directions. Amida Tathāgata made the Vow of accomplishing the ultimate salvation (the Twentieth Vow) to guide compassionately all the multitudinous beings. We already have the compassionate vow, which is called "the vow of planting roots of virtue," "the vow ensuring the birth of those who direct their thoughts [to the Pure Land]," and also "the vow of unfailing accomplishment of the ultimate salvation;" it can also be called "the vow of sincere mind and merit transference."

The [Twentieth] Vow says in the *Larger Sutra:*

If, when I attain Buddhahood, sentient beings in the lands of the ten directions who, having heard my Name, concentrate their thoughts on my land, plant roots of virtue, and sincerely transfer their merits toward my land with a desire to be born there should not eventually fulfill their aspiration, may I not attain perfect enlightenment.

It is also said in the same sutra:

Although they doubt these wisdoms, they still believe in retribution for evil and reward for virtue and so cultivate a store of merit, aspiring for birth in that land. Such beings are born in a palace.

It is also said in the same sutra:

Without a store of good from former lives,
One cannot hear this sutra;
But those who have strictly observed the precepts
Can hear the Right Dharma.

It is stated in the *Teaching Assembly of the Tathāgata of Infinite Life:*

If, when I attain Buddhahood, all the sentient beings in the countless lands who, having heard my Name expounded, make use of it as their own root of good and transfer its merit toward the Land of Utmost Bliss, should not be born there, may I not attain *bodhi.*

It is stated in the *Sutra on the Immeasurably Pure and Equal Enlightenment:*

Those who do not have this merit
Cannot hear the name of this sutra;
Only those who have strictly observed the precepts
Have now heard the Right Dharma.

Evil, arrogant, corrupt, and indolent people
Cannot readily accept this teaching;
But those who met Buddhas in their past lives
Will rejoice to hear the teaching of the World-honored One. 631a

It is rare to obtain human life,
And difficult to encounter a Buddha in this world;
Hard it is to attain the wisdom of faith;
Once you have heard the Dharma, pursue it with diligence.

The *Contemplation Sutra* states:

The Buddha further said to Ānanda, "Bear these words well in mind. To bear these words in mind means to hold fast to the Name of [the Buddha of Infinite Life]."

The *Amida Sutra* states:

[O]ne cannot attain birth in that land with few roots of good or a small store of merit.... [If you hear of Amida Buddha, hold fast to] his Name....

The Master of Kuang-ming Temple says:[182]

Although many other practices are called good acts, when compared with the Nembutsu they cannot match it. For this reason, the efficacy of the Nembutsu is widely praised in many sutras. For example, in the Forty-eight Vows in the *Larger Sutra* it is clarified that one can attain birth simply by exclusive recitation of Amida's Name. Also, the *Amida Sutra* says, "One can attain birth by exclusively reciting Amida's Name for one to seven days." Furthermore, the testimony of the Buddhas of the ten directions, countless as the sands of the Ganges River, has not been made in vain. In the passages on meditative and non-meditative good in this [*Contemplation*] *Sutra,* it is shown that one can attain birth simply by exclusively reciting the Name. These are a few of many examples. This completes an extensive exposition of the Nembutsu *samādhi.*

He also says:[183]

Again, one should deeply and decidedly believe that in the *Amida Sutra* Buddhas of the ten directions, countless as the sands of the Ganges River, give testimony to all ordinary people, encouraging them to seek birth with assurance....

The Buddhas' words and acts never disagree. When Śākyamuni urges all ordinary people to dedicate themselves to the exclusive recitation and exclusive practice with the assurance of their birth in that land after death, this teaching is equally praised, recommended, and testified to by all the Buddhas of the ten directions. Why? Because they all possess the great compassion that arises from the same enlightenment. One Buddha's teaching is the same as all Buddhas' teachings; all Buddhas' teachings are the same as one Buddha's teaching. It is just as expounded in the *Amida Sutra....*

[The sutra] urges all ordinary people to recite exclusively
Amida's Name singleheartedly for one to seven days, assur-
ing them of their unfailing attainment of birth. In the passage below, it is stated that in each direction there are
Buddhas as countless as the sands of the Ganges River who
all praise Śākyamuni:

> In the evil age of the five defilements, in this evil world,
> when evil sentient beings, evil passions, wrongdoings,
> and disbeliefs are rampant, Śākyamuni particularly
> praises Amida's Name and urges sentient beings to recite
> it, assuring them of their unfailing attainment of birth.

This is the testimony.

Further, the Buddhas of the ten directions, fearing that
sentient beings might not accept the teaching of one Buddha,
Śākyamuni, extend their tongues in one accord and simultaneously, covering with them the three thousand worlds and
expounding the words of truth and sincerity:

> Sentient beings, you should all accept what Śākyamuni
> has taught, praised, and testified to. When all ordinary
> people, regardless of whether their evil or merit is great
> or small and whether they practice for a long or short
> time, exclusively recite Amida's Name singleheartedly   631b
> for up to a hundred years or even one to seven days, they
> will certainly attain birth beyond any doubt.

This shows that one Buddha's teaching is testified to by
all the Buddhas. This is called "establishing faith with regard
to persons."

He also says:[184]

When I ponder the intent of the Buddha's Vow, I find that
he solely encourages right mindfulness and recitation of the
Name. In enabling us to attain birth quickly, this practice
cannot be compared with acts performed with mixed and

distracted thoughts. What this sutra and other scriptures widely praise in various places can be summarized as urging us to recite the Name. This one should know.

He also says:[185]

The passage [in the *Contemplation Sutra*] beginning with "The Buddha further said to Ānanda, 'Bear these words well in mind,'" shows that Śākyamuni entrusted Amida's Name to Ānanda so that it would be transmitted to distant generations. Although Śākyamuni has above expounded the benefit of both meditative and non-meditative practices, in view of the Buddha's Primal Vow, he meant to urge sentient beings to dedicate themselves solely to recite Amida Buddha's Name.

He also says:[186]

The Land of Utmost Bliss is the nirvana realm of
    non-action:
I fear it is difficult to be born by doing various good acts
    in accordance with given conditions.
Hence, the Tathāgata selected the essential method—
He urged us exclusively to be mindful of Amida
    singleheartedly.

He also says:[187]

As this cosmic period draws to a close, the five defilements
    flourish;
Sentient beings are so full of wrong views that they
    find it hard to have faith.
Although we are taught to dedicate ourselves wholly to
    the Nembutsu to take the path to the [Western Land],
Our faith is destroyed by others and so we find ourselves
    remaining as we were before.
We have always been like this since innumerable
    *kalpa*s ago;
It is not that we realize this for the first time in this life.

Because we have not encountered the excellent, strong
     power,
We have been transmigrating while unable to attain
     liberation.

He also says:[188]

Although the various Dharma gates all lead to liberation,
None of them surpasses birth in the Western Land
     through the Nembutsu.
When we recite the Nembutsu throughout life, or even
     ten times,
Or three or five times, the Buddha will come to welcome us.
Amida's Universal Vow has the strong power,
Enabling ordinary people who recite the Name to attain
     birth immediately.

He also says:[189]

All Tathāgatas provide skillful means;
The present sage Śākyamuni does the same.
As he expounds the Dharma in accordance with people's
     capacities, they all receive benefit;
Let each of them attain realization and understanding
     and enter the true gate....
The Buddha's teaching has many gates, numbering
     eighty-four thousand,
Precisely because the capacities of beings are different.
If you are seeking the eternal abode of peace and bliss,
First choose a practice of primary importance and,
     through it, enter the true gate.

He also says:[190]

From what I see and hear about the monks and laypeople
everywhere these days, there are different understandings
and practices—with the difference of exclusive and miscellaneous practices. If they but practice the Nembutsu with

singleness of mind, ten out of ten will be born. If they perform miscellaneous practices, not even one in a thousand will attain birth, because they lack sincere mind.

Master Yüan-chao's *Commentary on the Amida Sutra* states:

> The Tathāgata wishes to clarify the excellent merit of holding fast to the Name. First, he disparages other good acts as small roots of good. That is to say, all the acts of merit—for example, charity, observance of the precepts, construction of temples, making images, worshiping, chanting, meditation, repentance, and ascetic practices—are called small good acts, if they are not accompanied by true faith but are transferred toward the Pure Land with aspiration for birth there. They are not the cause of birth. If one holds fast to the Name in accord with this sutra, one will definitely attain birth. Hence, we realize that recitation of the Name is the act of many roots of good and many merits.
>
> Formerly I had this understanding, but people had doubts about this. Recently, I obtained a copy of the sutra engraved on a stone monument at Hsiang-yang and found that this text agreed with the hidden truth [of the *Amida Sutra*]. So people began to cultivate deep faith. The text reads:
>
> > Sons and daughters of good families, having heard an exposition of Amida Buddha, exclusively recite his Name with a concentrated and undistracted mind. It is through recitation of the Name that your karmic evils will be destroyed. This is the act of many virtues, many roots of good, and many merits.

631c

It is stated in the *Commentary*[191] by [Chih-yüan] of Mount Ku:

> Concerning "holding fast (*'shūji'*) to the Name," "*shū*" (fast) means to accept firmly; "*ji*" means to keep. Through the power of faith, one firmly accepts the Name in one's heart. Through the power of mindfulness, one keeps it without forgetting.

The *Larger Sutra* states:

It is difficult to encounter and behold a Tathāgata when he is in this world. Difficult to access, difficult to hear are the Buddhas' teachings and scriptures. It is also difficult to hear the excellent teachings for bodhisattvas, the *pāramitās* (perfections). Difficult too is it to meet a good teacher, to hear the Dharma, and perform the practices. But most difficult of all difficulties is to hear this sutra, have faith in it with joy, and hold fast to it. Nothing is more difficult than this. Thus have I formed my Dharma, thus have I expounded my Dharma, thus have I taught my Dharma. You must receive it and practice it by the method prescribed.

It is stated in the *Nirvana Sutra*:[192]

I have stated in this sutra, "The factor that makes all the sacred practices possible is the good teacher. Although the factors that make all the sacred practices possible are innumerable, if the good teacher is presented as one, it contains all the rest." I have expounded, "All evil acts are based on wrong views. Although the causes of all the evil acts are innumerable, if wrong views are presented as one, it contains all the rest." I have also stated, "The cause of highest, perfect *bodhi* is faith. Although the causes of *bodhi* are innumerable, if faith is presented as one, it contains all the rest."

It is also stated in the same sutra:[193]

Sons of good families, there are two kinds of faith: one is accepting in faith and the other is pursuing. Such people, although they accept the teaching in faith, cannot pursue it. Hence, they are described as possessing imperfect faith.

Again, there are two kinds of faith: one is the faith that arises from hearing, and the other is the faith that arises from reflection. These people's faith arises from hearing and not from reflection. Hence, they are described as possessing imperfect faith.

Again, there are two kinds [of faith]: one is to believe that
there is a path to enlightenment, and the other is to believe
that there are people who have attained it. These people's
faith only accepts that there is a path to enlightenment but
does not accept that there are people who have attained it.
This is described as possessing imperfect faith.

Again, there are two kinds [of faith]: one is to believe in
the right teaching, and the other is to believe in wrong teachings. To accept that there is the law of causality and that
Buddha, Dharma, and Sangha exist is to believe in the right
teaching. To reject the law of causality, to state that the Three
Treasures have different natures, and to believe in wrong
words and [wrong teachers, such as] Pūraṇa[-kāśyapa], is to
believe in wrong teachings. These people, although they
believe in the [Three] Treasures of Buddha, Dharma, and
Sangha, do not accept that the Three Treasures are the same
in essence; although they believe in the law of causality, they
do not accept that there are people who have attained the
Way. This is described as possessing imperfect faith, and
these people are the ones who have imperfect faith....

632a

Sons of good families, there are four good acts that bring
evil results. What are the four? The first is to recite sutras
in order to show that one is superior to others. The second is
to observe the precepts in order to gain profit. The third is to
practice charity in order to gain followers. The fourth is to
practice concentration and contemplation in order to reach
the realm of neither thought nor no-thought. These four good
acts bring evil results. Those who practice these four are
described as "those who sink and, after having sunk, emerge;
and after having emerged, sink again." Why do they sink?
Because they are desirous of the states of existence in the
three worlds. Why do they emerge? Because they see the
bright path. To see the bright path is to hear the teaching of
precepts (śīla), charity (dāna), and meditation (dhyāna). Why
do they sink again? Because their wrong views increase and

arrogance is produced. For this reason, I say in two verses in the sutra:

> If there are sentient beings who, desirous of various
>   states of existence,
> Perform good and evil acts in order to attain these
>   states,
> They lose sight of the path to nirvana.
> They are described as emerging briefly and sinking
>   again.
>
> Those who practice the Way in the dark ocean of birth
>   and death
> And attain liberation but still have evil passions,
> Are bound to receive evil results.
> They are described as emerging briefly and sinking
>   again.

For the Tathāgata, there are two kinds of nirvana: one is conditioned and the other is unconditioned. Conditioned nirvana lacks eternity, bliss, complete freedom, and purity; unconditioned nirvana possesses eternity, bliss, complete freedom, and purity....

These people deeply believe that the two kinds of precepts both bring about good results. Hence, they are described as possessing imperfect precepts. Such people lack faith and precepts and also, however much teaching they may hear, it is imperfect.

What is called "imperfect hearing"? To accept only half of the twelve divisions of the scriptures expounded by the Tathāgata and reject the other half—this is called "imperfect hearing." Also, even if one upholds these six divisions of scriptures, one cannot recite them and so one's exposition of the scriptures cannot benefit others; this is called "imperfect hearing." Further, having received the six divisions of the scriptures, one upholds, recites, and expounds them for the sake of disputation, in order to defeat others in discussions, to gain profit, or for secular purposes; this is called "imperfect hearing."

It is also stated in the same sutra:[194]

Sons of good families, the first and foremost true good teachers are bodhisattvas and Buddhas, the World-honored Ones. For what reason? Because of their three skillful controlling powers. What are the three? The first is extremely gentle words; the second is extremely stern rebukes; and the third is both gentle words and stern rebukes. Because of these, bodhisattvas and Buddhas are true good teachers.

632b   Again, sons of good families, Buddhas and bodhisattvas are considered to be great physicians; hence, they are called good teachers. For what reason? Because they know illnesses and the medicines to cure them, and they prescribe the medicine in correspondence with the illnesses. This is like a good physician, who is well acquainted with the eight kinds of medical arts. He first observes the symptoms, of which there are three types. What are the three? They are symptoms related to wind, fever, and water. To the patient of a wind disease, ghee is administered. To the patient of fever disease, crystalized sugar is given. To the patient of water disease, ginger infusion is prescribed. Because the physician knows well the root of the illness, he is able to administer the appropriate medicine and cure it. Hence, he is called a good physician.

Buddhas and bodhisattvas are like this. They know all the illnesses of ordinary people, which fall into three types: greed, anger, and ignorance. Those who have the illness of greed are urged to contemplate a human skeleton. Those who have the illness of anger are led to contemplate compassion. Those who have the illness of ignorance are made to contemplate the twelve conditioned originations. Because of this, the Buddhas and bodhisattvas are called good teachers. Sons of good families, just as a ferryman who safely carries people across the water is called a great ferryman, so it is with Buddhas and bodhisattvas; because they ferry sentient beings across the great ocean of birth and death, they are called good teachers.

It is stated in the *Garland Sutra:*[195]

When you think of your good teachers,
Think of them as your parents who gave birth to you.
They are like a nursing mother who nourished you
    with her milk.
They cause the elements of *bodhi* to grow in you.

They are like a physician who cures your illnesses,
Like a *deva* raining down nectar,
Like the sun showing us the right way,
And like the moon turning its pure orb.

It is also stated in the same sutra:[196]

The Tathāgata, the Great Compassionate One,
Appears in this world,
And for the sake of all sentient beings,
Turns the wheel of the supreme Dharma.

For the sake of sentient beings the Tathāgata
Diligently practiced the Way for innumerable *kalpa*s;
How could all the world repay
The benevolence of the Great Master?

The Master of Kuang-ming Temple says:[197]

How regrettable it is that sentient beings doubt what
    should not be doubted!
The Pure Land is before your eyes; it should not be denied.
Do not argue whether Amida embraces you or not;
What is essential is whether or not you singlemindedly
    direct your thoughts [toward the Pure Land].

They say [to each other] that from now until the time
    they attain Buddhahood,

They will repay the Buddha's benevolence by praising him
for a long *kalpa*.
If not blessed by the great power of Amida's Vow,
When and in which *kalpa* would we be able to escape
from this Sahā world?

How can you expect to reach the Treasure Land now?
It is indeed due to the power of the Great Master of the
Sahā world.
Without the exhortation of the Great Master, our good
teacher,
How can you enter the Pure Land of Amida?

By attaining birth in the Pure Land, repay your
indebtedness to the compassionate benevolence.

He also says:[198]

It is extremely difficult to meet an age in which a
Buddha appears;
Difficult it is for a person to realize the wisdom of faith.
To be able to hear the Dharma that is rarely met with
Is by far the most difficult of all.

To attain faith yourself and guide others to faith
Is the most difficult of all difficulties.
To guide all beings universally with great compassion
Is truly to repay your indebtedness to the Buddha's
benevolence.

He also says:[199]

Let us go home!

Do not stay in other lands.
Following the Buddha, let us return to our original home!
Once we have returned to our original land,
All our vows and practices will be spontaneously fulfilled.

Tears of joy and sorrow stream down. As we deeply reflect
    on ourselves,
We realize: If Śākyamuni Buddha had not awakened us,   632c
When would we be able to hear Amida's Name and Vow?
Although we feel the weight of the Buddha's
    compassionate benevolence, it is indeed difficult
    to repay it.

He also says:[200]

Beings of the ten directions have all been transmigrating in
the six realms without end. They have been interminably
floundering in the waves of desire and sinking in the sea of
suffering over many lifetimes. It is rare to meet with the
Buddha's Way and receive a human form, but I have now
received them. It is difficult to hear the Pure Land teaching,
but I have now heard it. It is hard to awaken faith, but I have
now awakened it.

[Concluding Remarks]

I truly realize that those who engage in exclusive performance
with mixed minds do not attain great joy. Hence, the master (Shan-
tao) said:[201]

These people do not feel gratitude for the Buddha's benevolence. Even when they perform practices they are arrogant
and disdainful, and their acts are always accompanied by the
desire for fame and wealth. Being naturally covered by self-
attachment, they do not associate with fellow believers and
good teachers. Accordingly, they choose to approach various
worldly affairs, thereby creating hindrances to their own and
others' performance of the right practice for birth.

How sad it is that the ordinary, ignorant people who possess
defilements and hindrances, from the beginningless past up to the
present, have had no opportunity for deliverance because they are

prone to perform the right and auxiliary acts in a mixed way and their minds vacillate between meditative and non-meditative practices. As I reflect upon the cycle of transmigration, I realize that it is difficult to take refuge in the Buddha's Vow-Power and enter the sea of great faith even in the passage of *kalpas* as numerous as the number of particles obtained by grinding the earth. How deplorable it is! I should deeply sorrow over this.

Generally speaking, sages of the Mahayana and the Hinayana and all good people hold to the auspicious Name of the Primal Vow as their own root of good. For this reason, they cannot awaken faith, realize Buddha wisdom, and understand Amida's intent in establishing the cause of birth; hence, they cannot enter his Land of Recompense.

[Conversion Through the Three Vows]

Now, I, Gutoku Shinran, disciple of Śākyamuni, having respectfully accepted the exposition of the master of discourse (Vasubandhu) and the exhortation of the master of this school (Shantao), left forever the temporary gate of the thousands of practices and various good acts, and departed from the teaching for birth beneath the twin *śāla* trees. Having converted to the true gate of cultivating the roots of good and the roots of virtue, I wholeheartedly awakened the aspiration for incomprehensible birth. However, I have now finally left the provisional true gate and turned into the sea of the best-selected vow. Having abandoned at once the aspiration for the incomprehensible birth, I am now assured of attaining the inconceivable birth. How significant is the vow of accomplishing the ultimate salvation (the Twentieth Vow)! Having entered, once and for all, the sea of the vow, I deeply realize the Buddha's benevolence. In order to repay his utmost virtue, I collect the essential passages of the true teaching and am always mindful of the sea of inconceivable virtue. More and more do I appreciate it, and especially receive it with gratitude.

[The Path of Sages]

I truly realize that the various teachings of the path of sages were intended for the period when the Buddha was in the world and for the Age of the Right Dharma, and not for the Ages of the Semblance Dharma, the Decadent Dharma, and the Extinct Dharma. The time for those teachings has already passed and they do not correspond to the capacities of people. The true teaching of the Pure Land Way, however, compassionately and equally leads to the Way the multitudes of defiled and evil beings of the period when the Buddha was in the world, the Ages of the Right Dharma, the Semblance Dharma, the Decadent Dharma, and the Extinct Dharma as well.

According to the Buddha's exposition and the masters' commentaries, sutras preached by different kinds of people fall into five groups: first, those expounded by the Buddha; second, those expounded by his holy disciples; third, those expounded by heavenly beings or saints; fourth, those expounded by spirits; and fifth, those expounded by apparitional beings. Of the five, the last four kinds of expositions cannot be relied upon. The three [Pure Land] sutras are the Great Sage's own exposition. 633a

The *Commentary on the Perfection of Great Wisdom Sutra* explains the four reliances as follows:

> When Śākyamuni was about to enter nirvana, he said to the monks, "From today on, rely on the Dharma, not on the people who expound it. Rely on the meaning, not on the words. Rely on wisdom, not on discriminative mind. Rely on the sutras that fully disclose the Buddha's true intent, not on those that do not.
>
> "Concerning reliance on the Dharma, the Dharma refers to the twelve divisions of scriptures. Follow them, not the people who expound them.
>
> "Concerning reliance on the meaning, the meaning is beyond discussion of whether or not one likes it, whether it

produces karmic evil or merit, or whether it is true or false. Words have meaning but the meaning is not the words. To give an illustration: when someone shows me where the moon is by pointing to it with his finger, I look only at the finger and not at the moon. The man would say, "I am showing you where the moon is by pointing to it. Why do you look only at my finger and not at the moon?" Similarly, words are like a finger pointing to the meaning; they are not the meaning itself. Hence, I say that you should not rely on words.

"Concerning reliance on wisdom, wisdom weighs and distinguishes good and evil; the discriminative mind always seeks pleasure and does not reach the right path to enlightenment. Hence, I say that you should not rely on the discriminative mind.

"Concerning reliance on the sutras that fully disclose the Buddha's true intent, of all the sages, the Buddha is foremost; of all the scriptures, the Buddha-Dharma is foremost; of all people, monks are foremost."

The Buddha regarded the sentient beings of an age in which there is no Buddha in the world as possessed of heavy karmic evil. They are the ones who have not cultivated the roots of good for seeing a Buddha.

Therefore, monks and laypeople of the latter age should discern the four reliances in practicing the Dharma.

Now, based on the true intent of the Buddha's teaching and the expositions made and transmitted by the masters of the past, I will clarify that the path of sages is provisional and the Pure Land path is true, and caution people against non-Buddhist teachings, which are perverted, false, and wrong. I will also determine the year of the Tathāgata Śākyamuni's passing into nirvana and make clear distinctions between the Ages of the Right Dharma, the Semblance Dharma, and the Decadent Dharma.

In connection with this, Master Tao-ch'o of Hsüan-chung Temple says:[202]

Those who practice the Way continuously and without cessation reach the stage of non-retrogression for the first time after ten thousand *kalpas*. Ordinary people of today are called "those of faith as light as feathers." They are also called "[bodhisattvas in] name only," "those not definitely established," and "ordinary beings outside the ranks." They have not yet departed from the burning house of samsara.

In the *Bodhisattva Ornament Sutra* (*P'u-sa ying-lo pen yeh*), the stages of practice leading to enlightenment are distinguished. Since [the course of stage-by-stage progression] is naturally set, this course is called the path of difficult practice.

[The Three Dharma Ages]

Master Tao-ch'o also says in the same work:

I will disclose the reason why the Pure Land teaching has arisen and urge people to follow this teaching by relating it to the times and the people. If the people, the teaching, and the times do not agree with each other, it is difficult to practice and enter the Way. The *Sutra on Mindfulness of the Right Dharma* (*Saddharma-smṛty-upasthāna-sūtra*) states:

When practitioners singleheartedly seek the Way,
They should always observe the times and the method
 of practice;
If the times are not opportune, the method of practice
 is not applicable.
This is called loss, not gain.

The reason is that it is just as one cannot make fire by rubbing wet wood, for the time is not opportune. It is also like seeking water by breaking dry wood and failing to obtain water. In this case, wisdom is lacking.

It is stated in the Moon Matrix section of the *Great Assembly Sutra:*

633b

275

During the first five hundred years after the Buddha's passing into nirvana, my disciples will be steadfast in learning wisdom. During the second five hundred years, they will be steadfast in learning meditation. During the third five hundred years, they will be steadfast in learning much teaching and chanting sutras. During the fourth five hundred years, they will be steadfast in constructing pagodas and temples, and performing meritorious acts and repentance. During the fifth five hundred years, the pure Dharma will be hidden and there will be much conflict and debate; but a little good Dharma will be still left, which they will practice steadfastly.

As I reflect on sentient beings of the present, I find that we are in the fourth five-hundred-year period after the Buddha's passing, and so this is the age in which we should repent for the evil done in the past, perform meritorious acts, and recite the Buddha's Name. When we recite the Name of Amida Buddha even once, our karmic evil which would cause us to transmigrate in birth and death for eighty *koṭi*s of *kalpa*s is eliminated. Such is the merit of one recitation of the Name. Those who constantly practice recitation are the ones who always repent themselves.

[Master Tao-ch'o] also says in the same work:

I will distinguish the duration of the sutras in the world. Śākyamuni Buddha's lifetime teachings lasted for five hundred years in the Age of the Right Dharma and for a thousand years in the Age of the Semblance Dharma. In the Age of the Decadent Dharma, which will last for ten thousand years, the number of sentient beings will decrease and the sutras will all disappear. The Tathāgata [Śākyamuni], out of pity for the sentient beings who suffer from the pain of burning, had this sutra (the *Larger Sutra*), in particular, survive and remain in the world for a hundred more years.

He also says in the same work:

The *Great Assembly Sutra* states:

> During the Age of the Decadent Dharma billions of sentient beings will practice the Way, but not even one will attain the end.

The present age is that of the Decadent Dharma and the world is an evil one with the five defilements. Only the Pure Land gate is open for us to pass through.

[The Last Dharma Age]

Now the multitudes of this evil and defiled world, ignorant of the distinctive features of the Age of the Decadent Dharma, criticize the manners of monks and nuns. People of the present, both monks and laypeople, should reflect on their own capacities.

Let us consider the teachings of the three ages. When we examine the time of the Tathāgata's complete nirvana, we find that it falls on the fifty-first year (the water/monkey year) of the reign of Mu, the fifth emperor of the Chou dynasty. From that [water/monkey year] to the first year of Gennin (the wood/monkey year) in this country it is two thousand one hundred and eighty-three years.[203] If we calculate based on the *Auspicious Kalpa Sutra* (*Bhadrakalpika-sūtra**), the *Benevolent King Sutra* (*Kāruṇikā-rājā-prajñāpāramitā-sūtra**), and the *Nirvana Sutra,* we find that six hundred and eighty-three years[204] have already passed since the Age of the Decadent Dharma began.

The *Candle of the Latter Dharma* (*Mappō-tōmyō-ki*) [by Saichō] reads as follows:

> The one who guides beings based on Oneness is the Dharma King; the one who reigns over the four seas with virtue is the Benevolent King. The Benevolent King and the Dharma King work together to enlighten beings and spread the teaching by harmonizing the supramundane truth with the mundane

truth. Consequently, the profound scriptures fill the whole country, and the beneficent teaching reaches everywhere under heaven.

Foolish monks all follow heaven's mandate and respectfully submit to strict punishment, while they are never at ease.

With regard to the Dharma, there are three ages and people are divided into three levels. The teaching for guiding us and the precepts change according to the times, and words of praise or condemnation are applied to people of different ages. In the three ages, practice of the Dharma thrives and declines in various ways, and people of the five five hundred-year periods attain wisdom and enlightenment differently. How can people be saved by only one path? How can they be disciplined by only one guiding principle? For this reason, I will clarify the distinctive features of the Ages of the Right Dharma, the Semblance Dharma, and the Decadent Dharma, and attempt to disclose the matters concerning observance and violation of the precepts in the sangha. There are three sections: first, ascertaining the theory of the Ages of the Right, Semblance, and Decadent Dharma; second, clarification of the matters concerning observance and violation of the precepts in the sangha; and third, scriptural evidence concerning these matters.

633c

First, ascertaining the theory of the Ages of the Right, Semblance, and Decadent Dharma: There are various different theories, one of which will be presented. K'uei-chi, a Mahayana master, cites the *Auspicious Kalpa Sutra* (actually, a passage adopted from the *Sutra on Maitreya's Ascent to the Tuṣita Heaven* [*Mi leng shang sheng ching*]), saying:

> After the Buddha's complete nirvana, the Right Dharma will last for five hundred years, and the Semblance Dharma for a thousand years. After this period of one thousand five hundred years, Śākyamuni's Dharma will perish.

The Age of the Decadent Dharma is not mentioned here. According to other explanations, [the Age of the Right Dharma lasts one thousand years. But,] since nuns do not observe the eight rules of respectful attitude and become indolent, the Age of the [Right] Dharma does not extend further [than five hundred years]. Hence, I do not adopt this theory.

The *Nirvana Sutra* says:

In the Age of the Decadent Dharma, one hundred and twenty thousand great bodhisattvas uphold the Dharma and keep it from perishing.

Since this statement concerns bodhisattvas of higher ranks, it does not suit our purposes.

Question: Then what are the main happenings during the fifteen hundred-year period?

Answer: It is stated in the *Mahāmāyā Sutra* (*Mo he mo i ching*):

During the first five hundred years after the Buddha's passing into nirvana, the seven holy sages, such as Mahā-kāśyapa, will successively uphold the Right Dharma and keep it from perishing. The Right Dharma will perish after five hundred years.

During the following century, the ninety-five kinds of non-Buddhist teachings will compete with each other for ascendancy. Then Aśvaghoṣa will appear and subdue all the non-Buddhist teachings.

During the seventh century, Nāgārjuna will appear in the world and tear up the banners of wrong views.

During the eighth century, monks will become self-indulgent and unruly in their behavior, and so only one or two will attain the fruit of the Way.

During the ninth century, male and female servants will be made into monks and nuns.

During the tenth century, when they hear the teaching of the contemplation of impurity, they will become angry and show no sign of interest.

During the eleventh century, monks and nuns will take wives and husbands, and thus break and abuse the precepts.

During the twelfth century, monks and nuns will have children.

During the thirteenth century, the color of the monks' robes will be changed to white.

During the fourteenth century, the four kinds of disciples will be like hunters, and will sell things belonging to the Three Treasures.

During the fifteenth century, two monks in the land of Kauśāmbī will engage in dispute and finally kill each other. As a result, the Buddha's teachings will be stored away in the dragons' palace.

This passage is also found in the *Nirvana Sutra,* fascicle eighteen, and in the *Benevolent King Sutra.* According to these sutras, after fifteen centuries there will be no precepts (*śīla*), meditation (*samādhi*), or wisdom (*prajñā*). Therefore, the *Great Assembly Sutra,* fascicle fifty-one, states:

During the first five hundred years after my passing into nirvana, monks and others will be steadfast in attaining liberation in accord with the Right Dharma. (The first attainment of the fruit of sagehood is described as "liberation.") During the next five hundred years, they will be steadfast in practicing meditation. During the next five hundred years, they will be steadfast in hearing much teaching. During the next five hundred years, they will be steadfast in constructing temples. During the last five hundred years, they will be steadfast in engaging in disputes and so the pure Dharma will be hidden away....

This passage means that during the first three of the five five hundred-year periods, the three learnings of precepts, meditation, and wisdom will be steadfastly upheld in due order. These three periods correspond to the Age of the Right Dharma, lasting five hundred years, and the Age of the Semblance Dharma, lasting a thousand years. The period after that, of constructing temples, is the Age of the Decadent Dharma. This is why K'uei-chi says in the *Commentary on the Diamond Sutra* (*Chin-kang pan-lo ching tsan shu*):

634a

> The Age of the Right Dharma lasts five hundred years and that of the Semblance Dharma lasts a thousand years. After the period of fifteen hundreed years, the Right Dharma will perish.

For this reason, we know that the age following this period is the Age of the Decadent Dharma.

Question: If that is so, to which age does the present period belong?

Answer: There are many theories concerning the years that have passed since the Buddha's nirvana. I will present two theories for now. First, Master Fa-shang and others, based on the *Chou Dynasty Record of Miraculous Events* (*Chou shou i chih*), say:

> The Buddha entered nirvana in the fifty-first year[205] (the water/monkey year) of the reign of Mu Wang-man, the fifth lord of the Chou dynasty.

According to this theory, from that water/monkey year to the present-day, twentieth year of Enryaku (the metal/snake year),[206] it is one thousand seven hundred and fifty years.

Second, Fei Ch'ang-fang and others, based on the *Spring and Autumn Annals* (*Ch'un ch'iu*) of the state of Lu, say:

The Buddha entered nirvana in the fourth year (the water/rat year)[207] of the reign of K'uang Wang-pan, the twenty-first lord of the Chou dynasty.

According to this theory, from that water/rat year to the present-day twentieth year of Enryaku (the metal/snake year)[208] is one thousand four hundred and ten years. Thus, the present period belongs to the end of the Age of the Semblance Dharma. The monks' behavior in this period is already the same as in the Age of the Decadent Dharma.

In the Age of the Decadent Dharma, only the words and teachings of the Buddha remain and neither practice nor enlightenment is possible. If there were precepts, there would be violation of the precepts. Since there are no longer precepts, what precept can one break to constitute violation of the precepts? Since no violation of the precepts is possible, how could there be observance of the precepts? Therefore, the *Great Assembly Sutra* says:

> After the Buddha's nirvana, Buddhists without precepts will fill the land.

Question: In the sutras and the Vinaya texts, those who have broken the precepts are refused permission to enter the sangha. Even those who have broken the precepts are thus treated; how much more so are those without precepts? If I am to repeat the remark about the Age of the Decadent Dharma, there are no precepts in this age. How could one feel the pain without a wound?

Answer: Your reasoning is wrong. The monks' behavior during the Ages of the Right, Semblance, and Decadent Dharma is extensively described in many sutras. Who is there, whether monk or layperson, within the sangha or outside it, who has not read about this? Why should they be too greedily attached to a wrong way of life to conceal the Right Dharma that is the support of the country? In the Age of the Decadent

Dharma of which we are speaking, there are monks in name only. However, we regard these nominal monks as true treasures of the world, for there are no other fields of merit. If in the Age of the Decadent Dharma there were some who observe the precepts, they would appear very strange [to us, as if] a tiger [were to appear] in the marketplace. Who would believe such a thing?

Question: The monks' behavior in the Ages of the Right, Semblance, and Decadent Dharma is described in various sutras. Is it stated in the sacred scriptures that in the Age of the Decadent Dharma nominal monks should be regarded as true treasures of the world?

Answer: It is stated in the *Great Assembly Sutra,* fascicle nine:

It is just as genuine gold is regarded as the priceless treasure. If there were no genuine gold, silver would be regarded as the priceless treasure. If silver were not available, brass, the spurious treasure, would be regarded as priceless. If there were no spurious treasure, copper or nickel, iron, pewter, or lead would be regarded as priceless. All of these are treasures in the world but the Buddha-Dharma is priceless. If there is no treasure of the Buddha, the *pratyekabuddha* is supreme. If there is no *pratyekabuddha,* the arhat is supreme. If there is no arhat, other sages are regarded as supreme. If there are no other sages, ordinary people who have attained meditative states are regarded as supreme. If there are no such ordinary people, those who strictly observe the precepts are regarded as supreme. If there are none who strictly observe the precepts, monks who have broken the precepts are regarded as supreme. If there are no such monks, monks in name only, who have shaved their heads and wear a monk's robe, are regarded as the supreme treasure. Compared with the ninety-five wrong paths, 634b they are by far the supreme and are worthy of the world's offerings. They are the foremost field of merit for sentient beings. For what reason? Because they show people that they are to be feared and respected. If one protects, supports, and respects such monks, one will before long attain the stage of insight [into the non-arising of all *dharmas*].

In the above passage, eight kinds of priceless treasure are presented, namely, the Tathāgata, *pratyekabuddhas*, *śrāvakas*, those who have attained the first three fruits of sagehood, ordinary beings who have attained meditative states, monks who observe the precepts, those who have broken the precepts, and monks in name only who have no precepts to observe. These are the priceless treasures of the Ages of the Right, Semblance, and Decadent Dharma. The first four are the treasures of the Age of the Right Dharma, the next three are the treasures of the Age of the Semblance Dharma, and the last is the treasure of the Age of the Decadent Dharma. From this we clearly know that the monks who have broken the precepts and those who have no precepts are equally true treasures.

Question: When I humbly read the above passages, I see that both monks who have broken the precepts and those who are monks in name only are all true treasures. For what reason is it stated in the *Nirvana Sutra* and the *Great Assembly Sutra* as follows:

If the king and the ministers make offerings to the monks who have broken the precepts, the three calamities will occur in the country and they will eventually fall into hell. Making offerings to the monks who have broken the precepts brings about such results. How much more so if they make offerings to the monks who have no precepts.

It follows then that the Tathāgata at times censures monks who have broken the precepts and at other times praises them. Would this not be the error of the one [Great] Sage making two contradictory judgments?

Answer: Your reasoning is not correct. The *Nirvana Sutra* and other sutras proscribe violation of the precepts in the Age of the Right Dharma. This is not meant for monks of the Ages of the Semblance and Decadent Dharma. Although the same terms are used their implications differ according to the times. The Great Sage proscribes or permits the same act according to the age. This is his intent. Therefore, he does not commit the fault of making two different judgments on one matter.

Question: How do you know that the *Nirvana Sutra* and other sutras proscribe violation of the precepts during the Age of the Right Dharma and do not address monks of the Ages of the Semblance and Decadent Dharma?

Answer: The exposition of the eightfold true treasure quoted above from the *Great Assembly Sutra* is the testimony. Depending on the age, these eight true treasures are all priceless. Since the monks who break the precepts in the Age of the Right Dharma corrupt the monks who observe the precepts, the Buddha strictly prohibits this and does not allow such monks to enter the sangha. Accordingly, the *Nirvana Sutra,* fascicle three, says:

> The Tathāgata has now entrusted the supreme Right Dharma to the kings, ministers, councilors, monks, and nuns.... If there are some who break the precepts and abuse the Right Dharma, the kings, ministers, and the four groups of Buddhists should correct them by taking disciplinary action against them. Such kings, ministers, and others will gain immeasurable merit.... They are my disciples, true *śrāvaka*s. The merit they gain will be immeasurable....

Such words of prohibition are found in many places. They are meant for the Age of the Right Dharma, not for the Ages of the Semblance and Decadent Dharma. The reason for this is that in the latter part of the Age of the Semblance Dharma and in the Age of the Decadent Dharma, the Right Dharma

is not practiced, and so there is no Dharma that can be abused. What act can be called abuse of the Dharma? There are no precepts to be broken, and so who can be called one who has broken the precepts? Further, there is no practice that the great king safeguards. How would the three calamities occur and how would the practice of precepts and wisdom be lost? Again, in the Ages of the Semblance and Decadent Dharma, there is no one who realizes enlightenment, and so how could the Buddha teach that the two kinds of sages be consulted with and protected? Hence, we know that the above descriptions all apply to the Age of the Right Dharma when the precepts are observed and violation of them is possible.

Next, during the first five hundred years in the one thousand-year period of the Semblance Dharma, observance of the precepts dwindles away and the breaking of precepts gradually increases. Although there are the precepts and practice of the Way, no enlightenment is possible. Hence, it is stated in the *Nirvana Sutra,* fascicle seven:

Kāśyapa Bodhisattva said to the Buddha, "World-honored One, according to the Buddha's exposition there are four kinds of devils. How can we distinguish the devils' teachings from the Buddha's? Among many sentient beings, some follow the devils' way and others follow the Buddha's. How can they know which way they are following?"

The Buddha said to Kāśyapa, "Seven hundred years after my nirvana, the devil Pāpīyas will gradually gain strength and make many attempts to destroy my Right Dharma. Suppose there is a hunter wearing a monk's robe; the devil Pāpīyas is like this. He will appear in the form

of a monk, nun, layman, or laywoman (i.e., the four groups
of Buddhists) in much the same way.... [He will say,]
'Monks are allowed to keep male and female servants, cows,
sheep, elephants, horses, and such daily necessities as copper and iron kettles and cauldrons and copper bowls of various sizes, and to engage in the cultivation of fields, planting seeds, buying and selling, and trade, and also to store
grains and rice. The Buddha, out of great compassion, takes
pity on sentient beings and so permits them to engage in
such activities and keep such things.' These remarks in
the sutras and the Vinaya are all devils' expositions."

It is already stated, "Seven hundred years after my nirvana, the devil Pāpīyas will gradually gain strength." Hence,
we know that at that time monks will at last desire and keep
the eight kinds of impure possessions. It is the devils' work
to make such false remarks. These sutras explain in detail
the monks' behavior with clear reference to the time, so they
should not be doubted. I have quoted only one passage, leaving the rest to your imagination.

Next, in the latter half of the Age of the Semblance
Dharma, observance of the precepts will decline and violation of the precepts will increase enormously. Therefore, it is
stated in the *Nirvana Sutra*, fascicle six:...

It is stated in the *Sutra on the Ten Wheels of Kṣitigarbha*
(*Daśacakra-kṣitigarbha-sūtra**):

Suppose there is someone who renounces the world according to the Buddhist rules and yet commits evil. Although
he is not a mendicant, he calls himself one; and although
he does not perform pure practices, he claims that he performs them. Such a monk opens the hidden storehouse
of all good and merit for all *deva*s, dragons, and *yakṣa*s,
and then becomes a good teacher of sentient beings.
Though he does not know contentment with little desire,
he shaves his head and beard and wears a monk's robe.

635a

By so doing, he increases the roots of good for the sake of sentient beings and shows the good path to all *deva*s and humans.... Although a monk who breaks the precepts is said to be a dead man, the power of observance of the precepts that still remains is like the cow's bezoar. Even though the cow dies, people make special efforts to obtain its bezoar. It is also like musk which is useful after the musk deer has died.

It is already stated,[209] "In the forest of *kālaka* trees, there is a persimmon tree." This illustrates the fact that, when the [Age of] the Semblance Dharma declines, only one or two monks who observe the precepts exist in the defiled world characterized by the breaking of precepts. It is also stated, "Although a monk who breaks the precepts is like a dead man, he is like the usefulness of the musk after the musk deer has died. He becomes a good teacher of sentient beings." Hence, we clearly know that in this period the breaking of precepts is finally permitted and the monk who breaks them is regarded as the field of merit for the world. This is the same as in the passage quoted earlier from the *Great Assembly Sutra*.

Next, after the end of the Age of the Semblance Dharma there are no precepts whatsoever. Recognizing the changing times, the Buddha, in order to save the people of the Age of the Decadent Dharma, praises the monks in name only to make them the field of merit in the world. The *Great Assembly Sutra*, fascicle fifty-two, says:

If, in the Age of the Decadent Dharma, there is a monk in name only who, in accord with my teaching, shaves his hair and beard and wears a monk's robe, and if there are donors who make offerings to him, such donors will gain immeasurable merit.

It is also stated in the *Sutra on the Wise and the Foolish* (*Hsien yü ching*):

In the last age in the future when the Dharma is about to perish (the Age of the Extinct Dharma), monks will take wives and [father] children. Yet you should pay homage to a group of four or more such monks just as you would to Śāriputra, Mahāmaudgalyāyana, and others.

It is also said in the same sutra:

If one beats and scolds monks who have broken the precepts, without knowing that they wear monk's robes, the offense is the same as causing blood to flow from the bodies of ten thousand *koṭi*s of Buddhas. If there are sentient beings who shave their hair and beards and wear the monk's robe for the cause of the Buddha-Dharma, even though they may not observe the precepts, they all already bear the seal of nirvana....

The *Great Compassion Sutra* says:

The Buddha said to Ānanda, "In the future, when the Dharma is about to perish, monks and nuns who have renounced the world in accord with my teaching will lead their children by the hand and wander together from one public house to another. They will commit impure acts while staying with my teaching. Despite their [indulging in] wine, they will be my disciples in this auspicious *kalpa* when a thousand Buddhas appear in the world. Afterward, Maitreya will become my successor, followed by others who will appear in succession until the last Tathāgata, Rocana. You should know, Ānanda, while following my teaching, people will become mendicants in name only and practice wrong acts and yet declare themselves mendicants. In appearance they resemble mendicants and always wear monks' robes. In the Auspicious Kalpa, when the Tathāgatas from Maitreya down to Rocana appear, such mendicants will, under these Buddhas, enter

complete nirvana without remainder. None will be left
behind. For what reason? Because among all such mendicants, some call the Buddha's name even once and
awaken faith even once; their acts of merit have not been
done in vain. This I know because I recognize everything
in the Dharma realm with the Buddha wisdom. . . . "

These sutras, referring to the specific age, regard monks
in name only in the future Age of the Decadent Dharma as
venerable masters of the world. If you seek to regulate the
behavior of the monks in name only in the Age of the Decadent Dharma with the rules of discipline meant for the Age
635b   of the Right Dharma, the teaching will run counter to the
people's capacity, and the people and the Dharma will not
fit each other. Accordingly, it is said in a Vinaya text:[210]

To enforce prohibition on that which should not be prohibited will mean abolishing the Vinaya rules established
with the Buddha's three supernatural faculties. Such an
act is an offense.

Having quoted above from the sutras, I have related the
different ages of the Dharma to the behavior of the monks.

Finally, in comparison with the teachings [in earlier ages],
the Right Dharma is destroyed in the Age of the Decadent
Dharma as a matter of natural development. The three modes
of action of sentient beings cannot be regulated, and their
four modes of deportment are against the Buddha's rules, as
described in the *Sutra Clearing Doubts Concerning the Semblance Dharma (Hsiang fa chüeh i ching)*. . . . It is also stated
in the *Sutra on the Buddha's Last Teaching (Wei chiao fa
lü)*. . . . Again, it is stated in the *Dharma Practice Sutra (Fa
hsing ching)*. . . . Also it is stated in the *Sutra on Mṛgāra's
Mother (Mṛgāramātṛ-sūtra*)*. . . . And it is stated in the *Benevolent King Sutra*. . . .

[Exhortations to Leave Non-Buddhist Ways and Take Refuge in the True Teaching]

I will discern the true and false teachings based on the various sutras, thereby cautioning people against the wrong and falsely attached view of non-Buddhist teachings.

The *Nirvana Sutra* says:[211]

> Once you have taken refuge in the Buddha, you should never again take refuge in various gods.

It is stated in the *Pratyutpanna Samādhi Sutra:*

> The laywomen who, having heard of this *samādhi,* wish to learn it ... should take refuge in the Buddha, Dharma, and Sangha. They should not follow other paths, worship gods or spirits, or seek lucky days.

It is stated in the same sutra:

> Laywomen who wish to learn this *samādhi* ... should not worship gods or spirits.

[Salvation of Demi-gods and Evil Spirits]

It is stated in Chapter Eight, "Constellations of the Devil King Pāpīyas," section two, in the Sun Matrix section of the *Great Assembly Sutra,* fascicle eight:

> Then [the saint] Kharoṣṭī said to the heavenly beings, "The moon and other heavenly bodies have their own area to cover. You give aid to the four kinds of sentient beings. What are the four? The human beings on earth, dragons, *yakṣas*, and others, down to scorpions. You give aid to all of them. In order to bring peace and happiness to all sentient beings, I have arranged constellations in position. Each of these has its own assigned work and allocated time, down to a moment. I will explain each in detail. Their activities are performed

harmoniously and augment each other in accordance with their locations and areas."

Kharoṣṭī joined his palms before the assembly and said, "I have thus arranged in position the sun and moon, periods of the year, and big and small constellations. What are the six seasons? The first and second months are the time of warmth. The third and fourth months are the time of sowing. The fifth and sixth months are the time of praying for rainfall. The seventh and eighth months are the time of ripening. The ninth and tenth months are the time of coldness. The eleventh and twelfth months are the time of heavy snow. Thus the twelve months are divided into six seasons.

635c "There are eight planets: Jupiter, Mars, Saturn, Venus, Mercury, the sun, the moon, and the planet of eclipse. There are also twenty-eight minor heavenly bodies, namely, from the constellation Kṛttikā to the constellation Bharaṇī. I have arranged these in position and have explained the laws regulating them. All of you, look and listen! All of you in this assembly, what do you think? Are the laws I adopted for placing them right or wrong? Are you or are you not delighted with the activities of the twenty-eight constellations and the eight major planets? Each of you, express your views as to whether you approve of them or not."

At that time, all the gods, saints, *asuras*, dragons, *kiṃnaras*, and others joined their palms and said, "Great saint, you are the most revered among gods. None among others, including dragons and *asuras*, surpasses you. Your wisdom and compassion are supreme. Since for innumerable *kalpas* you have taken pity on all sentient beings, without forgetting them, you have gained the reward of merits; your vows having been fulfilled, your merits are like an ocean. You know all things of the past, present, and future; there is none among gods who possesses wisdom like yours. No sentient being could operate the laws as you do with regard to the functions of day and night, moment and hour, big and small heavenly bodies, waxing and waning moon, and the cycle of the year. All of us are delighted with these. They give us peace and happiness. It is wonderful that you, the one of great virtue, thus give peace and comfort to sentient beings."

Then the saint Kharoṣṭī made this remark, "I have provided the cycle of the year of twelve months, and explained how I arranged the big and small constellations and the laws of time, such as moment and hour. I have also placed the four great heavenly kings on the four sides of Mount Sumeru, one king in each direction. They each reign over the sentient beings in each region. The heavenly king in the northern direction is Vaiśravaṇa; in his region there are many *yakṣa*s. The heavenly king in the southern direction is Virūḍhaka; in his region there are many *kumbhāṇḍa*s. The heavenly king in the western direction is Virūpākṣa; in his region there are many dragons. The heavenly king in the eastern direction is Dhṛtarāṣṭra; in his region there are many *gandharva*s. These kings protect all lands and towns throughout the four cardinal points and four intermediate directions. Spirits are also stationed to protect them."

At that time, the saint Kharoṣṭī made all the assembly—gods, dragons, *yakṣa*s, *asura*s, *kiṃnara*s, *mahoraga*s, humans, and non-human beings—rejoice beyond measure, saying, "How wonderful!" Then the gods, dragons, *yakṣa*s, *asura*s, and others made offerings to Kharoṣṭī day and night.

Next, after immeasurable ages, there will be another 636a saint, named Kālika. He will appear in the world and expound the laws governing the constellations and the big and small moons, and the essentials concerning times and seasons.

At that time, all the dragons, while dwelling with the sage on Mount Khalatiya, venerated and worshiped the saint Jyotīrasa. Using their power to the utmost, the dragons made offerings to the saint.

It is stated in Chapter Ten, "Nembutsu *Samādhi*," in the Sun Matrix section of the *Great Assembly Sutra*, fascicle nine:

> When Pāpīyas had presented this verse, there was in the assembly a devil woman named Darkness-Free. In the past she planted various roots of good. She said, "The mendicant Gautama is called 'Virtues.' If there are sentient beings who, having heard the Buddha's name, singlemindedly take refuge in him, no devil is capable of inflicting harm on them. Much less likely to receive harm from devils are beings who have seen the Buddha, have directly heard the Dharma from him, performed various methods of practice, and attained deep wisdom and extensive understanding.... An army of all devils, ten million *koṭi*s in number, could not inflict harm on them even for a moment. The Tathāgata has now opened the path to nirvana. I wish to go to the Buddha and take refuge in him."
>
> Then she expressed herself in verse for her father:...
>
> By practicing the teachings of all the Buddhas of the
>   three periods,
> I will deliver all suffering beings.
> Having attained complete freedom over all *dharma*s,
> I wish to be like the Buddha in the future.
>
> At that time, when Darkness-Free finished presenting this verse, five hundred devil women in the royal palace of her father, including her sisters and relatives, all awakened the *bodhi*-mind. At that time, having seen that all the five hundred women in the palace had taken refuge in the Buddha and awakened the *bodhi*-mind, the Devil King [Pāpīyas] became very angry, fear-ridden, and sorrowful.... Then the five hundred devil women stated in verse to Pāpīyas:
>
> If sentient beings take refuge in the Buddha,
> They will not fear even a thousand *koṭi*s of devils.
> Even more fearless are those who aspire to cross the
>   stream of birth and death

And reach the shore of the nirvana of non-action.

If there are persons who offer a piece of incense and
    a flower
To the Three Treasures of Buddha, Dharma, and
    Sangha,
And give rise to resolute and unflinching courage,
They cannot be destroyed by any number of devils....

Our immeasurable evil from the past
Is completely destroyed.
Since we have taken refuge in the Buddha sincerely
    and wholeheartedly,
We are sure of attaining the fruit of supreme *bodhi*.

When Devil King [Pāpīyas] heard these verses, his anger
and fear multiplied, troubling his mind. Emaciated and sorrowful, he sat alone in the palace.

At that time, Bodhisattva Mahāsattva Jyotīrasa hearing
the Buddha's exposition of the Dharma, made all sentient
beings become free of attachments and perform the four pure
practices....

[The Buddha said to Jyotīrasa,] "Bathe yourself, put on
clean robes, take only vegetarian food, refrain from eating
after noon, and do not eat acrid food. Choose a quiet place,
adorn a hall, and sit cross-legged with right mindfulness.   636b
Whether walking or sitting, contemplate the Buddha's physical characteristics without losing concentration. Do not take
any other objects or conceive of any other matters. For one
day and night or seven days and nights, do not engage in any
other acts. If you are sincerely mindful of the Buddha ... you
will see the Buddha. With small mindfulness, you will see a
small Buddha; with large mindfulness, you will see a large
Buddha.... With immeasurable mindfulness, you will see
the immeasurable and boundless Buddha body."

It is stated in Chapter Thirteen, "Protecting Stupas," in the
Sun Matrix section of the *Great Assembly Sutra,* fascicle ten:

> Then the devil Pāpīyas, surrounded all around by eighty *koṭi*s
> of his kinsmen, went to the place where the Buddha was.
> Having arrived there, he touched his head to the Buddha's
> feet and paid homage to him, the World-honored One. Then
> he said in verse: ...
>
>> All Buddhas of the three periods, with great compassion,
>> Accept my homage! I repent all the evil I have done.
>> In the two other treasures, Dharma and Sangha, too,
>> I sincerely take refuge in the same way.
>>
>> May I, today, make offerings to, worship,
>> And revere the Master of the World.
>> I will extinguish all evil forever and never again
>>   commit any evil;
>> Until the end of my life, I will take refuge in the
>>   Tathāgata's Dharma.
>
> After presenting this verse, the devil Pāpīyas said to the
> Buddha, "World-honored One, I pray that you, the Tathā-
> gata, always joyfully and compassionately embrace me and
> all sentient beings with the mind of equality and nondis-
> crimination."
>
> The Buddha said, "So I will do."
>
> Then the devil Pāpīyas greatly rejoiced and awakened
> the pure aspiration. He again touched his head to the
> Buddha's feet and paid homage to him, circumambulated him
> three times to the right, worshiped him with joined palms,
> and withdrew to one side. While remaining there, he looked
> at the World-honored One adoringly without tiring.

It is stated in Chapter Eight, "Evil Spirits Attaining Reverential Faith," in the Moon Matrix section of the *Great Assembly
Sutra,* fascicle five:

[The Buddha said,] "All of you, through elimination of wrong views, will gain ten kinds of merit. What are the ten? First, to attain tenderness and goodness of heart and so be accompanied by wise and good friends. Second, to believe in the law of karma and abstain from committing various evil acts, even at the sacrifice of your life. Third, to take refuge in and revere the Three Treasures and not to believe in gods. Fourth, to gain the right view and not to decide good or bad fortune according to the year, month, or day. Fifth, to be born in human or heavenly realms always and not to fall into the evil realms. Sixth, to attain clarity of mind in wisdom and goodness and so receive people's praise. Seventh, to abandon the secular world and always pursue the holy path. Eighth, to be free of both nihilistic and eternalistic views and accept the law of causation. Ninth, to always meet and see people of right faith, right practice, and right aspiration. Tenth, to be born in the good realms.

"If you transfer the roots of good acquired from eliminating wrong views toward highest, perfect *bodhi*, you will quickly accomplish the six perfections and attain perfect enlightenment in a Buddha land of goodness and purity. Having realized *bodhi*, while dwelling in that Buddha land you will adorn sentient beings with merits, wisdom, and all the roots of good. Such beings will come to be born in your land, no longer believe in gods, and become free of the fear of evil realms. After the end of their lives there, they will be reborn in good realms."

It is stated in Chapter Eight, "Evil Spirits Attaining Reverential Faith," in the Moon Matrix section of the *Great Assembly Sutra,* fascicle six:

> It is extremely difficult to encounter the Buddha's
>   appearance in the world;
> Difficult, too, is it to encounter the Dharma and the
>   Sangha.

636c

For sentient beings to attain pure faith is difficult;
To alienate yourself from various adverse conditions is
 difficult, too.

It is difficult to have pity on sentient beings;
To know contentment is of prime difficulty.
Difficult is it to be able to hear the Right Dharma;
To practice it well is most difficult of all.

If you know these difficulties and attain the [ten]
 equalities,
You will always enjoy happiness in the world;
The wise should always quickly realize
The ten equalities....

Then the World-honored One expounded the Dharma to
the multitudes of evil spirits, "Some evil spirits in the multitudes of evil spirits in the past awakened resolute faith but
later associated with evil teachers and came to perceive others' faults. For this reason, they were born as evil spirits."

[Divine Protection of the World
through the Buddhas' Benevolence]

It is stated in Chapter Nine, "Protection by the Heavenly
Kings," in the Moon Matrix section of the *Great Assembly Sutra*,
fascicle six:

Then, in order to inform people of the world, the World-honored One asked the heavenly king Great Brahmā, Lord of the
Sahā world, "Who protects and sustains the four continents?"
 The heavenly king Great Brahmā, Lord of the Sahā world,
said, "World-honored One of Great Virtue, the king of the
Tuṣita Heaven, together with countless hundreds of thousands of gods of the Tuṣita Heaven, protects and sustains
Uttarakuru, the northern continent. The king of the Heaven
of Free Enjoyment of Manifestations by Others, together with

countless hundreds of thousands of gods of the Heaven of Free Enjoyment of Manifestations by Others, protects and sustains Pūrvavideha, the eastern continent. The king of the Heaven of Enjoying Self-created Pleasures, together with countless hundreds of thousands of gods of the Heaven of Enjoying Self-created Pleasures, protects and sustains Jambudvīpa, the southern continent. The king of the Heaven of Restraining Well, together with countless hundreds of thousands of gods of the Heaven of Restraining Well, protects and sustains Aparagodānīya, the western continent.

"World-honored One of Great Virtue, the heavenly king Vaiśravaṇa, together with countless hundreds of thousands of *yakṣas*, protects and sustains Uttarakuru. The heavenly king Dhṛtarāṣṭra, together with countless hundreds of thousands of *gandharvas*, protects and sustains Pūrvavideha. The heavenly king Virūḍhaka, together with countless hundreds of thousands of *kumbhāṇḍas*, protects and sustains Jambudvīpa. The heavenly king Virūpākṣa, together with countless hundreds of thousands of dragons, protects and sustains Aparagodānīya.

"World-honored One of Great Virtue, seven constellations—arranged by the saint [Kharoṣṭī]—three luminaries, and three celestial maidens protect and sustain Uttarakuru. These seven constellations arranged by the saint are Śatabhiṣā, Dhaniṣṭhā, Pūrva-bhādrapadā, Uttara-bhādrapadā, Revatī, Aśvinī, and Bharaṇī. The three luminaries are Saturn, Jupiter, and Mars. The three celestial maidens are Kumbha, Mīna, and Meṣa.

637a

"World-honored One of Great Virtue, among the seven constellations arranged by the saint [Kharoṣṭī], Śata-bhiṣā, Dhaniṣṭhā, and Pūrva-bhādrapadā belong to the domain of Saturn, and Kumbha is its corresponding astrological house. Uttara-bhādrapadā and Revatī belong to the domain of Jupiter, and Mīna is its corresponding astrological house. Aśvini and Bharaṇī belong to the domain of Mars, and Meṣa is its corresponding astrological house. World-honored One of Great Virtue, these seven constellations arranged by the saint, three luminaries, and three celestial maidens protect and sustain Uttarakuru.

"World-honored One of Great Virtue, seven constellations arranged by the saint [Kharoṣṭī], three luminaries, and three celestial maidens protect and sustain Pūrvavideha. These seven constellations arranged by the saint are Kṛttikā, Rohiṇī, Mṛga-śiras, Ārdrā, Punar-vasu, Puṣya, and Āśleṣā. The three luminaries are Venus, Jupiter, and the moon. The three celestial maidens are Vṛṣa, Mithuna, and Karkaṭaka.

"World-honored One of Great Virtue, among the seven constellations arranged by the saint [Kharoṣṭī], Kṛttikā and Rohiṇī belong to the domain of Venus, and Vṛṣa is its corresponding astrological house. Mṛga-śiras, Ārdrā, and Punar-vasu belong to the domain of Jupiter, and Mithuna is its corresponding astrological house. Puṣya and Āśleṣā belong to the domain of the moon, and Karkaṭaka is its corresponding astrological house. World-honored One of Great Virtue, these seven constellations arranged by the saint, three luminaries, and three celestial maidens protect and sustain Pūrvavideha.

"World-honored One of Great Virtue, seven constellations arranged by the saint [Kharoṣṭī], three luminaries, and three celestial maidens protect and sustain Jambudvīpa. These seven constellations arranged by the saint are Maghā, Pūrva-phālgunī, Uttara-phālgunī, Hastā, Citrā, Svātī, and Viśākhā. The three luminaries are the sun, Mercury, and Venus. The three celestial maidens are Siṃha, Kanyā, and Tulā.

"World-honored One of Great Virtue, among the seven constellations arranged by the saint [Kharoṣṭī], Maghā, Pūrva-phālgunī, and Uttara-phālgunī belong to the domain of the sun, and Siṃha is its corresponding astrological house. Hastā and Citrā belong to the domain of Mercury, and Kanyā is its corresponding astrological house. Svātī and Viśākhā belong to the domain of Venus, and Tulā is its corresponding astrological house. World-honored One of Great Virtue, these seven constellations arranged by the saint, three luminaries, and three celestial maidens protect and sustain Jambudvīpa.

"World-honored One of Great Virtue, seven constellations arranged by the saint [Kharoṣṭī], three luminaries, and three celestial maidens protect and sustain Aparagodānīya. These seven constellations arranged by the saint are Anurādhā, Jyeṣṭhā, Mūla, Pūrvāṣāḍhā, Uttarāṣāḍhā, Śravaṇa, and Abhijit. The three luminaries are Mars, Jupiter, and Saturn. The three celestial maidens are Vṛścika, Dhanus, and Makara.

"World-honored One of Great Virtue, among the seven constellations arranged by the saint, Anurādhā and Jyeṣṭhā belong to the domain of Mars, and Vṛścika is its corresponding astrological house. Mūla, Pūrvāṣāḍhā, and Uttarāṣāḍhā belong to the domain of Jupiter, and Dhanus is its corresponding astrological house. Śravaṇa and Abhijit belong to the domain of Saturn, and Makara is its corresponding astrological house. World-honored One of Great Virtue, seven constellations arranged by the saint, three luminaries, and three celestial maidens protect and sustain Aparagodānīya.

"World-honored One of Great Virtue, among the four continents, Jambudvīpa is the most excellent. For what reason? Because the people of Jambudvīpa are courageous and wise, and their pure practices befit them. You, the Buddha, World-honored One, have appeared in it. For this reason, the four great heavenly kings all the more protect and sustain Jambudvīpa. There are in it sixteen great kingdoms. Four of them, Aṅga-Magadha, Vaṅgāmagadha, Avantī, and Cetī, are protected and sustained by the heavenly king Vaiśravaṇa, surrounded by a host of yakṣas. The four great kingdoms Kāśī, Kosala, Vaṃsa, and Malla are protected and sustained by the heavenly king Dhṛtarāṣṭra, surrounded by a host of gandharvas. The four great kingdoms Kuru, Vajjī, Pañcāla, and Sūrasena are protected and sustained by the heavenly king Virūḍhaka, surrounded by a host of kumbhāṇḍas. The four

637b

great kingdoms Assaka, Soma, Sorata, and Kamboja are protected and sustained by the heavenly king Virūpākṣa, surrounded by a host of dragons.

"World-honored One of Great Virtue, because the past heavenly saints protected and sustained the four continents, they have been positioned and arranged in this way. Later, in each country, dragons, *yakṣas*, *rākṣasas*, hungry ghosts, *piśācas*, *pūtanas*, *kaṭapūtanas*, and others were born in cities, villages, stupas, gardens, under trees, in cemeteries, mountain valleys, fields, rivers, springs, dams, or on jeweled islands in the sea or shrines—whether by egg, from a womb, from moisture, or through metamorphosis (i.e., the four modes of birth). Although dwelling in those places they have no territory of their own and have not yet received any teaching from others. Therefore, I pray that the Buddha arrange these spirits in position throughout the lands in Jambudvīpa in order to have them protect the lands and all sentient beings living there. We would rejoice at your arrangement." The Buddha said, "It is just as you say, Great Brahmā."

Then the World-honored One said in verse to clarify the essentials of this once more:

> In order to inform the people of the world,
> I, the Teacher, asked Brahmā:
> Who protects and sustains
> The four great continents?

> Brahmā, teacher of the heavens, [replied] thus:
> The kings of the Heaven
> Of Tuṣita, the Heaven of Free Enjoyment of Manifestations by Others,
> The Heaven of Enjoying Self-created Pleasures, and
> the Heaven of Restraining Well, with their followers,

> Protect and sustain
> The four great continents.

The four great heavenly kings
And their followers also protect and sustain them.

The twenty-eight constellations,
The twelve astrological houses,
And the twelve celestial maidens   637c
Protect and sustain the four great continents.

Dragons, spirits, *rākṣasa*s, and others,
Who have received no instructions from anyone,
Should be made to go and protect various regions
According to their place of birth.

Gods and spirits in various ways
Asked the Buddha to arrange them in position;
Taking pity on sentient beings,
They make the torch of the Right Dharma burn
    brilliantly.

Then the Buddha said to Bodhisattva Mahāsattva Moon
Matrix, "You, knower of purity, at the beginning of this auspicious *kalpa*, when the lifespan of human beings was forty
thousand years, Krakuccanda Buddha appeared in the world.
For the sake of immeasurable, countless hundred thousand
*koṭi*s of *nayuta*s of sentient beings, he stopped the wheel of
birth and death and turned the wheel of the Right Dharma;
he closed the evil paths and established the good paths and
the fruit of liberation.

"That Buddha entrusted the four continents to the heavenly king Great Brahmā, lord of the Sahā world, and to the
king of the Heaven of Free Enjoyment of Manifestations by
Others, the king of the Heaven of Enjoying Self-created Pleasures, the king of the Tuṣita Heaven, the king of the Heaven
of Restraining Well, and others. He did so in order to have
them protect and sustain the four continents, because he
takes pity on sentient beings in order to keep the seeds of the

Three Treasures multiplying and flourishing; in order to keep the vital energy of the earth, of sentient beings, and of the Right Dharma abiding long and increasing; and in order to keep sentient beings away from the three evil realms and lead them to the three good realms.

"As the cosmic period advanced, gods and humans deteriorated, all good acts and the pure Dharma became extinct, and great evil and addiction to evil passions increased. When the lifespan of human beings became thirty thousand years, Kanakamuni Buddha appeared in the world. He entrusted the four continents to the heavenly king Great Brahmā, lord of the Sahā world, and to other heavenly kings, from the king of the Heaven of Free Enjoyment of Manifestations by Others to the four great heavenly kings and their followers. He did so in order to have them protect and sustain the four continents and for other reasons, including keeping sentient beings away from the three evil realms and leading them to the three good realms.

"As the cosmic period further advanced, gods and humans deteriorated, the pure Dharma became extinct, and great evil and addiction to evil passions increased. When the lifespan of human beings became twenty thousand years, Tathāgata Kāśyapa appeared in the world. He entrusted the four continents to the heavenly king Great Brahmā, lord of the Sahā world, and to the king of the Heaven of Free Enjoyment of Manifestations by Others, the king of the Heaven of Enjoying Self-created Pleasures, the king of the Tuṣita Heaven, the king of the Heaven of Restraining Well, Kauśika Indra, the four great heavenly kings, and others, and their followers. In order to have them protect and sustain the four continents and for other reasons, including keeping sentient beings away from the three evil realms and leading them to the three good realms, Kāśyapa Buddha entrusted the four continents to Great Brahmā, the four great heavenly kings, and others, and also to many heavenly saints, the seven astrological houses,

638a

the twelve celestial maidens, the twenty-eight constellations, and others in order to have them protect and sustain the four continents.

"You, knower of purity, with the advance of the cosmic period we have reached the time of the evil world of strife with the defilement of the cosmic period, the defilement of evil passions, the defilement of sentient beings, and the defilement of great evil passions. This is the time when the lifespan of human beings is a hundred years, the pure Dharma has become completely extinct, and all kinds of evil darken the world. Just as seawater is of one taste, saltiness, the whole world is pervaded with the taste of great evil passions. Gangs of rascals, with skulls in their hands and their palms smeared with blood, kill each other. Among such evil sentient beings I have appeared in the world and attained enlightenment under the *bodhi* tree. I received alms from merchants, including Trapuṣa and Bhallika. Thus, for their sake, I have divided Jambudvīpa among gods, dragons, *gandharvas*, *kumbhāṇḍas*, *yakṣas*, and others, in order to have them protect and sustain it.

"Accordingly, all the bodhisattva *mahāsattvas* of the Buddha lands throughout the ten directions come and assemble here in a great multitude. In this Buddha land of Sahā, there are a hundred *koṭis* of suns and moons, a hundred *koṭis* of four continents, a hundred *koṭis* of four great oceans, a hundred *koṭis* of encircling iron mountains, a hundred *koṭis* of great encircling iron mountains, a hundred *koṭis* of Mount Sumerus, a hundred *koṭis* of four *asura* castles, a hundred *koṭis* of four great heavenly kings, a hundred *koṭis* of Heavens of the Thirty-three Gods, and so on, up to a hundred *koṭis* of abodes of neither thought nor non-thought—I will not enumerate all the numbers. In this Buddha land of Sahā I perform the Buddha's work. Assembled here in great multitude are all the kings of the Great Brahmā Heavens and their followers, the kings of Devil Heavens, the kings of Heavens of

Free Enjoyment of Manifestations by Others, the kings of the Heavens of Enjoying Self-created Pleasures, the kings of the Tuṣita Heavens, the kings of the Heavens of Restraining Well, the heavenly king Indras, the four great heavenly kings, the kings of *asuras*, the kings of dragons, the kings of *yakṣas*, the kings of *rākṣasas*, the kings of *gandharvas*, the kings of *kiṃnaras*, the kings of *garuḍas*, the kings of *mahoragas*, the kings of *kumbhāṇḍas*, the kings of hungry ghosts, the kings of *piśācas*, the kings of *pūtanas*, the kings of *kaṭapūtanas*, and so on, accompanied by their kinsmen, in order to hear the Dharma. Also, all the bodhisattva *mahāsattvas* and *śrāvakas* in this Buddha land of Sahā, with none excepted, have gathered here in order to hear the Dharma. I will now expound the most profound Buddha-Dharma for the sake of the great assembly that has gathered here. Moreover, in order to protect the world, I will arrange in position the spirits that have assembled in Jambudvīpa to have them protect and sustain it."

Then the World-honored One asked the heavenly king Great Brahmā, lord of the Sahā world, "To whom did the Buddhas of the past entrust these four continents so that they be protected and sustained?"

638b

The heavenly king Great Brahmā, lord of the Sahā world, replied, "The Buddhas of the past entrusted the four continents to me and Kauśika [Indra] so that we would protect and sustain them. But since we committed a fault, they stopped mentioning our names. Instead, they spoke to the other heavenly kings, constellations, luminaries, and astrological houses, ordering them to protect and sustain the four great continents."

The heavenly king Great Brahmā, lord of the Sahā world, and Kauśika Indra prostrated themselves at the Buddha's feet and said, "World-honored One of Great Virtue, Sugata of Great Virtue, we now repent our faults. We are like small children, stupid and ignorant. How can we announce our names in the presence of the Tathāgata? World-honored One of Great Virtue, please forgive us. Sugata of Great Virtue, please forgive us. The great assembly that has gathered here, please forgive us. We will teach others as we wish in our own territory and protect and sustain them, so that, in the end, we may lead sentient beings to the good realms. In the past, I received instructions from Krakuccanda Buddha, and have already made the seeds of the Three Treasures multiply and flourish. Similarly, we received instructions from Kanaka-muni Buddha and Kāśyapa Buddha, and diligently made the seeds of the Three Treasures multiply and flourish in order to keep the vital energy of the earth, sentient beings, and the taste of the Right Dharma—*maṇḍa*—abiding long in the world and increasing. Having received instructions from the World-honored One, even we can teach others as we wish in our own territory and carefully protect them in order to put an end to all strife and famine and perform other acts, including keeping the seeds of the Three Treasures from extinction, keeping the three kinds of vital energy dwelling long in the world and increasing, hindering evil acts of sentient beings, protecting and nurturing those who practice the Way, keeping sentient beings from falling into the three evil realms, leading them to the three good realms, and ensuring the Buddha-Dharma to abide long in the world."

The Buddha said, "It is very good of you, wonderful men, to do such acts."

Then the Buddha said to a hundred *koṭi*s of heavenly kings Great Brahmās, "I entrust to you the care of all beings who practice the Dharma, abide in the Dharma, and accord with the Dharma, thereby avoiding evil. You, leaders of sages, teach others as you wish in your own territory in the hundred *koṭi*s of the four continents. All the sentient beings are corrupt, evil, coarse, and rude; they torment and harm others and feel no pity for them. Having no fear for the next life, they incite and harass the minds of warriors (*kṣatriya*s), brahmans, merchants (*vaiśyas*), and slaves (*śūdras*), and also do the same even to the minds of animals. As a result of such acts of taking life and holding to wrong views, they invite untimely great winds and rains and cause impairment and diminution of the vital energy of the earth, sentient beings, and the Right Dharma. In such a case, stop them and lead them to abide in good acts.

638c

"You should also protect and nurture those sentient beings who seek good, who seek the Dharma, who aspire to cross to the other shore beyond birth and death, who practice the perfection of generosity (*dāna-pāramitā*), and so on up to the perfection of wisdom (*prajñā-pāramitā*)—and those sentient beings who perform practices in accord with the Dharma and engage in works in order to perform practices.

"If there are sentient beings who uphold and recite sutras and expound them and explain various scriptures for others, you should care for them with mindfulness and provide skillful means, so that they may gain strong powers, hear and not forget the teachings, accept in faith the distinctions of all *dharma*s, attain liberation from birth and death, practice the Noble Eightfold Path, and come into accord with the [five] roots of *samādhi*.

"If there are sentient beings in your territory who dwell in the Dharma, practice cessation and contemplation in proper order, come into accord with various *samādhi*s, and sincerely seek to realize the three kinds of *bodhi*,[212] you should guard them from hindrances, embrace them, kindly give alms to them, and keep them from running short of provisions.

"If there are sentient beings who give food and drink, clothing, and bedding, or who give medicine to the sick, you should make sure that the five benefits increase for the donors. What are the five? First, longer life; second, increase of wealth; third, increase of happiness; fourth, increase of good acts; and fifth, increase of wisdom. You yourselves will gain benefits and happiness for a very long time. As a result of this act, you will accomplish the six perfections, and before long you will attain the all-knowing wisdom."

Then the hundred *koṭi*s of heavenly king Brahmās, headed by the heavenly king Great Brahmā, lord of the Sahā world, together made this remark, "So it is, so it is. World-honored One of Great Virtue, in each of our own territories there are people who are corrupt, evil, coarse, and rude, who torment and harm others, feel no pity for them, and have no fear for the next life. We will stop them and make sure that the five benefits increase for the donors."

The Buddha said, "It is good of you to do so."

Then all the bodhisattva *mahāsattva*s, all the great *śrāvaka*s, all the gods, dragons, and others, including all the humans and non-humans, praised [the heavenly king Brahmās] and said, "How wonderful! Great valiant ones, you will ensure that this Dharma abides long in the world and that all sentient beings become free from the evil realms and quickly proceed to the good realms."

At that time, the World-honored One said in verse to clarify the essentials of this once more:

I say to Moon Matrix:
At the beginning of this Auspicious Kalpa,
Krakuccanda Buddha
Entrusted the four continents to Brahmā and others,

So that various evil be stopped,
The eye of the Right Dharma brighten,
All evil acts be abandoned,
Practitioners of the Dharma be protected,

The seeds of the Three Treasures multiply,   639a
The three kinds of vital energy increase,
Various evil realms cease to be,
And people be led to the good realms.

Kanakamuni also entrusted the four continents
To the king Great Brahmā and the heavenly kings
Of [the Heavens of] Free Enjoyment of Manifestations
  by Others, Enjoying Self-created Pleasures, and
  others,
Including the four great heavenly kings.

Next, Kāśyapa Buddha also entrusted them
To the king Great Brahmā, the four heavenly kings
Of [the Heaven of] Enjoying Self-created Pleasures
  and the other heavens,
Indra, the world-protecting kings,

And to all the heavenly saints of the past,
And arranged the constellations and luminaries
In position for the sake of the world,
So that they protect and sustain the sentient beings.

When the evil age of [the five defilements] has arrived
And the pure Dharma is about to perish,
I alone attain supreme enlightenment
And keep the people in peace and protected.

There are some in this assembly
Who often disturb and trouble me;
You teach the Dharma to them
To support and protect me.

Bodhisattvas throughout the ten directions
Have all, without exception, gathered here;
And heavenly kings, too,
Have come to this Buddha land of Sahā.

I asked the king Great Brahmā:
Who protected this world in the past?
[He replied:] Indra and Great Brahmā did,
But you have now instructed other heavenly kings.

Then Indra and King Brahmā
Asked the Teacher to forgive them their faults, saying:
In the territories where we rule as kings,
We will stop all evil.

We will make the seeds of the Three Treasures flourish,
And increase the three kinds of vital energy;
We will obstruct evil friends
And protect good ones.

It is stated in Chapter Ten, "Devils Attaining Reverential Faith," in the Moon Matrix section of the *Great Assembly Sutra*, fascicle seven:

At that time there were a hundred *koṭi*s of devils. They all rose from their seats at the same time, joined their palms and, facing the Buddha, touched their heads to his feet, and said to him, "World-honored One, we will muster up great courage and strive to protect and support the Buddha's Right Dharma, make the seeds of the Three Treasures flourish and abide long in the world, and make the vital energy of the earth, the vital energy of sentient beings, and the vital energy of the Dharma increase. If there are *śrāvaka* disciples of the World-honored One who abide in the Dharma, accord with the Dharma, and practice while keeping their three modes of action in harmony with the Dharma, we will protect and sustain all of them and see that they do not lack any necessities. . . .

In this Sahā world,
At the beginning of the Auspicious Kalpa,
Krakuccanda Tathāgata entrusted
The four [great] continents

To Indra and the heavenly king Brahmā
And had them protect and sustain them.

He made them multiply the seeds of the Three
    Treasures
And increase the three kinds of vital energy.

Kanakamuni, too, entrusted
The four [great] continents
To Brahmā, Indra, and other heavenly kings
And had them protect and sustain them.

Kāśyapa, too, did the same;
Entrusting the four [great] continents
To Brahmā, Indra, and the world-guardian kings,
He had them protect the practitioners of the Dharma.

He also made the heavenly saints of the past
And other heavenly saints
Arrange in position the astrological houses,
Constellations, and luminaries.

In the world of the five defilements I have appeared;
Having subdued devils, the adversaries,
I have formed a great assembly
And displayed the Buddha's Right Dharma. . . .

All the heavenly beings
All together said to the Buddha:
In the territories where we rule,
We will all protect the Right Dharma,

Make the seeds of the Three Treasures flourish,
And the three kinds of vital energy increase;
We will put an end to all disease and epidemics,
And terminate famine and strife.

It is stated in "Chapter on the Heavenly King Dhṛtarāṣṭra"
[of the *Great Assembly Sutra*]:

The Buddha said, "God of the sun and god of the moon, if you protect and sustain my Dharma I will enable you to enjoy long life and keep you from decline."

At that time, there were a hundred *koṭi*s of heavenly king Dhṛtarāṣṭras, a hundred *koṭi*s of heavenly king Virūḍhakas, a hundred *koṭi*s of heavenly king Virūpākṣas, and a hundred *koṭi*s of heavenly king Vaiśravaṇas. Together with their kinsmen they arose from their seats at the same time, adjusted their clothes, joined their palms, respectfully paid homage to the Buddha, and said, "World-honored One of Great Virtue, in our own territory we will sincerely protect and sustain the Buddha-Dharma, keep the seeds of the Three Treasures flourishing and abiding long in the world, and make all the three kinds of vital energy increase.... We now, with the same mind as our leader, heavenly king Vaiśravaṇa, protect the Buddha-Dharma in this Jambudvīpa and in the northern direction."

It is stated in the "Chapter on Patience," part sixteen, in the Moon Matrix section of the *Great Assembly Sutra*, fascicle eight:

The Buddha said, "So it is, so it is. It is just as you say. If there are beings who abhor pain and seek pleasure for their own sake, they should uphold the Buddhas' Right Dharma, thereby gaining the reward of immeasurable merit. If there are sentient beings who renounce the world to join my sangha, shave their beards and hair, and wear monk's robes, they all, without exception, bear the seal of nirvana, even if they do not observe the precepts. There may be some who have renounced the world but do not observe the precepts; acting unlawfully they cause distress to others, abuse, and revile them; holding swords and sticks in their hands they beat and tie them up, and even cut and slash them. There are other people who steal the robes and bowls of these monks and deprive them of daily necessities. Such people inflict harm on the true recompensed bodies of Buddhas of the three periods; they also gouge out the eyes of all heavenly beings.

Because they seek to destroy the Buddhas' Right Dharma and the seeds of the Three Treasures, they deny all heavenly beings the chance to obtain benefit and make them fall into hell. Consequently, the three evil realms grow larger and become full."

At that time, all heavenly beings, dragons, and others, down to all *kaṭapūtana*s, humans, and non-humans, together joined their palms and said, "We will regard as our teachers and elders all the *śrāvaka* disciples of the Buddha and those who, though they do not observe the precepts, shave their hair and beards and wear monk's robes on their shoulders. We will protect and support them, provide them with necessities, and see that they do not lack anything. If other heavenly beings, dragons, and others, down to *kaṭapūtana*s, cause distress to these monks and commit such acts as looking on them with malicious thoughts, we will all together impair their physical characteristics as heavenly beings, dragons, *kaṭapūtana*s, and so on, and make them ugly. We will also see that they do not live and take meals with us and that they do not laugh and sport with us in the same place. Such will be our punishment to them."

It is also stated:[213]

Give up divination, study right views, and resolutely and deeply believe in the causation of evil and meritorious acts.

[Warning of Disturbances by Devils and Evil Spirits]

It is stated in the *Śūraṅgama Samādhi Sutra:*

Those devils, spirits, and evil ones, accompanied by their respective followers, will each say, "I have attained supreme enlightenment." After my nirvana, during the Age of the Decadent Dharma, there will be many such devils, spirits, and evil ghosts. Swarming in the world, they will present

themselves as good teachers and cause sentient beings to fall
into the pit of attachment and wrong views, lose the way to
enlightenment, become deluded and confused, lose their judg-
ment, and derange their minds. Where these spirits pass families will collapse and disperse, and the members of those families will become devils of attachment and wrong views,
thereby losing the seeds of Tathāgatas.

It is stated in the *Sutra of Ritual Sprinkling* [*and Mantras*]
(*Kuan-ting shen chou ching*):

The thirty-six kings of spirits, accompanied by their kinsmen
spirits, ten thousand *koṭis* times the number of sands of the
Ganges River, will take turns to protect, while remaining
unseen, those who receive the Three Refuges.

It is stated in the *Sutra on the Ten Wheels of Kṣitigarbha:*

Those who correctly take refuge and disengage themselves
from delusive attachments and divination should never take
refuge in evil spirits or non-Buddhist teachings.

It is also stated in the same sutra:

There may be some who in various ways, to a lesser or greater
degree, cling to lucky or unlucky days, worship spirits . . . and
commit serious evil karma close to the act that leads to Avīci
hell. If they do not repent and extinguish such evil karma,
they should not become Buddhist mendicants and receive the
monks' full precepts. If you allow them to become Buddhist
mendicants and receive the monks' full precepts, you are committing a fault.

It is stated in the *Sutra on the Samādhi of Collecting All Merits* (*Sarva-puṇya-samuccaya-samādhi-sūtra**):

Do not turn toward non-Buddhist teachings; do not worship
non-Buddhist gods.

It is stated in the *Sutra on the Vows of the Buddha Medicine Master* (*Bhagavān-bhaiṣajyaguru-vaiḍūrya-prabhasya-pūrva-praṇidhāna-viśeṣa-vistara*):

> Sons and daughters of good families of pure faith, do not serve non-Buddhist gods until the end of your lives.

It is also stated in the same sutra:

> Those who believe in the false teachings of devils, non-Buddhists, and sorcerers, which are popular in the world and foretell fortune and misfortune, are most likely to have mistaken ideas. Engaging in divination, they will invite misfortune and kill various sentient beings. They will offer prayers to deities and invoke goblins and sprites to ask for good fortune and long life, only to find those prayers fruitless. Being foolish and deluded, they will believe in wrong teachings and cling to perverted views, ending in untimely death and falling into hell with no hope of an end to their terms there.... Eighth, they will suffer from unexpected poisoning, imprecation, and curses, and will be harmed by the spirits arising from corpses and others.

It is stated in the *Sutra on the Bodhisattva Precepts* (*Bodhisattva-bhūmi*):

> The rule of a Buddhist mendicant is not to pay homage to the king or parents, not to serve the six kinds of familial relatives, and not to worship spirits.

640a

It is stated in "Chapter on Upasena" in the *Sutra on the Buddha's Past Lives* (*Buddha-carita-saṃgraha-sūtra**), fascicle forty-two:

> At that time, there was a nephew of the three Kāśyapa brothers who was a brahman with his hair tied in the shape of a conch. His name was Upasena.... He always practiced and studied the way of heavenly saints with his two hundred and fifty disciples. He heard that his uncles, the three Kāśyapas,

had gone with all their disciples to the place of the Great Mendicant, shaved their hair and beards, and donned monk's robes. Having seen this, he faced his uncles and said in verse:

Uncles, you have worshiped fire in vain for a
    hundred years;
You have also practiced austerities in vain.
Today, do you abandon this practice
Just as a snake sloughs off its skin?

Then his uncles, the three Kāśyapas, all said together in verse to their nephew, Upasena:

Formerly, we worshiped the god of fire in vain
And practiced austerities to no purpose.
Today, we abandon this practice
Just as a snake casts off its skin.

It is stated in the [*Discourse on the*] *Awakening of Faith* [*in the Mahayana*]:

If sentient beings lack the power of the roots of good they may be deluded by devils, non-Buddhists, and spirits. These may appear in meditation manifesting various forms to terrify them, such as handsome men or women. If you meditate on the state of "mind only," these objects will disappear and will not cause any harassment to you any longer.

Sometimes they may manifest the forms of gods or bodhisattvas, or the forms of Tathāgatas, completely adorned with physical characteristics; they may teach you *dhāraṇī*s; or the virtues of generosity (*dāna*), observance of the precepts (*śīla*), forbearance (*kṣānti*), diligence (*vīrya*), meditation (*dhyāna*), and wisdom (*prajñā*) (i.e., the six perfections); or teach you that all things are equal, empty, formless, desireless, free of enemy or friend, having neither cause nor effect, and ultimately empty and tranquil—this is true nirvana. They may give you the knowledge of your past lives or your future. They may give you the power of knowing others' thoughts or unimpeded eloquence. They may make you attached to worldly fame and profit.

They may cause you to become angry or rejoice often, leaving you in an unstable state. You may become too gentle, too sleepy, feel your stomach heavy, become ill too often, or feel sluggish. You may have spates of diligence followed by negligence. You may give rise to disbelief, doubt, and much wavering thought. You may discard the excellent practices that you have been performing before and take up miscellaneous practices. You may be attached to worldly affairs and find yourself drawn to and entangled in them.

They may enable you to attain the states that partly resemble various *samādhis*; these are all non-Buddhist acquisitions and not true *samādhi*s. They may enable you to dwell in *samādhi* for one day, two days, three days, or up to seven days, while being naturally provided with aromatic and tasty food and drink, so that you will feel comfort in body and mind, without hunger or thirst, and thus become deeply attached to these states. Or they may cause you to take food immoderately, suddenly eating too much or too little, so that your complexion deteriorates.

640b

For this reason, practitioners should constantly be watchful with wisdom and keep their minds from falling into a net of depravity. Strive in right mindfulness. Neither grasp nor cling, and remove all these karmic hindrances. Know that all non-Buddhist *samādhi*s are accompanied by wrong views, attachment, and self-conceit, because they are rooted in avid desire for worldly fame, profit, and veneration.

[The Supremacy of Śākyamuni over Lao-tzu]

It is stated in the *Treatise Clarifying the True* (*Pien cheng lun*) [by Fa-lin]:

The chapters "Ten Clarifications" and "Nine Admonitions" in reply to the "ten differences and nine delusions" set forth by Li, the Taoist.

The first "difference" presented by the non-Buddhist says:

The Supreme Heavenly Lord Lao-tzu entrusted his spirit to the Hermit Lady Profoundly Wonderful, and was born from her left side. Śākyamuni entered the womb of Queen Māyā and was born from her right side....

The first clarification by the Buddhist is: Lao-tzu, against the established law, was conceived by a shepherdess and was born from her left side. The World-honored One, in accordance with the transforming and sustaining force of nature, was conceived by the sacred mother and was born from her right side.

A person of illumination (i.e., a bodhisattva) says: When I peruse the *Commentary on the Five Thousand Characters* (*K'ai wu ch'ien wen*) by Lü Ching-yü, Tai Shen, Wei Ch'u-hsüan, and others, and the lectures [on Lao-tzu] compiled by Emperor Yüan of the Liang dynasty and Chou Hung-cheng, I find that the title "Supreme Heavenly Lord" is used for the four persons: the Three Emperors, Yao, and Shun. The reason is that in ancient times there were these lords of great virtue who reigned over all the people; hence, they were called "Supreme Heavenly Lords." Kuo-chuang [in his commentary on the *Book of Chuang-tzu*] explains, "The person regarded as the wise man is the lord; those who are not recognized as such are retainers." Lao-tzu was not an emperor or lord. He is not included among the four persons who held this title. In what authoritative source is he described as "Supreme Heavenly Lord" as you thoughtlessly call him? Besides, such Taoist classics as the *Profoundly Wonderful* (*Hsüan-miao*), the *Central Platform* (*Chung-t'ai*), the *Red-sashed Jade Plate* (*Chu-t'ao-yü-cha*), and the *Record of Passing Through the Frontier* (*Ch'u-sai-chi*), state that Lao-tzu was born of his mother Li;

they do not mention "Hermit Lady Profoundly Wonderful."
So this description is not authentic; it is a groundless fiction.

Further, the *Precious Record of Hermit Sages* (*Hsien-jen yü lu*) says:

> Hermit sages do not take wives; hermit women do not
> take husbands. Although they have female forms they
> bear no children.

Such an auspicious event [as Lao-tzu's birth from Hermit Lady Profoundly Wonderful] would have been widely acclaimed. The fact, however, is that there is no mention of this in the *Record of History* (*Shih-chi*) or the *Book of Chou* (*Chou-shu*). To fabricate a false record and denounce the truth would be like trusting in the words of a liar.

In the *Book of Rites* (*Li-chi*) it is stated:

> One who retires from government office and has no rank
> is described as "shifted to the left."

The *Confucian Analects* (*Lun-yü*) says:

> It is against propriety to wear robes with the left side
> under the right.

If the left side is superior to the right, why do Taoists in their processions turn right, not left? The state decrees all end with, "as stated in the right." These are all examples of the established law of heaven.

The fourth "difference" presented by the non-Buddhist says:

> Lao-tzu lived in the days of Emperor Wen and the state
> teacher of the Chou dynasty when it was at its height.
> Śākyamuni lived in the days of Emperor Chuang and the
> teacher of Chi-pin (Kashmir).

The fourth clarification by the Buddhist is: Elder Yang (Lao-tzu) was a petty official in the government, humbly

serving in the archives. He did not live in the days of
Emperor Wen nor was he a state teacher of the Chou dynasty
when it was at its height. Śākyamuni was a prince and
attained the most honored enlightenment. His days correspond to the height of Emperor Chao and he was the teacher
of Jambudvīpa....

640c

The sixth "difference" presented by the non-Buddhist
says:

> Lao-tzu's life in the world began during the reign of
> Emperor Wen of [the Chou dynasty] and ended during
> the time of Confucius. Śākyamuni was born in the fam-
> ily of Śuddhodana; his period corresponds to the reign of
> Emperor Chuang.

The sixth clarification by the Buddhist is: Kāśyapa (incar-
nated as Lao-tzu) was born in the fire/hare year[214] of the reign
of Emperor Huan and died in the water/horse year[215] of the
reign of Emperor Ching. Although he is said to have died in
the time of Confucius, he did not live during the reign of Chi-
ch'ang (Emperor Wen). The Tamer of Beings (Śākyamuni)
was born in the wood/tiger year[216] of the reign of Emperor
Chao and died in the water/monkey year[217] of the reign of
Emperor Mu. He was the heir of Śuddhodana and appeared
before Emperor Chuang.

A person of illumination says: Confucius went to the kingdom of Chou, where he met Lao-tan (Lao-tzu) and asked him
about propriety. This is recorded in detail in the *Record of
History*. As to whether he was the teacher of Emperor Wen,
there is no authentic evidence. He appeared at the end of the
Chou dynasty; this can be found in the records, but that he
flourished at the beginning of the Chou dynasty lacks evidence in the historical documents....

The seventh "difference" presented by the non-Buddhist
says:

Lao-tzu was born during the Chou dynasty and, later in life, went into the desert. It is not known what became of him or where he died. Śākyamuni was born in the western land (India) and ended his life near the Ajitavatī River. [When he died] his disciples beat their chests in sorrow and a multitude of barbarian natives cried bitterly.

The seventh clarification by the Buddhist says: Lao-tzu was born at Lai-hsiang and buried at Huai-li. The details of this are known in the account of Ch'in-i's call of condolence, in which Lao-tzu is criticized for making people believe that he was "a hermit who hides himself in heaven." Gautama was born in the palace and died under the [twin] *śāla* trees. This became known in China during the reign of Emperor Ming of the Han dynasty and is recorded in a writing treasured in the imperial archives of Lan-t'ai.

A person of illumination says: It is stated in the "Inner Section" of the *Book of Chuang-tzu:*

When Lao-tan (Lao-tzu) died, Ch'in-i went to mourn him. He cried three times and then left the room. Lao-tzu's disciples were puzzled and asked, "Were you not the master's friend?" Ch'in-i replied, "When I went in, I saw young people mourning for Lao-tzu as if they had lost their father, and old people mourning for him as if they had lost their son. In ancient times, people spoke of 'a hermit who hides himself in heaven.' At first, I thought that Lao-tzu was exactly that type of person, but now I do not think so."

"Hide" means to withdraw; "heaven" means escape from bondage; "form" refers to the body. This passage means that at first Ch'in-i thought that Lao-tzu was a hermit who hid himself from worldly bondage, but now he sees that he was wrong. Ah, Lao-tzu sought to win people's sympathy by words of flattery; hence, he could not escape death. This means that he is not my friend....

The above are the ten clarifications of the Buddhist in reply to the ten differences set forth by the non-Buddhist.

The non-Buddhist asserts that the first difference is about left and right in the manner of birth; the Buddhist replies that from the time of birth there is a distinction of superior and inferior.

The Buddhist clarifies the matter: The custom of wearing clothes with the left side under the right is maintained by barbarians. In China, commands from the "right" are respected. So it is stated in the *Spring and Autumn Annals*:

> The prime minister receives no imperial commands, but the assistant ministers receive them. Is this not on the left (i.e., wrong)?

The *Record of History* states:

> Lin Hsiang-ju's contributions were great and his position was to the right of Lien-p'o. This made Lien-p'o feel humiliated.

It also states:

> Prime Minister Chang-i placed [the envoy from] Ch'in on the right and Wei on the left. Prime Minister Hsi-shou placed Han on the right and Wei on the left.

This is because the left side is not suitable. The *Book of Rites* says:

> "Left-sided" people who form groups and start riots shall be killed.

Does this not indicate that the right is superior and the left is inferior?

641a

Huang Fu-mi says in his *Biographies of Eminent Hermits (Kao shih chüan)*:

> Lao-tzu was a physiognomist in the state of Ch'u. He had

his house to the north of the Wo River, and studied under Ch'ang-ts'ung-tzu. When Ch'ang-tzu became ill, Li-erh (Lao-tzu) went to inquire after him.

Again, Chi-k'ang says:

Li-erh studied the arts of the nine hermits under Chüan-tzu.

When I examine various books, including one by T'ai-shih-kung, I cannot find any record that Lao-tzu was born from his mother's left side. Since there is no authentic source of information, this assertion is clearly unreliable.

As we all know, wielding a lance or moving a brush [with the right hand] is the first step in the martial or literary arts. It is just as the five ethers and three luminous bodies are the beginning of *yin* and *yang*. In the teaching of Śākyamuni, one turns to the right; this corresponds with human activities. The "left-hand" path of Chang-ling contradicts the law of heaven. Śākyamuni awakened compassion based on the realization of emptiness and responded to the needs of sentient beings. This shows how he manifested himself in this world.... Śākyamuni stood aloof from heaven and earth as the most revered one. His distinguished virtue was adored by all in the three worlds and the six realms....

The non-Buddhist remarks:

Lao-tzu set an example of filial piety and loyalty, thereby saving the world and the people. He was a paragon of compassion and love. Therefore, his teaching has been long transmitted without being altered by any of the hundred kings. His profound influence has benefited many generations, showing no sign of deviation for a myriad ages. Thus, his teaching has served as a standard, whether in ruling a kingdom or regulating the family.

In Śākyamuni's teaching, righteousness is discarded and parents are abandoned; benevolence and filial piety are not adopted. King Ajātaśatru killed his father, but it is declared that he did not commit any offense. Devadatta wounded his cousin [Śākyamuni] with an arrow, but we do not hear of any punishment imposed on him. If ordinary people are guided by [teachings such as] these, evil multiplies. If [Śākyamuni's] teaching becomes a standard, how can good be produced? This is the tenth "difference" showing that Lao-tzu's teaching conforms to the Way and Śākyamuni's teaching contradicts it.

The clarification of the Buddhist says: [According to the Taoist teaching,] righteousness is lower than the Way, propriety arises from lack of loyalty and sincerity, small benevolence is despised as the conduct of mean women, and great filial piety is practiced only by the rich. In addition, to laugh and sing at the occasion of bereavement is not the custom of the Chinese, and to beat trays at funerals is not the manner of the Chinese. [When Yüan-jang's mother died, he rode astride the coffin and sang. When Tzu-sang died, Tzu-kung made a call of condolence; Tzu-sang's four children looked at each other and laughed. Confucius was at the funeral, and laughed. When Chuang-tzu's wife died he beat the tray and sang.]

Therefore, the virtue of filial piety is taught to instruct such people, for it is intended for them to respect their parents. Also, the virtue of loyalty is taught to them in order to have them respect their king. It is through the profound benevolence of the wise ruler that the teaching of such virtues spread to all countries; it is through the great filial piety of the sacred king that the benevolent ruling reaches throughout the four seas.

The Buddhist sutras say:

Since the subject of mental activity transmigrates in the six realms, there is no being that has not been one's father or mother. Since beings change their abodes in the three worlds of birth and death, who can distinguish friends from enemies?

It is also stated:

> With the eye of wisdom covered over by ignorance, people come and go in birth and death. While repeating comings and goings, they commit various acts through which they become each other's parents and children. Enemies often become friends, and friends often become enemies.

Hereupon, Buddhist mendicants abandon the secular world and turn toward the true. They regard all beings as equal to their parents and relatives. They discard worldly prosperity and seek the Way. They treat all beings as their parents. [They universally practice the right mind and look upon others as equal to their parents.]

Taoism esteems serene emptiness but you place greater importance on love. The law is to be enforced equally but you discriminate between friends and enemies. Is this not unreasonable? It is recorded in history books that rivalry for power results in abandoning one's parents; Duke Hua of Ch'i and Emperor Mu of Ch'u are examples of this. Is it not a mistake to slander the [Great Sage] (Śākyamuni) on these grounds?

Here ends the tenth point clarifying that Taoism is inferior [to Buddhism]. . . .

The two emperors (Fou Hsi and Nu Wa) ruled the land and transformed the people with their virtue. [The *Sutra on the Four Continents Surrounding Sumeru* (*Hsü mi ssu yü ching*) says: "Bodhisattva Responding-to-Voice appeared as Fou Hsi, and Bodhisattva Auspicious appeared as Nu Wa."] The three sages set forth their teachings [in the *Sutra on the Questions of Bodhisattva Emptiness-Tranquility* (*K'ung chi so wen ching*)]: "Kāśyapa appeared as Lao-tzu, Bodhisattva Māṇavaka appeared as Confucius, and Bodhisattva Pure Light appeared as Yen-hui"] and expounded the Way in the period of defilement. The Yellow Emperor and Lao-tzu enthusiastically expounded the teaching of "returning to oneness by emptying one's self." The Duke of Chou and Confucius promoted study of the arts of poetry, composition, propriety, and music. Manifesting the virtue of modesty and maintaining simple and sincere disposition are steps to sagehood. The three kinds of awe and the five constant virtues are causes for birth in human and heavenly realms. These teachings are in tacit agreement with the Buddhist truth but they are not correct and exhaustive discussions of it. It is like asking a deaf mute the way; he may be able to show you the direction but cannot tell the exact distance. It is also like asking a rabbit or a horse about crossing the river; it can tell you how to cross it but does not know its depth.

These examples show that the Yin and Chou dynasties were not fit for the spread of Śākyamuni's teaching. It is like a child unable to look directly at blazing flames or dazzling light, or like a coward unable to listen well to the shuddering sound of a sudden clap of thunder. Thereupon, on seeing rivers and ponds swelling, Emperor Chao became fearful of the birth of a divine being (Śākyamuni). On seeing clouds and a rainbow change color, the queen of Emperor Mu rejoiced at the [Great Sage's] death. [The *Chou Dynasty Record of Miraculous Events* says: On the eighth day of the fourth month, in the twenty-fourth year of the reign of Emperor Chou, all rivers and springs swelled and overflowed. On the fifteenth day of the second month, in the fifty-second year of the reign of Emperor Mu, violent winds arose; trees were blown down, the sky darkened with black clouds, and a ghastly white rainbow appeared.] Such being the case, how could the teaching be received across the rivers of the Pamirs? How could the sincere pursuit of the Dharma cross the Himalayas? The *Vimalakīrti[-nirdeśa]-sūtra* says, "It is the fault of the blind, not the fault of the sun or the moon." If a thorough investigation were to be made, it would harm your nature of "Chaos."

[The Buddhist truth] is beyond your understanding.

This is the first point disclosing your blindness.

The second point of the Buddhist concerning the construction of statues and pagodas:

From the time of Emperor Ming of the Han dynasty to the end of the Ch'i and Liang dynasties, more than two hundred people, including kings, nobles, officials, and monks, nuns, laymen, and laywomen (i.e., the four groups of Buddhists), sensed the presence of the most sacred being, though invisible, and saw a miraculous light with their own eyes.

Some saw the impression of the Buddha's foot on Mount Wan and a brilliant Buddha image on the waters of Hu-tu; others saw the [Buddha's] image appearing like the full moon at the foot of Mount Ch'ing-t'ai and a stupa outside the Yungmen gate. Emperor Nan-p'ing perceived an auspicious image, and Emperor Wen-hsüan received a sacred tooth relic in his dream. Emperor Hsiao succeeded in casting a golden image of the Buddha at the first attempt, while the Emperor of Sung tried to cast one four times without success. There are a number of such examples—too many to mention them all. How can you overlook these miraculous signs even with your blind eyes?

There is no virtue that is not contained—this is *nieh-p'an* (nirvana). There is no place that is not reached—this is *pu-t'i (bodhi)*. There is nothing that wisdom does not pervade—this is *fo-t'o* (Buddha). These Chinese words represent Sanskrit terms. If expressed in these two languages, "Buddha" is clearly to be entrusted in. How do you explain this? *Fo-t'o*

is translated as *ta-chueh* ("great awakening") in Chinese. *Pu-t'i* is translated as *ta-tao* ("Great Way"). *Nieh-p'an* is translated as *wu-wei* ("non-action"). Although you tread the earth of enlightenment all day, you do not know that the Great Way is a different name for enlightenment. Although you receive your bodily form from the great awakening, you do not know that "great awakening" is a translation of "Buddha."

Chuang-chou (Chuang-tzu) says:

> After you have the great awakening, you will realize a great dream.

Kuo[-hsiang] says in his commentary:

> Awakening refers to a sage. The reason is that those who have distress in their hearts are all dreaming.

The commentary also says:

> Confucius and Tzu-yu were not able to reach the true understanding beyond words; hence, theirs was not the great awakening.

A man of virtue says: "The teaching of Confucius does not go beyond this."

Nirvana, which is tranquility and illumination, cannot be known by consciousness or wisdom. Words fail to reach it, and mental activity ceases to function [trying to grasp it]. Hence, one forgets words to describe it. The Dharma body is possessed of the three virtues and four excellent qualities; it is tranquil and free of obstacles. Hence, it is described as "liberation." This means that through true understanding one attains cessation of troubles. Although Confucius was a sage, he cannot compare with the Buddha in spiritual accomplishments. I say this, for Liu-hsiang's *Two Records of Antiquity* (*Liu-hsiang ku*) states:

> One hundred fifty years after Buddhist sutras were transmitted to China, Lao-tzu composed the *Five Thousand-character Discourse* (*Tao te ching*).

Both Chou (Chuang-tzu) and Lao-tzu, no doubt, read Buddhist sutras. In their words and teachings evidence for this is found here and there. We should ponder on this....

The *Sutra on Mindfulness of the Right Dharma* says:

If people do not observe the precepts, gods will decrease and *asura*s will increase. Good dragons will lose their power and evil dragons will gain in power. When evil dragons have power, they will cause frost and hail to fall from the sky and violent winds and torrential rain will occur out of season. Then the five kinds of crops will not yield good harvest, epidemics will arise one after another, and the people will starve and kill each other.

If people observe the precepts, gods will grow in majestic glory, *asura*s will decrease, evil dragons will lose their power, and good dragons will gain in power. When good dragons have power, wind and rain will come at the right time and the four seasons will be harmonious. The nourishing rain will fall, bringing abundant crops. People will be at peace, and arms will cease to be used. Epidemics will not occur....

A man of virtue says: The Taoist says in the *Book of Hidden Truth of the Great Heaven (Yin shu)* and the *Book of Supreme Truth (Wu shang chen shu)*: "The Lord of the supreme Great Way rules in the Great Gossamer Net Heaven, which is infinitely vast and of fifty-five layers, on Mount Jade Capital, where there is a seven-jeweled stage, golden floor, and jade desk. Attended by hermit youths and hermit ladies, he dwells outside the Thirty-two Heavens and the three worlds."

The *Chart of the Five Divine Peaks (Shen-ch'üan wu yüeh t"u)* reads: "The Celestial Honored One of the Great Way governs at T'ai-hsüan-tu (Capital of Great Profundity), located in the province of Jade Light, the prefecture of Golden Truth, the district of Heavenly Protection, the county of Primordial Illumination, the village of Settled Aspiration. No calamities infiltrate there."

The *Scripture of Spirits (Ling shu ching)* has this to say: "Great Gossamer Net Heaven lies at the top of the heavens in 555,555 layers."

The *Chart of the Five Divine Peaks* says: "'*Tu*' means capital. The highest Lord of Gods (Lao-tzu), the supreme Great Way, the Way of Ways, remaining in tranquility, dwells in the Capital of Great Profundity."   642a

The *Inner Sound of the Heavens* (*Chu t'ien nei yin*) says: "Gods, together with hermits, beat drums in the storied palace. They have an audience with the Lord of the Way at the Jade Capital and entertain him."

If we examine the *Catalog of Taoist Scriptures* (*Tao chiao mu lu*) dedicated to the emperor by the Taoist, we find that all people say, "According to Lu Hsiu-ching, a man of the Sung, there are one thousand two hundred and twenty-eight volumes." They did not originally include miscellaneous works and the writings of So-and-so "tzu." Now the Taoist lists two thousand forty volumes. Among them are many titles taken from the *Catalog of Literature of the Book of Han* (*Han shui wen chih*); eight hundred and eighty-four are arbitrarily listed as Taoist scriptures. . . .

Upon investigation, we find that T'ao-shu was Fan-li. He intimately served Kou-chien, the king of Yüeh. The king and all his ministers were taken prisoners by the kingdom of Wu, and had to eat excrement and drink urine; they suffered untold misery. Further, Fan-li's son was murdered by the kingdom of Ch'i. If his father possessed the art of transforming one's body, why could he not transform himself and escape?

In the *Record of the Creation of Heaven and Earth* (*Tsao li t'ien ti chi*) it is recorded, "Lao-tzu was conceived in the womb of the consort of Emperor Yu." That is to say, Lao-tzu was Emperor Yu's child. It also says, "His position was an official in the Office of Archives." This shows that he was Emperor Yu's retainer. The *Scripture on Converting the Barbarians* (*Hua hu ching*) says, "Lao-tzu was Tung-fang Shuo of the Han dynasty." If this is so, since Emperor Yu was killed by the western barbarians, why did Lao-tzu not, out of love for him, give him a divine amulet to save his life? . . .

We have referred to Lu Hsiu-ching's catalog; there is no authentic text. It is amazing that there are so many errors. Hsiu-ching's catalog was obviously fraudulent. *Hsüan Tu-kuan's Catalog* (*Hsüan tu lu*) [based on it] is the worst of all fakes.

[Exhortation to Take Refuge
in the Buddha]

It is also stated in the same work:

The *Great [Nirvana] Sutra* states:

There are ninety-six paths; only the single path of the Buddha is the right path. The other ninety-five are all non-Buddhist paths (i.e., the ninety-five wrong paths).

I (Emperor Wu) have discarded the non-Buddhist paths and taken refuge in the Tathāgata. If there are lords who make the same vow, they should each awaken the *bodhi*-mind. Lao-tzu, the Duke of Chou, Confucius, and others guided people as disciples of the Tathāgata, but they were originally in the wrong. They taught only worldly good, unable to bring people beyond the state of ordinary beings to sagehood. Lords, ministers, nobles, kings, and their families should turn from false paths and follow the true one, abandon wrong paths and enter the right one. It is stated in the Buddhist scripture, the *Discourse on the Establishment of Truth* (*Ch'eng shih lun*):

To follow non-Buddhist paths with great reverence and follow the Buddha-Dharma with little reverence is a wrong view. If your reverence for both is equal, your acts are neutral, neither good nor evil. To serve the Buddha with strong resolution and to serve Lao-tzu with little concern is pure faith. "Pure" means thoroughly pure, within and without, with complete extinction of defilements and delusion. "Faith" is to believe in the right and reject the wrong; hence, such people are called the Buddha's disciples of pure faith. Others are all wrong-viewed; they cannot be called persons of pure faith....

Give up the wrong teaching of Lao-tzu and enter the true teaching of the Dharma.

642b

The Master of Kuang-ming Temple says:[218]

The Buddhas of the zenith, countless as the sands of the
    Ganges River,
Extend their tongues for the sake of the beings of this
    Sahā world
Who commit the ten evil acts and the five grave offenses,
    entertain much doubt, and slander the Dharma,
Believe in wrong paths, serve spirits, offer food to gods
    and devils,

Who, with delusory thoughts, seek benevolence and
    benefits,
Only to find that misfortune and calamities increase more
    and more,
Or who, lying in bed with sickness for many years,
Become deaf and blind, have broken legs and paralyzed
    hands—

Those who serve gods and yet receive such retributions—
Why do they not abandon such beliefs and practice
    mindfulness of Amida?

It is stated in T'ien-t'ai's *Steps to the Dharma Realm* (*Fa-chieh tz'u ti*):

The first is to take refuge in the Buddha. The [*Nirvana*] *Sutra* says:

Those who take refuge in the Buddha should never again take refuge in various non-Buddhist gods.

333

It also says:

Those who take refuge in the Buddha will not fall into evil realms.

The second [step] is to take refuge in the Dharma. It is said, "Take refuge in and practice what the Great Sage taught, whether his teachings or theoretical principles."

The third is to take refuge in the Sangha. It is said, "The mind takes refuge in the company of those who have renounced the world and follow the right practice of the three vehicles." The same sutra says:

One never again takes refuge in non-Buddhist paths.

Master Tz'u-yün says:

In India, methods of worship are compiled in the Vedas, and in China they are found in the *Book of Rites*. They do not lead to liberation from the world. From the perspective of the true, they are provisional means to guide the people of the world.

[Hungry Ghosts]

Master Che-kwan of Koryo says:[219]

Hungry ghosts are called *preta*s in Sanskrit. Their places of habitation are found in various realms. Hungry ghosts with much merit become spirits of mountains and forests or of graveyards. Those without merit dwell in filthy places, receive no food or drink, and are constantly whipped. Forced to dam up rivers and oceans, they suffer immeasurable pain. Those who harbor flattery and deception in their hearts and have committed the five grave offenses and the ten evil acts that belong to the lowest degree of karmic evil receive the recompense of this state of existence.

Master Shen-chih comments on this:[220]

Concerning the realm of hungry ghosts, "hungry" means constantly starving, and "ghost" means that which returns. According to the *Book of Shih* (*Shih-tzu*), in ancient times a dead person was called "one who has returned." Also heavenly spirits are called spiritual beings, and earth spirits are called earth-gods.... In form, they resemble human beings or they are like beasts. The mind that is not honest is described as "flattery" and "deception."

Master Tai-chih says:[221]

"Spirits" refers to spiritual beings. They all belong to the four realms of the gods, the *asura*s, the hungry ghosts, and hell.

[Devils' Disturbances]

Master Chieh-tu says:[222]

Devils are classified in evil realms.

The *Discourse on Cessation and Contemplation,* in the section on devils' activities, says:

Second, I will clarify the way devils appear: Whether they belong to the upper or lower class, they are called devils. When we look into the details of their differences, we find that there are no more than three kinds: 1) spirits that irritate practitioners, 2) spirits that seduce practitioners at fixed hours, and 3) devil spirits. The ways these three kinds of devils appear vary.

642c

Genshin, based on the *Discourse on Cessation and Contemplation,* says:[223]

Devils obstruct enlightenment by taking advantage of practitioners' evil passions. Spirits cause illness and deprive them of the root of life.

The *Confucian Analects* says:

Chi-lu asked, "Should we worship spirits?"

Confucius said, "You should not worship spirits. Why should people worship them?"

[Epilogue]

When I humbly contemplate matters, I find that in the various teachings of the path of sages, both practice and enlightenment have long become unrealizable, and the true teaching of the Pure Land Way is now flourishing as the sure way to enlightenment.

Despite this fact, monks of various temples, being blind in discerning the teachings, are unable to distinguish true from provisional ways. Confucian scholars in the capital, confused about practices, cannot tell the difference between right and wrong paths. Thus, the scholar-monks of Kōfukuji Temple presented a petition to the retired emperor [Gotoba-in] (Takanari) in the first part of the second month in the fire/hare year of the Jōgen era[224] during the reign of Emperor [Tsuchimikado-in] (Tamehito).

Lords and vassals who opposed the Dharma and justice bore indignation and resentment [to the Nembutsu teaching]. Thus, Master Genkū, the great founder who promulgated the true teaching of the Pure Land Way, and a number of his followers were, without proper investigation of their crimes, indiscriminately sentenced to death or, deprived of their priesthood, exiled under criminals' names. I was one of them. Hence, I am neither priest nor layman, and so I took "Toku" as my surname. Master Genkū and his disciples spent five years in exile in remote provinces.

On the seventeenth day of the eleventh month in the first year of Kenryaku, the metal/sheep year,[225] during the reign of Emperor [Sado-no-in] (Morinari), Master Genkū was pardoned by imperial order and returned to the capital. After that he lived at Ōtani, north of Toribeno at the western foot of Higashiyama, Kyoto. In the second year of Kenryaku, he passed away at the hour of the horse (midday) of the twenty-fifth day of the first month. At his death, there appeared incalculable miraculous signs, as stated in his biography.

I, Gutoku Shinran, disciple of Śākyamuni, abandoned sundry practices and took refuge in the Primal Vow in the first year of Kennin, the metal/rooster year.[226] In the wood/ox year of the Genkyū era,[227] with the master's kind permission, I copied his *Collection of Passages on the Nembutsu Chosen in the Original Vow*. In the same year, on the fourth day of the middle part of the fourth month, the master in his own hand inscribed my copy with the title inside, *"Collection of Passages on the Nembutsu Chosen in the Original Vow,"* and the words, *"Namu amida butsu:* The fundamental act for the attainment of birth is the Nembutsu," and also my new name, "Shakkū, disciple of Śākyamuni." On the same day, I borrowed the master's portrait and copied it. In the same second year [of Genkyū], on the ninth day of the latter part of the seventh intercalary month, the master inscribed my copy of the portrait with *"Namu amida butsu"* and with this passage of the true teaching: "If, when I become a Buddha, all sentient beings in the ten directions who call my Name even ten times fail to be born in my land, may I not attain perfect enlightenment. This Buddha, having attained Buddhahood, now dwells in the Pure Land. You should know that his weighty vows are not in vain. Sentient beings who call his Name will unfailingly attain birth." On the same day, he also wrote on the portrait my new name, [Zenshin,] to which my former name "Shakkū" was changed according to a revelation in a dream. The master was then seventy-three years old.

643a

The *Collection of Passages on the Nembutsu Chosen in the Original Vow* was compiled at the request of the chancellor, the ordained layman (Lord Tsukinowa Kanezane, Buddhist name Enshō). The essentials of the true teaching of the Pure Land Way and the profound doctrine of the Nembutsu are contained in it. Those who read it can easily understand. It is indeed an incomparable and supreme collection of fine passages, an unsurpassed and profound scripture. Out of the thousands of people who received his teaching, personally or otherwise, over many days and years, very few were allowed to read and copy this book.

Nevertheless, I was allowed to copy it and also make a copy of Genkū's portrait. This is the benefit of the exclusive practice of the act of right assurance; this is a sure proof of my future attainment of birth. With tears of sorrow and joy, I have noted the above story.

What a joy it is that I place my mind in the ground of the Buddha's Universal Vow and let my thoughts flow into the sea of the inconceivable Dharma! I deeply acknowledge the Tathāgata's compassion and appreciate the master's benevolence in instructing me. As my joy increases, my feeling of indebtedness deepens. Hereupon, I have collected the essentials of the true teaching, and have gleaned important passages of the Pure Land Way. I think only of the Buddha's deep benevolence, and do not concern myself with people's abuse. May those who read this attain joyful faith of the Vow-Power, either by the cause of faithful acceptance of the teaching or by the condition of doubt and abuse, and realize the supreme fruition in the Land of Peace and Provision.

It is stated in the *Collection of Passages on the Land of Peace and Bliss:*

> I have collected true words so that they may help others practice the way for birth. For my wish is that those who have attained birth may lead those who come after them and those who aspire for birth may follow their predecessors, thus following one after another endlessly and uninterruptedly until the boundless sea of birth and death is exhausted.
>
> For this reason, priests and laypeople of the last age should respectfully accept this teaching in faith. This one should bear in mind.

A verse in the *Garland Sutra* says:

> When people see a bodhisattva
> Perform various practices,

Some give rise to good thoughts and others conceive
    evil thoughts;
But the bodhisattva embraces them both.

End of Chapter VI: Revealing the Transformed
Buddhas and Lands

Obscuring the light and mixing with the dust is the
    beginning of establishing contact with beings;
Attaining Buddhahood and manifesting the eight
    major events shows the end of the Buddha's mission.

Notes

1. In the *Commentary on the Larger Sutra* (*Wu liang shou ching lien i shu wen tsan*).

2. Shinran's note says: Also known as the *Larger Sutra on Amida* and the *Sutra on the Twenty-four Vows*.

3. This description should read: *Sutra on the Lotus of Compassion*, fascicle three, "Chapter on Giving Predictions to Bodhisattvas."

4. *Discourse on the Ten Stages* (*Daśabhūmika-vibhāṣā*), "Chapter on Entry into the First Stage."

5. Refers to Nāgārjuna's *Provision for Bodhi* (*Bodhi-saṃbhāra**).

6. In the *Discourse on the Ten Stages*, "Chapter on the Specific Features of the First Stage."

7. In the *Discourse on the Ten Stages*, "Chapter on the Purification of the First Stage."

8. In the *Discourse on the Ten Stages*, "Chapter on the Easy Practice."

9. In the *Discourse on the Pure Land* (*Sukhāvatīvyūha-upadeśa**).

10. Part of the Chinese term for "condensed form."

11. In the *Discourse on the Pure Land*.

12. In the *Collection of Passages on the Land of Peace and Bliss* (*An le chi*).

13. The *Commentary on the Perfection of Great Wisdom Sutra* (*Mahāprajñā-pāramitā-upadeśa**).

14. In the *Collection of Passages on the Land of Peace and Bliss*.

15. In the *Collection of Passages on the Land of Peace and Bliss*.

16. In the *Hymns of Birth in the Pure Land* (*Wang sheng li tsan chieh*).

17. In the *Hymns of Birth in the Pure Land*.

18. In the *Hymns of Birth in the Pure Land*.

19 In the *Hymns of Birth in the Pure Land.*

20 In the *Hymns of Birth in the Pure Land.*

21 In the *Essential Meaning of the Contemplation Sutra (Hsüan i fen).*

22 In the *Essential Meaning of the Contemplation Sutra.*

23 In the *Method of Contemplation of Amida Buddha (Kuan nien fa men).*

24 In the *Method of Contemplation of Amida Buddha.*

25 In the *Hymns on the Pratyutpanna Samādhi (Pan chou tsan).*

26 In Kyeong-heung's *Commentary on the Larger Sutra.*

27 In Kyeong-heung's *Commentary on the Larger Sutra.*

28 In Kyeong-heung's *Commentary on the Larger Sutra.*

29 In Kyeong-heung's *Commentary on the Larger Sutra.*

30 In Kyeong-heung's *Commentary on the Larger Sutra.*

31 In the *Larger Sutra.*

32 In Kyeong-heung's *Commentary on the Larger Sutra.*

33 In Kyeong-heung's *Commentary on the Larger Sutra.*

34 In Kyeong-heung's *Commentary on the Larger Sutra.*

35 In Kyeong-heung's *Commentary on the Larger Sutra.*

36 The *Discourse on the Awakening of Faith in the Mahayana (Mahāyāna-śraddhotpāda-śāstra*).*

37 In the *Commentary on the Amida Sutra (A mi t'o ching i shu)* by Master Yüan-chao.

38 In his *Commentary on the Contemplation Sutra (Kuan ching shu).*

39 In his *Commentary on the Larger Sutra.*

40 In his *Discourse on the Nembutsu Samādhi, the King of Jewels (Nien fo san mei pao wang lun).*

41 Refers to the *Larger Sutra.*

42 In Nāgārjuna's *Discourse on the Ten Stages,* "Chapter on the Easy Practice."

43 In the *Commentary on Vasubandhu's Discourse on the Pure Land (Wang sheng lun chu).*

44 In the *Hymns of Birth in the Pure Land.*

45 In the *Shorter Pure Land Liturgy of the Nembutsu Chant in Five Stages* (*Wu hui fa shih tsan*).

46 In the *Commentary on the Non-meditative Good* (*San shan i*).

47 In the *Commentary on the Non-meditative Good*.

48 In the *Hymns of Birth in the Pure Land*.

49 In the *Commentary on the Non-meditative Good*.

50 The *Hymns of Birth in the Pure Land*.

51 The *Commentary on the Non-meditative Good*.

52 The *Commentary on the Non-meditative Good*.

53 The *Commentary on Vasubandhu's Discourse on the Pure Land*.

54 In the *Commentary on the Contemplation Sutra*.

55 This phrase appears in Shan-tao's *Essential Meaning of the Contemplation Sutra*.

56 The *Nirvana Sutra*, "Chapter on the Sacred Practice."

57 The *Nirvana Sutra*, "Chapter on Virtuous King."

58 The *Nirvana Sutra*, "Chapter on Expounding the Dharma like a Lion."

59 The *Nirvana Sutra*, "Chapter on Expounding the Dharma like a Lion."

60 The *Garland Sutra* (*Avataṃsaka-sūtra*), "Chapter on Clarification of Difficulties."

61 In the phrase "ocean of the One Vehicle" mentioned above; see note 55.

62 In the *Essential Meaning of the Contemplation Sutra*.

63 In the *Hymns on the Pratyutpanna Samādhi*.

64 In the *Larger Sutra*.

65 In the *Teaching Assembly of the Tathāgata of Infinite Life* (*Sukhāvatī-vyūha-sūtra*).

66 In the *Commentary on the Meditative Good* (*Ting shan i*).

67 In the passage that says, "Amida's transcendent powers are unhindered; they work everywhere according to one's wishes."

68 In the *Commentary on the Introductory Part* (*Hsü fen i*).

69 In the *Commentary on the Non-meditative Good*.

70 In the *Hymns on the Pratyutpanna Samādhi.*

71 In the *Commentary on the Non-meditative Good.*

72 The *Nirvana Sutra,* "Chapter on the Sacred Practice."

73 The *Nirvana Sutra,* "Chapter on the Sacred Practice."

74 In the *Teaching Assembly of the Tathāgata of Infinite Life.*

75 The *Nirvana Sutra,* "Chapter on the Lion's Roar."

76 The *Nirvana Sutra,* "Chapter on Kāśyapa."

77 The *Nirvana Sutra,* "Chapter on Kāśyapa."

78 The *Garland Sutra,* "Chapter on Entry into the Dharma Realm," Chin version.

79 The *Garland Sutra,* T'ang version.

80 The *Garland Sutra,* "Chapter on Bhadraśrī Bodhisattva," T'ang version.

81 In the *Teaching Assembly of the Tathāgata of Infinite Life.*

82 In the *Commentary on the Non-meditative Good.*

83 The *Essential Meaning of the Contemplation Sutra.*

84 The *Commentary on the Introductory Part.*

85 The *Commentary on the Meditative Good.*

86 In the *Commentary on the Amida Sutra.*

87 In Chieh-tu's *Notes for Memory (Wen ch'ih chi)* to the *Commentary on the Amida Sutra.*

88 In the *Teaching Assembly of the Tathāgata of Infinite Life.*

89 In the *Larger Sutra.*

90 In the *Teaching Assembly of the Tathāgata of Infinite Life.*

91 The *Nirvana Sutra,* "Chapter on Kāśyapa."

92 In the *Commentary on the Non-meditative Good.*

93 In the phrase, "having heard the Name."

94 In the *Commentary on the Meditative Good.*

95 Quoted above from Shan-tao's work, the *Commentary on the Meditative Good* (see note 66).

[96] The full title of this sutra is: *Sutra on the Way of Salvation of Humans by Amida, the Perfectly Enlightened One, That Transcends All Buddhas*, translated by Tripiṭaka Master Chih-ch'ien.

[97] In the *Sutra on the Immeasurably Pure and Equal Enlightenment (Sukhāvatīvyūha-sūtra)*.

[98] The *Nirvana Sutra*, "Chapter on the Lion's Roar."

[99] In the *Hymns on the Pratyutpanna Samādhi*.

[100] In the *Hymns of Birth in the Pure Land*.

[101] In the *Teaching Assembly of the Tathāgata of Infinite Life*.

[102] In the *Contemplation Sutra*.

[103] In the *Hymns on the Pratyutpanna Samādhi*.

[104] In the *Hymns of Birth in the Pure Land*.

[105] In the *Method of Contemplation of Amida Buddha*.

[106] In the *Commentary on the Introductory Part*.

[107] In the *Commentary on the Non-meditative Good*.

[108] In the *Collection of Passages on the Pure Land Teaching (Lun shu ching t'u wen)*.

[109] In the *Teaching Assembly of the Tathāgata of Infinite Life*.

[110] Quoted by Tsung-hsiao in his *Collection of Passages on the Land of Bliss*.

[111] Quoted by Tsung-hsiao in his *Collection of Passages on the Land of Bliss*.

[112] In the *Hymns on the Pratyutpanna Samādhi*.

[113] In the *Hymns of the Nembutsu Liturgy (Fa shih tsan)*.

[114] In the *Hymns on the Pratyutpanna Samādhi*.

[115] The *Nirvana Sutra*, "Chapter on What the Multitudes Heard."

[116] In the *Hymns of the Nembutsu Liturgy*.

[117] The *Nirvana Sutra*, "Chapter on Actual Illnesses."

[118] The *Nirvana Sutra*, "Chapter on the Sacred Practice."

[119] The *Nirvana Sutra*, "Chapter on the Sacred Practice."

[120] The *Nirvana Sutra*, "Chapter on Kāśyapa."

[121] In the *Teaching Assembly of the Tathāgata of Infinite Life.*

[122] The *Śūraṅgama Samādhi Sutra*, fascicle one.

[123] In the *Commentary on the Non-meditative Good.*

[124] In the *Hymns of the Nembutsu Liturgy.*

[125] In the *Ten Causes of Birth* (*Ōjōjūin*).

[126] The *Sutra on the Ten Wheels of Kṣitigarbha* (*Daśacakra-kṣitigarbha-sūtra**).

[127] In the *Teaching Assembly of the Tathāgata of Infinite Life.*

[128] In the *Essential Meaning of the Contemplation Sutra.*

[129] In the *Commentary on the Meditative Good.*

[130] In the *Larger Sutra.*

[131] The *Nirvana Sutra,* "Chapter on the Four Aspects."

[132] In the *Nirvana Sutra,* "Chapter on the Four Dependables."

[133] In the *Nirvana Sutra,* "Chapter on the Sacred Practice."

[134] In the *Nirvana Sutra,* "Chapter on the Sacred Practice."

[135] In the *Nirvana Sutra,* "Chapter on the Virtuous King."

[136] In the *Nirvana Sutra,* "Chapter on the Virtuous King."

[137] In the *Nirvana Sutra,* "Chapter on the Virtuous King."

[138] In the *Nirvana Sutra,* "Chapter on Kāśyapa."

[139] In the *Nirvana Sutra,* "Chapter on Kāśyapa."

[140] In the *Nirvana Sutra,* "Chapter on the Sacred Practice."

[141] In the *Nirvana Sutra,* "Chapter on Kāśyapa."

[142] In the *Nirvana Sutra,* "Chapter on Kāśyapa."

[143] In the *Nirvana Sutra,* "Chapter on the Lion's Roar."

[144] In the *Essential Meaning of the Contemplation Sutra.*

[145] In the *Commentary on the Introductory Section.*

[146] In the *Commentary on the Meditative Good.*

[147] In the *Hymns of the Nembutsu Liturgy.*

[148] In the *Hymns of the Nembutsu Liturgy.*

[149] In the *Hymns of the Nembutsu Liturgy.*

[150] In Kyeong-heung's *Commentary on the Larger Sutra.*

[151] The *Nirvana Sutra,* "Chapter on Kāśyapa."

[152] The *Nirvana Sutra,* "Chapter on Kāśyapa."

[153] Quoted in Fei-hsi's *Discourse on the Nembutsu Samādhi, the King of Jewels.*

[154] The *Sutra on the Way of Salvation of Humans by Amida, the Perfectly Enlightened One, That Transcends All Buddhas.*

[155] The *Sutra on the Immeasurably Pure and Equal Enlightenment.*

[156] In the *Teaching Assembly of the Tathāgata of Infinite Life.*

[157] In the *Hymns of the Nembutsu Liturgy.*

[158] The passage quoted here is, in fact, in the "Chapter on Giving Predictions to Bodhisattvas."

[159] In the *Larger Sutra.*

[160] In the *Teaching Assembly of the Tathāgata of Infinite Life.*

[161] In the *Commentary on the Meditative Good.*

[162] In Kyeong-heung's *Commentary on the Larger Sutra.*

[163] The *Discourse Clearing Doubts about the Pure Land Teaching* (*Shih ching t'u ch'ün i lun*).

[164] In the *Essential Meaning of the Contemplation Sutra.*

[165] In the *Essential Meaning of the Contemplation Sutra.*

[166] In the *Commentary on the Introductory Part.*

[167] In the *Commentary on the Introductory Part.*

[168] In the *Commentary on the Non-meditative Good.*

[169] In the *Commentary on the Introductory Part.*

[170] In the *Commentary on the Introductory Part.*

[171] In the *Commentary on the Non-meditative Good.*

[172] In the *Hymns of Birth in the Pure Land.*

[173] In the *Hymns of Birth in the Pure Land.*

[174] In the *Method of Contemplation of Amida Buddha.*

[175] In the *Hymns of the Nembutsu Liturgy.*

[176] In the *Hymns on the Pratyutpanna Samādhi.*

[177] In the *Hymns on the Pratyutpanna Samādhi.*

[178] the *Essential Meaning of the Contemplation Sutra.*

[179] In the *Commentary on the Meditative Good.*

[180] The *Hymns of the Nembutsu Liturgy.*

[181] The *Hymns of the Nembutsu Liturgy.*

[182] In the *Commentary on the Meditative Good.*

[183] In the *Commentary on the Non-meditative Good.*

[184] In the *Commentary on the Non-meditative Good.*

[185] In the *Commentary on the Non-meditative Good.*

[186] In the *Hymns of the Nembutsu Liturgy.*

[187] In the *Hymns of the Nembutsu Liturgy.*

[188] In the *Hymns of the Nembutsu Liturgy.*

[189] In the *Hymns on the Pratyutpanna Samādhi.*

[190] In the *Hymns of Birth in the Pure Land;* this is quoted in Chih-sheng's *Collection of Liturgical Passages from Various Scriptures.*

[191] The *Commentary on the Amida Sutra.*

[192] The *Nirvana Sutra,* "Chapter on Kāśyapa."

[193] The *Nirvana Sutra,* "Chapter on Kāśyapa."

[194] The *Nirvana Sutra,* "Chapter on the Virtuous King."

[195] The *Garland Sutra,* "Chapter on Entry into the Dharma Realm."

[196] The *Garland Sutra,* "Chapter on Entry into the Dharma Realm."

[197] In the *Hymns on the Pratyutpanna Samādhi.*

[198] In the *Hymns of Birth in the Pure Land.*

[199] In the *Hymns of the Nembutsu Liturgy.*

[200] In the *Hymns of the Nembutsu Liturgy.*

[201] In the *Hymns of Birth in the Pure Land.*

[202] In the *Collection of Passages on the Land of Bliss.*

203 Should read: "two thousand one hundred and seventy-three years."

204 Should read: "six hundred and seventy-three years."

205 Should read: "fifty-third year," 949 B.C.E.

206 801 C.E.

207 609 B.C.E.

208 801 C.E.

209 In the *Nirvana Sutra.*

210 The *Four-Part Vinaya (Dharmaguptaka-vinaya).*

211 The *Nirvana Sutra,* "Chapter on the Nature of Tathāgata."

212 The *bodhi* of the *śrāvaka,* the *pratyekabuddha,* and the bodhisattva.

213 In the *Garland Sutra,* "Chapter on the Ten Stages."

214 714 B.C.E.

215 519 B.C.E.

216 1027 B.C.E.

217 949 B.C.E.

218 In the *Hymns of the Nembutsu Liturgy.*

219 In *T'ien-t'ai's Discourse on the Fourfold Teachings (T'ien t'ai ssu chiao i).*

220 In his *Commentary on T'ien-t'ai's Discourse on the Fourfold Teachings (T'ien t'ai ssu chiao i chi chieh).*

221 In the *New Notes to the Commentary on the Ullambana Sutra (Yü lan p'en ching shu hsin chi).*

222 In the *Subsidiary Discourse on the Contemplation Sutra (Kuan ching fou hsin lun).*

223 In the *Collection of Essential Passages Concerning Birth.*

224 1207 C.E.

225 1211 C.E.

226 1201 C.E.

227 1205 C.E.

Glossary

Abhijit: One of the twenty-eight constellations; corresponds to four stars in Aquarius. *See also* twenty-eight constellations.

accommodated body: One of the three bodies of the Buddha; the manifestation of a transformed body of a Buddha in correspondence with the beings to be saved. *See also* three bodies of the Buddha.

act of right assurance: The fourth of the five right acts established by Shantao; it is to recite Amida's Name singlemindedly. *See also* Amida; Name; Shan-tao.

adamantine mind or adamantine faith: Faith of the Other-Power; since this quality is in essence Amida's wisdom and compassion, it is indestructible, hence, "adamantine." *See also* faith of the Other-Power.

agada: A medicine with miraculous healing power, or a medicine for deathlessness.

Āgamas: A body of scriptures containing the early teachings of the Buddha.

Age of the Decadent Dharma: The period of ten thousand years following the Age of the Semblance Dharma, in which only the teaching of the Buddha exists but correct practice is no longer possible. *See also* Age of the Semblance Dharma; five five hundred-year periods; three ages of the Dharma.

Age of the Extinct Dharma: The age that follows the Age of the Decadent Dharma; in this period the Buddha-Dharma becomes completely extinct. This period lasts for a very long time until the next Buddha appears in the world. *See also* Age of the Decadent Dharma; three ages of the Dharma.

Age of the Right Dharma: The period of five hundred years after the Buddha's passing into nirvana, in which his teaching is properly practiced and enlightenment can be attained. *See also* five five hundred-year periods; three ages of the Dharma.

Age of the Semblance Dharma: The period of a thousand years following the Age of the Right Dharma, in which the Buddha's teaching is practiced but enlightenment is no longer possible. *See also* Age of the Right Dharma; five five hundred-year periods; three ages of the Dharma.

aggregates. *See* five aggregates.

Ajātaśatru ("Unborn Enemy"): The son of King Bimbisāra and Queen Vaidehī; he imprisoned his father and left him to die in jail, thus usurping the throne of Magadha. He also imprisoned his mother. Later he repented his evil act and became a disciple of the Buddha. *See also* Bimbisāra; Magadha; Vaidehī.

Ajita ("Unconquerable"): The name of a bodhisattva identified with Maitreya. *See also* Maitreya.

Ajitavatī: A river in Central India; the Buddha passed into nirvana on the western side of this river.

āmalaka: The name of a plant bearing edible fruits, which are also used for medicinal purposes.

Amida: The name of the Buddha who dwells in the Pure Land, from the Sanskrit amita ("infinite"), which stands for Amitābha ("Infinite Light") and Amitāyus ("Infinite Life"). Amida is one of the most popular Buddhas and is mentioned in more than two hundred sutras, of which the *Sutra on the Buddha of Infinite Life (Larger Sutra)* is the most important, as one of the canonical texts of Pure Land Buddhism in China and Japan. According to this sutra, Amida was previously a king; when he met the Buddha Lokeśvararāja, he wished to himself become a Buddha. He then renounced the world and became a mendicant called Dharmākara. Dharmākara made Forty-eight Vows and performed various bodhisattva practices to fulfill them. After many eons his vows were fulfilled and he became the Buddha of Infinite Light and Life—Amida. His land is called Sukhāvatī, "the land of utmost bliss," also known as the Pure Land and the Western Paradise. For purposes of meditative practice, the Pure Land sutras describe Amida's land as being in the west. As Amida promised in the Eighteenth Vow, those who have joyful faith and recite his Name, a practice called the Nembutsu, are assured of rebirth in the Pure Land. Amida is a transcendent Buddha, as contrasted to a historical Buddha, and is generally regarded as a recompensed-body Buddha. The tradition of Buddhism centering around Amida arose in India and further developed in China and Japan. Amida is thus the principal Buddha in the Jōdo, Shin, and other Pure Land schools. In Esoteric Buddhism, Amida is one of the five Buddhas that dwell in the five cardinal directions. *See also* Dharmākara; Eighteenth Vow; Esoteric Buddhism; Forty-eight Vows; Jōdo Shinshū; Nembutsu; Pure Land; Pure Land school; Shin school; *Larger Sutra;* three bodies of the Buddha.

Amida Sutra (Sukhāvatīvyūha-sūtra): The Chinese translation of this text by Kumārajīva has been used as one of the three basic canonical texts of Pure Land Buddhism; the title of the Sanskrit text is *Sukhāvatīvyūha,* "Glorious Adornment of Sukhāvatī" ("land of bliss") (See *The Smaller Sutra on Amitāyus,* in *The Three Pure Land Sutras,* Revised Second Edition, translated by INAGAKI Hisao, Numata Center, 2003.) The *Amida Sutra* briefly describes blissful aspects of the Pure Land (Sukhāvatī) and mentions that innumerable Buddhas of the six directions praise Amida's virtue and testify to the truth of this sutra. It then explains that one who holds fast to Amida's Name (i.e., recitation of the Nembutsu) will be born in his land. It is also referred to as the *Smaller Sutra* or the *Sutra on the Buddha of Infinite Life. See also* Amida; *Amida Sutra;* Kumārajīva; Nembutsu; Pure Land; Pure Land school.

Ānanda ("Happiness" or "Joy"): A cousin of the Buddha who was his close disciple and personal attendant, and who was renowned for his ability to recite all of the Buddha's sermons from memory.

Aṅga-Magadha: One of the sixteen great kingdoms in India at the time of the Buddha. *See also* sixteen great kingdoms.

Anurādhā: One of the twenty-eight constellations; corresponds to four stars in Scorpio. *See also* twenty-eight constellations.

anuttara-samyak-saṃbodhi: Highest, perfect enlightenment. *See also bodhi.*

Aparagodānīya: One of the four great continents that lie in the four directions around Mount Sumeru; this continent lies to the west of Mount Sumeru; it is round, its inhabitants enjoy a lifespan of five hundred years, and cows are used as currency there. *See also* four great continents; Mount Sumeru.

Araṇemi ("Not disputing"): The name of the king mentioned in the *Sutra of the Lotus of Compassion;* he made fifty-two vows and became the Buddha of Immeasurable Life. *See also* Samudrareṇu.

Ārdrā: One of the twenty-eight constellations; corresponds to eight stars in Orion. *See also* twenty-eight constellations.

arhat ("one who is worthy" of offerings): A saint who has completely eradicated evil passions and attained liberation from the cycle of birth and death (samsara); arhatship is the highest of the four stages of spiritual attainment in the Hinayana; when capitalized, the term is also one of the ten epithets of a Buddha. *See also* Hinayana; samsara.

Āryadeva (ca. third century): Disciple of Nāgārjuna and author of the *Hundred-verse Discourse* (*Śata-śāstra**), a foundational text of the Three Discourse school. *See also* Nāgārjuna; Mādhyamika school; Three Discourse school.

Āśleṣā: One of the twenty-eight constellations; corresponds to eight stars in Hydra. *See also* twenty-eight constellations.

Assaka: One of the sixteen great kingdoms in India at the time of the Buddha. *See also* sixteen great kingdoms.

asura: A kind of evil spirit that is constantly engaged in warring against the Hindu gods. In Buddhism, they became one of the eight kinds of superhuman beings that protect Buddhism.

asura castle: Refers to the four *asura* kings' castles that exist under the sea on the four sides of Mount Sumeru. *See also* Mount Sumeru.

asura's harp: A harp possessed by *asura*s which produces music without anyone playing it. *See also asura.*

Aśvaghoṣa: A great exponent of the Mahayana who flourished in the first century C.E.; the author of an epic poem on the life of the Buddha, the *Buddha-carita,* and the probable author of the *Discourse on the Awakening of Faith in the Mahayana. See also Discourse on the Awakening of Faith in the Mahayana;* Mahayana.

Aśvinī: One of the twenty-eight constellations; corresponds to three stars in Aries. *See also* twenty-eight constellations.

Auspicious Kalpa: The present cosmic period, in which a thousand Buddhas are believed to appear in the world. *See also kalpa.*

Auspicious Name: Amida's Name that contains immeasurable virtues capable of removing all karmic evils. *See also* Amida.

auxiliary acts: Of the five right acts, the first three and the last are called auxiliary; the fourth, exclusive recitation of Amida's Name, is called "the act of right assurance." *See also* act of right assurance; Amida; five right acts.

avaivartika: The stage of non-retrogression. *See also* bodhisattva stages.

Avalokiteśvara ("Lord of beholding [people of the world]"): The name of a great bodhisattva who represents Amida's great compassion. Amida often appears in a triad with Avalokiteśvara on his left and Mahāsthāmaprāpta on his right. *See also* Amida; bodhisattva; Mahāsthāmaprāpta.

Avantī: One of the sixteen great kingdoms in India at the time of the Buddha. *See also* sixteen great kingdoms.

Avīci hell: The hell of interminable pain and suffering; those who have committed the five grave offenses and abused the Dharma are consigned to this hell. *See also* five grave offenses; hell.

Bhallika. *See* Trapuṣa.

Bharaṇī: One of the twenty-eight constellations; corresponds to the Musca Borealis. *See also* twenty-eight constellations.

Bimbisāra: The fifth king of the Śaiśnāga dynasty in Magadha and a follower of the Buddha. In his later years he was imprisoned by his son Ajātaśatru and died in confinement. *See also* Ajātaśatru; Magadha.

birth and death. *See* samsara.

birth beneath the twin *śāla* trees: A form of birth in the Transformed Land attained by followers of the Nineteenth Vow; the "twin *śāla* trees" is the place where Śākyamuni entered nirvana. *See also* Nineteenth Vow; nirvana; Śākyamuni; Transformed Land; twin *śāla* trees.

Bob-wi: A seventh-century Korean master of the Consciousness Only school and the author of the *Commentary on the Larger Sutra* (lost). *See also* Consciousness Only school.

bodhi: Enlightenment; the state of the highest perfection of wisdom; the state of undefiled purity and eternal bliss. *See also* three kinds of *bodhi*.

bodhi-mind (*bodhicitta*): The bodhisattva's aspiration to attain enlightenment (*bodhi*) and save other beings from suffering. *See also bodhi;* bodhisattva.

Bodhiruci: An Indian monk who was invited to Ch'ang-an, China, in 693; he produced translations of fifty-three scriptures, including Vasubandhu's *Discourse on the Pure Land,* and is said to have converted the Chinese monk-scholar T'an-luan to Pure Land Buddhism. *See also Discourse on the Pure Land;* Pure Land school; T'an-luan; Vasubandhu.

bodhisattva: In the Mahayana, one who has made vows to attain enlightenment and save suffering beings through embarking on a course of practice known as the six perfections (*pāramitā*s), which requires an immensely long period of time to complete. One who has accomplished the bodhisattva practices and completed the ten bodhisattva stages is a Buddha. *See also* bodhisattva stages; Mahayana; six perfections.

bodhisattva-*piṭaka:* The body of Mahayana teachings of the bodhisattva path. *See also* Mahayana.

bodhisattva stages: The spiritual stages that must be accomplished by a bodhisattva who has awakened aspiration for enlightenment (*bodhicitta*) and made vows, culminating in the attainment of Buddhahood. Ten stages were established in Indian Buddhism; Chinese Buddhists later developed a system of fifty-two stages. In these stages, one is expected to perform various practices for innumerable eons over many lifetimes. *See also bodhicitta;* bodhisattva; fifty-two stages; ten stages.

bodhi tree: The tree under which a Buddha attains enlightenment.

borderland: A figurative expression for the Transformed Land. *See also* Transformed Land.

Brahmā: Originally, the creator god in Hinduism, incorporated into Buddhism as a tutelary god.

Brahmā Heaven: One of the heavens of the world of form. *See also* three worlds.

Buddha-contemplation *samādhi:* Concentration of the mind in order to visualize Buddhas, especially Amida. *See also* Amida; *samādhi.*

Buddhahood: The state of being a Buddha; the goal of the bodhisattva path.

Buddha land: A cosmic world or realm in which a particular Buddha dwells.

Buddha-nature: The potentiality of becoming a Buddha; the essential nature of the Buddha.

Buddha of Infinite Life: Refers to Amida Buddha; infinite life is one of his two major attributes, along with infinite light. *See also* Amida.

Buddha of Infinite Light: Refers to Amida Buddha; infinite light is one of his two major attributes, along with infinite life. *See also* Amida.

Buddha vehicle: The Mahayana teaching that enables all beings to attain Buddhahood. *See also* Mahayana.

burning house: A metaphor from the *Lotus Sutra* that refers to the three realms of transmigration. *See also Lotus Sutra;* three realms of transmigration.

campaka: A fragrant tree.

capital of tranquility and non-action: Refers to Amida's Pure Land which is the state of nirvana free of disturbances by evil passions and delusions. *See also* Amida; evil passions; nirvana; Pure Land.

Cetī: One of the sixteen great kingdoms in India at the time of the Buddha. *See also* sixteen great kingdoms.

Chang-lun: A military officer at the time of Kao Tsung in the Southern Sung dynasty; in his later years he built a hall in his residence where he practiced the Nembutsu with his family. *See also* Nembutsu.

Ch'an school (Japan, Zen): A major Mahayana school that teaches exclusive practice of meditation as its soteriological path; the word *ch'an* is a transliteration of the Sanskrit *dhyāna* (meditation). According to tradition, one day when the Buddha was with an assembly of disciples on Mount Gṛdhrakūṭa (Vulture Peak) in India, he lifted up a flower that had been offered to him by a god. None among his disciples understood the meaning of this gesture except Mahākāśyapa, who indicated his realization by smiling. The Buddha then proclaimed that he would transmit directly to Mahākāśyapa the essence of Buddhism. Thus the Ch'an school, unlike other Buddhist schools, does not rely on a specific set of scriptural texts for its doctrinal basis but instead on "the transmission outside the scriptures," the direct teaching and transmission of the mystic truth of Ch'an from master to disciple. From Mahākāśyapa the tradition was transmitted to his disciple, then to the latter's disciple, and so on, in India until the twenty-eighth patriarch, Bodhidharma, brought Ch'an to China in 529. After an interview with Emperor Wu-ti, Bodhidharma went to live on Mount Sung, where he meditated day and night, finally transmitting the tradition to his successor Hui-k'o, the second patriarch of the Ch'an school in China. Ch'an flourished remarkably in China after the sixth patriarch Hui-neng, developing into several subschools. From the eighth century on it was introduced into Japan, where it is known as the Zen school. The two major Zen schools, Rinzai and Sōtō, were brought to Japan by Eisai in 1191 and Dōgen in 1227, respectively. A third school, the Ōbaku, was established in 1654. According to Ch'an (Zen), Buddhas and their lands are not established outside of one's mind. Practitioners are encouraged to realize Buddhahood directly through the concentrated practice of meditation, using meditative techniques designed to help them transcend ordinary dualistic thought, such as meditating on *kōans*, paradoxical conundrums that cannot be grasped by logical or conceptual means, often in the form of anecdotes of past masters.

Chapter on the Universal Gate" of the *Lotus Sutra:* This chapter explains that Avalokiteśvara manifests thirty-three incarnations to save suffering beings. *See also* Avalokiteśvara; *Lotus Sutra.*

Che-kwan: A Korean T'ien-t'ai monk of the mid-tenth century, author of *T'ien-t'ai's Discourse on the Fourfold Teachings (T'ien t'ai ssu chiao i).* At the request of the king of Wu-yueh, he brought T'ien-t'ai scriptures to China, which had been lost there due to war. *See also* T'ien-t'ai school.

Chia-hsiang: An alternative name for the Chinese monk Chi-tsang, so called because he lived at the Chia-hsiang Temple. *See also* Chi-tsang.

Chieh-tu (ca. twelfth century): A master of the Vinaya school and a disciple of Yüan-chao; he was a devoted practitioner of Pure Land Buddhism. *See also* Pure Land school; Vinaya school; Yüan-chao.

Chih-i (538–597): The third patriarch of the T'ien-t'ai school, popularly known as Master T'ien-t'ai or Master Chih-che. The author of many works, he is regarded as the founder of the T'ien-t'ai school due to his great contribution to the systematization of its teachings. *See also* T'ien-t'ai school.

Chih-sheng: A Vinaya master of the T'ang dynasty; well known as the compiler of the *K'ai-yüan Era Catalog of Scriptures (K'ai yüan shih chiao lu). See also* Vinaya school.

chin bird: A poisonous bird that feeds on snakes; its green feathers, when soaked in wine, are used to create poison.

Ch'ing-wen: A T'ien-t'ai master of the Sung dynasty. *See also* T'ien-t'ai school.

Chi-tsang (549–623). A Chinese monk who systematized the doctrine of the Three Discourse school by writing the *Essentials of the Three Discourses (San lun hsüan i). See also* Chia-hsiang; Three Discourse school.

Citrā: One of the twenty-eight constellations; corresponds to Spica and three stars in Virgo. *See also* twenty-eight constellations.

Collection of Passages on the Nembutsu Chosen in the Original Vow (Senchaku Hongan Nembutsu Shū; translated by Morris J. Augustine and KONDŌ Tesshō, Numata Center, 1997): An important Pure Land text composed by Hōnen in 1198 at the request of the chancellor, Fujiwara Kanezane. The text justifies the Nembutsu as the most effective method of salvation, and its appearance marked the independence of the Jōdo school, the Japanese school of Pure Land Buddhism. *See also* Hōnen;Jōdo Shinshū; Nembutsu; Pure Land school.

Collection of Passages on the Land of Peace and Bliss (An le chi): An important Pure Land text written by Tao-ch'o based mainly on the *Contemplation Sutra*. *See also Contemplation Sutra;* Pure Land school; Tao-ch'o.

Commentary on the Larger Sutra (Wu liang shou ching lien i shu wen tsan): A work by Kyeong-heung, a Korean monk of the latter half of the seventh century, who was originally a scholar of the Consciousness Only school. *See also* Kyeong-heung; Consciousness Only school.

Commentary on Vasubandhu's Discourse on the Pure Land (Wang sheng lun chu): T'an-luan's principal work and the foundation for the later development of Pure Land Buddhism, this text was especially valued by Shinran. *See also* Pure Land school; Shinran; T'an-luan; Vasubandhu.

Confucianism: An ethical, religious system of China originating in the teaching of Confucius; it centers around filial duty and emphasizes the virtues of benevolence and propriety. More specifically, Confucianism teaches the five constant virtues to be followed by all people: benevolence, righteousness, propriety, wisdom, and sincerity. The original individualistic ethical ideal developed into a political one; Confucius sought to establish the norm of ethics for the king. His influence was so great that the number of his disciples is said to have been three thousand. After his death, Confucian sanctuaries were built throughout China and its teachings spread far and wide in China and beyond—Confucianism formed the basic ethical norm of Korea, Vietnam, and Japan. *See also* Confucius.

Confucius (ca. 551–479 B.C.E.): Chinese philosopher and political scientist, author of the *Analects (Lun-yü)*; his teachings formed the basis of Confucianism. Born in a poor family in the state of Lu in Shan-tung province, initially he was a minor public servant but his extensive knowledge of the Chinese classics led him into a career as the founder of a private institute and then as a political advisor to Lu and other kingdoms. While traveling throughout the country, he preached his ideal of moral political philosophy to various leaders. His moral teaching, centering on humanistic principles and filial duty, spread widely in Chinese society and became a dominant school of thought known as Confucianism. *See also* Confucianism.

Consciousness Only school: A philosophical and psychological school of Mahayana Buddhism founded in the fourth century by Vasubandhu, which developed out of the Yogācāra tradition. The Chinese Tripiṭaka master Hsüan-tsang transmitted the teaching to China, where it thrived as the Fa-hsiang school. It was then transmitted to Japan, where it was known as the Hossō school, and became popular as one of the six schools of

Buddhism in the Nara period. *See also* Hossō school; Hsüan-tsang; Tripiṭaka master; Vasubandhu; Yogācāra.

contemplation. *See samādhi.*

contemplation of impurity: A meditative practice in which the meditator perceives through contemplation (*samādhi*) that all that he is attached to is impure, and thus his clinging and greed are removed. *See also samādhi.*

contemplation of the true Buddha body: The ninth of the thirteen contemplations (*samādhis*) in the *Contemplation Sutra,* which shows how to visualize Amida's true body. *See also* Amida; *Contemplation Sutra; samādhi.*

Contemplation Sutra (Amitāyurdhyāna-sūtra*): Also called the *Sutra on Visualization of the Buddha of Infinite Life,* one of the three major Pure Land sutras, translated into Chinese by Kālayaśas in the period 424–442. (See *The Sutra on Contemplation of Amitāyus,* in *The Three Pure Land Sutras,* Revised Second Edition, translated by INAGAKI Hisao, Numata Center, 2003.) The sutra begins with a tragic event involving King Bimbisāra and Queen Vaidehī. When Vaidehī requested the Buddha to teach her the way of salvation, he showed her various Buddha lands. She particularly wanted to be born in Amida's Pure Land, so Śākyamuni presented thirteen contemplations and nine levels of non-meditative good as the way of attaining birth there. *See also* Amida; Bimbisāra; Kālayaśas; non-meditative good; Pure Land; Śākyamuni; Vaidehī.

cosmic period (*kalpa*): A period of cosmic change, of which there are four major changes: 1) the creation of the universe; 2) the continued existence of the universe; 3) the destruction of the universe; and 4) the complete annihilation of the universe. In the second period, human lifespan is at first immeasurable but gradually decreases until it reaches ten years; then it gradually increases until it reaches eighty thousand years, from which it decreases until it reaches ten years. The present period is that of declining lifespan, especially the worst period when human lifespan is between a hundred and ten years and the five defilements are very strong. *See also* five defilements; *kalpa.*

cow-headed sandalwood (*gośīrṣa-candana*): The most fragrant sandalwood produced in the region of Mount Gośīrṣa ("cow head") in India.

crosswise going-out: Refers to the provisional Pure Land teachings corresponding to the Nineteenth and Twentieth Vows, which lead practitioners to the Transformed Land. *See also* crosswise transcendence; Nineteenth Vow; Pure Land school; Transformed Land; Twentieth Vow.

crosswise transcendence: Refers to the true Pure Land teaching corresponding to the Eighteenth Vow. *See also* crosswise going-out, Eighteenth Vow; Pure Land school.

dāna-pāramitā ("perfection of giving"): One of the six perfections (*pāramitā*s). *See also* six perfections.

Darkness-Free: Daughter of the devil king Pāpīyas. *See also* Pāpīyas.

definitely assured stage: The stage in which one is assured of attaining enlightenment; same as the stage of non-retrogression. *See also* boshisattva stages; stage of non-retrogression.

deva: A god, commonly used to refer a Hindu deity. The realm of the *deva*s is one of the six realms of samsara. *See also* six realms; three good realms.

Devadatta ("God-given"): A cousin of the Buddha who became his disciple but later tried to murder him and assume leadership of the sangha. Devadatta incited Prince Ajātaśatru to kill his father, King Bimbisāra, and usurp the throne. *See also* Ajātaśatru; Bimbisāra.

devils of the five aggregates: Refers to the five aggregates, or constituent elements of one's existence. The aggregates often cause hindrances to the practice of Buddhism; hence, they are called devils. *See also* five aggregates; four kinds of devils.

Dhaniṣṭhā: One of the twenty-eight constellations; corresponds to a star in Aquarius and two stars in Pegasus. *See also* twenty-eight constellations.

Dhanus: One of the twelve astrological houses; corresponds to Sagittarius.

dhāraṇī: A mystic phrase, spell, or incantation.

dharma: Any phenomenon, thing, element, or attribute; the elements that make up the perceived phenomenal world.

Dharma: The truth, law; the teachings of the Buddha.

Dharma base: The basic principle of all *dharma*s; equivalent to Dharma-nature. *See also* Dharma-nature.

Dharma body. *See* three bodies of the Buddha.

Dharma-body bodhisattva: A bodhisattva who has realized the Dharma body.

Dharma body of equality: The body of the Buddha or bodhisattva who has realized the truth of universal equality, or nondiscrimination.

Dharma body of non-action: The Buddha's Dharma body, which is completely tranquil like nirvana but, at the same time, is capable of displaying all kinds of pure altruistic activity. *See also* Dharma body.

Dharma gate: A teaching, a method of guiding beings to liberation.

Dharmākara ("Store of the Dharma"): The name of the bodhisattva who made the Forty-eight Vows and became Amida. *See also* Amida; Forty-eight Vows.

Dharma King: Refers to the Buddha.

Dharmakṣema (385–433): An Indian monk who came to China via Kucha and Tun-huang in 412 and produced translations of the *Nirvana Sutra,* the *Sutra of Golden Splendor,* and other texts. *See also Nirvana Sutra.*

Dharma-nature: The essential nature of all that exists; same as true suchness and the Dharma body. *See also* Dharma body; true suchness.

Dharma realm: The sphere of ultimate reality; objects of mental conception in general; the entire universe. *See also* ultimate reality.

Dhṛtarāṣṭra: One of the four great heavenly kings, the guardian god of the East. *See also* four great heavenly kings.

Dīpaṅkara ("Making Light"): The name of a past Buddha.

Discourse on the Awakening of Faith in the Mahayana (Mahāyānaśraddhotpāda-śāstra*): An important work in the Mahayana ascribed to Aśvaghoṣa; it first gives an ontological explanation of one's existence in relation to ultimate reality and ends with a discussion of soteriological methods, including birth in the Pure Land. *See also* Aśvaghoṣa; Mahayana; Pure Land.

Discourse on the Pure Land (Sukhāvatīvyūha-upadeśa*): Also referred to as the *Discourse on the Sutra of the Buddha of Infinite Life,* an important work by Vasubandhu, translated into Chinese by Bodhiruci. The author first presents the "Verses of Aspiration in the Pure Land," and then sets forth the Pure Land practice in the form of the five mindful practices by way of explaining the verses. He describes in detail the seventeen glorious features of the Pure Land, the eight virtues of Amida, and the four transcendent activities of the bodhisattvas dwelling in the Pure Land. Vasubandhu's profession of faith in Amida, "with singleness of mind, I take refuge in the Tathāgata of unhindered light shining throughout the ten directions," forms the essential ideal of Shin Buddhism. *See also* Amida; Bodhiruci; five mindful practices; Pure Land; Shin school; Vasubandhu.

Discourse on the Ten Stages (Daśabhūmika-vibhāṣā): Nāgārjuna's commentary on the *Sutra on the Ten Stages,* which is part of the *Garland
Sutra.* In Kumārajīva's Chinese translation of the text, Nāgārjuna's
exposition begins with the first stage and ends halfway through the second stage. Of the thirty-five chapters, the ninth chapter, "Easy Practice," has been widely used as one of the canonical texts of Pure Land
Buddhism in China and Japan. In this chapter Nāgārjuna presents the
recitation of the names of the Buddhas and bodhisattvas as an easy and
effective way of reaching the stage of non-retrogression and also professes his devotion to Amida. *See also* Amida; *Garland Sutra;* Kumārajīva; Nāgārjuna; Pure Land school; stage of non-retrogression; *Sutra on
the Ten Stages;* ten stages.

dragonflower tree: The type of tree under which Maitreya will attain Buddhahood when he descends to earth from the Tuṣita Heaven. *See also*
Maitreya; Tuṣita Heaven.

dust-motes' *kalpas*: *Kalpas* as numerous as all the dust particles of the universe. *See also kalpa.*

eight aspects (of the Buddha's activity): The eight glorious features of Amida's
merit explained by Vasubandhu in his *Discourse on the Pure Land:* 1)
the seat; 2) physical glory; 3) speech; 4) mental activity; 5) congregation;
6) sovereign power; 7) lordship; and 8) unfailing sustenance. *See also*
Amida; *Discourse on the Pure Land;* Vasubandhu.

eight directions: The four cardinal points of north, south, east, and west and
the four intermediate directions.

eighteen special qualities: The characteristics of a Buddha: 1) absence of
imperfections of the body; 2) clear speech in guiding beings to enlightenment; 3) perfect concentration; 4) nondiscriminative thought; 5) possessing a perfectly settled mind; 6) knowing and accepting all *dharmas*;
7) limitless resolve to save sentient beings; 8) unceasing effort to save
sentient beings; 9) spiritual correspondence with all other Buddhas; 10)
omniscience; 11) complete liberation from all bonds; 12) complete knowledge of all aspects of liberation; 13) manifesting excellent physical forms
to guide sentient beings to salvation; 14) employing subtle words to teach
sentient beings; 15) pure mental acts to teach sentient beings and remove
their ignorance and passions; 16) complete knowledge of the past lives
of all beings; 17) complete knowledge of all future events; and 18) complete knowledge of all events in the present life.

Eighteenth Vow: The most important of all the Forty-eight Vows made by
Dharmākara, this vow promises that those who have sincere joyful faith
and recite Amida's Name will attain birth in the Pure Land: "If, when

I attain Buddhahood, sentient beings in the lands of the ten directions who sincerely and joyfully entrust themselves to me, desire to be born in my land, and call my Name even ten times should not be born there, may I not attain perfect enlightenment." The phrase "call my Name even ten times (i.e., ten recitations of the Nembutsu) is the traditional reading long established in Pure Land Buddhism in China and Japan, although the literal meaning of this phrase is "think of me even ten times" (see the BDK edition of *The Larger Sutra on Amitāyus* in *The Three Pure Land Sutras,* Revised Second Edition, translated by INAGAKI Hisao, Numata Center, 2003, p. 16). There are two other vows that assure beings of birth in the Pure Land, the Nineteenth and Twentieth, but in Shinran's interpretation the joyful faith presented in the Eighteenth Vow is the pure faith of Other-Power, not mixed with practitioners' self-power calculations, and so it is the cause of birth in the True Recompensed Land. The implications of this vow are fully explained in Chapter III, "Revealing the True Faith," in the *Kyōgyōshinshō*. *See also* Amida; Dharmākara; Forty-eight Vows; Name; Nineteenth Vow; Other-Power; Pure Land; self-power; Shinran; store of merit and wisdom; True Recompensed Land; Twentieth Vow.

eight events: The eight major events that all Buddhas who appear in this world must experience: 1) descending from the Tuṣita Heaven; 2) being conceived in the mother's womb; 3) birth; 4) renunciation of the world; 5) defeating devils; 6) enlightenment; 7) preaching the Dharma; and 8) passing into nirvana.

eight excellent qualities: The water of the ponds in the Pure Land has these eight qualities: it is pure, cool, smooth, sweet, moistening, comforting, thirst-quenching, and nourishing. *See also* Pure Land.

eight kinds of impure possessions: Monastics are not allowed to own the following: 1) land, houses, gardens, and forests; 2) vegetables and plants; 3) grains; 4) male or female servants; 5) domestic animals; 6) money and treasures; 7) ivory carvings; and 8) pots and kettles.

eight kinds of medical arts: The methods for curing 1) physical illness, 2) eye diseases, 3) womb diseases, 4) children's illnesses, 5) scabs, 6) poisonings, 7) wrong thoughts; and 8) possession of knowledge of astrology.

eight rules of respectful attitude: The eight special rules to be observed by nuns toward monks: 1) a nun, regardless of seniority, must pay respect to a monk, regardless of his age or standing; 2) a nun should not rebuke a monk; 3) a nun must not criticize a monk who has committed a fault; 4) a female novice must receive the full precepts from a monk; 5) a nun who has committed a transgression must repent before the monks; 6) nuns must receive instructions from the assembly of monks twice a month; 7) during the summer retreat, nuns should learn the Dharma from monks morning and evening; and 8) after the summer retreat, nuns should follow the monks to observe the ceremony of confession.

eight wisdoms: The eight undefiled wisdoms attained by those who have entered sagehood by destroying their evil passions through clear cognition of the Four Noble Truths. *See also* evil passions; Four Noble Truths.

eight worldly concerns: Gain and loss; calumny and praise; flattery and censure; pleasure and pain.

Eleventh Vow: One of the Forty-eight Vows made by Dharmākara, "If, when I attain Buddhahood, humans and devas in my land should not dwell in the definitely assured stage and unfailingly reach nirvana, may I not attain perfect enlightenment." Shinran calls this "the vow of unfailing attainment of nirvana" and "the vow of realization of great nirvana." The implications of this vow are fully explained in Chapter IV, "Revealing the True Enlightenment," in the *Kyōgyōshinshō*. *See also* Dharmākara; Forty-eight Vows; Shinran.

elixir: A material used for alchemy, said to turn iron into gold.

embryonic state: Refers to an intermediate state of rebirth attained by Pure Land devotees who cultivate merit by good acts but do not entirely entrust themselves to Amida; they are reborn in lotus buds in the Pure Land and remain there for five hundred years without being able to see or hear the Buddha, Dharma, or Sangha. *See also* Pure Land.

emptiness (*śūnyatā*): The absence of substantiality of the self and all phenomena (*dharma*s); what ordinary people think of as truly existent phenomena are empty of inherent substance because all *dharma*s arise only in dependence on causes and conditions (the law of causality, *pratītyasamutpāda*). Through direct insight into emptiness, enlightened sages are liberated from their attachment to the self and *dharma*s, thus attaining *prajñā* (transcendent wisdom). *See also* law of causality; *prajñā*.

"enduring": The name of an herb said to grow in the Himalayas.

enlightenment. *See bodhi.*

eraṇḍa: A kind of plant that grows in India, which has beautiful red flowers and a strong unpleasant smell. It is said that anyone who eats the fruit of this plant will die of insanity. Often contrasted with *candana* (sandalwood), which has a sweet scent.

Esoteric Buddhism: A form of Buddhism that combines Mahayana teachings with ritual and meditative techniques explicated in texts called tantras. Also referred to as Tantric Buddhism or Vajrayana Buddhism; the Japanese branch of Esoteric Buddhism is the Shingon school. *See also* Shingon school.

essential gate: Specifically, the teaching of the Nineteenth Vow, or the explicit teaching of the *Contemplation Sutra*. *See also Contemplation Sutra;* Nineteenth Vow; true gate; Universal Vow.

evil passions (*kleśa*): Mental functions that disturb and defile the mind and body. They are considered the cause of transmigration in samsara; by extinguishing them, one becomes an arhat. In the Mahayana, through recognizing the nonsubstantiality of the evil passions, a bodhisattva attains liberation and realizes *bodhi*. *See also* arhat; *bodhi;* bodhisattva; Mahayana; samsara.

Fa-chao: (766–822): A Chinese Pure Land master who disseminated the Nembutsu chant in five different pitches and tones. *See also* Nembutsu; Pure Land school.

faith of the Other-Power: In Shin Buddhism, faith is endowed by Amida as contrasted with the kind of faith generated by devotees through their own efforts, which is called "faith of self-power." Faith of the Other-Power originates from the Eighteenth Vow and is the true cause for birth in the Pure Land. *See also* Amida; Eighteenth Vow; Other-Power; Pure Land.

Fa-lin (572–640): A monk well versed in both Buddhist and Taoist teachings, he composed the *Treatise Clarifying the True (Pien ch'eng lun)* in order to refute Taoist views. *See also* Taoism.

Fei-hsi: An eighth-century Chinese Ch'an (Zen) master, author of the *Treatise on the Nembutsu Samādhi—The King of Treasures (Nien fo san mei pao wang lun)*. *See also* Ch'an school.

fifth gate in the phase of "going out": The last of the five results of the five mindful practices, that is, returning to this world of suffering to save beings. *See also* five gates; five mindful practices.

fifty-two stages: A system popularly used in China and Japan to describe the various stages of spiritual advancement passed through by the Buddhist practitioner, from that of an ordinary, unenlightened person to Buddhahood. The fifty-two stages are as follows: 1) the ten stages of understanding, 2) the ten stages of dwelling, 3) the ten stages of practice, 4) the ten stages of merit transference, 5) the ten bodhisattva stages (*bhūmi*s), 6) the rank next to the Buddha, and 7) Buddhahood. *See also* bodhisattva stages; ten stages.

first fruit (*srota-āpatti-phala*): The "fruit of entering the stream," the first of the four stages of sagehood in the Hinayana. *See also* Hinayana; stream-winner.

first stage: The first of the ten bodhisattva stages, called the stage of joy; corresponds to the forty-first of the fifty-two stages. *See also* bodhisattva stages; fifty-two stages; stage of joy; ten stages.

five aggregates (*pañca-skandha*): The five constituent elements of living beings: 1) matter, or form, 2) perception, 3) conception, 4) volition, and 5) consciousness.

five constant virtues: The five Confucian virtues: benevolence, righteousness, propriety, knowledge, and sincerity. *See also* Confucianism.

five defilements: The five marks of a period of general degeneration, consisting of degradation of the 1) *kalpa,* or eon, 2) views, 3) passions, 4) human condition, and 5) human lifespan.

five desires: The desire for wealth, good food and drink, fame, or sleep; the desires that arise concerning the objects of the five sense perceptions. *See also* sense objects; sense perceptions.

five Dharma gates: The five kinds of acts of bodhisattvas: acts of body, speech, mind, wisdom, and skillful means. *See also* bodhisattva.

five ethers: Different theories pertain to this concept; according to one, the five ethers are the five elements that create all phenomena, the invisible, the beginning of form, the beginning of all things, the beginning of substance, and the absolute. Another theory explains that they are the five atmospheric influences of rain, good weather, heat, cold, and wind.

five evil acts. *See* five grave offenses.

five evil realms: The five lower samsaric states of existence through which living beings transmigrate: 1) the realm of heavenly beings (*deva*s), 2) the realm of human beings, and the realms of 3) animals, 4) hungry ghosts, and 5) hell. *See also* hell; hungry ghost; samsara.

five eyes: The five properties of vision possessed by the Buddha, also called the five kinds of perfectly illuminating eyes: 1) the human eye, 2) heavenly eye, 3) the wisdom eye, 4) the Dharma eye, and 5) the Buddha eye.

five five hundred-year periods: According to the *Great Assembly Sutra,* the history of Buddhism after the Buddha's death is divided into five five hundred-year periods: 1) in the first period, Buddhist practitioners are able to attain liberation, 2) in the second, they steadfastly practice meditation, 3) in the third, they eagerly listen to the Buddhist teaching, 4) in the fourth, their practice consists of building temples and stupas, and 5) in the fifth, they engage in doctrinal disputes. These periods represent the gradual decline of Buddhist practice and correspond to the Ages of the Right, Semblance, and Decadent Dharma. *See also Great Assembly Sutra;* three ages of the Dharma.

five gates: The five results of the five mindful practices: 1) the gate of approach; 2) the gate of great assembly; 3) the gate of residence; 4) the gate of the chamber; and 5) the gate of playing in the garden. *See also* five mindful practices.

five grave offenses: The most serious offenses of Buddhist followers, commission of which consigns one to the Avīci hell. They are interpreted in slightly different ways in the Hinayana and Mahayana schools. The most commonly used version is that of the Hinayana: 1) killing one's father, 2) killing one's mother, 3) killing an arhat, 4) causing the Buddha's body to bleed, and 5) causing disunity in the Buddhist order (sangha). The Mahayana version, which Shinran presents in Chapter III, "Revealing the True Faith," in the *Kyōgyōshinshō,* is: 1) destroying stupas, burning sutra repositories, or stealing property belonging to the Three Treasures; 2) slandering the teaching of the three vehicles by saying that it is not the sacred teaching of the Buddha, obstructing and depreciating it, or hiding it; 3) beating and rebuking monks and nuns, whether they observe the precepts, have received no precepts, or have broken the precepts; enumerating their transgressions, confining them, forcing them back into secular life, forcing them to do menial work, levying tax duties on them, or putting them to death; 4) killing one's father, killing one's mother, causing blood to flow from the body of the Buddha, destroying the harmony of the sangha, or killing an arhat; and 5) rejecting the law of causality and constantly performing the ten evil acts throughout one's life. *See also* arhat; Avīci hell; Hinayana; law of causality; Mahayana; Shinran; ten evil acts; Three Treasures; three vehicles.

five inconceivables: The teaching that there are five powers that are beyond human understanding: 1) the number of sentient beings, which neither increases nor decreases; 2) karma power; 3) dragons' power to cause rain to fall; 4) meditation power to produce miracles, and 5) the power of the Buddha-Dharma.

five kinds of suffering: Birth, old age, sickness, and death, and the pain of parting from loved ones.

five mindful practices: The five practices for attaining birth in the Pure Land, outlined by Vasubandhu in his Discourse on the Pure Land: 1) worshiping Amida, 2) praising his virtue by invoking his Name, 3) aspiring for birth in the Pure Land, 4) practicing contemplation on Amida, the Pure Land, and the bodhisattvas dwelling there, and 5) transferring merit to other sentient beings in order to save them from suffering. *See also* Amida; Discourse on the Pure Land; Pure Land; Vasubandhu.

five powers: The five powers obtained by the practice of the five roots of good: 1) the power of firm faith in the Buddha and the Buddha-Dharma; 2) the power of great effort; 3) the power of mindfulness; 4) the power of deep concentration; and 5) the power of deep insight into the true nature of reality. *See also* five roots of good.

five precepts: The five basic precepts undertaken by all Buddhists: not to kill, not to steal, not to commit adultery or engage in sexual misconduct, not to lie, and not to ingest intoxicants.

five right acts: The five acts to be practiced for gaining birth in the Pure Land established by Shan-tao: 1) chanting the three Pure Land sutras, etc.; 2) contemplation of Amida, bodhisattvas, and the Pure Land; 3) worshiping Amida; 4) recitation of Amida's Name (i.e., the Nembutsu); and 5) praising and making offerings to Amida. *See also* Amida; Name; Nembutsu; Pure Land; Shan-tao; three Pure Land sutras.

five roots of good: The good spiritual elements that lead one to enlightenment: 1) faith in the Three Treasures and the Four Noble Truths; 2) making efforts to do good; 3) being mindful of the true Dharma; 4) concentration; and 5) insight into the true nature of reality. *See also* Four Noble Truths; Three Treasures.

Five Thousand-character Discourse: Refers to Lao-tzu's *Tao te ching,* the fundamental text of Taoism. *See also* Lao-tzu; Taoism.

five vehicles: The teachings for the five kinds of beings—bodhisattvas, *pratyekabuddhas, śrāvakas, devas,* and human beings; also refers generally to these five kinds of beings. *See also* bodhisattva; *deva; pratyekabuddha; śrāvaka.*

"flower passage" concerning One Mind: Refers to the first line of Vasubandhu's *Verses of Aspiration for Birth (Sukhāvatīvyūha-upadeśa-kārikā*):* "World-honored One, with singleness of mind, I take refuge in the Tathāgata of Unhindered Light Shining Throughout the Ten Directions." Vasubandhu's profession of singleminded devotion to Amida, i.e., the One Mind, forms the central part of Shinran's concept of faith. *See also* Amida; One Mind; Shinran; Vasubandhu.

Forty-eight Vows: The vows made by Dharmākara; upon their fulfillment he became Amida Buddha. The Forty-eight Vows are fully explicated in the *Larger Sutra*. *See also* Amida; Dharmākara; *Larger Sutra*.

forty special qualities of the Buddhas: According to Nāgārjuna, Buddhas possess forty special qualities, such as the ability to fly in the air at will and the ability to manifest innumerable transformed bodies. *See also* Nāgārjuna.

four bases of consciousness: Of the five aggregates, the first four—form, perception, conception, and volition—are the bases of the fifth aggregate, consciousness. *See also* five aggregates.

four bases of mindfulness: A fourfold practice of mindfulness: 1) contemplating one's body as defiled, 2) contemplating one's perception as painful, 3) contemplating one's mind as impermanent, and 4) contemplating things in general (*dharmas*) as devoid of fixed selfhood.

four bases of transcendent knowledge: 1) Transcendent knowledge based on the concentration of will, 2) transcendent knowledge based on the concentration of effort, 3) transcendent knowledge based on the concentration of thought, and 4) transcendent knowledge based on the concentration of investigation into the principle of reality.

four correct strivings: 1) To strive to eliminate evil that has been done, 2) to strive not to commit evil, 3) to strive to do good, and 4) to strive to increase the good that has been done.

four dependable sages: Originally, the four groups of bodhisattvas mentioned in Chih-i's commentary on the *Lotus Sutra;* they are 1) bodhisattvas in the ten stages of understanding and in the five preliminary stages, 2) those in the ten stages of dwelling, 3) those in the ten stages of practice and the ten stages of merit transference, and 4) those in the highest ten stages of bodhisattvahood and in the rank next to the Buddha. *See also* Chih-i; fifty-two stages; *Lotus Sutra*.

four elements: The four elements that constitute material things (*dharmas*): 1) the earth element, which represents solidity and supports things; 2) the water element, which moistens and contains things; 3) the fire element, which represents heat and matures things; and 4) the wind element, which represents motion and causes things to grow.

four excellent qualities: Nirvana is characterized by these four qualities: eternity, bliss, freedom of action, and purity. *See also* nirvana.

four fearlessnesses: In the Buddha's teaching of the Dharma, these four fearlessnesses represent: 1) confidence that the Buddha thoroughly knows all *dharmas*, 2) confidence that he has exhausted all evil passions, 3) confidence in disclosing the elements that hinder the realization of enlightenment; and 4) fearlessness in expounding the method of liberation.

four great continents: The four large land masses of different shapes lying in the ocean around Mount Sumeru, each in one of the cardinal directions. They are: Pūrvavideha to the east, 2) Jambudvīpa to the south, 3) Aparagodānīya to the west, and 4) Uttarakuru to the north. *See also* Aparagodānīya; Jambudvīpa; Pūrvavideha; Uttarakuru.

four great heavenly kings: The guardian gods of the four directions: 1) Dhṛtarāṣṭra in the east, 2) Virūḍhaka in the south, 3) Virūpākṣa in the west, and 4) Vaiśravaṇa in the north. They are the kings of the four great continents around Mount Sumeru. *See also* four great continents; Mount Sumeru.

four groups of Buddhists: Monks, nuns, laymen, and laywomen. Also called the four groups of disciples.

four kinds of devils: Ordinarily, the following are called "devils": 1) evil passions, 2) the five aggregates, 3) death, and 4) the king of devils (Pāpīyas) in the Heaven of Free Enjoyment of Manifestations by Others. In Chapter VI, "Revealing the Transformed Buddhas and Lands," in the *Kyōgyōshinshō,* the term refers to the spurious sutras and Vinaya rules expounded by devils, and those who believe in them. *See also* five aggregates; Heaven of Free Enjoyment of Manifestations by Others; Pāpīyas.

four kinds of gifts: The prescribed items that may be offered to the Buddha: 1) food and drink, 2) clothing, 3) a bed, and 4) medicine.

four kinds of nourishment: 1) Food and drink that sustain one's body; 2) pleasant sensations that nourish one's body; 3) volition and desire that sustain one's body; and 4) consciousness that sustains one's body.

four kinds of pleasure: According to the *Nirvana Sutra,* the pleasure of nirvana is distinguished into four kinds: 1) the state of neither pain nor pleasure attained by destruction of all pleasures; 2) the pleasure of tranquility; 3) the pleasure of omniscience; and 4) the pleasure of indestructibility. *See also Nirvana Sutra.*

four kinds of practice: The four practices in Pure Land Buddhism established by Shan-tao: 1) the practice of worshiping Amida and his attendant bodhisattvas; 2) the exclusive practice of reciting the Nembutsu; 3) the uninterrupted practice of the Nembutsu; and 4) the sustained practice of the Nembutsu throughout one's life. *See also* Amida; Nembutsu; Pure Land school; Shan-tao.

four kinds of soldiers: 1) Soldiers riding elephants; 2) soldiers riding horses; 3) soldiers riding carts; and 4) infantry.

four major prohibitions: The most serious of all offenses for monks: 1) sexual intercourse, 2) stealing, 3) killing a person, and 4) lying about one's spiritual attainment. Committing any one of these results in expulsion from the sangha.

four modes of birth: According to Buddhist mythology, the four ways living beings are born in samsara: 1) birth from womb, 2) birth from an egg, 3) birth from moisture, and 4) birth by metamorphosis.

four modes of deportment: Walking, standing, sitting, and lying down.

Four Noble Truths: The basic doctrine of Buddhism: 1) the truth of suffering, i.e., that life is characterized by suffering; 2) the truth regarding the cause of suffering, i.e., that the cause of suffering is evil passions; 3) the truth regarding the extinction of suffering, i.e., that nirvana is the state in which all suffering is extinguished; and 4) the truth regarding the path to nirvana, i.e., that following the Noble Eightfold Path leads beings to nirvana. *See also* Noble Eightfold Path; evil passions; nirvana.

four realms: The four unfortunate realms of transmigration in samsara: the hell realm and the realms of hungry ghosts, animals, and *asuras*. *See also* samsara; six realms; three realms of transmigration.

four reliances: A set of guidelines on how to study the Dharma, taught by the Buddha to his disciples before his parinirvāṇa: 1) to rely on the Dharma, not on those who expound it, 2) to rely on the meaning, not merely on the words, 3) to rely on wisdom, not on discriminative mind, and 4) to rely on the sutras that fully disclose the Buddha's true intent, not on those that do not.

four right practices: The four activities of bodhisattvas in the Pure Land, explained by Vasubandhu in his *Discourse on the Pure Land:* 1) appearing in other lands to teach the Dharma, 2) visiting other Buddhas simultaneously and in a flash of thought, 3) making offerings to all Buddhas without discriminative thought, and 4) preaching the Dharma as do the Buddhas. *See also* bodhisattva; *Discourse on the Pure Land;* Pure Land, Vasubandhu.

four streams: Also called the four violent streams and the four kinds of evil passions, so called because they are the cause of beings' drifting in the ocean of samsara: 1) desire—various evil passions that arise in the world of desire, 2) existence—delusions concerning samsaric existences in the worlds of form and non-form, 3) wrong views—wrong views that arise in the three worlds, and 4) ignorance—inveterate ignorance of all sentient beings in the three worlds. *See also* evil passions; samsara; three worlds.

four unhindered wisdoms: 1) Thorough knowledge and command of words and sentences explaining the Dharma; 2) thorough knowledge of the meanings of the teachings; 3) absence of impediment in communicating in various dialects; and 4) absence of impediment in preaching to people according to their capacity.

four virtues: The four virtues that bodhisattvas must possess in order to teach the Dharma: 1) truthfulness, 2) generosity, 3) the ability to remove passions and desires, and 4) wisdom.

four wisdoms: The four kinds of wisdom realized by an enlightened being: 1) great, perfect mirror wisdom, 2) the wisdom of realizing the equality of all things, 3) the wisdom of wondrous observation, and 4) the wisdom of manifesting metamorphoses.

gandharva: A heavenly musician and attendant of Indra that lives on the smell of food; one of the eight kinds of superhuman beings who protect Buddhism.

Garland Sutra (*Avataṃsaka Sutra*): A Mahayana sutra said to have been delivered by the Buddha during the first three weeks of his enlightenment; it describes the mystical state of enlightenment on an unparalleled grand scale. *See also* Mahayana.

garuḍa: A mythological giant bird said to eat dragons; one of the eight kinds of superhuman beings that protect Buddhism.

Gautama: The family name of Prince Siddhārtha, who became the Buddha; often used to refer to Śākyamuni. *See also* Śākyamuni; Siddhārtha.

Genkū. *See* Hōnen.

Genshin (942–1017): A Tendai monk and a great exponent of Pure Land thought; the sixth of the Seven Patriarchs of Shin Buddhism, well known as the author of the *Collection of Essential Passages Concerning Birth* (*Ōjōyōshū*). *See also* Pure Land school; Seven Patriarchs; Shin school; Tendai school.

great assembly: The assembly of all the bodhisattvas and sages in the Pure Land. *See also* bodhisattva; Pure Land.

Great Assembly Sutra (*Mahāvaipulyamahāsaṃnipāta-sūtra*): A Mahayana sutra in which the Buddha explains to other Buddhas and bodhisattvas the Mahayana principles, such as the theory of emptiness. This sutra is also strongly characterized by esotericism. *See also* emptiness; Mahayana.

Great Being: A synonym for a bodhisattva *mahāsattva*. *See also mahāsattva*.

Great Encircling Adamantine Mountain: The outermost mountain range, made of iron, which encircles the universe of the three thousand great thousand worlds, i.e., this world system. *See also* three thousand great thousand worlds.

great faith: The faith that is awakened by the Other-Power, which is the cause of birth in the Pure Land and attainment of enlightenment. *See also* joyful faith; Other-Power; Pure Land.

great joy: The joy that attends one's attainment of the faith of the Other-Power. *See also* joyful faith; Other-Power.

great practice: Refers to the practice of reciting the Name of Amida, i.e., the Nembutsu, so called because this act originates from the Seventeenth Vow and contains all the merits and virtues of true suchness; this act constitutes the karmic energy for attaining birth in the Pure Land. *See also* Amida; Name; Nembutsu; Pure Land; Seventeenth Vow; true suchness.

Great Sage: Refers to the Buddha.

great treasure-ocean of merits: Amida's complete merit and virtue. *See also* Amida.

Great Vehicle. *See* Mahayana.

Gutoku (literally, "short-haired ignorant person"): The name assumed by Shinran when he was exiled to northern Japan in 1207. From that time on he called himself "Gutoku Shinran." *See also* Shinran.

harītakī: A kind of plant that grows in India and Southeast Asia; its fruits are bitter and are often used as medicine.

Hastā: One of the twenty-eight constellations; corresponds to four stars in Corvus. *See also* twenty-eight constellations.

Heaven of Enjoying Self-created Pleasures (Nirmāṇarati): The fifth of the six heavens in the world of desire; so called because the *deva*s dwelling there can freely create objects of pleasure and enjoy them. *See also deva;* three worlds.

Heaven of Free Enjoyment of Manifestations by Others (Paranirmitavaśa-vartin): The sixth heaven in the world of desire. *See also* three worlds.

Heaven of Restraining Well (Suyāma or Yāma): The third of the six heavens in the world of desire; so called because the *devas* dwelling there enjoy pleasure at appropriate times. *See also deva;* three worlds.

Heaven of the Thirty-three Gods (Trāyastriṃśa): The second of the six heavens in the world of desire; it is located atop Mount Sumeru and is reigned over by Indra. *See also* Indra; Mount Sumeru; three worlds.

hell (*naraka*): The lowest state of samsaric existence, where those who have committed the five grave offenses are reborn and suffer torment for many eons. There are eight scorching hells and eight freezing hells; of these, the Avīci hell is the most painful. *See also* Avīci hell; five grave offenses; four realms; samsara; six realms; three realms of transmigration.

Hinayana ("Lesser Vehicle"): A term applied by Mahayana Buddhists to various early schools of Buddhism whose primary soteriological aim is individual salvation. The stages of spiritual attainment in the Hinayana path are those of the stream-winner, once-returner; non-returner, and arhat. The term Theravāda ("Way of the Elders") is more properly used to refer to the Hinayana schools. *See also* arhat; Mahayana; non-returner; once-returner; stream-winner.

Hōnen (1133–1212): The founder of the Japanese Pure Land school (Jōdoshū). He was born in Kume in Mimasaka Province (present-day Okayama Prefecture) and at the age of fifteen went to Mount Hiei, where he studied Tendai doctrine. At forty-three, seeking the way to liberation, he discovered the writings of Shan-tao and from that time considered himself a follower of Shan-tao and practiced the Nembutsu exclusively. He left Mount Hiei and lived in Yoshimizu, where he propagated the Nembutsu among people from all walks of life. In 1198, he composed the *Senchaku Hongan Nembutsu Shū (Collection of Passages on the Nembutsu Chosen in the Original Vow)*, which marked the founding of the Japanese Pure Land School. In 1206, his school was persecuted by the authorities and he was exiled to Tosa in Shikoku, but was pardoned in 1211 and returned to Kyoto, where he died the following year. *See also Collection of Passages on the Nembutsu Chosen in the Original Vow;* Jōdo school; Nembutsu; Pure Land school; Shan-tao; Tendai school.

Hossō school: A school of Japanese Buddhism, a continuation of the Chinese Fa-hsiang school, which was based on the Yogācāra school. *See also* Consciousness Only school; Yogācāra school.

Hsüan-tsang (600–664): A Chinese Tripiṭaka master who traveled to India via Central Asia; he reached the Nālanda Monastery in the kingdom of Magadha in 630, where he studied Consciousness Only doctrine intensively under Śīlabhadra for five years. Hsüan-tsang returned to China in 645, bringing with him six hundred and fifty-seven Sanskrit Buddhist texts, relics of the Buddha, etc. Under the patronage of the emperor, and with the assistance of other monk-scholars, he translated seventy-five scriptures into Chinese, including the Prajñāpāramitā sutras, Abhidharma and Yogācāra texts, as well as the basic text of the Fa-hsiang, or Hossō, school. At the request of Emperor T'ai-tsung, he wrote a well-known account of his travels, *The Great T'ang Dynasty Record of the Western Regions* (translated by Li Rongxi; Numata Center, 1996). *See also* Consciousness Only school; Hossō school; Magadha; Prajñāpāramitā sutras; Tripiṭaka master.

hungry ghost (*preta*): Beings who inhabit one of the three lower realms of the six realms of existence; they suffer the torment of insatiable hunger. *See also* six realms.

icchantika: One who has no stock of good roots and thus no possibility of attaining Buddhahood.

imperfect faith: Not accepting the entire Buddhist teachings; also, believing in the Buddha-Dharma but not accepting that there are practitioners who have realized it.

imperfect hearing: Not accepting the entire Buddhist teachings; also, chanting sutras only for impure reasons, in order to gain fame and profit, etc.

incomprehensible birth: The mode of birth in the Transformed Land which followers of the Twentieth Vow attain. *See also* birth beneath the twin *śāla* trees; inconceivable birth; Transformed Land; Twentieth Vow.

inconceivable birth: The mode of birth in the True Recompensed Land which followers of the Eighteenth Vow attain. *See also* birth beneath the twin *śāla* trees; Eighteenth Vow; incomprehensible birth; True Recompensed Land.

Indra: The lord god of the Heaven of the Thirty-three Gods, the second of the six heavens in the world of desire. Originally a Hindu deity, in Buddhism Indra is considered to be a god who protects Buddhism and its followers. *See also* Heaven of the Thirty-three Gods; three worlds.

Infinitely Enlightened One: An epithet for Amida. *See also* Amida.

insight into the non-arising of all *dharmas* (*anutpattika-dharma-kṣānti*): A higher spiritual awakening in which one recognizes that no phenomenon (*dharma*) really arises or perishes; insight into emptiness. *See also* *dharma;* emptiness.

Jambudvīpa: In Buddhist cosmology, the triangular continent situated to the south of Mount Sumeru, corresponding to the Indian subcontinent; the name derives from the word *jambu* (mango) because this continent is said to produce a good deal of this fruit. *See also* four great continents; Mount Sumeru.

Jambūnada gold: A type of purplish-tinged gold said to be produced in the river that runs through the mango groves of the northern part of Jambudvīpa. *See also* Jambudvīpa.

Jīvaka: A famous physician and the son of King Bimbisāra's younger brother; said to have cured the Buddha's illness. *See also* Bimbisāra.

Jōdo: The Pure Land of a Buddha, especially Amida's Pure Land. In the Mahayana many Buddhas' lands, established as the result of the vows of the Buddhas when they were bodhisattvas, are conceived of as existing beyond the realms of samsara. These Buddha lands can be visualized through prescribed methods of contemplation and are also offered as places of habitation for bodhisattvas and sentient beings who seek to practice the Way and realize enlightenment. When the term is used without further specification, it means Amida's Pure Land. *See also* Amida; bodhisattva; Buddha land; Mahayana; Pure Land; samsara.

Jōdo Shinshū: A Japanese Buddhist school founded by Shinran; popularly called Shin Buddhism or the Shin school. It offers a way of salvation for all human beings, regardless of their spiritual capacity, by enabling them to attain birth in Amida's Pure Land through faith of the Other-Power, accompanied by the practice of the Nembutsu. Though he is popularly credited with establishing this school, Shinran did not claim to be the founder but professed that he was simply following the teachings of his predecessors, known as the Seven Patriarchs. Shinran's doctrinal system centering around absolute trust in Amida's salvific power is explicated in the *Kyōgyōshinshō.* The date of the foundation of this school is popularly given as 1224, when this work is believed to have been completed in a draft stage. This school is the largest religious denomination in Japan. *See also* Amida; faith of the Other-Power; Nembutsu; Other-Power; Pure Land; Pure Land school; Seven Patriarchs; Shinran; Shin school.

Jōdoshū: A Japanese Buddhist school founded by Hōnen (or Genkū) in 1175 based on the teaching of Shan-tao that the exclusive practice of the

Nembutsu promised in Amida's Vow is the cause of birth in the Pure Land. He declared the independence of a Pure Land school totally dedicated to the Nembutsu, which came to be known as Jōdoshū. Hōnen began to spread the Nembutsu teaching at his hermitage in Kyoto; soon many people came to listen to his teaching. From among numerous scriptures, he chose as the basic canonical texts the following: 1) the *Larger Sutra,* 2) the *Contemplation Sutra,* 3) the *Amida Sutra,* and 4) Vasubandhu's *Discourse on the Pure Land.* The essential teaching of this school is explicated in Hōnen's *Collection of Passages on the Nembutsu Chosen in the Original Vow* (composed in 1198). After Hōnen's death, the Jōdo school was divided into four subschools: 1) the Chinzei, founded by Benchō; 2) the Seizan, founded by Shōkū; 3) the Chōrakuji, founded by Ryūkan; and 4) the Kuhonji, founded by Chōsai. Apart from those, there were two other branches, one started by Kōsai and the other by Shinran. Shinran's Jōdo Shinshū has attained remarkable development and gained a dominant position among all the Pure Land schools. *See also* Amida; *Amida Sutra; Collection of Passages on the Nembutsu Chosen in the Original Vow; Contemplation Sutra; Discourse on the Pure Land;* Hōnen; Jōdo Shinshū; *Larger Sutra;* Nembutsu; Shan-tao.

joyful faith: Faith of the Other-Power originating from the Eighteenth Vow; the entrusting and joyful heart endowed to us by Amida, which is the cause of birth in the Pure Land. *See also* Amida; Eighteenth Vow; faith of the Other-Power; Pure Land.

Jyeṣṭhā: One of the twenty-eight constellations; corresponds to Antares and two stars in Scorpio. *See also* twenty-eight constellations.

Jyotīrasa: A hermit said to have lived near the Himalayas.

kālaka tree: A kind of plant, resembling a persimmon tree, which bears poisonous fruit.

Kālayaśas: A monk from Central Asia, who traveled to China in the early Yüan-chia era (424–453) and translated two sutras, including the *Contemplation Sutra. See also Contemplation Sutra.*

Kālika: A hermit.

kalpa: An eon, an immensely long period of time; its length is metaphorically explained, for instance, as the period required for one to empty a castle full of poppy seeds by taking away one seed every three years. *Kalpa* is also a period of great cosmic change. *See also* cosmic period.

Kamboja: One of the sixteen great kingdoms in India at the time of the Buddha. *See also* sixteen great kingdoms.

Kanakamuni: The fifth of the seven past Buddhas. *See also* seven past Buddhas.

Kanyā: One of the twelve astrological houses; corresponding to Virgo.

Kao-yü (d. 742): A famous Chinese monk said to have recited the Nembutsu five thousand times a day and to have chanted the *Amida Sutra* three hundred thousand times during his life. *See also Amida Sutra;* Nembutsu.

Kapilavastu: The capital city of the Śākya clan in northeast India, where Śākyamuni was born; in his later years it was occupied by the Kosala clan. *See also* Śākyamuni.

karāla worm: ("black worm"): A type of worm that during birth tears through its mother's body.

Karkaṭaka: One of the twelve astrological houses; corresponds to Cancer.

karma ("action"): Any action of body, speech, or mind (thought), which may be either morally good, bad, or neutral. The concept of karma is connected with the Buddhist theory of transmigration, since most actions create either a positive or negative seed in one's consciousness that leads to birth in samsara. *See also* samsara.

karma-consciousness: The basic consciousness that stores all one's karmic seeds and gives rise to existence in the next life.

Kāśī: One of the sixteen great kingdoms in India at the time of the Buddha. *See also* sixteen great kingdoms.

Kāśyapa: The sixth of the seven past Buddhas and the third of the one thousand Buddhas of the Auspicious Kalpa. *See also* Auspicious Kalpa; seven past Buddhas.

kaṭapūtana: A foul-smelling and deformed spirit; those of the warrior caste (*kṣaitrya*) who have committed unworthy acts are said to be reborn as spirits of this type and undergo the same suffering as hungry ghosts (*pretas*). *See also* hungry ghost.

Kauśāmbī: One of the sixteen kingdoms that flourished at the time of the Buddha; King Udayana of this kingdom was a patron of the Buddha. *See also* sixteen great kingdoms.

Kauśika Indra: The name of the god Indra when he was reborn as a human. *See also* Indra.

Kegon school: A school of Japanese Buddhism, corresponding to the Chinese Hua-yen school; both schools are based on the teachings of the *Garland Sutra*. *See also Garland Sutra.*

Khalatiya: A mountain near the Himalayas.

Kharoṣṭī: One of the former incarnations of Śākyamuni. Born at the beginning of the Auspicious Kalpa to a widowed queen who had intercourse with an ass, he was abandoned but was raised by a female *rākṣasa* and later became a hermit. *See also* Auspicious Kalpa; *rākṣasa;* Śākyamuni.

kiṃnara: A god of music, one of the eight kinds of superhuman beings that protect Buddhism.

king of devils: An epithet for Pāpīyas, said to dwell in the Heaven of Free Enjoyment of Manifestations by Others. *See also* Heaven of Free Enjoyment of Manifestations by Others; Pāpīyas.

Kosala: One of the sixteen great kingdoms in India at the time of the Buddha. *See also* sixteen great kingdoms.

koṭi: A large unit of measurement, said to equal ten million.

Krakucchanda: The fifth of the seven past Buddhas and the second of the one thousand Buddhas of the Auspicious Kalpa; according to the *Dīgha Nikāya,* one of the early Buddhist texts in the Pali Canon, he was born in the country called "Peace," when the lifespan of human beings was thirty thousand years in duration, and attained Buddhahood under an *udumbara* tree. *See also* Auspicious Kalpa; Pali Canon; seven past Buddhas; *udumbara.*

Kṛttikā: One of the twenty-eight constellations; corresponds to Pleiades. *See also* twenty-eight constellations.

Kumārajīva (344–413): A Buddhist monk-scholar and translator. Born of an Indian father and Kuchan mother, who was the sister of a king of Kucha, he entered monkhood at seven and studied both the Mahayana and Hinayana in northwest India and elsewhere. Invited to Chang-an in 401, he translated thirty-five sutras and discourses, including the Prajñā-pāramitā sutras, the *Lotus Sutra,* and the *Amida Sutra.* He also lectured on the Mādhyamika discourses and laid the foundation of the Three Discourse school. It is said that he had three thousand disciples, of who four, including Seng-chao, are especially famous. *See also Amida Sutra; Lotus Sutra;* Mādhyamika school; Prajñāpāramitā sutras; Seng-chao; Three Discourse school.

Kumbha: One of the twelve astrological houses; corresponds to Aquarius.

kumbhāṇḍa: A type of demon that is under the command of the Four Heavenly Kings; it is believed to consume human vital energy. *See also* four great heavenly kings.

Kuru: One of the sixteen great kingdoms in India at the time of the Buddha. *See also* sixteen great kingdoms.

Kyeong-heung: A Korean monk of the latter half of the seventh century who was a follower of the Consciousness Only school; the author of many works, including the *Commentary on the Larger Sutra. See also Commentary on the Larger Sutra;* Consciousness Only school.

Land of Bliss: Refers to Amida's Pure Land. *See also* Amida; Pure Land.

Land of Immeasurable Light: Refers to Amida's Pure Land. *See also* Amida; Pure Land.

Land of Peace and Bliss: Refers to Amida's Pure Land. *See also* Amida; Pure Land.

Land of Peace and Provision: Refers to Amida's Pure Land. *See also* Amida; Pure Land.

Land of Recompense: Another term for the True Recompensed Land, the Buddha land rewarded to Amida upon fulfillment of his vows and practice; specifically, Amida's Pure Land. *See also* Amida; Pure Land; True Recompensed Land.

Land of Utmost Bliss: Refers to Amida's Pure Land. *See also* Amida; Pure Land.

Lao-tzu ("Old Master"): A contemporary of Confucius, looked upon as the founder of Taoism; said to be the author of the *Tao te Ching,* the foundational text of Taoism. *See also* Taoism.

Larger Sutra: Commonly abbreviated name for the *Sutra on the Buddha of Infinite Life (Sukhāvatīvyūha-sūtra),* also called the *Larger Sutra on the Buddha of Infinite Life;* the most important of the three Pure Land sutras, in which Amida's vows and the Pure Land are fully recounted and the way of salvation through faith and the Nembutsu is presented.(See *The Larger Sutra on Amitāyus,* in *The Three Pure Land Sutras,* Revised Second Edition, translated by INAGAKI Hisao, Numata Center, 2003.) *See also* Amida; Nembutsu; Pure Land; three Pure Land sutras.

law of causality (*pratītyasamutpāda*): The Buddhist doctrine of dependent co-arising which says that all phenomena (*dharmas*) arise in relation to causes and conditions and in turn are the causes and conditions for the arising of other phenomena. Nothing exists independently of its causes and conditions. *See also* twelve causations.

Lei T'zu-tsung (386–448): A Chinese monk who was a member of the White Lotus Society and practiced the Nembutsu *samādhi*. *See also* Nembutsu *samādhi;* White Lotus Society.

li: A Chinese measure of length equal to three hundred sixty paces, or about one thousand eight hundred and ninety feet; often used to translate the Indian unit of measurement, *yojana*. *See also yojana*.

Liu Ch'eng-chih (352–410): A Chinese monk who was well versed in Taoism and other philosophies; together with Lei T'zu-tsung he joined the White Lotus Society and practiced the Nembutsu *samādhi*. *See also* Nembutsu *samādhi;* White Lotus Society.

Liu Tzu-hou (772–819): A Chinese Buddhist scholar of the T'ang dynasty.

Lokeśvararāja ("World-sovereign King"): The name of a Buddha; the teacher of Dharmākara Bodhisattva. *See also* Dharmākara.

Lord Preacher of this Sahā world: Refers to Śākyamuni, who is responsible for guiding people in the Sahā world, which consists of Mount Sumeru at the center and the four continents that surround it. *See also* four great continents; Mount Sumeru; Sahā world.

Lotus-store world: Originally, Vairocana's Buddha land; also used to refer to Amida's Pure Land. *See also* Amida; Pure Land; Vairocana.

Lotus Sutra: The popular, abbreviated name for the *Sutra of the Lotus of the Wonderful Dharma (Saddharmapuṇḍarīka-sūtra)*. (See BDK edition, *The Lotus Sutra,* translated by KUBO Tsugunari and YUYAMA Akira, Numata Center, 1993); one of the most important Mahayana sutras in East Asian Buddhism, it presents the One-Vehicle teaching; the T'ien-t'ai (Tendai) and Nichiren schools were established on the basis of this sutra. *See also* Mahayana; Nichiren school; One Vehicle; T'ien-t'ai school.

Mādhyamika school: "The School of the Middle"; along with the Yogācāra school, one of the two principal Mahayana philosophical schools in India. Based on Nāgārjuna's *Discourse on the Middle (Madhyamaka-kārikā)*, this school emphasizes the emptiness of all apparently existing phenomena. The truth of the middle way lies in the fact that things are neither existent nor nonexistent. The Mādhyamika discourses were translated into Chinese by Kumārajīva, and served as the foundational texts of the Three Discourse school (Sanlun school), which was transmitted to Japan where it was known as the Sanron school. *See also* emptiness; Kumārajīva; Nāgārjuna; Three Discourse school; Yogācāra school.

Magadha: A kingdom in northern India at the time of Śākyamuni Buddha.

Maghā: One of the twenty-eight constellations; corresponds to nine stars in Hydra. *See also* twenty-eight constellations.

mahāparinirvāṇa: Great, complete nirvana, usually a description of the nirvana of the Buddha. *See also* nirvana.

mahāsattva ("great being"): Synonym for a bodhisattva.

Mahāsthāmaprāpta ("Possessed of Great Power"): One of the two bodhisattvas attending Amida; he represents Amida's wisdom. *See also* Amida.

Mahayana: ("Great Vehicle'): One of the two major schools of Buddhism, along with the Hinayana. The Mahayana aims at bringing all sentient beings to Buddhahood. Followers of the Mahayana are called bodhisattvas. At the outset of their careers, they make vows to save all beings, and in order to realize them they cultivate wisdom and accumulate merits. When their vows are fulfilled, they become Buddhas. Although historical evidence shows that the Mahayana arose a few centuries after the Buddha's passing, Mahayanists believe that the essential part of the Mahayana teaching was revealed by the Buddha through some transcendental means such as *samādhi.* The development of the Mahayana resulted in a great outpouring of Buddhist literature, including the *Garland Sutra,* the Prajñāpāramitā ("Perfection of Wisdom") sutras, the *Nirvana Sutra,* and other sutras such as the three Pure Land sutras. The Mahayana is the primary form of Buddhism practiced in northern Vietnam, Nepal, Bhutan, Tibet, China, Mongolia, Korea, and Japan. *See also* bodhisattva; *Garland Sutra;* Hinayana; *Nirvana Sutra;* Prajñāpāramitā sutras; three Pure Land sutras.

mahoraga: A type of supernatural being said to have the body of a human and the head of a snake; a god of music; one of the eight kinds of superhuman beings that protect Buddhism.

Maitreya ("Friendly One"): A bodhisattva of the highest stage, who is now dwelling in the Tuṣita Heaven; after the end of his life there he will appear in this world to become the next Buddha. *See also* bodhisattva; ten stages; Tuṣita Heaven.

Makara: One of the twelve astrological houses; corresponds to Capricorn.

Malla: One of the sixteen great kingdoms in India at the time of the Buddha. *See also* sixteen great kingdoms.

maṇḍa: The most refined of the four products derived from cow's milk; used as a metaphor for the supreme teaching of the Buddha.

māndārava: A beautiful and fragrant flower, its name translates as "heavenly wonderful flower."

maṇi-gem: A precious gem of a globular shape with a short pointed top, called the "wish-fulfilling gem."

Mañjuśrī ("Beauty and Glory"): The name of a bodhisattva who represents the wisdom and enlightenment of all Buddhas; often portrayed mounted on a lion, attending Śākyamuni.

mantra: A verbal formula, charm, or incantation.

Master of Kuang-ming Temple. *See* Shan-tao.

Master of Shuryōgon-in: Refers to Genshin, who lived in the hall of this name on Mount Hiei. *See also* Genshin.

meditative good: One of two kinds of practice presented in the *Contemplation Sutra* for attaining birth in the Pure Land, along with the practice of non-meditative good. Concerning the practice of meditative good, the sutra presents thirteen contemplations centering on Amida as a method of attaining birth in the Pure Land. *See also* Amida; *Contemplation Sutra;* non-meditative good; Pure Land.

merit transference: Generally, the term refers to transferring the merit one has accumulated to another; transferring one's merit in order to attain Buddhahood; or bodhisattvas' transference of merit to sentient beings to save them. In Shin Buddhism, the term refers specifically to Amida's transference of his merit to sentient beings to enable them to attain birth in the Pure Land. *See also* Amida; bodhisattva; Pure Land; Shin school.

Meṣa: One of the twelve astrological houses; corresponds to Aries.

middle and lower sages of the two vehicles: *Pratyekabuddhas* and *śrāvaka*s. *See also pratyekabuddha; śrāvaka;* two vehicles.

middling and inferior vehicles: The vehicles of the *pratyekabuddha* and the *śrāvaka,* respectively. *See also pratyekabuddha; śrāvaka;* two vehicles.

Mīna: One of the twelve astrological houses; corresponds to Pisces.

Mithuna: One of the twelve astrological houses; corresponds to Gemini.

Moon Matrix: The name of a bodhisattva.

Mount Laṅkā: The mountain in Sri Lanka where the *Laṅkāvatāra Sutra* was delivered.

Mount Sumeru: In Buddhist cosmology, the highest mountain rising from the center of the world; it has four sides, is narrowest in the center, and is surrounded by eight mountain ranges; in the ocean between the seventh and eighth of these ranges are the four great continents inhabited by human beings. *See also* four great continents.

Mṛga-śirā: One of the twenty-eight constellations; corresponds to three stars in Orion. *See also* twenty-eight constellations.

Mūla: One of the twenty-eight constellations; corresponds to nine stars in Scorpio. *See also* twenty-eight constellations.

Nāgārjuna: An influential exponent of Mahayana Buddhism, who lived around the second or third century C.E. He is regarded as the founder of eight Mahayana schools, and revered especially as the founder of the Mādhyamika (Middle Way) school. In the Shin Buddhist tradition, he is considered the first of the Seven Patriarchs; his *Discourse on the Ten Stages,* especially the "Chapter on Easy Path," is one of the canonical texts of Pure Land Buddhism. *See also Discourse on the Ten Stages;* Mādhyamika school; Mahayana; Pure Land school; Seven Patriarchs; Shin school; Three Discourse school.

Name: Amida's Name; in Shin Buddhism the Name is believed to perform Amida's salvific activity; hence, the term does not refer to the figure of Amida but to the phrase *"Namu amida butsu,"* which signifies devotees' taking refuge in Amida Buddha and indicates the unity of Amida and those to be saved. *See also* Amida; Shin school.

Namu amida butsu: Literally, "I take refuge in Amida Buddha." Recitation of this phrase is the practice of the Nembutsu. *See also* Name; Nembutsu.

naraka. See hell.

naturalness: The state of things as they really are, suchness; ultimate truth or ultimate reality. Also refers to the working of Amida's Vow-Power, which is beyond all human understanding. *See also* Amida; suchness; ultimate reality; Vow-Power.

nayuta: A large unit of numerical measurement, said to be equal to ten million or one hundred billion.

Nembutsu: Literally, "thinking of or remembering the Buddha"; meditation on the Buddha; more popularly, the term refers to the recitation of Amida's Name, repetition of the phrase *"Namu amida butsu"* as a non-meditative devotional practice. *See also* Amida; Name; *Namu amida butsu.*

Nembutsu *samādhi:* Concentration *(samādhi)* on Amida's Name through repeated recitation of it; the term also refers to contemplation of Amida's physical manifestations. *See also* Amida; Nembutsu; *samādhi.*

Nichiren school: A sect of Japanese Buddhism founded in the thirteenth century by the monk Nichiren (1222–1282). Its teachings are based on extolling the supremacy of the *Lotus Sutra* above all other teachings. The central practice advocated in this school is the recitation of the title of the *Lotus Sutra, "Namu myōhō renge kyo." See also Lotus Sutra.*

nine classes. *See* nine grades of aspirants.

nine grades of aspirants: In the *Contemplation Sutra,* aspirants for the Pure Land are divided into nine types according to their varied devotional practices; there are three main classes, highest, middle, and lowest; each of these three classes is further divided into three levels of highest, middle, and lowest. *See also Contemplation Sutra;* Pure Land.

Nineteenth Vow: The nineteenth of the Forty-eight Vows made by Dharmākara, who became Amida Buddha upon their fulfillment: "If, when I attain Buddhahood, sentient beings in the lands of the ten directions who awaken aspiration for enlightenment, do various meritorious deeds, and sincerely desire to be born in my land, should not, at their death, see me appear before them surrounded by a multitude of sages, may I not attain perfect enlightenment." Shinran calls this "the vow of performing meritorious acts," "the vow of Amida's appearance at one's death to guide one to birth in the Pure Land," "the vow of Amida's coming to receive the aspirant," and "the vow of sincere mind and aspiration." The Forty-eight vows are explicated in the *Larger Sutra. See also* Amida; Dharmākara; essential gate; Forty-eight Vows; *Larger Sutra;* Pure Land; Shinran; store of merit.

ninety-five wrong paths: The ninety-five kinds of wrong (i.e., non-Buddhist) teachings that were in existence at the time of the Buddha.

nirvana: Liberation from samsara, a state in which all evil passions are extinguished and the highest wisdom attained; *bodhi,* enlightenment. *See also bodhi;* evil passions; samsara.

Nirvana Sutra: A sutra delivered by the Buddha before entering *parinirvāṇa.* There are two versions, Hinayana and Mahayana. The Hinayana version, extant in Pali and Chinese, first gives an account of the Buddha's last days, beginning with his departure from Rajagṛha and ending in his *parinirvāṇa* at Kuśinagara, and goes on to describe how his body was cremated and that his relics (*śarīras*) were distributed among eight kingdoms; this version also expounds part of the Buddha's teaching. The Mahayana version is extant in Tibetan and Chinese, and partially in Sanskrit. There are four Chinese versions: 1) the "Northern" text of forty fascicles, 2) the text in six fascicles, 3) the text in two fascicles, and 4) a revised text of thirty-six fascicles, called the "Southern" text. Many important Mahayana ideas are comprised in the Mahayana versions of the sutra, such as 1) the eternal presence of the Buddha's body (the Dharma body), 2) all beings have Buddha-nature, and 3) even *icchantika*s can become Buddhas. The sutra also contains a detailed account of Ajātaśatru's tribulations and his attainment of liberation. Shinran held this sutra in high esteem and extensively quotes from it in the *Kyōgyōshinshō. See also* Ajātaśatru; Buddha-nature; Hinayana; *icchantika;* Mahayana; *parinirvāṇa;* Shinran; three bodies of the Buddha.

Noble Eightfold Path: The eight aspects of practice for attaining nirvana, as taught by the Buddha in the fourth of the Four Noble Truths: 1) right view; 2) right thought; 3) right speech; 4) right action; 5) right livelihood; 6) right effort; 7) right mindfulness; and 8) right meditation. *See also* Four Noble Truths.

nonduality: Ultimate reality, in which one perceives no dualistic existences, such as birth and death, samsara and nirvana. *See also* ultimate reality.

nondual mind: Nondiscriminative mind; the mind that perceives things as they are beyond the duality of subject and object.

non-human: *Deva*s, dragons, demigods, and other supernatural beings.

non-meditative good: One of the two types of practice for attaining birth in the Pure Land presented in the *Contemplation Sutra,* along with the practice of meditative good. The nine kinds of non-meditative good are presented in relation to the nine grades of aspirants. *See also Contemplation Sutra;* meditative good; nine grades of aspirants; Pure Land.

non-practice: The practice of the bodhisattvas in the Pure Land or those in or above the eighth stage; these bodhisattvas perform practices in accord with true suchness and so they are not at all attached to their actions. *See also* bodhisattva; Pure Land; ten stages; true suchness.

non-returner (*anāgāmin*): The third of the four stages of spiritual attainment in the Hinayana; one who has attained this stage is no longer subject to rebirth in the world of desire. *See also* Hinayana; three worlds.

not definitely established: Said of those who follow the Twentieth Vow and practice the Nembutsu with self-power, who will be born in the Transformed Land. *See also* Nembutsu; rightly established stage; self-power; Transformed Land; Twentieth Vow; wrongly established stage.

once-returner (*sakṛdāgāmin*): The second of the four stages of spiritual attainment in the Hinayana; one who has attained this state is subject to rebirth only once in each of the human and the heavenly realms of the three worlds before attaining nirvana. *See also* Hinayana; nirvana; three worlds.

One Buddha Vehicle of the Vow: In Shin Buddhism, the absolute one way of attaining Buddhahood for all beings based on Amida's Vows. *See also* One Vehicle of the Universal Vow.

"one-child" stage: Originally, refers to the stage of a bodhisattva who looks upon all sentient beings as his/her only child; this spiritual state is equated with Buddha-nature. *See also* bodhisattva; bodhisattva stages; Buddha-nature.

one Dharma principle: The ultimate, undifferentiated, and all-inclusive reality principle; same as true suchness. *See also* true suchness.

One Mind: Exclusive devotion to Amida, professed by Vasubandhu in the opening verse of his *Discourse on the Pure Land;* Shinran took this as the faith of the Other-Power; in Chapter III, "Revealing the True Faith" in the *Kyōgyōshinshō,* he discusses the relationship between the One Mind and the three minds in the three Pure Land sutras and concludes that they are implicitly the same in meaning. *See also* Amida; *Contemplation Sutra; Discourse on the Pure Land;* faith of the Other-Power; *Larger Sutra;* Shinran; three Pure Land sutras; Vasubandhu.

One Mind in the *Amida Sutra:* The phrases in the *Amida Sutra,* "hold fast [to the Name]" and "holds fast to his Name ... with a concentrated and undistracted mind," are interpreted by Shinran as indicating the One Mind with which aspirants recite the Name in order to attain birth in the Pure Land. In its implicit meaning, this mind is the same as the faith of the Other-Power. *See also Amida Sutra;* faith of the Other-Power; Name; One Mind; Pure Land; Shinran.

One Mind of Other-Power: Faith of the Other-Power that is the cause of one's birth in the Pure Land. *See also* faith of the Other-Power; Pure Land.

One Most Honored in Heaven: An epithet for the Buddha.

Oneness: Absolute oneness; the essential nature of all that exists; same as true suchness. *See also* true suchness.

One Vehicle: The teaching that carries all beings to enlightenment; another term for the Mahayana. *See also* Mahayana.

One Vehicle of the Universal Vow: The teaching that leads all beings to Buddhahood; Amida's law of salvation based on the Primal Vow. *See also* Amida; One Buddha Vehicle of the Vow; Primal Vow.

Other-Power: The power originating from Amida's Primal Vow. *See also* Amida; faith of the Other-Power; Primal Vow.

other shore: The other side of the ocean of samsara, i.e., nirvana. *See also* nirvana; samsara.

Pali Canon: The earliest compilation of Buddhist texts, compiled in the fifth-fourth centuries B.C.E. and recorded in writing at the beginning of the first century C.E. It consists of the the Sutra-*piṭaka,* the Vinaya-*piṭaka,* and the Abhidharma-*piṭaka,* i.e., Tripiṭaka. *See also* Tripiṭaka.

Pañcāla: One of the sixteen great kingdoms in India at the time of the Buddha. *See also* sixteen great kingdoms.

Pāpīyas: The king of the devils, who abides in the Heaven of Free Enjoyment of Manifestations by Others. *See also* Heaven of Free Enjoyment of Manifestations by Others.

parable of two rivers and a white path: In this parable of the Shin Buddhist path, Shan-tao employs the metaphors of "water" and "fire" to refer to greed and anger, respectively. *See also* Shan-tao.

*pāramitā*s. *See* six perfections.

pārijāta: A fragrant tree said to grow in the palace of Indra. *See also* Indra.

parinirvāṇa: Complete nirvana, commonly used to describe the nirvana of the Buddha. *See also* nirvana.

path of difficult practice: One of the two kinds of practice distinguished by Nāgārjuna in his *Discourse on the Ten Stages,* along with the path of easy practice; this is the bodhisattva practice that involves painstaking effort for a long period of time. *See also* bodhisattva; *Discourse on the Ten Stages;* Nāgārjuna; path of easy practice.

path of easy practice: One of the two kinds of practice distinguished by Nāgār-juna in his *Discourse on the Ten Stages,* along with the path of difficult practice; in this path one concentrates on recitation of the names of Buddhas and bodhisattvas, especially Amida's Name, with sincere faith, thereby quickly reaching the stage of non-retrogression. *See also* bodhi-sattva; *Discourse on the Ten Stages;* Nāgārjuna; path of difficult practice; stage of non-retrogression.

path of insight: The stage of a bodhisattva in which one destroys all passions and delusions; equated with the stage of joy. *See also* stage of joy; ten stages.

path of sages: The way of attaining enlightenment through one's own power,or self-power, in this world; one of the two paths to enlightenment, along with the Pure Land path, distinguished by Tao-ch'o. *See also* Pure Land path; self-power; Tao-ch'o.

perfections. *See* six perfections.

Perfectly Enlightened One: An epithet for the Buddha.

person of illumination: One who has mastered the deepest teaching of Buddhism; also an epithet for a bodhisattva. *See also* bodhisattva.

person of pure karmic perfection: One who has accomplished the pure mer-itorious acts; refers to Amida. *See also* Amida.

phase of going forth: One of the two phases of Amida's merit transference through which aspirants travel the path to enlightenment (*bodhi*). In this phase, Shinran distinguishes four aspects of approach: 1) learning the essentials of the *Larger Sutra,* 2) accepting the Name and practic-ing the Nembutsu, 3) entrusting oneself to Amida wholeheartedly and attaining pure joyful faith, and 4) attaining *bodhi. See also* Amida; *bodhi;* joyful faith; *Larger Sutra;* merit transference; Name; Nembutsu; phase of returning; Shinran.

phase of returning: One of the two phases of Amida's merit transference. After one is born in the Pure Land and realizes enlightenment (*bodhi*) in the phase of going forth, one returns to the realms of samsara to save other sentient beings. This altruistic activity of a bodhisattva is made possible by Amida through his Twenty-second Vow. *See also* Amida; *bodhi;* bodhisattva; merit transference; phase of going forth; Pure Land; samsara; Twenty-second Vow.

piśāca: A fierce-looking spirit similar to a *rākṣasa. See also rākṣasa.*

piṭaka: Literally, "basket." Refers to a collection or body of scriptures. *See also* bodhisattva-*piṭaka;* Tripiṭaka.

Planet of Eclipse. *See* Rāhu.

Po Lo-t'ien (772–846): One of the greatest Chinese Buddhist poets of the T'ang dynasty.

prajñā: Transcendent wisdom; one of the six perfections to be practiced by bodhisattvas. *See also* bodhisattva; six perfections.

Prajñāpāramitā (Perfection of Wisdom) sutras: The name of a large body of important and influential Mahayana sutras expounding the doctrine of emptiness; most are contained in Hsüan-tsang's translation consisting of six hundred fascicles. *See also* emptiness; Hsüan-tsang; Mahayana.

pratītyasamutpāda. See law of causality.

pratyekabuddha ("solitary enlightened one"): One of the two kinds of Hinayana sages, along with *śrāvakas,* who seek to reach the stage of arhat and attain nirvana. A *pratyekabuddha* attains emancipation by observing the principle of the law of causality without the guidance of a teacher, and does not teach others. *See also* arhat; Hinayana; law of causality; nirvana; *śrāvaka.*

pratyutpanna samādhi: A practice of concentration (*samādhi*) in which one visualizes being in the presence of all the Buddhas, attained by concentrating on Amida and reciting his name for a period ranging from a week to three months. This practice, explicated in the *Pratyutpanna Samādhi Sutra,* has been widely practiced in India, China, and Japan as a method of visualizing Amida. *See also* Amida; *Pratyutpanna Samādhi Sutra; samādhi.*

Pratyutpanna Samādhi Sutra: A Mahayana sutra that explicates the practice of this meditative method (translated by Paul Harrison, Numata Center, 1998). *See also pratyutpanna samādhi.*

Primal Vow: Refers generally to the Forty-eight Vows taken by Dharmākara, who became Amida on their completion; specifically, the Eighteenth Vow. *See also* Amida; Dharmākara; Eighteenth Vow; Forty-eight Vows.

provisional "person": Refers to human beings, who are provisional existences composed of the five aggregates and are in essence unsubstantial. Explaining the karmic continuation of personality of the aspirant to be born in the Pure Land, T'an-luan says in the *Commentary on Vasubandhu's Discourse on the Pure Land,* "The provisional 'person' in this defiled land and the provisional 'person' in the Pure Land are neither exactly the same nor definitely different." *See also Commentary on Vasubandhu's Discourse on the Pure Land;* five aggregates; Pure Land; T'an-luan.

Punar-vasu: One of the twenty-eight constellations; corresponds to Gemini. *See also* twenty-eight constellations.

puṇḍarīka: A white lotus blossom.

Pūraṇa-kāśyapa: One of the six masters at the time of the Buddha. *See also* six masters.

pure karmic act: The pure merit that Amida transfers to aspirants, which is contained in his Name. *See also* Amida; Name.

Pure Land: Generally, any Buddha land; specifically, refers to Sukhāvatī, ("land of utmost bliss"), the Buddha land in the West reigned over by Amida. *See also* Amida; Buddha land.

Pure Land path: The system of practice and faith for attaining birth in the Pure Land through the power of Amida's Primal Vow; along with the path of sages, one of the two paths leading to enlightenment. *See also* Amida; path of sages; Primal Vow; Pure Land.

Pure Land school: A school of Mahayana Buddhism founded in the fifth century in China and brought to Japan, where it was established as an independent school by Hōnen. The salvific goal of this school centers on attaining rebirth in Amida's Pure Land through faith in Amida and recitation of the Nembutsu. *See also* Amida; faith of the Other-Power; Hōnen; Jōdoshū; Mahayana; Nembutsu; Pure Land; Shin school.

pure mind: The undefiled mind of wisdom that bodhisattvas of the eighth or higher stages attain. *See also* bodhisattva; ten stages.

Pūrvāṣāḍhā: One of the twenty-eight constellations; corresponds to four stars in Sagittarius. *See also* twenty-eight constellations.

Pūrva-bhādrapadā: One of the twenty-eight constellations; corresponds to two stars in Pegasus. *See also* twenty-eight constellations.

Pūrva-phālgunī: One of the twenty-eight constellations; corresponds to five stars in Hydra. *See also* twenty-eight constellations.

Pūrvavideha: One of the four great continents, it lies to the east of Mount Sumeru. *See also* four great continents; Mount Sumeru.

Puṣya: One of the twenty-eight constellations; corresponds to four stars in Cancer. *See also* twenty-eight constellations.

pūtana: A type of spirit that attends Dhṛtarāṣṭra and protects the eastern direction together with *gandharva*s. *See also* Dhṛtarāṣṭra; *gandharva.*

Rāhu: The name of a fabled planet believed to cause eclipses of the sun and moon.

Rājagṛha: The capital of Magadha at the time of the Buddha; the present-day city of Rajgir. *See also* Magadha.

rākṣasa: A kind of demon possessing supernatural power and said to bewitch and eat humans; one of the classes of demons in Indian mythology that were adopted as guardians of Buddhism.

reality principle of tranquility and equality: From the viewpoint of ultimate reality, all things are absolutely tranquil and free of disturbances of evil passions and delusions. *See also* evil passions; ultimate reality.

realm of neither thought nor non-thought: The highest stage of spiritual attainment within samsara; the highest of the four stages in the world of non-form. *See also* samsara; three worlds.

realm of sloth and pride: Another name of the Transformed Land; those who are addicted to pleasures while seeking enlightenment are born in this realm and are unable to proceed to the Pure Land. *See also* Transformed Land.

recompensed body: The body of a Buddha rewarded for his vows and practices; one of the three bodies of the Buddha. *See also* three bodies of the Buddha.

Recompensed Land: The Buddha land rewarded for Amida's vows and practices where those of the true faith of the Eighteenth Vow will be reborn. *See also* Amida; Eighteenth Vow; True Recompensed Land.

Revatī: One of the twenty-eight constellations; corresponds to eight stars in Andromeda and seven stars in Pisces. *See also* twenty-eight constellations.

right act. *See* act of right assurance.

Right Dharma: The Buddha-Dharma; the teaching of truth expounded by the Buddha.

rightly established stage: Said of those who have attained the proper foundation for attaining birth in the Pure Land and realizing nirvana. *See also* nirvana; not definitely established; Pure Land; wrongly established stage.

right practice: Along with sundry practices, one of the two kinds of practice for birth in the Pure Land established by Shan-tao; a set of five devotional acts centering on recitation of Amida's Name. *See also* Amida; five right acts; Name; Shan-tao; sundry practices.

Rocana: The name of the last of the thousand Buddhas who will appear during the Auspicious Kalpa. *See also* Auspicious Kalpa.

Rohiṇī: One of the twenty-eight constellations; corresponds to Hyades and two stars in Taurus. *See also* twenty-eight constellations.

roots of good (*kuśala-mūla*): Meritorious acts, such as the absence of greed, anger, and ignorance (the three poisons), which produce good karmic results. As a provisional method of attaining birth in the Pure Land, the Pure Land sutras encourage planting roots of good. Shinran teaches that the truly meritorious good is comprised in Amida's Name itself. *See also* Amida; Name; Pure Land; Shinran.

roots of *samādhi:* The five roots of concentration (*samādhi*), identical to the five roots of good. *See also* five roots of good; *samādhi.*

Sacred Name: Refers to Amida's Name. *See also* Amida; Name.

Sage of the Upper Vehicle: Refers to a Buddha.

sages' family: One of the six divisions of the bodhisattva stages; corresponds to the ten stages. *See also* bodhisattva stages; ten stages.

Sahā world: The world system that consists of Mount Sumeru at the center and the four great continents surrounding it; i.e., the world of human beings' existence. *See also* four great continents; Mount Sumeru.

Śākyamuni: The historical Buddha, who lived in India in the fifth century B.C.E. and whose life and teachings form the basis for Buddhism.

samādhi: A mental state of concentration, focusing the mind on one point; also a transcendent mental state attained by the repeated practice of concentration, such as visualizing a Buddha or Buddha land and realizing emptiness. *See also* Buddha land; emptiness.

samādhi of moonlight love: A concentrative practice (*samādhi*) wherein one causes sentient beings to open up their minds of good, just as moonlight causes the blue lotus flowers to bloom; also, this *samādhi* gives delight to Buddhist practitioners just as the moonlight gives joy to people; through this *samādhi* the Buddha removed Ajātaśatru's physical and mental suffering. *See also* Ajātaśatru; *samādhi.*

samādhi of the single practice: The practice of concentration (*samādhi*) that entails exclusive recitation of the Nembutsu. *See also* Nembutsu.

samādhi of true suchness: The practice of concentration (*samādhi*) in which one realizes things as they are (i.e., true suchness) without delusory discriminations.

samādhi of universal equality: The practice of concentration (*samādhi*) in which one simultaneously visualizes all the innumerable Buddhas.

Samantabhadra ("Universally Gracious"): The name of a great bodhisattva who represents the ultimate principle, meditation, and practice of all Buddhas; also the right-hand attendant of Śākyamuni; often portrayed mounted on a white elephant.

samsara: The cycle of birth and death through which beings transmigrate due to karmic causes; the world of suffering, contrasted with the bliss of nirvana. *See also* karma; nirvana.

Samudrareṇu ("Sea-sand"): A brahman and King Araṇemi's minister, who is mentioned in the *Sutra of the Lotus of Compassion;* one of the former incarnations of Śākyamuni.

samyaksaṃbuddha ("perfectly enlightened one"): One of the ten titles of the Buddha.

Sanlun school. *See* Three Discourse school.

Sanron school. *See* Three Discourse school.

Śāriputra ("Son of Śāri"): One of the ten great disciples of the Buddha, well known for his intelligence.

Śata-bhiṣā: One of the twenty-eight constellations; corresponds to nine stars in Aquarius and one star in Equuleus. *See also* twenty-eight constellations.

selected Primal Vow: In a broad sense, this refers to all Forty-eight Vows of Dharmākara but specifically to the Eighteenth Vow. *See also* Dharmākara; Eighteenth Vow; Forty-eight Vows; Primal Vow.

self-power: A practitioner's own spiritual power, in contrast to the Other-Power of Amida. Since one's self-power is limited and defiled by the evil passions and delusion, it cannot bring about higher spiritual states or birth in the Pure Land. Shinran teaches us to abandon self-power and entrust ourselves to Amida's Other-Power. *See also* Amida; evil passions; Other-Power; Pure Land; Shinran.

Seng-chao (384–414): One of the four leading disciples of Kumārajīva and the author of many works, he was well versed in the philosophy of emptiness. *See also* emptiness; Kumārajīva.

sense bases: The six objects of sensation and perception corresponding to the six sense organs: visual color and form, sound, odor, taste, tactile objects, and mental objects. *See also* sense consciousnesses; sense organs; sense perceptions.

sense consciousnesses: The consciousnesses corresponding to the six sense organs (eyes, ears, nose, tongue, body, and mind) and their corresponding objects; the consciousnesses that arise due to visual, auditory, olfactory, gustatory, tactile, and mental perceptions. *See also* sense bases; sense organs; sense perceptions.

sense organs: The six sense organs of the eyes, ears, nose, tongue, body, and mind. *See also* sense bases; sense consciousnesses; sense perceptions.

sense perceptions: The perceptions that correspond to the six sense organs— visual, auditory, olfactory, gustatory, tactile, and mental perceptions. *See also* sense bases; sense consciousnesses; sense organs.

seven factors of enlightenment: 1) Distinguishing the correct teaching from wrong teachings; 2) making efforts to practice the correct teaching; 3) rejoicing in the correct teaching; 4) eliminating torpor and attaining ease and relaxation; 5) being mindful so as to maintain equilibrium of concentration and insight; 6) concentration; and 7) mental detachment from external objects, thereby securing equanimity.

seven holy sages: The seven great teachers who successively transmitted the Dharma after the Buddha's *parinirvāṇa:* Mahākāśyapa, Ānanda, Upagupta, Śīlananda, Utpala, Ox-mouth, and Treasure-god.

seven jewels: Gold, silver, beryl, crystal, sapphire, rosy pearl, and cornelian.

seven past Buddhas: The seven Buddhas who appeared in this world: 1) Vipaśyin, 2) Śikhin, 3) Viśvabhū, 4) Krakucchanda, 5) Kanakamuni, 6) Kāśyapa, and 7) Śākyamuni.

Seven Patriarchs: The seven masters who especially contributed to the development of Shin Buddhism before Shinran. They are: Nāgārjuna and

Vasubandhu of India; T'an-luan, Tao-ch'o, and Shan-tao of China; and Genshin and Hōnen of Japan. *See also* Genshin; Hōnen; Nāgārjuna; Shan-tao; Shinran; Shin school; T'an-luan; Tao-ch'o; Vasubandhu.

seventeen aspects of the Pure Land: The seventeen glorious features of the Pure Land as explained by Vasubandhu in his *Discourse on the Pure Land*. They are: 1) purity, 2) vastness, 3) essential nature, 4) luminous appearance, 5) manifold precious adornments, 6) magnificent illumination, 7) supreme sensations, 8) water, earth, and sky, 9) rain, 10) light, 11) wonderful name, 12) Lord Buddha, 13) kinsmen, 14) nourishment, 15) freedom from a ictions, 16) gate of the great principle, and 17) fulfillment of all aspirations. *See also Discourse on the Pure Land;* Pure Land; Vasubandhu.

Seventeenth Vow: The seventeenth of the Forty-eight Vows taken by Dharmākara, who became Amida Buddha upon their fulfillment: "If, when I attain Buddhahood, innumerable Buddhas in the lands of the ten directions should not all praise and glorify my Name, may I not attain perfect enlightenment." Chapter II, "Revealing the True Practice," in the *Kyōgyōshinshō* is based on this vow. Shinran refers to this vow by various names: "the vow that the Name shall be glorified by all the Buddhas," "the vow that the Name shall be praised by all the Buddhas," "the vow that the Name shall be lauded by all the Buddhas," "the vow accomplishing the going-forth aspect of merit transference," and the "vow of the Nembutsu chosen from among many practices." *See also* Amida; Dharmākara; Forty-eight Vows; Name; Nembutsu; Shinran.

seven treasures: The seven kinds of precious items possessed by a wheel-turning monarch: the wheel *(cakra)*, elephants, horses, gems, excellent ladies, attendants, and generals. *See also* wheel-turning monarch.

Shan-tao (613–681): Also known as the Master of Kuang-ming Temple; disciple of Tao-ch'o, and the fifth of the Seven Patriarchs of Shin Buddhism. He successfully attained visualization of Amida and the Pure Land, and also practiced the Nembutsu many times a day. His four-fascicle *Commentary on the Contemplation Sutra (Kuan ching shu)* has played an important role in disseminating the Pure Land teaching in China and Japan. *See also* Amida; *Contemplation Sutra;* Nembutsu; Pure Land; Seven Patriarchs; Shin school; Tao-ch'o.

Shen-chih (1042–1091): A T'ien-t'ai master. *See also* Tien-t'ai school.

Shin school: Another term for Shin Buddhism and a popular name for the Jōdo Shinshū school founded by Shinran. *See also* Jōdo Shinshū; Shinran.

Shingon school: Japanese school of Esoteric Buddhism founded by the monk Kūkai in the eighth century. *See also* Esoteric Buddhism.

Shinran. *See* Translator's Introduction, pp. xiv–xv.

Siddhārtha ("All Objectives Accomplished"): The name of a prince of Magadha in northeast India, who later became Śākyamuni ("the sage [muni] of the Śākya clan"), i.e., the Buddha. *See also* Śākyamuni.

Siṃha: One of the twelve astrological houses; corresponds to Leo.

single path: The enlightenment of true suchness, and also the path leading to it. *See also* true suchness.

śirīṣa: An acacia tree.

six kinds of familial relatives: Father, mother, brothers, sisters, wife, and children.

six masters: Six religious teachers in central India at the time of the Buddha—Pūraṇa-kāśyapa, Maskarī-gośālīputra, Sañjayī-vairaṭīputra, Ajita-keśakambala, Kakuda-kātyāyana, and Nirgrantha-jñātiputra; critical of the orthodox Hindu teachings, they traveled around India expounding their own religio-philosophical views.

six perfections (*pāramitā*s): The six types of practices to be perfected by bodhisattvas on the path to Buddhahood. They are: 1) generosity (*dāna*), 2) observance of the precepts (*śīla*), 3) patience (*kṣānti*), 4) effort (*vīrya*), 5) meditation (*dhyāna*), and 6) wisdom (*prajñā*).

six realms: The six samsaric states of existence into which beings may be born: the realm of hell, the realm of the hungry ghosts, the realm of animals, the realm of humans, the realm of *asura*s, and the realm of *deva*s. *See also asura; deva;* hungry ghost; samsara.

six supernatural powers: Six transcendent faculties attributed to a Buddha, bodhisattva, or arhat; they are: 1) the ability to go anywhere at will and to transform oneself or other objects at will, 2) divine eyes capable of seeing anything at any distance, 3) divine ears capable of hearing any sound at any distance, 4) the ability to know others' thoughts, 5) the ability to know one's former lives and the former lives of others, and 6) the ability to destroy all evil passions.

sixteen great kingdoms: The major kingdoms that flourished in India at the time of the Buddha, variously named in different traditions. According to the *Great Assembly Sutra* quoted by Shinran they are: Aṅga-Magadha, Vaṅgāmagadha, Avantī, Cetī, Kāśī, Kosala, Vaṃsa, Malla, Kuru, Vajjī, Pañcāla, Sūrasena, Assaka, Soma, Sorata, and Kamboja. *See also Great Assembly Sutra.*

sixty-two views: The sixty-two wrong views held by people at the time of the Buddha.

Smaller Sutra. See Amida Sutra.

Soma: One of the sixteen great kingdoms in India at the time of the Buddha. *See also* sixteen great kingdoms.

Sorata: One of the sixteen great kingdoms in India at the time of the Buddha. *See also* sixteen great kingdoms.

spirit arising from a corpse: A kind of evil spirit which a devil conjures from a corpse and uses to inflict harm on people.

śrāvaka ("word-hearer"): Originally, a disciple of the Buddha, one of those who heard him expound the teachings directly; later, the term came to refer to one of the two kinds of Hinayana sages, along with *pratyekabuddha*s; generally, one who seeks to attain nirvana. *See also* Hinayana; *pratyekabuddha*.

Śravaṇa: One of the twenty-eight constellations; corresponds to three stars in Aries and three stars in Sagittarius. *See also* twenty-eight constellations.

Śrāvastī: A kingdom in central India (present-day Sāhetmāhet in Gonda Province); the Buddha often stayed at the Jeta Grove monastery outside the capital of this kingdom.

stage of definite assurance: The bodhisattva stage in which one is assured of attaining enlightenment; corresponds to the rightly established stage. *See also* bodhisattva stages; rightly established stage; ten stages.

stage of insight: The stage of having attained insight into the non-arising of all *dharma*s. *See also* insight into the non-arising of all *dharma*s.

stage of joy: The forty-first stage in the fifty-two-stage scale, or the first of the ten bodhisattva stages. In this stage one partially awakens undefiled wisdom for the first time and becomes assured of reaching Buddhahood, and so is filled with joy. Also called the stage of non-retrogression. *See also* bodhisattva stages; fifty-two stages; stage of non-retrogression; ten stages.

stage of learning: In the Hinayana, all the stages of spiritual attainment below that of arhat; in these stages one still has more to learn. *See also* arhat; Hinayana.

stage of no more learning: In the Hinayana, the stage of an arhat, attained by extinguishing all evil passions; at this stage one does not have anything more to learn. *See also* arhat; evil passions; Hinayana.

stage of non-retrogression: The bodhisattva stage in which one realizes part of the undefiled wisdom and will advance to Buddhahood without regressing to lower stages. Until one reaches this stage, one is liable to fall back to lower stages. This stage is equated with the stage of joy, or the first of the ten bodhisattva stages. *See also* bodhisattva stages; fifty-two stages; stage of joy, ten stages.

stage of teaching others: Attained by bodhisattvas above the eighth stage, in which they can freely teach and guide sentient beings. *See also* bodhisattva stages; fifty-two stages; ten stages.

stages of understanding and practice: The eleventh to the thirtieth stages in the system of the fifty-two stages leading to Buddhahood. *See also* bodhisattva stages; fifty-two stages.

stone-liquid: A material used for alchemy.

store of expediency: The expedient Pure Land teachings represented by the Nineteenth and the Twentieth Vows, meant to lead aspirants to the Other-Power teaching of the Eighteenth Vow. *See also* Eighteenth Vow; Nineteenth Vow; Other-Power; Pure Land; Twentieth Vow.

store of merit: Refers to the teaching of the Nineteenth Vow, which provides the way of birth in the Pure Land through transference to it of the merit received from the practice of the meditative and non-meditative good; the Pure Land promised for such aspirants is the Transformed Land. *See also* meditative good; merit transference; Nineteenth Vow; non-meditative good; Pure Land; Transformed Land.

store of merit and wisdom: Refers to the teaching of the Eighteenth Vow, which is consummated with merit and wisdom. *See also* Eighteenth Vow.

store of virtue: Refers to the teaching of the Twentieth Vow, which provides the way of birth in the Pure Land through transference to it of the merit of recitation of the Nembutsu; in the explicit sense this is still a self-power practice that promises attainment of birth in the Transformed Land. *See also* merit transference; Nembutsu; Pure Land; self-power; Transformed Land; Twentieth Vow.

stream-winner (*srota-āpanna*): The first of the four stages of spiritual attainment in the Hinayana; one who has entered the stream of the Dharma by destroying various wrong views. *See also* Hinayana.

Subhūti: One of the ten disciples of Śākyamuni renowned for his deep understanding of emptiness. *See also* emptiness.

suchness: Things as they are; thus-ness; same as true suchness. *See also* true suchness.

sudarśana: A medicinal tree that grows in the Himalayas, said to purify eyesight and the auditory organs.

Sudarśana: Another name for Ajātaśatru. *See also* Ajātaśatru.

sudden teaching: The teaching that leads one to the rapid attainment of enlightenment.

Śuddhodana ("Pure Rice"): The king of Kapilavastu and the father of Siddhārtha (Śākyamuni). *See also* Kapilavastu; Śākyamuni; Siddhārtha.

Sugata ("Well-gone"): One of the ten epithets of the Buddha.

Sunakṣatra: A disciple of Śākyamuni who later disobeyed him; he gave rise to the wrong view of rejecting the law of causality and as a result fell into the Avīci hell while alive. *See also* Avīci hell; law of causality; Śākyamuni.

sundry practices: Along with right practice, one of the two kinds of practice for birth in the Pure Land established by Shan-tao; sundry practices are those other than the five right practices centering on the Nembutsu. *See also* Nembutsu; Pure Land; right practice; Shan-tao.

supramundane path: The path leading to the undefiled wisdom of the Buddha and bodhisattvas.

śūraṅgama samādhi: The practice of concentration (*samādhi*) that is capable of extinguishing the three poisons, i.e., greed, hatred, and ignorance; it is explicated in the *Śūraṅgama Samādhi Sutra.*

Śūrasena: One of the sixteen great kingdoms in India at the time of the Buddha. *See also* sixteen great kingdoms.

Sutra on Contemplation of the Buddha of Infinite Life. See Contemplation Sutra.

Sutra on the Buddha of Infinite Life. See Larger Sutra.

Sutra on the Immeasurably Pure and Equal Enlightenment: The earliest of the five extant Chinese translations of the *Larger Sutra,* produced by Lokakṣema (Chih Lou-chia-ch'en) during the Later Han dynasty, between 147–186. *See also Larger Sutra.*

Sutra on the Ten Stages (*Daśabhūmika-sūtra*): The name given to the "Chapter on the Ten Stages" of the *Garland Sutra;* Nāgārjuna's commentary on this, the *Discourse on the Ten Stages,* is an important Shin Buddhist scripture, quoted often by Shinran in the *Kyōgyōshinshō. See also Discourse on the Ten Stages; Garland Sutra;* Nāgārjuna; Shinran; Shin school.

Sutra on the Way of the Salvation of Humans by Amida, the Perfectly Enlightened One, That Transcends All Buddhas: The second oldest Chinese translation of the *Larger Sutra,* produced by Chih Ch'ien during the Wu dynasty, between 223–228. *See also Larger Sutra.*

Svātī: One of the twenty-eight constellations; corresponds to four stars in Virgo. *See also* twenty-eight constellations.

Tamer of Beings: An epithet for the Buddha.

T'an-luan (476–542): The third of the Seven Patriarchs of Shin Buddhism; first studied the Buddhist philosophy of emptiness, and then sought the Taoist way of longevity. On meeting the monk Bodhiruci, he converted to Pure Land Buddhism. His *Commentary on Vasubandhu's Discourse on the Pure Land* is a classic text of the Pure Land school and provides a doctrinal basis for his successors, especially Shinran. *See also* Bodhiruci; *Commentary on Vasubandhu's Discourse on the Pure Land;* emptiness; Pure Land school; Seven Patriarchs; Shinran; Shin school; Taoism; Vasubandhu.

Tao-ch'o (562–645): The fourth of the Seven Patriarchs of Shin Buddhism; he entered the priesthood at age fourteen and became well versed in the *Nirvana Sutra;* at age forty, during a visit to Hsüan-chung Temple, he read an inscription in praise of T'an-luan and became an aspirant for the Pure Land. He repeated the Nembutsu as many as seventy thousand times a day, and gave more than two hundred lectures on the *Contemplation Sutra.* His Pure Land thought is fully presented in the *Collection of Passages on the Land of Peace and Bliss. See also Collection of Passages on the Land of Peace and Bliss; Contemplation Sutra;* Nembutsu; *Nirvana Sutra;* Pure Land; Seven Patriarchs; Shin school; T'an-luan.

Taoism: An indigenous Chinese religious philosophy based on the teachings of Lao-tzu collected in the *Tao te ching.* Taoism, which arose as a popular religion in the Later Han dynasty (25–220), is based on belief in the invisible, underlying principle of the universe called the "Tao" (Way), and the balance of *yin* and *yang.* In contrast to the more practical social philosophy of Confucianism, Taoism advocates withdrawal from secular engagements. Taoism spread throughout China, eventually becoming a dominant religion that coexisted with the Confucian sociopolitical structure of

Chinese society. Along with Lao-tzu, the Yellow Emperor is believed to be one of the founders of Taoism. *See also* Confucianism; Lao-tzu; Yellow Emperor; *yin* and *yang.*

Tathāgata ("Thus-come"): An epithet for a Buddha, popularly construed as meaning "one who has come from thusness." *See also* thusness.

Tathāgata of Unhindered Light: Refers to Amida; "unhindered light" is one of the twelve kinds of light possessed by Amida. *See also* Amida; twelve kinds of light.

Tathāgata of Unhindered Light Shining Throughout the Ten Directions: Vasubandhu refers to Amida by this name in his *Discourse on the Pure Land. See also* Amida; *Discourse on the Pure Land;* twelve kinds of light; Vasubandhu.

Teaching Assembly of the Tathāgata of Infinite Life: One of the five extant Chinese translations of the *Larger Sutra,* produced by Bodhiruci during the T'ang dynasty, between 706–713. *See also* Bodhiruci; *Larger Sutra.*

Tendai school: Japanese form of the T'ien-t'ai school, brought to Japan from China in the eighth century by the monk Saichō. *See also* T'ien-t'ai school.

ten directions: The eight directions, comprised of the four cardinal directions (north, east, south, and west), the four intermediate directions (northeast, southeast, southwest, and northwest), plus the zenith and nadir. As a general term, it refers to the entire sphere of reality; everywhere.

ten equalities: The mind of equanimity does not discriminate in regard to any of the following ten things: 1) sentient beings, 2) *dharmas*, 3) purity, 4) generosity (*dāna*), 5) precepts (*śīla*), 6) forbearance or patience (*kṣānti*), 7) effort (*vīrya*), 8) meditation (*dhyāna*), 9) wisdom (*prajñā*)—these last six are the six perfections; and 10) the purity of all *dharmas.* Those who have attained this mind will obtain superior rewards and enter the state of fearlessness. *See also* dharma; six perfections.

ten evil acts: The ten evil acts of body, speech, and mind: 1) killing living beings, 2) stealing, 3) committing adultery, 4) telling lies, 5) uttering harsh words, 6) uttering words that cause enmity between people, 7) engaging in idle talk, 8) greed, 9) anger, and 10) wrong views.

ten powers: The powers attributed to a Buddha: 1) the ability to distinguish right and wrong, 2) knowing the karmas of all sentient beings of the past, present, and future, and their outcome, 3) knowing all forms of meditation, 4) knowing the superior and inferior capacities of sentient beings, 5) knowing what sentient beings desire and think, 6) knowing the different levels of existence of sentient beings, 7) knowing the results of various methods of practice, 8) knowing the transmigratory states of all sentient beings and the courses of karma they follow, 9) knowing the past lives of all sentient beings and the nirvanic state of nondefilement, and 10) knowing how to destroy all evil passions. *See also* evil passions; karma; nirvana.

ten stages (*bhūmis*): The final ten of the fifty-two stages attained by bodhisattvas on the path to Buddhahood. They are the stages of: 1) joy (*pramuditā-bhūmi*), 2) purity (*vimalā-bhūmi*), 3) radiance (*prabhākarī-bhūmi*), 4) blazing (*arciṣmatī-bhūmi*), 5) difficult to conquer (*sudurjayā-bhūmi*), 6) manifestation (abhimukhī-bhūmi), 7) far-reaching (*dūraṃgamā-bhūmi*), 8) immovable (*acalā-bhūmi*), 9) wondrous wisdom (*sādhumatī-bhūmi*), and 10) Dharma cloud (*dharmameghā-bhūmi*). *See also* bodhisattva stages; fifty-two stages.

third meditation heaven: The third of the four meditation heavens in the world of form. *See also* three worlds.

Thirteenth Vow: The thirteenth of the Forty-eight Vows made by Dharmākara, who became Amida upon their fulfillment: "If, when I attain Buddhahood, my lifespan should be limited, even to the extent of a hundred thousand *koṭi*s of *nayuta*s of *kalpa*s, may I not attain perfect enlightenment." Also called "the vow of infinite life." As the result of this vow, Amida became the Buddha of Infinite Life. *See also* Amida; Dharmākara; Forty-eight Vows.

thirty-two physical marks of excellence: Buddhas and wheel-turning monarchs are said to possess thirty-two special physical characteristics, such as a protuberance on the top of the head, white curls of hair between the eyebrows, and so on. *See also* wheel-turning monarch.

three ages of the Dharma: The three periods of the Dharma after the Buddha's nirvana: 1) the Age of the Right Dharma lasting for five hundred years after the Buddha's nirvana, in which his teaching is properly practiced and enlightenment can be attained; 2) the Age of the Semblance Dharma, the period of a thousand years following the Age of the Right Dharma, in which the Buddha's teaching is practiced but enlightenment is no longer possible; 3) the Age of the Decadent Dharma, the period of ten thousand years following the Age of the Semblance Dharma, in which only the teaching of the Buddha exists but correct practice is no longer possible. After the three ages of the Dharma comes the Age of the Extinct Dharma, in which the Dharma becomes totally extinct. *See also* Age of the Decadent Dharma; Age of the Extinct Dharma; Age of the Right Dharma; Age of the Semblance Dharma; five five hundred-year periods.

three bodies of the Buddha (*trikāya*): The three bodies in which a Buddha may take form: the Dharma body (*dharmakāya*), the primordial body of a Buddha, which is identical with true suchness, nirvana; the recompensed body (*saṃbhogakāya*), a body of enjoyment acquired by Buddhas upon the absolute perfection of their practice; and the accommodated body or transformed body (*nirmāṇakāya*), an infinite number of forms in which Buddhas, out of their great compassion, reveal themselves to help living beings. *See also* accommodated body; recompensed body; true suchness; two kinds of Dharma bodies.

three calamities: According to Buddhist mythology, there are three minor calamities that will occur at the end of the world: cosmic fire, worldwide floods, and strong winds that destroy everything. The terms also refers to the three minor calamities that occur at a time of major cosmic changes: 1) killing with knives and swords, 2) prevalence of epidemics, and 3) famine.

Three Discourse school (Chinese, Sanlun; Japanese, Sanron): A school of Mahayana Buddhism founded in the fifth century in China, which drew its doctrinal basis from three Mādhyamika texts: Nāgārjuna's *Discourse on the Middle* (*Madhyamaka-kārikā*) and *Twelve-gate Discourse* (*Dvāda-śadvāra-śāstra**) and the *Hundred-verse Discourse* (*Śata-śāstra**) by Āryadeva. The doctrine was systematized by Chi-tsang. *See also* Chi-tsang; Āryadeva; Mādhyamika school; Mahayana; Nāgārjuna.

Three Emperors: The three legendary emperors of ancient China: 1) Fou Hsi, who is said to have invented the Chinese system of writing from mystic diagrams seen on the back of a tortoise, and also taught people how to cook the flesh of animals for food; 2) Shen Nung, the fabled teacher of animal husbandry, etc.; 3) and the Yellow Emperor. *See also* Yellow Emperor.

three evil realms: The three lower realms of rebirth in samsara: the realm of hell, the realm of hungry ghosts, and the realm of animals. *See also* four realms; hungry ghost; samsara; six realms; three realms of transmigration.

three gates of liberation: Liberation attained through the realization of emptiness, formlessness, and desirelessness.

three good realms: The three higher realms of rebirth in samsara—the realm of humans, the realm of *asura*s, and the realm of *deva*s. *See also asura; deva;* samsara.

three grades of aspirants: The higher, middle, and lower grades of aspirants for birth in the Pure Land, as distinguished in the *Larger Sutra*. *See also Larger Sutra;* Pure Land.

three insights: Insights into the nature of *dharmas*: 1) insight into reality through hearing the sacred sound, 2) insight into reality by coming into accord with it, and 3) insight into the non-arising of all *dharmas*. *See also* insight into the non-arising of all *dharmas*.

three Kāśyapa brothers: Three brothers of the Kāśyapa clan who became the Buddha's disciples: Uruvilvā Kāśyapa, Nadī Kāśyapa, and Gayā Kāśyapa; they formerly were Brahmanists.

three kinds of awe: According to Chinese notions of moral virtue, three things that people of virtue should respect: Heaven's mandate, the words (teachings) of great humans, and the words (teachings) of sages.

three kinds of *bodhi:* The three distinct types of enlightenment achieved by those of the three vehicles: *śrāvakas, pratyekabuddhas,* and bodhisattvas respectively. *See also bodhi;* bodhisattva; *pratyekabuddha; śrāvaka;* three vehicles.

three kinds of compassion: 1) "Small compassion," the compassion that arises from merely perceiving sentient beings; this is awakened in the minds of ordinary people or followers of the Hinayana; 2) "medium compassion," the compassion that arises from the observation of the component elements (aggregates) of sentient beings; this is awakened in the minds of arhats or bodhisattvas below the first stage; 3) "great compassion," the compassion that arises from the realization of emptiness; this is awakened in the minds of bodhisattvas of the first stage or higher. *See also* arhat; bodhisattva; bodhisattva stages; emptiness; first stage; five aggregates; Hinayana; ten stages.

three kinds of glorious accomplishment: The Pure Land, Amida, and the bodhisattvas in the Pure Land. *See also* Amida; bodhisattva; Pure Land.

three kinds of illness difficult to cure: A reference to the three kinds of people difficult to save. *See also* three kinds of people who are difficult to save.

three kinds of people who are difficult to save: 1) Those who have committed the five grave offenses, 2) those who have abused the Dharma, and 3) those who have no stock of merit (*icchantikas*) and, hence, no possibility of becoming a Buddha. *See also* five grave offenses; *icchantika.*

three kinds of pleasure: According to T'an-luan, 1) external pleasure, or pleasure arising from the five sense perceptions, 2) internal pleasure, or pleasure arising from meditation in the world of form, and 3) the pleasure of the Dharma music, or bliss arising from wisdom, which arises from love of the Buddha's merit. *See also* sense perceptions; three worlds.

three kinds of sensation: Painful, pleasant, and neutral (neither painful nor pleasant).

three kinds of vital energy: The vital energy of the earth, of sentient beings, and of the Right Dharma. *See also* Right Dharma.

three learnings: 1) Observance of the precepts (*śīla*), 2) meditation (*samādhi*), and 3) cultivation of wisdom (*prajñā*).

three luminous bodies: The sun, moon, and stars.

three meritorious acts: According to the *Contemplation Sutra* these are: 1) caring for one's parents, attending to one's teachers and elders, compassionately refraining from killing, and doing the ten good deeds; 2) taking the three refuges, keeping the various precepts, and refraining from breaking the rules of conduct; and 3) awakening aspiration for enlightenment (*bodhi*-mind), believing deeply in the law of causality, chanting the Mahayana sutras, and encouraging people to follow the Mahayana teachings. *See also bodhi*-mind; *Contemplation Sutra;* law of causality; Mahayana.

three minds: In the *Contemplation Sutra,* the three minds are sincere mind, deep mind, and the mind aspiring for birth by merit transference. In the Eighteenth Vow in the *Larger Sutra,* they are sincere mind, joyful faith, and desire for birth. *See also Contemplation Sutra;* Eighteenth Vow; *Larger Sutra.*

three modes of action: The three types of action, of body (i.e., physical acts), of speech, and of mind (i.e., thoughts) done by human beings that produce karmic seeds.

three painful states of existence. *See* three realms of transmigration.

three poisons: Greed, or craving; anger, or hatred; and ignorance, or delusion.

three Pure Land sutras: The three main canonical texts of the Pure Land school—the *Larger Sutra,* the *Contemplation Sutra,* and the *Amida Sutra* (also known as the *Smaller Sutra*). (See the BDK edition, *The Three Pure Land Sutras,* Revised Second Edition, translated by INAGAKI Hisao, Numata Center, 2003.) *See also Amida Sutra; Contemplation Sutra; Larger Sutra;* Pure Land school.

three realms of transmigration: The three lowest of the six realms of rebirth in samsara, the realms of hell, hungry ghosts, and animals. Also called the three painful states of existence or the three realms of suffering. *See also* four realms; samsara; six realms.

three refuges: Taking refuge in the Buddha, Dharma, and Sangha.

three sages: Three famous sages of ancient China: Lao-tzu, Confucius, and Yen-hui, Confucius' chief disciple. *See also* Confucius; Lao-tzu.

three stages of sagehood: Refers to thirty of the fifty-two stages leading to Buddhahood, that is, the ten stages of dwelling, those of practice, and those of merit transference. *See also* fifty-two stages.

three supernatural faculties: The three special faculties attained by a Buddha, bodhisattva, or arhat: 1) the ability to know one's former lives and those of others, 2) the ability to know one's future destiny and that of others, and 3) the ability to know all the suffering of the present life and of removing its root cause, i.e., the evil passions. *See also* arhat; bodhisattva; evil passions.

three thousand great thousand worlds (*trisāhasra-mahāsāhasra-lokadhātavaḥ*): A unit of the world system containing a thousand million worlds. A thousand worlds, each having Mount Sumeru at its center, make a small one thousand world; a thousand of these worlds make a medium one thousand world; a thousand of these worlds make a great one thousand world; through triple multiplication, the term becomes "three thousand great thousand worlds." It is said that a Buddha reigns over such a world system of this dimension.

three thousand worlds. *See* three thousand great thousand worlds.

Three Treasures: Buddha, Dharma, and Sangha.

three vehicles: The Buddhist teachings and practice for *śrāvaka*s, *pratyekabuddha*s, and bodhisattvas, respectively. *See also* bodhisattva; *pratyekabuddha*; *śrāvaka*.

three virtues: The three virtues of the Buddha—the Dharma body, *prajñā*, and liberation.

three worlds: The three classifications of samsaric states of existence: the world of desire (*kāmadhātu*), this world of suffering; the world of form (*rūpadhātu*) inhabited by those who have severed all desires but still experience the world as form; and the world of non-form (*ārūpyadhātu*), inhabited by those who have severed all desires and attachment to form but have not yet attained enlightenment. *See also* samsara.

three times: Past, present, and future.

thusness (*tathatā*): The state of things as they are; ultimate reality; true suchness. *See also* true suchness; ultimate reality.

T'ien-t'ai school (Japanese, Tendai): A school of Mahayana Buddhism based on the *Lotus Sutra;* also the popular name of the monk Chih-i who systematized T'ien-t'ai school teachings. *See also* Chih-i; *Lotus Sutra;* Tendai school.

tranquility and non-action: Descriptive term for the nirvana realm of the Pure Land. *See also* nirvana; Pure Land.

transformed body. *See* accommodated body; three bodies of the Buddha.

Transformed Land: The land provisionally manifested by Amida to take in followers of the Nineteenth and Twentieth Vows, that is, practitioners of the Nembutsu and other meritorious acts with self-power; this land is manifested in different forms according to the different natures of the aspirants' devotional practices. *See also* Amida; Nembutsu; Nineteeth Vow; self-power; Twentieth Vow.

transmigration. *See* samsara; three realms of transmigration.

Trapuṣa: With his younger brother Bhallika, one of the Buddha's first disciples. He and his brother met the Buddha four weeks after his enlightenment and offered him food; Trapuṣa became a lay Buddhist and Bhallika became a Buddhist monk.

Treasure Land: Refers to the Pure Land.

Treasure-store (Ratnagarbha): The name of a Buddha. The son of the brahman Samudrareṇu and King Araṇemi's minister, he renounced the world and became the Buddha of this name; under his guidance, Amida, Śākyamuni, and other Buddhas awakened aspiration for *bodhi* and became Buddhas. *See also* Amida; Araṇemi; *bodhi;* Śākyamuni; Samudrareṇu.

Tripiṭaka ("three baskets"): The three divisions of the Buddhist canon. In the Pali Canon, the divisions are the Sutras (the Buddha's teachings), the Vinaya (the monastic code), and the Abhidharma (commentaries on the Buddha's teachings). *See also* Pali Canon.

Tripiṭaka master: One who is well versed in all the three divisions of the Buddhist canon; a title of respect for a monk with an extensive knowledge of Buddhism. *See also* Tripiṭaka.

true and provisional vows: The true vow is the Eighteenth Vow; the provisional vows are the Nineteenth and Twentieth Vows. *See also* Eighteenth Vow; Nineteenth Vow; Twentieth Vow.

true gate: Specifically, the teaching of the Twentieth Vow, or the explicit teaching of the *Amida Sutra. See also Amida Sutra;* essential gate; Twentieth Vow; Universal Vow.

true mind: True faith endowed by Amida; same as joyful faith. *See also* joyful faith.

true reality: 1) Ultimate reality, true suchness; 2) the conception of nirvana as complete extinction in the Hinayana. *See also* Hinayana; nirvana; true suchness; ultimate reality.

True Recompensed Land: Amida's land of infinite light and life where followers of the Eighteenth Vow are reborn and attain enlightenment. It is distinguished from the provisional Transformed Lands that are established for followers of the Nineteenth and Twentieth Vows. *See also* Amida; Eighteenth Vow; Nineteenth Vow; Pure Land; Recompensed Land; Transformed Land; Twentieth Vow.

true suchness: Ultimate reality; things as they are; thusness. *See also* thusness; ultimate reality.

Tsung-hsiao (1151–1214): The compiler of the *Collection of Passages on the Land of Bliss (Le-pang wen-lei).*

Tulā: One of the twelve astrological houses; corresponds to Libra.

Tuṣita Heaven: The fourth of the six heavens in the world of desire, in which the future Buddha Maitreya now dwells preaching the Dharma to *devas. See also deva;* Maitreya; three worlds.

Twelfth Vow: The twelfth of the Forty-eight Vows made by Dharmākara, who became Amida Buddha upon their fulfillment: "If, when I attain Buddhahood, my light should be limited, illuminating even a hundred thousand *koṭi*s of *nayuta*s of Buddha lands, may I not attain perfect enlightenment." This is called "the vow of infinite light," based on which Amida became a Buddha of infinite light. *See also* Amida; Dharmākara; Forty-eight Vows.

twelve causations: The twelve links (*nidāna*) in the chain of the law of causality that explain the origin of the condition of birth and death (samsara) to which living beings are bound: 1) basic ignorance (*avidyā*), 2) blind volition (*saṃskāra*), 3) consciousness (*vijñāna*), 4) name and form (*nāmarūpa*), i.e., mental functions and the formation of physical elements, 5) the six sense bases (*ṣaḍāyatana*), 6) contact with the external sense objects (*sparśa*), 7) sensations (*vedanā*), 8) desire or craving (*tṛṣṇā*), 9) grasping or clinging (*upādāna*), 10) existence (*bhāva*), 11) birth (*jāti*), and 12) old age and death (*jarā-maraṇa*). *See also* law of causality; samsara; sense bases; sense objects.

twelve divisions of scriptures: The classical division of the Buddhist scriptures into twelve types according to their different styles of exposition: 1) *sūtra*, the Buddha's exposition of the Dharma in prose; 2) *geya*, verses that repeat ideas already expressed in prose; 3) *gāthā*, verses containing ideas not expressed in the prose section of a sutra; 4) *nidāna*, narratives of happenings in the past which explain a person's present state; 5) *itivṛttaka*, narratives of past lives of the Buddha's disciples; 6) *jātaka*, narratives of past lives of the Buddha; 7) *adbhuta-dharma*, accounts of miracles performed by the Buddha or deities; 8) *avadāna*, an exposition of the Dharma through allegories; 9) *upadeśa*, discussions of doctrine, often in question-and-answer form; 10) *udāna*, an exposition of the Dharma by the Buddha without awaiting questions or requests from his disciples; 11) *vaipulya*, an extensive exposition of principles of truth; and 12) *vyākaraṇa*, prophecies by the Buddha regarding his disciples' attainment of Buddhahood.

twelve kinds of light: According to the *Larger Sutra,* Amida possesses the following kinds of light: 1) infinite light, 2) boundless light, 3) unhindered light, 4) incomparable light, 5) light of the king of flame, 6) pure light, 7) light of joy, 8) light of wisdom, 9) unceasing light, 10) inconceivable light, 11) ineffable light, and 12) light outshining the sun and moon. *See also* Amida; *Larger Sutra.*

Twentieth Vow: The twentieth of the Forty-eight Vows, as explicated in the *Larger Sutra,* made by Dharmākara, who became Amida Buddha upon their fulfillment: "If, when I attain Buddhahood, sentient beings in the lands of the ten directions who, having heard my Name, concentrate their thoughts on my land, plant roots of virtue, and sincerely transfer their merits toward my land with a desire to be born there should not eventually fulfill their aspiration, may I not attain perfect enlightenment." Shinran calls this vow by various names: "the vow of planting roots of virtue," "the vow ensuring the birth of those who direct their thoughts [to the Pure Land]," "the vow of unfailing accomplishment of the ultimate salvation," "the vow of sincere mind and merit transference," and "the vow of the true gate." Those who practice according to this vow are to be born in the Transformed Lands. *See also* Amida; Dharmākara; Forty-eight Vows; *Larger Sutra;* merit transference; Name; store of virtue; true gate.

twenty-eight constellations: The celestial sphere is divided into twenty-eight sections along the ecliptic, to which are allocated the twenty-eight constellations, from Spica to Corvus.

twenty-five bodhisattvas: The bodhisattvas mentioned in the *Sutra on the Ten Ways of Attaining Birth (Shih wang sheng ching)*, including Avalokiteśvara and Mahāsthāmaprāpta; they accompany Amida to welcome aspirants to the Pure Land. *See also* Amida; Avalokiteśvara; Mahāsthāmaprāpta; Pure Land.

twenty-five states of existence: The three worlds are divided into twenty-five states of existence, which include the four great continents, the four evil realms, the six heavens in the world of desire, the Brahmā Heaven, the Heaven of No-thought, the Heaven of Pure Abode, the Four Meditation Heavens, and the Four Heavens of Space-abodes. *See also* four great continents; three worlds.

twenty-nine aspects: According to Vasubandhu, there are seventeen glorious aspects of the Pure Land, eight of Amida, and four of the bodhisattvas in the Pure Land; together these glorious aspects of the Pure Land number twenty-nine. *See also* Amida; Pure Land; Vasubandhu.

twenty-ninth state of existence: On attaining the stage of stream-winner the practitioner will be subject to transmigration no more than twenty-eight more times before attaining nirvana, that is, seven times each in the human and heavenly realms and fourteen times in the intermediate states between death and rebirth. *See also* nirvana; stream-winner.

Twenty-second Vow: The twenty-second of the Forty-eight Vows, as explicated in the *Larger Sutra,* made by Dharmākara, who became Amida Buddha upon their fulfillment: "If, when I attain Buddhahood, bodhisattvas in the Buddha lands of the other directions who visit my land should not ultimately and unfailingly reach the stage of becoming a Buddha after one more life, may I not attain perfect enlightenment. Excepted are those who wish to teach and guide sentient beings in accordance with their original vows. For they will wear the armor of great vows, accumulate merit, deliver all beings from birth and death, visit Buddha lands to perform the bodhisattva practices, make offerings to Buddha Tathāgatas throughout the ten directions, enlighten countless sentient beings as numerous as the sands of the Ganges River, and establish them in highest, perfect enlightenment. Such bodhisattvas transcend the course of practice of ordinary bodhisattvas, manifest the practices of all the bodhisattva stages, and cultivate the virtues of Samantabhadra." This vow is called "the vow of unfailing attainment of the rank next to Buddha," "the vow of attainment of Buddhahood after one lifetime," and also "the vow of the merit transference for our return to this world." Based on the fulfillment of this vow, those born in the Pure Land where they attain enlightenment can freely visit other worlds to save beings. *See also* Amida; Dharmākara; Forty-eight Vows; *Larger Sutra;* merit transference; Pure Land.

twin *śāla* trees: Originally, the trees under which Śākyamuni entered complete nirvana; Shinran uses this term to refer to the Transformed Land where the followers of the Nineteenth Vow are to be born. *See also* birth beneath the twin *śāla* trees; Nineteeth Vow; nirvana; Śākyamuni; Shinran; Transformed Land.

two emperors: Two legendary rulers of China, Fou Hsi and Nu Wa, his sister and successor.

two fruits of reward: The reward for one's past karma is of two kinds: one's physical existence and environment; the former is the principal reward, and the latter the dependent reward. In the case of Amida, the glorious physical features and mental activities of Amida himself and the bodhisattvas who attend him are the principal reward, and the Pure Land is the dependent reward. *See also* Amida; karma; Pure Land.

two kinds of delusion: Delusion that arises from false discrimination and innate and more deeply rooted delusion.

two kinds of Dharma bodies: According to T'an-luan, Buddhas and bodhisattvas have two kinds of Dharma bodies: 1) the Dharma body of the Dharma-nature which is identical with ultimate reality; and 2) Dharma bodies of expediency, which are their manifestations as accommodated or transformed bodies. *See also* accommodated body; Dharma-nature; three bodies of the Buddha; ultimate reality.

two kinds of good acts: Practices of meditative good and non-meditative good as presented in the *Contemplation Sutra*. *See also Contemplation Sutra;* meditative good; non-meditative good.

two kinds of practice: Shan-tao distinguishes the Pure Land practices into two: 1) right practice that ensures birth in the Pure Land, which is further distinguished into five right acts; and 2) sundry practices. *See also* five right acts; Pure Land; Shan-tao; sundry practices.

two kinds of seeing: 1) Seeing Buddha-nature with the eyes and 2) realizing it through hearing. *See also* Buddha-nature.

two kinds of recompensed glorious adornments: Amida's glorious physical manifestations and the Pure Land. *See also* Amida; Pure Land.

two kinds of wisdom: 1) The wisdom of knowing ultimate reality; and 2) the wisdom of knowing the discriminative aspects of existence. *See also* ultimate reality.

two sages: The two Buddhas Amida and Śākyamuni. *See also* Amida; Śākyamuni.

two vehicles: The teachings and paths of practice for *śrāvaka*s and *pratyeka-buddha*s. *See also pratyekabuddha; śrāvaka.*

Tzu and Seng: Two rivers in Shan-tung Province, China; the waters of each are different but on entering the sea they are said to "become of one taste."

Tz'u-min (680–748): Founder of the Tz'u-min school of Pure Land Buddhism; he studied Buddhism in India for thirteen years and received the Nembutsu teaching; on returning to China, he continued to practice the Nembutsu and spread it widely. *See also* Nembutsu; Pure Land school.

Tz'u-yun (964–1032): A T'ien-t'ai monk who built a hermitage near Mount T'ien-t'ai where he practiced the Nembutsu *samādhi;* he propagated both T'ien-t'ai and Nembutsu teachings. *See also* Nembutsu; Nembutsu *samādhi;* T'ien-t'ai school.

uḍumbara: A kind of fig tree that is said to bloom only once in three thousand years; used to describe the rare appearance of a Buddha.

ultimate reality: Ultimate truth; things as they really are, true suchness; the state of enlightenment in which ultimate reality is apprehended.

unconditioned *dharma* (*asaṃskṛta*): The state of existence beyond change; the noumenal world; ultimate reality; nirvana; true suchness. The term is contrasted with conditioned *dharma* (*saṃskṛta*), which refers to the phenomenal world or the world of transience. *See also dharma;* nirvana; true suchness.

Unhindered One: Refers to a Buddha.

Universal Vow: Refers to Amida's Primal Vow; also the Other-Power teaching of the Eighteenth Vow of the *Larger Sutra. See also* Amida; Eighteenth Vow; essential gate; Primal Vow; true gate.

universe of a thousand million worlds. *See* three thousand great thousand worlds.

Upasena: A brahman.

Uttara-aṣāḍhā: One of the twenty-eight constellations, corresponding to six stars in Sagittarius. *See also* twenty-eight constellations.

Uttara-bhādrapadā: One of the twenty-eight constellations, corresponding to one star in Pegasus and one star in Andromeda. *See also* twenty-eight constellations.

Uttarakuru: One of the four great continents surrounding Mount Sumeru; this continent lies to the north of it. *See also* four great continents.

Uttara-phālgunī: One of the twenty-eight constellations, corresponding to twenty-two stars in Crater and Hydra. *See also* twenty-eight constellations.

Vaidehī: King Bimbisāra's wife; imprisoned by her son, Ajātaśatru, she requested the Buddha to teach her the way of liberation from suffering. This led to the delivery of the *Contemplation Sutra*. *See also* Ajātaśatru; Bimbisāra; *Contemplation Sutra*.

Vairocana: (Japanese, Dainichi and Birushana; literally, "illuminating"): The principal Buddha in the *Garland Sutra* and in the Shingon school; in the *Garland Sutra*, he is a Recompensed Buddha dwelling in the Lotus-store World and emitting great floods of light to illumine countless worlds. *See also Garland Sutra;* Lotus-store World ; Shingon school.

Vaiśravaṇa: One of the four great heavenly kings, the guardian god of the North. *See also* four great heavenly kings.

Vajjī: One of the sixteen great kingdoms in India at the time of the Buddha. *See also* sixteen great kingdoms.

vajra: Adamant; a very hard material that is identified with diamond or the essential substance of gold; often used as an analogy for something that is indestructible, e.g., the Buddha's wisdom or faith of the Other-Power.

Vaṃsa: One of the sixteen great kingdoms in India at the time of the Buddha. *See also* sixteen great kingdoms.

Vangāmagadha: One of the sixteen great kingdoms in India at the time of the Buddha. *See also* sixteen great kingdoms.

Varṣakāra: A minister of King Bimbisāra. *See also* Bimbisāra.

vārṣika: A fragrant tree that blooms during the rainy season.

Vasubandhu (320–400): A great exponent of the Abhidharma and Yogācāra philosophy, especially the Consciousness Only school; author of the *Abhidharma-kośa*, the *Discourse on the Consciousness Only Doctrine,* and the *Discourse on the Pure Land*. The second of the Seven Patriarchs of Shin Buddhism. *See also* Abhidharma; Consciousness Only school; *Discourse on the Pure Land;* Seven Patriarchs; Shin school; Yogācāra.

vertical going-out: Refers to the teachings of the path of sages for the gradual attainment of enlightenment (*bodhi*) requiring many *kalpa*s of practice, such as is taught in the Hossō and Three Discourse schools. *See also bodhi;* crosswise going-out; crosswise transcendence; Hossō school; *kalpa;* path of sages; Three Discourse school; vertical transcendence.

vertical transcendence: Refers to the Mahayana teachings for the rapid attainment of enlightenment *(bodhi),* such as is taught in the Kegon, Tendai, and Shingon schools. *See also bodhi;* crosswise going-out; crosswise transcendence; Kegon school; Mahayana; Shingon school; Tendai school; vertical going-out.

Vinaya: Precepts and rules of conduct for monastics; along with the Abhidharma and the Sutras, one of the three divisions of the Buddhist Canon (Tripiṭaka). *See also* Tripiṭaka.

Vinaya school: Buddhist school based on the Vinaya texts. *See also* Vinaya.

virtuous masters: Refers particularly to the Seven Patriarchs of Shin Buddhism. *See also* Seven Patriarchs; Shin school.

Virūḍhaka: One of the four great heavenly kings; the guardian god of the south. *See also* four great heavenly kings.

Virūpākṣa: One of the four great heavenly kings; the guardian god of the west. *See also* four great heavenly kings.

Viśākhā: One of the twenty-eight constellations, corresponding to four stars in Libra. *See also* twenty-eight constellations.

vow-mind: Amida's wish to save all sentient beings. *See also* Amida.

vow of great compassion: Amida's Vow of salvation, particularly the Seventeenth Vow and the Twelfth and Thirteenth Vows. *See also* Seventeenth Vow; Thirteenth Vow; Twelfth Vow.

vow of sincere mind and joyful faith: The Eighteenth Vow. *See also* Eighteenth Vow.

vow of unfailing attainment of nirvana: The Eleventh Vow. *See also* Eighteenth Vow.

vows of light and life: The vow of infinite light (Twelfth Vow) and the Vow of infinite life (Thirteenth Vow). *See also* Thirteenth Vow; Twelfth Vow.

Vow-Power: The power generated by Amida's Primal Vow to fulfill that vow. *See also* Amida; Primal Vow.

Vṛṣa: One of the twelve astrological houses, corresponding to Taurus.

Vṛścika: One of the twelve astrological houses, corresponding to Scorpio.

Way: The ultimate state of enlightenment; *bodhi;* also refers to the Buddhist path. *See also bodhi.*

Western Land: Amida's Pure Land. *See also* Amida; Pure Land.

wheel of the Dharma: The Buddha's teaching, which is taught interminably and without hindrance, like the precious wheel of the wheel-turning monarch. *See also* Dharma; wheel-turning monarch.

wheel-turning monarch (*cakravartin*): The ideal king, as conceived of in Indian philosophy, who rules the world with a special wheel (*cakra*) that flies through the air and destroys his enemies; said to possess seven treasures, including the wheel. *See also* seven treasures.

White Lotus Society: Originally founded by Hui-yüan in 402 on Mount Lu in China, the objective of this sect was to practice meditation on Amida in accordance with the *Pratyutpanna Samādhi Sutra,* with a view to attaining rebirth in the Pure Land. This marked the beginning of Pure Land Buddhism in China. This type of Nembutsu *samādhi* flourished from the end of the T'ang dynasty through the Sung dynasty. In the twelfth century, Tzu-yüan became a Pure Land follower and built a hermitage called "White Lotus" in which to practice meditation and promulgate the teaching; his tradition was called the "White Lotus school." This school introduced a new development in the fourteenth century by adopting the theory of the appearance of the future Buddha Maitreya in the world. A member of the sect, Han Shan-tong, formed a clandestine religious group that proposed to change the political regime and realize an ideal world through Maitreya's grace. In 1351, he staged an armed uprising against the government with three thousand followers but was captured and killed. This incident triggered prolonged social disturbance in China, leading to a number of uprisings. By the beginning of the Yüan dynasty, this and similar groups associated with the White Lotus school were banned by secular authorities. *See also* Amida; Maitreya; Nembutsu *samādhi; Pratyutpanna Samādhi Sutra;* Pure Land school.

wisdom-perfection: (*prajñā-pāramitā*): One of the six perfections. *See also* six perfections.

womb palace: A figurative expression for the Transformed Land; though born in the Pure Land, aspirants who harbor doubt are enclosed in lotus buds, as in a mother's womb, and are unable to see the Buddha and bodhisattvas or hear the Dharma. *See also* Pure Land; Transformed Land.

World Eye: An epithet for the Buddha.

Glossary

World Hero: An epithet for the Buddha.

World-honored One: One of the ten titles of the Buddha.

worldly paths: The miscellaneous practices of ethical and religious good performed with relative thoughts and judgments; these practices end in repeating the cycle of birth and death (samsara) and do not lead to the transcendent wisdom of a Buddha or bodhisattva. *See also* bodhisattva; samsara.

World Valiant One: An epithet for the Buddha.

wrongly established stage: The stage attained by those who follow the Nineteenth Vow and practice the Nembutsu and other good acts with self-power; they will be born in the Transformed Land. *See also* Nembutsu; Nineteenth Vow; not definitely established; rightly established stage; self-power; Transformed Land.

yakṣa: A kind of demon, fearsome in appearance; a type of demigod; one of the eight kinds of supernatural beings who protect Buddhism.

Yao and Shun: Legendary emperors of China, renowned for their ideal rule of the country.

Yellow Emperor: A legendary monarch of China, said to have established the system of weights and measures, musical scales, standards of clothing, the monetary system, etc.; along with Lao-tzu, believed to be one of the founders of Taoism. *See also* Lao-tzu; Taoism.

yin and *yang:* In Taoism, the balance of the negative and positive principles, or energies, of the universe. *See also* Taoism.

Yogācāra school: Along with the Mādhyamika school, one of the two major Mahayana schools of Indian Buddhism. According to tradition, it was founded by Maitreya; the original teachings advocated realization of ultimate reality through the meditative practice of unity (*yoga*). The fourth-century Indian masters Asaṅga and Vasubandhu further developed Yogācāra doctrines but as they devoted more attention to the systematization of the teaching of "consciousness only" (*vijñapti-mātra*) rather than the meditative practice itself, the name "Consciousness Only" came to be used for the Yogācāra school. The monk-scholars Sthiramati, Dignāga, and Dharmapāla further developed the doctrines of this school and it was later transmitted to China where it was known as the Fa-hsiang school. *See also* Consciousness Only school; Mādhyamika school; Mahayana; Maitreya; Vasubandhu.

yojana: An Indian unit of distance, roughly equivalent to seven to nine miles, based on the distance the royal army could march in one day; one *yojana* is equivalent to forty Chinese *li*. *See also li.*

Yüan-chao (1048–1116): First studied the T'ien-t'ai teachings and later became a master of the Vinaya school; when he became ill he realized his powerlessness and took refuge in Amida. *See also* Amida; T'ien-t'ai school; Vinaya school.

Yung-ch'in: A Vinaya master and Yüan-chao's disciple; he is said to have practiced the Nembutsu thirty thousand times a day. *See also* Nembutsu; Vinaya school; Yüan-chao.

Bibliography

Hirota, Dennis, et al., trans. "The Teaching, Practice and Realization of the Pure Land Way," in the *Collected Works of Shinran*. Kyoto: Jōdo Shinshū Hongwanji-ha, 1997. Translation of the entire text with notes and glossary.

Inagaki, Hisao, et al., trans. *The Kyō Gyō Shin Shō*. Kyoto: Ryukoku Translation, Ryukoku University, 1966. Translation of Shinran's own comments and important quotations with the original text, romanized transcription, and notes.

Inagaki, Saizo, trans. *Kyōgyōshinshō*. Buddhist Publication Series No. 2. Kyoto: English Publication Bureau, Hompa Hongwanji, 1954. Introductory essay and translation of the General Preface, the Chapter on the True Teaching, and part of the Chapter on the True Practice.

Sugihira, Shizutoshi, trans. *Kyōgyōshinshō Monrui. The Eastern Buddhist*, Vol. 8, nos. 3–4. Annotated translation of the General Preface, the Chapter on the True Teaching, and part of the Chapter on the True Practice.

Suzuki, D. T., trans. *The Kyōgyōshinshō*. Kyoto: Shinshū Otani-ha, 1973. Translation of the first four chapters.

Yamamoto, Kosho, trans. *Kyōgyōshinshō*. Tokyo: Karinbunko, 1958. Translation of the entire text with footnotes and glossary.

Index

A

Abhaya 142

Abhidharma-kośa 167

abode(s) 6, 8, 16, 54, 175, 181, 263, 305, 326

accommodated body. *See* body of the Buddha

act of right assurance (*see also* right act) xviii, 57–8, 76, 93, 244, 245, 338

acts of body, speech, and mind (*see also* three modes of action) 90, 103, 143, 193, 245

agada medicine 115

Āgamas 28

Age of the Decadent Dharma 79, 249, 250, 273, 274, 276–7, 278–9, 281–6, 288, 290, 314

Age of the Extinct Dharma 71, 79, 273, 289

Age of the Right Dharma 273, 274, 276, 278–9, 281–6, 290

Age of the Semblance Dharma 79, 221, 273, 274, 276, 278, 281–6, 287, 288

Aid to Bodhi (*see also* Provision for *Bodhi*) 14

Ajātaśatru 3, 12, 136–55, 239, 325

Ajita 236

Ajitakeśakambala 141, 145

Ajitavatī River 322

Amida xiii, xiv, xv, xvi, xvii, xviii, xx, 4, 5, 9, 17, 21, 24, 25, 26, 28, 29, 33, 34, 35, 36, 37, 39, 40, 41, 43, 44, 45, 46, 47, 50, 51, 52, 55, 56, 58, 59, 60, 63, 67, 68, 69, 71, 75, 76, 77, 78, 79, 80, 83–4, 85, 87, 88, 89, 90, 91, 92, 93, 94, 98, 99, 100, 101, 103, 105, 111, 112, 117, 119, 121, 124, 125, 129, 130, 131, 132, 133, 163, 164, 165, 166, 167, 169, 171, 172, 173, 174, 177, 178, 180, 189, 194, 196, 197, 199–201, 217, 218, 219, 221, 222, 223–4, 226, 227, 228, 233–4, 238, 239, 243–5, 246, 248, 250, 254, 256, 258, 260, 261, 262, 263, 264, 269, 280, 271, 272, 276, 333, 343

Light of 3, 4, 34, 59, 80

Amida Sutra (*see also* Smaller *Sutra*) xix, 37, 42, 54, 70, 91, 92, 244, 259, 260, 261, 264

Amitāyurdhyāna-sūtra. See Contemplation *Sutra*

A mi t'o ching i shu. See Commentary on the *Amida Sutra*

Amoghapāśakalpa-rāja. See Sutra on Amoghapāśa's Divine Manifestation and Mantra

anāgamin. See non-returner

Ānanda 5–6, 7, 8, 11, 102, 158, 197–9, 208, 235, 259, 262, 289

Aṅga-Magadha 301

An le chi. See Collection of Passages on the Land of Peace and Bliss

423

A List of the Volumes of the BDK English Tripiṭaka

(First Series)

Abbreviations

Ch.:	Chinese
Skt.:	Sanskrit
Jp.:	Japanese
Eng.:	Published title
T.:	Taishō Tripiṭaka

Vol. No.		Title	T. No.
45-II	*Ch.*	Yu-p'o-sai-chieh-ching （優婆塞戒經）	1488
	Skt.	Upāsakaśīla-sūtra (?)	
	Eng.	The Sutra on Upāsaka Precepts	
46-I	*Ch.*	Miao-fa-lien-hua-ching-yu-po-t'i-shê （妙法蓮華經憂波提舍）	1519
	Skt.	Saddharmapuṇḍarīka-upadeśa	
46-II	*Ch.*	Fo-ti-ching-lun （佛地經論）	1530
	Skt.	Buddhabhūmisūtra-śāstra (?)	
	Eng.	The Interpretation of the Buddha Land	
46-III	*Ch.*	Shê-ta-ch'eng-lun （攝大乘論）	1593
	Skt.	Mahāyānasaṃgraha	
	Eng.	The Summary of the Great Vehicle	
47	*Ch.*	Shih-chu-p'i-p'o-sha-lun （十住毘婆沙論）	1521
	Skt.	Daśabhūmika-vibhāṣā (?)	
48, 49	*Ch.*	A-p'i-ta-mo-chü-shê-lun （阿毘達磨俱舍論）	1558
	Skt.	Abhidharmakośa-bhāṣya	
50–59	*Ch.*	Yü-ch'ieh-shih-ti-lun （瑜伽師地論）	1579
	Skt.	Yogācārabhūmi	
60-I	*Ch.*	Ch'êng-wei-shih-lun （成唯識論）	1585
	Eng.	Demonstration of Consciousness Only (In Three Texts on Consciousness Only)	
60-II	*Ch.*	Wei-shih-san-shih-lun-sung （唯識三十論頌）	1586
	Skt.	Triṃśikā	
	Eng.	The Thirty Verses on Consciousness Only (In Three Texts on Consciousness Only)	
60-III	*Ch.*	Wei-shih-êrh-shih-lun （唯識二十論）	1590
	Skt.	Viṃśatikā	
	Eng.	The Treatise in Twenty Verses on Consciousness Only (In Three Texts on Consciousness Only)	
61-I	*Ch.*	Chung-lun （中論）	1564
	Skt.	Madhyamaka-śāstra	
61-II	*Ch.*	Pien-chung-pien-lun （辯中邊論）	1600
	Skt.	Madhyāntavibhāga	

Vol. No.		Title	T. No.
75	*Ch.*	Fo-kuo-yüan-wu-ch'an-shih-pi-yen-lu （佛果圜悟禪師碧巖録）	2003
	Eng.	The Blue Cliff Record	
76-I	*Ch.*	I-pu-tsung-lun-lun （異部宗輪論）	2031
	Skt.	Samayabhedoparacanacakra	
76-II	*Ch.*	A-yü-wang-ching （阿育王經）	2043
	Skt.	Aśokarāja-sūtra (?)	
	Eng.	The Biographical Scripture of King Aśoka	
76-III	*Ch.*	Ma-ming-p'u-sa-ch'uan （馬鳴菩薩傳）	2046
	Eng.	The Life of Aśvaghoṣa Bodhisattva (In Lives of Great Monks and Nuns)	
76-IV	*Ch.*	Lung-shu-p'u-sa-ch'uan （龍樹菩薩傳）	2047
	Eng.	The Life of Nāgārjuna Bodhisattva (In Lives of Great Monks and Nuns)	
76-V	*Ch.*	P'o-sou-p'an-tou-fa-shih-ch'uan （婆藪槃豆法師傳）	2049
	Eng.	Biography of Dharma Master Vasubandhu (In Lives of Great Monks and Nuns)	
76-VI	*Ch.*	Pi-ch'iu-ni-ch'uan （比丘尼傳）	2063
	Eng.	Biographies of Buddhist Nuns (In Lives of Great Monks and Nuns)	
76-VII	*Ch.*	Kao-sêng-fa-hsien-ch'uan （高僧法顯傳）	2085
	Eng.	The Journey of the Eminent Monk Faxian (In Lives of Great Monks and Nuns)	
76-VIII	*Ch.*	Yu-fang-chi-ch'ao: T'ang-ta-ho-shang-tung-chêng-ch'uan （遊方記抄: 唐大和上東征傳）	2089-(7)
77	*Ch.*	Ta-t'ang-ta-tz'ŭ-ên-ssŭ-san-ts'ang-fa-shih-ch'uan （大唐大慈恩寺三藏法師傳）	2053
	Eng.	A Biography of the Tripiṭaka Master of the Great Ci'en Monastery of the Great Tang Dynasty	
78	*Ch.*	Kao-sêng-ch'uan （高僧傳）	2059
79	*Ch.*	Ta-t'ang-hsi-yü-chi （大唐西域記）	2087
	Eng.	The Great Tang Dynasty Record of the Western Regions	

Vol. No.		Title	T. No.
80	*Ch.*	Hung-ming-chi （弘明集）	2102
81–92	*Ch.*	Fa-yüan-chu-lin （法苑珠林）	2122
93-I	*Ch.*	Nan-hai-chi-kuei-nei-fa-ch'uan （南海寄歸内法傳）	2125
	Eng.	Buddhist Monastic Traditions of Southern Asia	
93-II	*Ch.*	Fan-yü-tsa-ming （梵語雜名）	2135
94-I	*Jp.*	Shō-man-gyō-gi-sho （勝鬘經義疏）	2185
94-II	*Jp.*	Yui-ma-kyō-gi-sho （維摩經義疏）	2186
95	*Jp.*	Hok-ke-gi-sho （法華義疏）	2187
96-I	*Jp.*	Han-nya-shin-gyō-hi-ken （般若心經秘鍵）	2203
96-II	*Jp.*	Dai-jō-hos-sō-ken-jin-shō （大乘法相研神章）	2309
96-III	*Jp.*	Kan-jin-kaku-mu-shō （觀心覺夢鈔）	2312
97-I	*Jp.*	Ris-shū-kō-yō （律宗綱要）	2348
	Eng.	The Essentials of the Vinaya Tradition	
97-II	*Jp.*	Ten-dai-hok-ke-shū-gi-shū （天台法華宗義集）	2366
	Eng.	The Collected Teachings of the Tendai Lotus School	
97-III	*Jp.*	Ken-kai-ron （顯戒論）	2376
97-IV	*Jp.*	San-ge-gaku-shō-shiki （山家學生式）	2377
98-I	*Jp.*	Hi-zō-hō-yaku （秘藏寶鑰）	2426
98-II	*Jp.*	Ben-ken-mitsu-ni-kyō-ron （辨顯密二教論）	2427
98-III	*Jp.*	Soku-shin-jō-butsu-gi （即身成佛義）	2428
98-IV	*Jp.*	Shō-ji-jis-sō-gi （聲字實相義）	2429
98-V	*Jp.*	Un-ji-gi （吽字義）	2430
98-VI	*Jp.*	Go-rin-ku-ji-myō-hi-mitsu-shaku （五輪九字明秘密釋）	2514

Vol. No.		Title	T. No.
98-VII	*Jp.*	Mitsu-gon-in-hotsu-ro-san-ge-mon （密嚴院發露懺悔文）	2527
98-VIII	*Jp.*	Kō-zen-go-koku-ron （興禪護國論）	2543
98-IX	*Jp.*	Fu-kan-za-zen-gi （普勧坐禪儀）	2580
99–103	*Jp.*	Shō-bō-gen-zō （正法眼藏）	2582
104-I	*Jp.*	Za-zen-yō-jin-ki （坐禪用心記）	2586
104-II	*Jp.* *Eng.*	Sen-chaku-hon-gan-nen-butsu-shū （選擇本願念佛集） Senchaku Hongan Nembutsu Shū	2608
104-III	*Jp.* *Eng.*	Ris-shō-an-koku-ron （立正安國論） Risshōankokuron or The Treatise on the Establishment of the Orthodox Teaching and the Peace of the Nation (In Two Nichiren Texts)	2688
104-IV	*Jp.* *Eng.*	Kai-moku-shō （開目抄） Kaimokushō or Liberation from Blindness	2689
104-V	*Jp.* *Eng.*	Kan-jin-hon-zon-shō （觀心本尊抄） Kanjinhonzonsho or The Most Venerable One Revealed by Introspecting Our Minds for the First Time at the Beginning of the Fifth of the Five Five Hundred-year Ages (In Two Nichiren Texts)	2692
104-VI	*Ch.*	Fu-mu-ên-chung-ching （父母恩重經）	2887
105-I	*Jp.* *Eng.*	Ken-jō-do-shin-jitsu-kyō-gyō-shō-mon-rui （顯淨土眞實教行証文類） Kyōgyōshinshō: On Teaching, Practice, Faith, and Enlightenment	2646
105-II	*Jp.* *Eng.*	Tan-ni-shō （歎異抄） Tannishō: Passages Deploring Deviations of Faith	2661
106-I	*Jp.* *Eng.*	Ren-nyo-shō-nin-o-fumi （蓮如上人御文） Rennyo Shōnin Ofumi: The Letters of Rennyo	2668
106-II	*Jp.*	Ō-jō-yō-shū （往生要集）	2682